Transforming Early Head Start Home Visiting

Research on home visiting shows that Early Head Start (EHS) home-based programs benefit from additional training and resources that streamline philosophy and content. In this essential guide, Walsh and Mortensen propose that alignment with Family Life Education's (FLE) strengths-based methodology results in greater consistency through a model of prevention, education, and collaboration with families.

This text is the first to outline linkages between FLE and EHS home visiting. It explores a qualitative study of FLE integrated in a current EHS home-based program and application of FLE methodology to home visiting topics. This approach will influence professional practice and provide a foundation for developing evidence-based home visiting practices. Online content accompanies the text, with videos demonstrating the FLE approach in action and discussion questions to encourage engagement with and understanding of the core material.

Transforming Early Head Start Home Visiting: A Family Life Education Approach is essential reading for upper-level undergraduate and masters students in family studies and early childhood education, as well as practitioners working with children and families.

Bridget A. Walsh is an Associate Professor of Human Development and Family Studies at the University of Nevada, Reno. In 2016, NCFR awarded her with the honor of CFLE of the year. She is co-chair of the NCFR home visiting focus group. She is chair of the Coaching Workgroup of the Ounce of Prevention's Community of Practice, Professional Development for home visitors.

Jennifer A. Mortensen is an Assistant Professor of Human Development and Family Studies at the University of Nevada, Reno. She is a fellow with the Doris Duke Fellowship for the Promotion of Child Well-Being. She is also a CFLE and co-chair of the NCFR home visiting focus group. Her research focuses on parenting and childcare for families with infants and toddlers. She draws inspiration for this work from her time as a teacher at Early Head Start.

Transforming Early Head Start Home Visiting

A Family Life Education Approach

Bridget A. Walsh and Jennifer A. Mortensen

NEW YORK AND LONDON

First published 2020
by Routledge
52 Vanderbilt Avenue, New York, NY 10017

and by Routledge
2 Park Square, Milton Park, Abingdon, Oxon, OX14 4RN

Routledge is an imprint of the Taylor & Francis Group, an informa business

© 2020 Taylor & Francis

The right of Bridget A. Walsh and Jennifer A. Mortensen to be identified as authors of this work has been asserted by them in accordance with sections 77 and 78 of the Copyright, Designs and Patents Act 1988.

All rights reserved. No part of this book may be reprinted or reproduced or utilized in any form or by any electronic, mechanical, or other means, now known or hereafter invented, including photocopying and recording, or in any information storage or retrieval system, without permission in writing from the publishers.

Trademark notice: Product or corporate names may be trademarks or registered trademarks, and are used only for identification and explanation without intent to infringe.

Library of Congress Cataloging-in-Publication Data
A catalog record for this title has been requested

ISBN: 978-1-138-03709-0 (hbk)
ISBN: 978-1-138-03711-3 (pbk)
ISBN: 978-0-429-29825-7 (ebk)

Typeset in Bembo
by Integra Software Services Pvt. Ltd.

Visit the eResources URL:
www.routledge.com/9781138037113

To my supporters—Lori, Mike, and Todd

To my first classroom of babies—thank you for sending me on this entire journey

Contents

List of Illustrations	*ix*
Foreword	*xii*
Preface	*xiv*
Acknowledgments	*xvii*

1	Introduction to Family Life Education: A Historical Perspective	1
2	The State of Early Head Start Home Visiting	15
3	Family Life Education: A Foundation for Early Head Start Home Visiting	29
4	Family Life Education Approach to Home Visiting: A Qualitative Study	49
5	Reflective Practice	82
6	Building and Supporting Relationships	103
7	Supporting Development and Learning	129
8	Health and Safety	159
9	Observing Behavior, Development, and Environments	187
10	Guidance of Infant/Toddler Behavior	214
11	Partnering with and Supporting Families	240
12	Diversity and Inclusion with an Emphasis on Supporting Families of Infants/Toddlers with Special Needs	266
13	Professionalism	296

viii   *Contents*

14   Supporting Competencies in Adults   318

15   Promises and Challenges for the Interface of Home Visiting and
     Family Life Education   346

16   Training to Promote a Family Life Education Approach to Early Head
     Start Home Visiting   354

     Appendix A: Introduction to Early Head Start Home Visiting:
     One Program's Description   *382*
     Appendix B: Competencies for Pre-Service Home Visitors
     Alignment (available as an e-resource)
     Appendix C: FLE as an Enhancement to Parents
     as Teachers   *395*
     Appendix D: How to Become Certified in Family
     Life Education   *402*
     Index   *408*

Illustrations

Figures

16.1	Video Perceptions by Time and Group	365
C.1	Logic Model for Parents as Teachers Curriculum	396

Tables

4.1	Participant Characteristics	53
4.2	Coding Analysis	60
5.1	Family Life Education Concepts and Resources that Align with Reflective Practices	87
5.2	Family Life Education Concepts and Resources that Align with Reflective Practices	88
5.3	Family Life Education Concepts and Resources that Align with Reflective Practices	89
5.4	Family Life Education Concepts and Resources that Align with Reflective Practices	90
5.5	Family Life Education Concepts and Resources that Align with reflective Practices	91
5.6	Family Life Education Concepts and Resources that Align with Reflective Practices	92
6.1	Family Life Education Concepts and Resources that Align with Building and Supporting Relationships	109
6.2	Family Life Education Concepts and Resources that Align with Building and Supporting Relationships	110
6.3	Family Life Education Concepts and Resources that Align with Building and Supporting Relationships	111
6.4	Family Life Education Concepts and Resources that Align with Building and Supporting Relationships	112
6.5	Family Life Education Concepts and Resources that Align with Building and Supporting Relationships	113
6.6	Family Life Education Concepts and Resources that Align with Building and Supporting Relationships	114
7.1	Family Life Education Concepts and Resources that Align with Supporting Development and Learning	135
7.2	Family Life Education Concepts and Resources that Align with Supporting Development and Learning	136

x *Illustrations*

7.3	Family Life Education Concepts and Resources that Align with Supporting Development and Learning	138
7.4	Family Life Education Concepts and Resources that Align with Supporting Development and Learning	139
7.5	Family Life Education Concepts and Resources that Align with Supporting Development and Learning	140
7.6	Family Life Education Concepts and Resources that Align with Supporting Development and Learning	141
8.1	Family Life Education Concepts and Resources that Align with Health and Safety	168
8.2	Family Life Education Concepts and Resources that Align with Health and Safety	169
8.3	Families And Individuals In Societal Contexts Concepts and Resources that Align with Health And Safety	170
8.4	Family Life Education Concepts and Resources that Align with Health and Safety	171
8.5	Family Life Education Concepts and Resources that Align with Health and Safety	173
8.6	Family Life Education Concepts and Resources that Align with Health and Safety	174
9.1	Family Life Education Concepts and Resources that Align with Observing Behavior, Development, and Environments	194
9.2	Family Life Education Concepts and Resources that Align with Observing Behavior, Development, and Environments	195
9.3	Family Life Education Concepts and Resources that Align with Observing Behavior, Development, and Environments	196
9.4	Family Life Education Concepts and Resources that Align with Observing Behavior, Development, and Environments	198
9.5	Family Life Education Concepts and Resources that Align with Observing Behavior, Development, and Environments	201
10.1	Family Life Education Concepts and Resources that Align with Guidance of Infant/Toddler Behaviors	221
10.2	Family Life Education Concepts and Resources that Align with Guidance of Infant/Toddler Behaviors	223
10.3	Family Life Education Concepts and Resources that Align with Guidance of Infant/Toddler Behaviors	224
10.4	Family Life Education Concepts and Resources that Align with Guidance of Infant/Toddler Behaviors	225
11.1	Family Life Education Concepts and Resources that Align with Partnering with and Supporting Families	245
11.2	Family Life Education Concepts and Resources that Align with Partnering with and Supporting Families	246
11.3	Family Life Education Concepts and Resources that Align with Partnering with and Supporting Families	248
11.4	Family Life Education Concepts and Resources that Align with Partnering with and Supporting Families	249
11.5	Family Life Education Concepts and Resources that Align with Partnering with and Supporting Families	250

11.6	Family Life Education Concepts and Resources that Align with Partnering with and Supporting Families	252
11.7	Family Life Education Concepts and Resources that Align with Partnering with and Supporting Families	253
12.1	Family Life Education Concepts and Resources that Align with Diversity and Inclusion	272
12.2	Family Life Education Concepts and Resources that Align with Diversity and Inclusion	274
12.3	Family Life Education Concepts and Resources that Align with Diversity and Inclusion	276
12.4	Family Life Education Concepts and Resources that Align with Diversity and Inclusion	277
12.5	Family Life Education Concepts and Resources that Align with Diversity and Inclusion	279
12.6	Family Life Education Concepts and Resources that Align with Diversity and Inclusion	281
13.1	Family Life Education Concepts and Resources that Align with Professionalism	304
13.2	Family Life Education Concepts and Resources that Align with Professionalism	305
13.3	Family Life Education Concepts and Resources that Align with Professionalism	306
13.4	Family Life Education Concepts and Resources that Align with Professionalism	307
14.1	Family Life Education Concepts and Resources that Align with Supporting Competencies in Adults	324
14.2	Family Life Education Concepts and Resources that Align with Supporting Competencies in Adults	327
14.3	Family Life Education Concepts and Resources that Align with Supporting Competencies in Adults	329
14.4	Family Life Education Concepts and Resources that Align with Supporting Competencies in Adults	331
16.1	Video Web Links	358
16.2	Inter-Rater Reliability of Videos	359
16.3	Sample Characteristics	361
16.4	Coding Analysis	363
16.5	FLE Content Knowledge by Group	367
16.6	Coding Analysis	369

Foreword

Mr. Justin Petkus is dually certified as a Child Life Specialist and Family Life Educator, and was recognized by the National Council on Family Relations as the 2018 Certified Family Life Educator of the Year, and in 2019 by the Association of Child Life Professionals as an annual research award recipient. He is a PhD Candidate specialized in Clinical and Health Psychology at the University of Luxembourg in the Integrative Research Unit on Social and Individual Development (INSIDE) within the Institute for Health and Behaviour, and is a Co-Founder of Pediatric Potential Inc., a non-profit organization committed to strengthening the wellbeing of children and families around the world through research, teaching and outreach to improve pediatric health care experiences and enhance access to pediatric psychosocial care.

When I embarked on implementing the first family life education model and approach to Early Head Start home visiting in the United States in 2014, I had a clear goal in mind: to establish intentionality to the home visiting role. A scope of practice for home visitors was lacking, and it was reflected in the mixed approaches to home visiting that my team applied, respectively.

Identity-based practice is elemental in all professions. Role identity enables professionals to deliver purpose driven work rooted in understanding the *how* and *why* of what they do. Recipients of any service in any industry are better served when their expectations match the role of the provider. Identity formation in the Early Head Start home visiting profession has largely been at a microlevel. That is, purpose and motivations are often formulated by individual home visitors, individual supervisor's expectations, and agencies interpretation of Head Start performance standards and not by macrolevel home visiting professional standards of practice.

In their book *Transforming Early Head Start Home Visiting: A Family Life Education Approach*, Bridget A. Walsh and Jennifer A. Mortensen present a long-awaited call to action: an identity for Early Head Start home visitors as family life educators. At last, the case for the interface of Early Head Start home visiting and family life education is articulated though a synthesis of empirical research and first-hand account success stories. The book drives home visiting research and practice forward for scholars and is an essential practical guide for students, educators, home visitors, and Early Head Start administrators.

A measure of success in the first family life education home visiting program was when the home visitors established a mutual sense of identity in their respective roles. It was when the home visitors identified as family life education providers, that they reached a paradigm shift from operating as tertiary and secondary therapeutic interventionalists to foremost primary and secondary coaching preventionists. Training home visitors using a visual scope of practice framework was vital in this identity building process. In turn, families became catalysts in their own lives, limiting the reliance on the home visitor. Home visitors learned how to be *with* families to empower, deconstructing their thought of needing to do *for* families to rescue.

Walsh and Mortensen strengthen home visitors' scope of practice by aligning the ten content areas of family life education to Early Head Start home visiting, and the foundational principles of education, prevention, and strengths-based approaches they share. This is the next step in the professionalization of home visiting, and will assist in the elevation and training rigor of the Early Head Start home visiting workforce. As Walsh and Mortensen outline, newly developed professional development modules in family life education home visiting are an effective start in doing so.

The foundational groundwork for the future of family life education in Early Head Start home visiting has been paved by the passionate researchers and practitioners cited in this book. Collaborative efforts between current experts and their tenacious work with those to come, will be necessary to solidify family life education as the professional home and theoretical framework for Early Head Start home visitors. The National Council on Family Relations (NCFR), the Administration for Children and Families Office of Head Start, and the Head Start Early Childhood Learning and Knowledge Center (ECLKC) are key stakeholders to this aim.

I conclude with a quote by ancient Chinese philosopher Lao Tzu, which I believe can serve as a reminder when thinking about the responsibility of family life education in home visits with children and their families:

> Go to the people. Live with them. Learn from them. Start with what they know. Build with what they have. But with the best leaders, when the work is done, the task accomplished, the people will say "We have done this ourselves."
>
> (Lao Tzu)

Justin M. Petkus, MS, CFLE, CCLS

Preface

- Why is home visiting (HV) important to families?
- Why is family life education (FLE) important to maintaining and to building protective factors in families?
- What do family life educators offer families they work with and serve in the context of home visiting?
- How do family life educators work with families in the context of home visits?
- I am unsure of what do after graduating with a family degree and earning a Certified Family Life Educator (CFLE) credential. Is home visiting a way for me to work with families and to put my degree and credential into practice?
- There are so many approaches to home visiting. How will my family training prepare me to be a home visitor?

All home visitors—regardless of the program's goals or mission—work with families, and family life educators have a foundation in applying family science knowledge to work with families. Family life education (FLE) is delivered through a myriad of ways, such as through home visits, and FLE needs continue to grow and adapt for twenty-first century families (see Mitchell, Hughes, & Curtiss, 2014). This text endeavors to further the interface of home visiting and family life education and to respond to the above questions.

While some have hypothetically considered these questions, others actively engage in exploring the interface of FLE and Early Head Start-Home Based Option (EHS-HBO). For example, the account of an Early Head Start/Head Start agency that hired CFLEs for home visiting positions (see Petkus, 2015) is inspiring yet realistic. This book strives to provide justification for becoming passionate about this interface and the idea of incorporating FLE into EHS-HBO. We shadowed numerous home visits at the aforementioned EHS-HBO program using a FLE approach to guide their work. We'd like to make those visits come to life for a broader audience and to build upon their existing work.

Early Head Start emphasizes a more holistic approach to home visiting through a two-generation focus on assisting parents and children. A curriculum like Parents as Teachers (PAT) may not be enough to adequately prepare an EHS home visitor; they have comprehensive responsibilities to the whole family and need the philosophical underpinnings of the CFLE type approach (Roggman, personal communication, March, 28, 2018).

This book commences by introducing the reader to the evolvement of FLE. Then the current state of EHS-home-based services are addressed with insight as to how FLE might offer an important role in the delivery of EHS-HBO. Principles of FLE are addressed to provide further support for the interface of FLE and EHS-home-based services. Empirical material on one program's application of FLE to EHS home visiting is explored.

The second half of this book focuses on the alignment of home visiting pre-service competencies with FLE content areas. The purpose of the second half of the book is also to explore CFLE approved programs as pre-service training for home visitors. Then, the authors discuss future areas for researchers and practitioners to explore. Finally, the authors share findings and results of implementing professional development modules to promote the practice of FLE in EHS-home based services. The videos within the four modules (links to the videos can be found in Chapter 16) may incite ideas about strengthening the interface of FLE and EHS-home based services.

The Appendices strengthen and extend the content of the book chapters. There are videos and discussion questions for each chapter to help bring the ideas in this book to life.

For the extremely reluctant reader, we understand that change and trans-formation are often challenging even if they reflect good intensions and enlightened ethos. To acknowledge your concerns, the EHS-HBO that made an effort to hire CFLEs and to switch from a toy-bag centered approach to a FLE approach had 100% staff turnover (see Chapter 4). The exploration of the interface of FLE and EHS-HBO comes from being cognizant of the challenges and the strengths in the home visiting field. The reality is that we expect home visitors to motivate families to change, and we expect CFLEs to teach families and to change lives as well. In this book, the reader will find qualitative studies that were conducted to explore the interface of EHS home visiting and FLE, the synthesis of up-to-date empirical research, systematic reviews, databases of evidence-based approaches, and first-hand accounts, with the intent to shape the thinking, the training, and the practice of future generations of home visitors and family life educators.

A mix of state, private, and federal funds support home visiting and EHS and the Maternal, Infant and Early Childhood Home Visiting (MIECHV) program are both examples of federal funding (see Harrison & May, 2018). Home visiting experiences bipartisan support given the emphasis on evidence-based programs and return on investment (see Harrison & May, 2018; Walsh, 2019). We are in a time of unprecedented support for home visiting, yet federal funding has remained flat, and there is a pronounced appetite for professiona-lization of home visitors (Walsh, 2019). The need for family-centered services remains. Now is a time for advocates of young children and families to dream

xvi *Preface*

of universal home visiting or of getting all families that are eligible for home visiting to volunteer to enroll and having quality services that can meet their needs.

There is a need in higher education to engage in the pre-service training of home visitors. As a program of study, Human Development and Family Studies (or Family Science) (HDFS) is gaining popularity, with an estimated more than 400 colleges and universities offering this major. At our university, HDFS majors have increased 44% and minors have tripled over a recent period. Many students in our HDFS program desire a clear link between their studies and professions. This is a sentiment shared by most of our colleagues. In fact, the National Council on Family Relations created a "We Are Family Science" website to help students and professionals identify links between HDFS training and professions. In a recent study of professionals, participants agreed that FLE would be a viable approach to EHS home visiting, and many participants indicated that training in FLE would be valuable for most home visitors (see Walsh, Mortensen, Edwards, & Cassidy, in press). *Transforming Early Head Start Home Visiting: A Family Life Education Approach* is the first book that explores this important interface.

References

Harrison, C. L., & May, A. (2018). Home visiting: Improving children's and families well-being. Retrieved from http://www.ncsl.org/research/human-services/home-visiting-improving-children-s-and-families-well-being.aspx

Mitchell, E. T., Hughes, R. Jr., & Curtiss, S. L. (2014). Family life education. In L. H. Ganong, & M. Coleman (Eds.), *The social history of the American family: An encyclopedia* (pp. 497–499). Thousand, Oaks, CA: Sage.

Petkus, J. (2015). A first-hand account of implementing a Family Life Education model: Intentionality in Head Start home visiting. In M. J. Walcheski, & J. S. Reinke (Eds.), *Family life education: The practice of family science* (pp. 325–331). Minneapolis, MN: National Council on Family Relations.

Walsh, B. A. (2019). The interface of FLE and EHS home-based services: Past, present, and future. *CFLE Network, 32,* 11–13.

Walsh, B. A., Mortensen, J. A., Edwards, A. L., & Cassidy, D. (in press). The practice of family life education within Early Head Start home visiting. *Family Relations.*

Acknowledgments

Thank you to Justin Petkus, MS, CFLE, CCLS for starting us on this journey and for writing the foreword for this book. We would like to thank Head Start for Kent County's Home Visiting team with a special thanks to Ibrahim Skenderovic and the wonderful home visitors and families that let us into their lives. We would like to thank Michelle Cossar for her openness to learning about this book and for sharing her profound work with children and families. This site provided many helpful insights and it was extremely motivating to witness family life education in their daily home visiting services.

We express gratitude to Sherry Waugh, Jamie Selby, Martie Fine, Karyn Leanos, Maria Reyes-Vargas, Shauna Herrick, and Tracy Casbarro. We also express gratitude to Milagro Guardado, CFLE and EHS home visitor. Thank you to Atzimba Bravo for sharing her story and for opening her home to careful observations. Thank you to Catherine Rutledge for her guidance and knowledge on how to best serve families of infants/toddlers with special needs. Thank you to Rose Steffen, Shelby Peterson, Sergio Trejo, and Ellen Rahn for your support and hard work with projects related to this book.

We would like to thank our co-leader of the NCFR Home Visiting Focus Group, Dr. Carla Peterson (Nancy Rygg Armbrust Professor of Early Childhood Development and Education at Iowa State University). We would like to thank the NCFR Home Visiting Focus Group, particularly Dawn Cassidy. We would like to also thank Dr. Claire Valloton of Michigan State University, Dr. Lori Roggman of Utah State University, and The Collaborative for the Understanding of the Pedagogy of Infant/Toddler Development at large. We express gratitude to Keira Hambrick for her sharing her expertise and for her unwavering support throughout this process.

We thank the readers for the work you do or will do on behalf of families. Our hope is that this book will help you explore the interface of family life education and EHS-HBO services in your thinking and in your important work with families.

1 Introduction to Family Life Education
A Historical Perspective

Historically, FLE has been incorporated into a variety of educational and social enterprises (Lewis-Rowley, Brasher, Moss, Duncan, & Stiles, 1993). This is partially due to the multidisciplinary and multi-professional nature of FLE (Arcus, Schvaneveldt, & Moss, 1993; Darling & Cassidy, 2014; Duncan & Goddard, 2017; Lewis-Rowley et al., 1993) yet it is a unique profession (Hans, 2015). Before we discuss how a FLE approach within the EHS HV program structure could advance the study and practice of the interface between FLE and EHS home visiting, we will briefly remember the past and provide an overview of key events and cornerstones that promoted the evolution of FLE.

Jane Addams's Hull House—1889. In 1889, Jane Addams's Hull House in Chicago was a catalyst for solving social problems by using intellectual thought. It created a sense of community and helped poor people learn skills and take classes (Downey, 2009). "Addams' highly successful model of family life education, which included home visits, interactive learning, and individualized group learning goals, developed concurrently with the charity organization movement" (Darling & Cassidy, 2014, p. 19). Contemporary family life educators accept that home visitation by a trained individual can support family strengths and needs in the home environment (Darling & Cassidy, 2014; Duncan & Goddard, 2017; Petkus, 2015; Walsh, 2017). People who worked at the Hull House, such as Frances Perkins, reported that working there was transformative learning and she saw first-hand the social problems of the world and the importance of community building (Downey, 2009). This model embraced community building and collaboration between the poor and the settlement workers, which in the twenty-first century are tenets that remain central to family life education (Darling & Cassidy, 2014).

Morrill Land Grant Act of 1862 and 1890. FLE, the application of family science, is often housed in the following academic programs: human development and family studies, human development and family science, child and family studies, family science, or similar nomenclature. The FLE profession is a relatively young area but has roots in home economics (Bredehoft, 2001; Lewis-Rowley et al., 1993; Walsh, DeFlorio, Burnham, & Weiser, 2017) and family sociology (Lewis-Rowley et al., 1993). The progress made in home economics to help family science get to its current form is partially

2 Introduction to Family Life Education

contributed to the Morrill Acts of 1862 and 1890. The two acts helped create land grant universities (Russo, 2010). The first act, signed into law by President Abraham Lincoln, provided funds to promote liberal and practical education (Russo, 2010). Because of the first Morrill Act, subject matter central to family and home were enhanced (Lewis-Rowley et al., 1993). The second Morrill Act resulted in 17 historically Black land grant colleges (Russo, 2010) and required each land grant school to establish an agricultural school (Walsh et al., 2017). Approximately 155 years later, communities, youth, and families still benefit from these acts becoming law (Allen-Diaz, 2012).

1900s–1920s. Family fields and social work were conceived as distinct academic areas in tertiary education (Lewis-Rowley et al., 1993). Social work is often associated with home visiting by the public, yet the process and objectives of home visiting have been ignored by most social work historians (Holbrook, 1983). The first White House Conference on Child Welfare was held in 1909 (Lewis-Rowley et al., 1993) and the key messages of this conference were the value of home life to a valuable society and how poverty should not disrupt home life (Conference on the care of dependent children, 1909). Another notable event, the passage of the Smith-Lever Act in 1914, established Cooperative Extension Service at land grand universities in each state, of which education about home management, often provided in the home, was the major thrust (Lewis-Rowley et al., 1993; Scholl, 2013). Extension programs are thought to have commenced prior to 1914 or the passage of the Smith-Lever Act, and family and consumer science (formerly home economics) was highly important to Extension service from its nascent stages (Scholl, 2013).

1921–1950s. During the 1920s, parent education experienced growth and attention (Darling & Cassidy, 2014). Parent education includes activities, services, resources, and processes that support parents and caregivers to increase their efficacy in raising children (Jacobson, 2015). During the 1940s, parent education was viewed as prevention and focuses were mixed between mental health and family perspectives (Lewis-Rowley et al., 1993).

The National Council on Family Relations (NCFR) was founded in 1938 by Paul Sayre, Ernest Burgess, and Sidney E. Goldstein to focus on family research, practice, and policy (Czaplewski, 2011). In its current form, NCFR has an annual national conference, state and affiliate conferences, three scholarly journals, newsletters and reports, and policy briefs (NCFR, n.d.). NCFR is the main professional organization for family science professionals and the Certified Family Life Educator (CFLE) credential (NCFR, n.d.).

1951–1990s. In the 1950s, an increasing divorce rate, disparity in sexual behavior standards, and disagreement about what sex education should include were of large concern to family life educators (Lewis-Rowley et al., 1993). Work in Canada, in the form of a conference, focused on the family in 1964 and formed the foundation for the Vanier Institute of the Family, which was founded in 1965, and some of their major accomplishments in the 1970s included statements about the qualifications of family life educators (Darling & Cassidy, 2014). Today, the Vanier Institute of the Family partners with organizations to promote positive family life in Canada (The Vanier Institute of the Family, 2018).

The Children, Youth and Families at Risk (CYFAR) program targets at-risk youth and families to implement and deliver educational services, and has been doing so since 1991 through federal funding (United States Department of Agriculture, n.d.). The CYFAR work is one example of expanding the traditional conceptualization of FLE by providing it to disadvantaged families considered at greatest risk due to socioeconomic status (Duncan & Goddard, 2017).

Expansion and Professionalization of FLE[1]

Framework for Lifespan Family Life Education—1987

The major content areas of FLE were identified in the Framework for Lifespan Family Life Education (Arcus, 1987), which has been revised several times since its inception (Bredehoft, 2001; Bredehoft & Walcheski, 2011). The framework reflects the following: (a) a broad definition of FLE, (b) learning (knowledge, skills, and attitudes), and (c) various ages and stages of family members (Arcus, 1987; Bredehoft, 2001). The framework has several uses, including assisting program developers, implementers, and assessors with content guidelines (Arcus et al., 1993; Bredehoft, 2001). The topics in the first framework included:

(a) human development and sexuality,
(b) interpersonal relationships,
(c) family interaction,
(d) family resource management,
(e) education about parenthood,
 (f) ethics, and
(g) family and society (see Arcus, 1987).

The second iteration of the framework by Bredehoft (1997, as cited in Bredehoft, 2001) included nine areas, and the third iteration by Bredehoft and Walcheski includes ten areas (2011, as cited in Reinke & Walcheski, 2015). The ten areas are specified later in this chapter.

First CFLEs—1985

The National Council on Family Relations (NCFR) started to develop certification for family life educators in the 1960s (Darling & Cassidy, 2014). In 1985, standards and criteria for the Certified Family Life Educator certification program were approved (Darling, Fleming, & Cassidy, 2009). CFLEs represent

4   *Introduction to Family Life Education*

a concerted effort that sheds light on the value of family life education as a practice with known standards and requirements (Cassidy, 2015).

Academic Program Review—1996

In 1996, the NCFR initiated the academic program review, which allowed academic colleges and universities to demonstrate coursework in the ten FLE content areas (Darling et al., 2009). Candidates with coursework in the ten content areas from a CFLE-approved academic program could apply to become a provisional CFLE through an abbreviated application process (Darling et al., 2009). After accruing work experience germane to the ten FLE content areas, provisional CFLEs are eligible to apply for full CFLE status.

National CFLE Exam—2007

The National Council on Family Relations launched a national exam for the CFLE credential (Darling, Cassidy, & Rehm 2017) that replaced the portfolio process for candidates (Reinke & Walcheski, 2015). The portfolio process was time-consuming and prone to subjectivity by reviewers. This exam offered an additional pathway to obtaining CFLE provisional status by offering an option for candidates without full content area coursework in the ten content areas in a CFLE approved program to sit for a national exam.

Code of Ethics—2009

In 1992, ethics became a top-priority of NCFR members and approximately six years later they released ethical principles after an iterative process (Adams, Gilbert, Dollahite, & Keim, 2015). In 2009, the NCFR unveiled a code of ethics for CFLEs (Darling et al., 2017) that exists in addition to the FLE content area of professional ethics and practice (see Palm, 2018). The code of ethics includes 36 principles and it must be read and signed before an individual can become a CFLE. The code of ethics conveys professional expectations and was based on the guidelines created by the Minnesota Council on Family Relations (MNCFR, 2009). There are a series of steps to assist professionals with ethical dilemmas, these are: identification of relationships, application of principles, identification of contradictions/tensions, identification of possible solutions, and selection of actions (see MNCFR, 2016) for parent and family life educators (Palm, 2018).

Principles of Family Life Education—1993

Seven operational principles of family life education were introduced in 1993 (Arcus et al., 1993). The operational principles are guides for practice and are generally accepted by professionals in family life education (Arcus et al., 1993). These are:

1. Family life education is relevant to individuals and families throughout the lifespan.
2. Family life education should be based on the needs of individuals and families.
3. Family life education is a multidisciplinary area of study and multi-professional in its practice.
4. Family life education programs are offered in many different settings.
5. Family life education takes an educational rather than a therapeutic approach.
6. Family life education should present and respect differing family values.
7. Qualified educators are crucial to the successful realization of the goals of family life education.

(Arcus et al., 1993, pp. 15–20)

These principles formed the foundation for the Framework for Lifespan Family Life Education (Bredehoft, 2001). In the twenty-first century, these principles of FLE have been firmly sorted into foundational principles (education, prevention, strengths-based approach, a foundation in research and theory) and operational principles (culture, context, content, practice) (Darling et al., 2017). The foundations of family life education model (FFLE) underscores foundational principles of FLE with changes in operational principles across time (Darling, Cassidy, & Rehm, 2019).

Levels of Family Involvement Model—1995

FLE is more educational than clinical (Arcus et al., 1993; Doherty, 1995). Doherty's (1995) Levels of Family Involvement (LFI) model promoted the perspective of viewing FLE and family therapy as part of a continuum rather than disparate professions. Since LFI was first presented more than two decades ago, it has received criticism (see Myers-Walls, Ballard, Darling, & Myers-Bowman, 2011) and a response to this criticism (Doherty & Lamson, 2015).

It is appropriate to consider the LFI model in the context of home visiting services. Doherty (1995) stated that FLE includes activities such as home visits that are designed to promote the efficacy of families (Doherty, 1995). This LFI model was designed to assist professionals in considering the depths of family's needs, the kinds of services warranted by the family's needs, and the importance of the match between the professional's skills and family's needs (Doherty & Lamson, 2015). The five levels of the LFI model include:

1. minimal emphasis on family or institution centered,
2. information and advice or collaborative dissemination of information,
3. feelings and support or working with family members' feelings and need for support,

6 *Introduction to Family Life Education*

4. brief focused intervention or psychoeducational intervention for complex or chronic family concerns, and
5. family therapy.

(Doherty, 1995; Doherty & Lamson, 2015)

Doherty (1995) asserted that level one (minimal emphasis on family) and level five (family therapy) do not directly apply to FLE. The LFI showcases the diversity of skills needed when working with families and does not suggest that FLE is subservient to family therapy nor that level five encompasses the other levels (Doherty & Lamson, 2015).

Feelings and support, or level three, might be an appropriate level for FLE. Whether in a group or one-on-one, participants should feel free to express themselves and be encouraged to try new ways of doing family life. The most common errors made by the professional include:

> (a) moving too quickly back to the cognitive level because of personal discomfort; (b) cutting off a parent by turning the issue back to the group too quickly; (c) giving premature advice before the parent had had the chance to tell the story; and (d) probing too deeply into the sources of the parent's distress, thereby becoming too intrusive in an effort to help.

(Doherty, 1995 pp. 354–355)

Intervention, or the fourth level, is also germane to FLE, particularly in the context of home visiting given its emphasis on families at risk, such as teen parents with problems, or families involved in mental health challenges and/or child protective services. At this level, it is important to recognize the importance of referrals to family therapists and the collaborative work with families, therapists, and other professionals (Doherty, 1995).

Domains of Family Practice Model—2011

What would you include in a 30-second elevator speech on the definition of FLE? It would be helpful to define it as including strengths-based work with families as well as other foundational and operational principles (see Chapter 3). The content of FLE could be emphasized particularly for inclusion of topics that are germane to family life (Darling et al., 2017; Myers-Walls et al., 2011) including knowledge and skills in the ten FLE content areas.

One further approach is to delineate how it is similar to and different from other areas of family practice, such as family therapy (FT) and family case management (FCM), as developed by Myers-Walls et al. (2011) in their domains of family practice model. Myers-Walls et al. somewhat praised Doherty's (1995) LFI model, but mostly presented criticisms including that it was narrowly focused on differences and that family case management, as a segment of social work, needed to be included. Thus, Myers-Walls et al.'s (2011) domains of family practice model underscored similarities of all three domains—FLE, FT, and FCM—including their shared vision of "Strong, healthy families" (p. 362). They also have similarities, such as valuing the family as a system, the operational principles of context and culture, research-based practice, and professional practice and ethics (Myers-Walls et al., 2011).

As Doherty (1995) indicated, there are also differences between areas of family practice. FLE focuses on the present and future, whereas FT focuses on the past, present, and future, and FCM is mostly focused on the present (Myers-Walls et al., 2011). For example, a family life educator would talk with a family about their immediate needs and future goals and collaborate to form an action plan with the family to support those goals. A family therapist would desire to learn about family of origin contexts and would return to those to break cycles in the present and future. A family case manager would want the families to have their immediate needs met, such as finding free or low-cost legal advice, diapers for a new infant, or getting the family enrolled in a public assistance program.

Framework for Best Practices in Family Life Education—2012

Best practices are those that have evidence of effectiveness (Ballard & Taylor, 2012). The Framework for Best Practices in FLE emphasizes program content, program design, and the family life educator; the aforementioned three components should work in tandem with context, culture, and the needs and strengths of the population (Ballard & Taylor, 2012; Ballard, Tyndall, Baugh, Bergeson, & Littlewood, 2016).

Program content emphasizes the ten FLE content areas, which are: (1) families and individuals in societal contexts, (2) internal dynamics of families, (3) human growth and development across the lifespan, (4) human sexuality across the lifespan, (5) interpersonal relationships, (6) family resource management, (7) parent education and guidance, (8) family law and public policy, (9) professional ethics and practice, and (10) family life education methodology (NCFR, 2015). Earlier in this chapter, we stated that the major content areas of FLE were identified in the Framework for Lifespan Family Life Education (Arcus, 1987). In addition to the revisions made to the Framework, which helped evolve the content areas, there has been empirical research to make the content areas what they are in the twenty-first century. For instance, Darling, Fleming, and Cassidy (2009) conducted a practice analysis survey of family professionals, including CFLEs and non-certified family professionals, to further validate the content areas as a foundation for best practices in program content. Human growth and development across the lifespan was considered the content area that was most germane to professional practices, whereas family law and public policy was considered the least germane to practice; however, none of the ten content areas were considered not applicable to practice (Darling et al., 2009). While some family professionals may fully embrace content areas deemed less

8   Introduction to Family Life Education

desirable to practice, such as family law and public policy (e.g., Baumle, 2018; Bogenschneider, 2014; Fricke, Walsh, & Barghouti, 2017; Henderson & Martin, 2002), others may lack an understanding of policy and law, particularly in regard to applications of it to their practice, or they may work in an environment that discourages involvement with policy, to name a few reasons (Darling et al., 2017; Darling et al., 2009).

Program design is a component of best practices that focuses on methods of FLE (Ballard & Taylor, 2012). FLE methodology is a content area that focuses on practice or methods more so than content (Ballard & Taylor, 2012). The other two content areas that emphasize practice or methods more so than content are professional ethics and practice and family law and public policy (Darling et al., 2017). A parenting program that uses the strengths based approach would ask parents to start each session by making positive statements and the FLEs would promote their strengths as well as collaborate with them to reframe negative statements (Ballard et al., 2016). Focusing on strengths may set the stage for empowerment and building efficacy and confidence (Ballard et al., 2016).

The role of the professional delivering FLE is crucial to best practices and to success with working with families (Ballard et al., 2016). The family life educator's training, credentials, and experiences are important to the processes, goals, and outcomes of FLE. Family life educators must be skilled at providing research-based information to families and deliver it in a way that makes sense to each family (Ballard & Taylor, 2012). CFLEs are often suited to deliver a wide variety of programs and services, and at times program specific training is warranted to deliver a specific program (Ballard et al., 2016). Family life educators should have training that embodies cultural competence (Ballard & Taylor, 2012) to work with all families, particularly families that have backgrounds and characteristics that are different from their own.

Best Practices in Online FLE—2012

In its present state, FLE includes online learning experiences (Darling et al., 2017). As early as 1999, it was noted that the Internet has an important place in FLE (Hughes, Bowers, Mitchell, Curtiss, & Ebata, 2012). Online FLE includes education and experiences via technology and media that are intended to promote families' strengths and positive outcomes. There are five steps to online FLE program development, which are: problem analysis, program content, instructional design, program implementation, and program evaluation (Hughes et al., 2012). Family life educators may be faced with two online FLE planning situations, either converting a face-to-face program to online delivery, or developing an online program without having a template of this program or experiences with it face-to-face (Hughes, Ebata, Bowers, Mitchell, & Curtiss, 2015). It is important to keep in mind that planning FLE experiences for face-to-face and online delivery share similarities but there are also unique design issues with both and they work in tandem in hybrid approaches (Hughes et al., 2015).

A recent survey of CFLEs demonstrated that most CFLEs have positive views of technology, particularly that it is useful and increases effectiveness and productivity (Walker, 2017). It is likely that future CFLEs enrolled in NCFR approved programs will engage with a variety of technology, such as a flipped classroom (Roehl, Reddy, & Shannon, 2013) and infographics (Allen, 2017; Berke, 2017). All in all, this suggests that CFLEs trained in CFLE-approved programs enter the workforce well-versed in the challenges and strengths of using technology to reach goals and achieve outcomes.

Family Life Coaching: A Technique for Family Life Educators—2014

FLE can include individual education in contexts such as coaching (Darling et al., 2017). Family life coaching is an optimal technique for family life educators (Myers-Walls, 2014). Whether such a technique is a domain of family practice—with similarities to and differences from FLE, family case management, and family therapy—is an issue that may be further explored (see Allen & Huff, 2014; Myers-Walls, 2014). A few qualitative studies have been conducted on family life coaching to explore the training and competencies (Kruenegel-Farr, Allen, & Machara, 2016) and perspectives of family practitioners to support family life coaching as a domain of family practice (Allen & Huff, 2014).

Allen and Huff (2014, 2015) have argued for the inclusion of family life coaching as an additional domain of family practice in Myers-Walls et al.'s (2011) model. Similarly, Allen (2016) has asserted that some components of family life coaching are similar to FLE and coaching psychology, while others are novel. On the contrary, a rebuttal as to why family life coaching is a technique rather than a domain of family practice has also been asserted (Myers-Walls, 2014).

FLE Model of Home Visiting—2015

Is FLE, or components of it, viable for promoting home visiting effectiveness? Machir (2014) made the case for CFLEs as home visitors. Petkus (2015) introduced a FLE approach to home visiting with EHS-HBO. He applied the domains of family practice model (Myers-Walls et al., 2011) to EHS HV to create boundaries. In particular, he asserted that operating in all three domains (FT, FCM, and FLE) creates ill-defined roles for home visitors and uncertainties about how families view their roles (Petkus, 2015). Home visitors should operate mostly in the FLE domain (Petkus, 2015) but home visitors often feel that they operate in all three domains, which creates burn-out and lack of a professional focus and identity. Chapter 4 in this book specifically explores

10   *Introduction to Family Life Education*

how the paradigm shifted from a toy-centered approach that included home visitors operating in all three domains of family practice to a FLE-only approach within one EHS-HBO. The aforementioned qualitative study in Chapter 4 was integral to spawn answers to the call for further conceptualizing and articulating Petkus's model. It is going to take practitioners and researchers, both generalists and specialists, who are versed in FLE and Early Head Start home visiting to position families at the forefront of planning and delivery and to fully prepare the next generation of home visitors for contemporary families.

Answering the Call: How to Strengthen a FLE Approach to EHS Home Visiting

We suggest that a FLE approach to EHS HV would provide an additional dimension of family-centered training to program staff, and the integration of CFLEs as EHS home visitors would elevate the training rigor of the current EHS HV workforce (Walsh, Mortensen, Edwards, & Cassidy, in press). There are many ways FLE aligns with and has the potential to strengthen the core dimensions of EHS HV (Walsh, 2017, 2019; Walsh et al., in press). Some of these ways include:

- Shared assumptions of EHS HV align with FLE principles
- Current limitations of EHS HV and areas where further research and innovation is needed in the EHS HV approach or a call-to-action or questions to enhance EHS HV
- Foundation of FLE principles, including operational components, complements the aims and practices of EHS home visiting programs
- Lessons learned from one EHS-HBO that transitioned from a special toy-centered child approach to a FLE approach
- Alignment of HV competencies with FLE competencies
- Survey research and narratives as a foundation for exploring future directions of the practice of FLE within EHS HV
- Professional development modules that target FLE for the audience of in-service EHS home visitors
- Exploration of the idea of FLE as an enhancement to the established curriculum of Parents as Teachers (PAT)

Summary

FLE has a long history that can be traced to the 1700s and then to cornerstones in the 1800s, such as Jane Addam's Hull House and the two Morrill Acts. This chapter highlights a number of hallmarks and advancements (e.g., the first CFLEs in the 1980s; the domains of family practice model, which was published in *Family Relations* in 2011) that are essential to the expansion and professionalization of FLE. Contemporary developments in FLE include family life coaching and a FLE approach to Early Head Start home visiting. This chapter closes with an overview of this book: how to strengthen a FLE approach to Early Head Start home visiting.

Key Concepts

- Academic program review
- Best practices in online family life education
- CFLE exam
- Code of ethics
- Domains of family practice model
- Family life coaching
- Family life education model of home visiting
- Framework for best practices in family life education
- Framework for lifespan family life education
- Jane Addams's Hull House
- Levels of family involvement model
- Morrill Land Grant Acts
- Principles of family life education

Recommended Readings

Duffee, J. H., Mendelsohn, A. L., Kuo, A. A., Legano, L. A., Earls, M. F., & Council on Community Pediatrics, Council on Early Childhood, Committee on Child Abuse and Neglect (2017). Early childhood home visiting. *Pediatrics*, 140(3). E20172150

Zigler, E. F., & Freedman, J. (1987). Head Start: A pioneer of family support. In S. L. Kagan, D. R. Powell, B. Weissbound, & E. F. Zigler (Eds.), *America's family support programs, perspectives, and prospects* (pp. 57–76). New Haven, CT: Yale University Press.

Note

1 Some of the content in this section (Expansion and Professionalization of FLE) is adapted from Walsh, B. A., Mortensen, J. A., Peterson, C. A., Cassidy, D., & CUPID (in press). Competency alignment and certification for pre-service home visitors. *Family Relations*.

References

Adams, R. A., Gilbert, K. R., Dollahite, D. C., & Keim, R. E. (2015). The development and teaching of the ethical principles and guidelines for family scientists. In M. J. Walcheski, & J. S. Reinke (Eds.), *Family life education: The practice of family science* (pp. 291–302). Minneapolis, MN: National Council on Family Relations.

12 Introduction to Family Life Education

Allen, K. (2016). *Theory, research, and practical guidelines for family life coaching*. Switzerland: Springer.

Allen, K. (2017). Reaching students where they are: Teaching family science through technology. *CFLE Network, 30.4*, 10–11.

Allen, K., & Huff, N. L. (2014). Family coaching: An emerging family science field. *Family Relations, 63*, 569–582. doi: 10.1111/fare.12087

Allen, K., & Huff, N. L. (2015). Family coaching: An emerging family science field. In M. J. Walcheski, & J. S. Reinke (Eds.), *Family life education: The practice of family science* (pp. 61–72). Minneapolis, MN: National Council on Family Relations.

Allen-Diaz, B. (2012). 150 years after Morrill Act, land-grant universities are key to healthy California. *California Agriculture, 66*, 2.

Arcus, M. (1987). A framework for life-span family life education. *Family Relations, 36*, 5–10.

Arcus, M. E., Schvaneveldt, J. D., & Moss, J. J. (1993). The nature of family life education. In M. E. Arcus, J. D. Schvaneveldt, & J. J. Moss (Eds.), *Handbook of family life education: Foundations of family life education* (pp. 1–25). Newbury Park, CA: Sage.

Ballard, S. M., & Taylor, A. C. (2012). Best practices in family life education. In S. M. Ballard & A. C. Taylor (Eds.), *Family life education with diverse populations* (pp. 1–18). Thousand Oaks, CA: Sage.

Ballard, S. M., Tyndall, L. E., Baugh, E. J., Bergeson, C. B., & Littlewood, K. (2016). Frameworks for best practices in family life education: A case example. *Family Relations, 65*, 393–406. doi: 10.1111/fare.12200

Baumle, A. K., (2018). Legal counseling and the marriage decision: The impact of same-sex marriage on family law practice. *Family Relations, 67*, 192–206. doi: 10.1111/fare.12294

Berke, D. (2017). Infographics as a teaching tool for family life educators or "A picture is worth a thousand words!" *CFLE Network, 30*(4), 13–14.

Bogenschneider, K. (2014). *Family policy matters: How policymaking affects families and what professionals can do* (3rd ed.). New York: Taylor & Francis.

Bredehoft, D. J. (2001). The framework for life span family life education revisited and revised. *The Family Journal: Counseling and Therapy for Couples and Families, 9*, 134–139.

Bredehoft, D. J., & Walcheski, M. J. (Eds.). (2011). *The Family Life Education Framework* [Poster and PowerPoint presentation]. Minneapolis, MN: National Council on Family Relations.

Cassidy, D. (2015). Family life education: Advancing the profession. In M. J. Walcheski, & J. S. Reinke (Eds.), *Family life education: The practice of family science* (pp. 311–323). Minneapolis, MN: National Council on Family Relations.

Conference on the care of dependent children. (1909). *Proceedings of the Conference on the care of dependent children: Held at Washington, DC, January 25, 26, 1909. Special message of the President of United States recommending legislation desired by the Conference … and transmitting the proceedings of the Conference. Communicated to the two houses of Congress on February 15, 1909*. Washington, [U.S.]: Govt. print. off.

Czaplewski, M. J. (2011). NCFR history book. Retrieved https://history.ncfr.org/

Darling, C. A., & Cassidy, D. (2014). *Family life education: Working with families across the lifespan* (3rd ed.). Long Grove, IL: Waveland.

Darling, C. A., Cassidy, D., & Rehm, M. (2017). Family life education: Translational family science in action. *Family Relations, 66*, 741–752. doi: 10.1111/fare.12286

Darling, C. A., Cassidy, D., & Rehm, M. (2019). The foundations of family life education model: Understanding the field. *Family Relations*. Advance online publication. doi: 10.1111/fare.12372

Darling, C. A., Fleming, W. M., & Cassidy, D. (2009). Professionalization of family life education: Defining the field. *Family Relations, 58*, 330–345.

Doherty, W. J. (1995). Boundaries between parent and family education and family therapy: The levels of family involvement model. *Family Relations, 44*, 353–358. doi: 10.2307/584990

Doherty, W. J., & Lamson, A. L. (2015). The levels of family involvement model: 20 years later. In M. J. Walcheski, & J. S. Reinke (Eds.), *Family life education: The practice of family science* (pp. 39–46). Minneapolis, MN: National Council on Family Relations.

Downey, K. (2009). *The woman behind the New Deal: The life and legacy of Frances Perkins— Social security, unemployment insurance, and the minimum wage.* New York: Anchor Books.

Duncan, S. F., & Goddard, H. W. (2017). *Family life education: Principles and practices for effective Outreach* (3rd ed.). Thousand Oaks, CA: Sage.

Fricke, A. B., Walsh, B. A., & Barghouti, J. A. (2017). Tri-parenting: Legal developments and strengths. *Family Focus, 74*, 18–19.

Hans, J. D. (2015). The science of family life education: History, status, and practice. In M. J. Walcheski, & J. S. Reinke (Eds.), *Family life education: The practice of family science* (pp. 3–8). Minneapolis, MN: National Council on Family Relations.

Henderson, T. L., & Martin, K. J. (2002). Cooperative learning as one approach to teaching family law. *Family Relations, 51*, 351–360. doi: 132.174.250.16

Holbrook, T. (1983). Going among them: The evolution of the home visit. *Journal of Sociology and Social Welfare, 10*, 112–135.

Hughes, R. Jr., Bowers, J. R., Mitchell, E. T., Curtiss, S., & Ebata, A. T. (2012). Developing online family life prevention and education programs. *Family Relations, 61*, 711–727. doi: 10.1111/j.1741-3729.2012.00737.x

Hughes, R. Jr., Ebata, A. T., Bowers, J., Mitchell, E. T., & Curtiss, S. L. (2015). Strategies for designing online family life education programs. In M. J. Walcheski, & J. S. Reinke (Eds.), *Family life education: The practice of family science* (pp. 131–140). Minneapolis, MN: National Council on Family Relations.

Jacobson, A. L. (2015). Parenting education and guidance. In M. J. Walcheski, & J. S. Reinke (Eds.), *Family life education: The practice of family science* (pp. 61–72). Minneapolis, MN: National Council on Family Relations.

Kruenegel-Farr, D. S., Allen, K., & Machara, M. E. (2016). Family and parent coaching certification processes: What do current programs do? *Family Science Review, 21*, 77–93.

Lewis-Rowley, M., Brasher, R. E., Moss, J. J., Duncan, S. F., & Stiles, R. J. (1993). The evolution of education for family life. In M. E. Arcus, J. D. Schvaneveldt, & J. J. Moss (Eds.), *Handbook of family life education: Foundations of family life education* (pp. 26–50). Newbury Park, CA: Sage.

Machir, J. (2014). Certified Family Life Educators as home visitors: Making the case. Retrieved from https://www.ncfr.org/cfle-network/past-issues/spring-2014/certified-family-life-educators-home-visitors-maki

Minnesota Council on Family Relations (MNCFR) (2009). *Ethical thinking and practice for parent and family life education.* Minneapolis, MN: Ethics Committee, Parent and Family Education Section.

Minnesota Council on Family Relations (MNCFR) (2016). *Ethical thinking and practice for parent and family life education.* Minneapolis, MN: Ethics Committee, Parent and Family Education Section.

Myers-Walls, J. A. (2014). Comments and reflections on family coaching: An emerging Family Science field. *Family Relations, 63,* 583–588. doi: 10.1111/fare.12097

Myers-Walls, J., Ballard, S., Darling, C., & Myers-Bowman, K. (2011). Reconceptualizing the domains and boundaries of family life education. *Family Relations, 60,* 357–372. doi: 10.1111/j.1741-3729.2011.00659.x

NCFR. (n.d.) NCFR history. Retrieved https://www.ncfr.org/history

NCFR (2015). Family life education content areas: Content and practice guidelines. In M. J. Walcheski & J. S. Reinke (Eds.), *Family life education: The practice of family science* (pp. 143–155). Minneapolis, MN: National Council on Family Relations.

Palm, G. (2018). Professional ethics and practice in family life education. In *Tools for ethical thinking and practice in family life education* (4th ed., pp. 1–10). Minneapolis, MN: National Council on Family Relations.

Petkus, J. (2015). A first-hand account of implementing a Family Life Education model: Intentionality in Head Start home visiting. In M. J. Walcheski, & J. S. Reinke (Eds.), *Family life education: The practice of family science* (pp. 325–331). Minneapolis, MN: National Council on Family Relations.

Reinke, J., & Walcheski, M. (2015). Introduction—family life education: The practice of family science. In M. J. Walcheski, & J. S. Reinke (Eds.), *Family life education: The practice of family science* (pp. vii–xii). Minneapolis, MN: National Council on Family Relations.

Roehl, A., Reddy, S. L., & Shannon, G. J. (2013). The flipped classroom: An opportunity to engage millennial students through active learning strategies. *Journal of Family & Consumer Sciences, 105,* 44–49.

Russo, C. J. (2010). *Encyclopedia of law and higher education.* Thousand Oaks: CA: Sage.

Scholl, J. (2013). Extension family and consumer sciences: Why it was included in the Smith-Lever Act of 1914. *Journal of Family and Consumer Sciences, 105,* 8–16.

The Vanier Institute of the Family. (2018). Our founders: Georges and Pauline Vanier. Retrieved http://vanierinstitute.ca/about-us/our-founders/

United States Department of Agriculture. (n.d.). Children, youth and families at risk (CYFAR). Retrieved https://nifa.usda.gov/program/children-youth-and-families-risk-cyfar

Walker, S. (2017). Technology use by Certified Family Life Educators. *CFLE Network, 30* (4), 15–17.

Walsh, B. A. (2017). Setting the stage for families in poverty as catalysts: A family life education approach to Early Head Start Home Visiting. *Family Focus, 73,* 8–10.

Walsh, B. A. (2019). The interface of FLE and EHS home-based services: Past, present, and future. *CFLE Network, 32,* 11–13.

Walsh, B. A., DeFlorio, L., Burnham, M. M., & Weiser, D. A. (2017). *Introduction to human development and family studies.* New York: Taylor & Francis.

Walsh, B. A., Mortensen, J. A., Edwards, A. L., & Cassidy, D. (in press). The practice of family life education within Early Head Start home visiting. *Family Relations.*

2 The State of Early Head Start Home Visiting

Research on home visiting has blossomed in recent years as home visiting programs have become an increasingly popular way to deliver services to vulnerable families. This expansion is partially due to the establishment of the Maternal, Infant, and Early Childhood Home Visiting (MIECHV) program, which contributes funding to home visiting programs that are backed by solid scientific evidence of effectiveness (i.e., evidence-based) (Rodrigue & Reeves, 2015). Early Head Start (EHS) home visiting is one of the most prominent home visiting programs, but—as with most home visiting programs—research tends to find only small to moderate effects of the program on child and family wellbeing. More recently, researchers have focused their efforts on the quantity and quality of home visits to try to isolate the essential components that promote positive family outcomes (Raikes et al., 2006; Roggman et al., 2008). Nonetheless, home visiting approaches, including EHS, remain somewhat of a "black box" given programs' diverse approaches for home visiting delivery. This chapter explores how home visiting supports vulnerable families, provides an overview of the EHS home visiting approach, reviews current research on the effectiveness of home visiting, and identifies what research tells us about under which conditions EHS is most effective. In the following chapter, we extend these ideas to explore how family life education methodology or Certified Family Life Educators as home visitors could effectively address the need for a consistent and enhanced evidence-based curriculum to EHS HV.

The Importance of Home Visiting for Vulnerable Families

Home visiting programs, such as EHS, play an important role in the lives of the families they serve. Families living in poverty can experience stress due to food insecurity, hunger, inadequate medical care, the inability to provide such basic needs as food, clothing, and shelter to their children, dangerous neighborhoods, and a myriad of other factors. These compounding stressors create situations in which families are vulnerable to poor outcomes. Families living in poverty are more likely to experience issues related to domestic violence, addiction, and mental health concerns (Evans, 2004; Azzi-Lessing, 2013). Children growing up in poverty are also more likely to develop behavioral and social problems, are at greater risk for academic failure (Bradley & Corwyn, 2002; Miller & Chen, 2013),

16 State of Early Head Start Home Visiting

with increased risk-taking in adolescence continuing to perpetuate poor adult outcomes (Evans & Cassells, 2014). Home visiting programs can help vulnerable families capitalize on existing strengths in a variety of ways. Home visiting programs may connect families to helpful community resources, improve parent–child interactions, offer parents social support, improve family relations, and support child development and school readiness.

In general, there is a great body of scientific evidence that supports home visiting programs as effective in improving family and child wellbeing. The national database, Home Visiting Evidence of Effectiveness (HomVEE), was developed in 2009 by the U.S. Department of Health and Human Services to monitor the effectiveness of various home visiting programs (Sama-Miller et al., 2017). Each year, the HomVEE program reviews new research on current home visiting programs. In addition to EHS home visiting, other prominent programs include Healthy Families America (HFA) and Nurse Family Partnership (NFP). Each of the aforementioned program models has specific guidelines that emphasize activities and processes differently. Across a variety of program models, results from the HomVEE database suggest that, in general, home visiting programs are effective in:

- improving child health and development
- fostering child school readiness
- improving family economic self-sufficiency
- providing linkages and referrals to community support programs
- improving maternal wellbeing
- improving positive parenting practices
- reducing child maltreatment, and
- reducing juvenile delinquency, family violence, and crime.

(Sama-Miller et al., 2017)

It is important to note that no single home visiting model has proven to be a "magic bullet" that improves all aspects of family and child wellbeing. Most program models find favorable effects in achieving some, but not all, of the above outcomes. The HomVEE database classifies a home visiting program as evidence-based when evaluation by multiple quality research studies has documented its effectiveness in improving at least two of the above outcomes (Administration for Children and Families [ACF], 2018a). The HomVEE database classifies EHS home visiting as an evidence-based model because researchers have found significant effects in the majority of the outcome domains listed above. The following sections explore the background of Early Head Start home visiting and current research within the program.

Background on EHS Home Visiting

In 1965, President Lyndon B. Johnson and the United States Congress authorized funding for the Head Start Project (ACF, 2018b). Head Start was developed in response to the nation's increasing awareness of the deleterious effects of poverty, and the recognition that quality education can make a difference in the lives of impoverished families. Head Start programs provide free early childhood education to preschool-age children, child development services, parental support, and health and nutrition education to families who live below the federal poverty line (Zigler & Muenchow, 1992).

In the decades following the establishment of the Head Start Project, researchers in neuroscience and human development documented the critical importance of children's experiences during the first few years of life. Policy makers paid attention to this research, and Early Head Start (EHS) was added as part of the 1994 Head Start Reauthorization Act, which expanded funding for services to pregnant women and families with infants and toddlers (Raikes & Love, 2002). EHS is a two-generation program, meaning that the program focuses on supporting parents in addition to their young children. EHS home visiting operates on the principle of improving children's wellbeing via strengthening children's experiences and relationships at home (ACF, 2002). Improving children's wellbeing begins with strengthening parents' skills to foster quality parent–child relationships and home learning environments (Chazan-Cohen et al., 2013).

Some EHS programs provide services via center-based childcare (similar to Head Start), while others provide services via home-based visiting programs, or a mix of center-based and at-home services. For the most part, pregnant women and children are eligible for services if the family is eligible for public assistance, the child is homeless or in foster care, or the family's income falls at or below the federal poverty line. According to the 2019 federal poverty guidelines, a family of four earning $25,750 annually would qualify for EHS (U.S. Department of Health and Human Services, 2019).

All EHS programs are based on and must adhere to the Head Start Program Performance Standards (HSPPS; ACF, 2016), but granting agencies develop EHS programs in accordance to the needs of families in their communities (Raikes & Love, 2002). According to the HSPPS:

> A home-based program must provide home visits and group socialization activities that promote secure parent–child relationships and help parents provide high-quality early learning experiences in language, literacy, mathematics, social and emotional functioning, approaches to learning, science, physical skills, and creative arts. A program must implement a research-based curriculum that delivers developmentally, linguistically, and culturally appropriate home visits and group socialization activities that support children's cognitive, social, and emotional growth for later success in school.
>
> (HSPPS § 1302.35; ACF, 2016)

Given this clear purpose, EHS home visiting programs primarily focus on promoting healthy child development, positive family relationships, and collaboration with the community (ACF, 2002, 2004). The HSPPS specify that home visits must occur once per week (a minimum of 46 visits per year) for at least 90 minutes, and that a minimum of 22 group parent socialization activities must be held over the program year (§ 1302.22).

Individual programs have the flexibility to plan the structure and content of home visits, as long as they meet the guidelines set forth in the HSPPS § 1302.35 (ACF, 2016). Section B stipulates that in terms of *home-based program design*, all home visits must be planned jointly with the parents and home visitor and incorporate information from ongoing assessment. Section C stipulates that *home visiting experiences* must set goals and use a curriculum that implement:

1. age and developmentally appropriate, structured, child-focused learning experiences;
2. strategies and activities that promote parents' ability to support the child's cognitive, social, emotional, language, literacy, and physical development;
3. strategies and activities that promote the home as a learning environment that is safe, nurturing, responsive, and language- and communication-rich;
4. research-based strategies and activities that recognize bilingualism and biliteracy as strengths for children who are dual language learners; and,
5. follow-up activities with families to discuss learning experiences provided in the home between each visit, address concerns, and inform strategies to promote progress toward school readiness goals.

(HSPPS § 1302.35, ACF, 2016)

Furthermore, Section D stipulates that any *home-based curriculum* used by EHS must be developmentally appropriate, research-based, and focused on promoting parents' roles as their child's teacher. Notably, the HSPPS also mandate that staff must be adequately supported to implement the curriculum with fidelity through support, feedback, and supervision (HSPPS § 1302.35, ACF, 2016).

Additionally, training for EHS home visitors is outlined in the HSPPS § 1302.91 (ACF, 2016) as follows:

i. have a minimum of a home-based CDA credential or comparable credential, or equivalent coursework as part of an associate's or bachelor's degree; and,
ii. demonstrate competency to plan and implement home-based learning experiences that ensure effective implementation of the home visiting curriculum and promote children's progress across the standards described in the Head Start Early Learning Outcomes Framework: Ages Birth to Five, including for children with disabilities and dual language learners, as appropriate, and to build respectful, culturally responsive, and trusting relationships with families.

While complying with these expectations, EHS home visitors may have varying levels of higher education in a variety of disciplines. A CDA credential, or Child Development Associate, is an avenue for training in early care and education, including home visiting for families with children ages birth to five (Council for Professional Recognition [CPR], 2017). The CDA is a competency-based credential, requiring that professionals demonstrate their competence in a variety of areas including: facilitating the environment, child development, guidance related to social and emotional development, positive relationships with families, a well-run program, and commitment to professionalism. The CDA is a common education requirement for home visiting programs. For example, the recently revised Head Start Performance Standards listed the CDA Credential as the minimum educational requirements for all home visitors (Administration for Children and Families [ACF], 2016). Home visitors may also come from social work, early childhood education, family science, or be paraprofessionals from the community. Some programs also employ family- and child-specific home visitors to help families achieve different goals (Peterson et al., 2007). According to a national survey of Early Head Start families, approximately 27% had a home visitor with an Associate's degree, 43% a Bachelor's degree, and 8% a graduate/professional degree (ACF, 2015). For families who had home visitor without an Associate's degree, 79% had a CDA credential (ACF, 2015).

The HSPPS also mandate that EHS programs "implement a research-based, coordinated coaching strategy for education staff" (§ 1302.93, ACF, 2016). At a minimum, this involves identifying areas in which staff members are in need of support, and providing opportunities for "intensive coaching," observation, feedback, and modeling of best practices. Intensive coaching opportunities must align with the program's goals and curriculum, be delivered by a well-trained coach, and be used as opportunities for professional growth.

What Research Tells Us about EHS Home Visiting

The following sections provide an overview of the scientific research on the effectiveness of EHS home visiting. First, we examine the overall effectiveness of EHS home visiting in improving child development, school readiness, and parent wellbeing. Second, we examine the conditions under which EHS home visiting seems to have the biggest impact.

The Effectiveness of EHS Home Visiting

Much of the data about the effectiveness of EHS home visiting comes from the Early Head Start Research and Evaluation Project (EHSRE; ACF, 2002, 2004). Initiated in 1996, the EHSRE was a collaboration with multiple research universities and 17 EHS programs around the U.S, representing about 3,000 families. Some EHS sites provided only home visiting, only center-based childcare, or a combination of the two. Thirteen sites provided home visiting (or combination) services. The study was a randomized experiment, meaning that families eligible for EHS services were randomly sorted into two groups: EHS services (program), and no EHS services (control). Researchers assessed children and parents at various time points throughout the program, as well as after the program ended upon kindergarten entry (ACF, 2002). The randomized experimental design allowed researchers to compare the children and families who received EHS home visiting services to those who did not receive such services, and to attribute differences in their outcomes to effects of the EHS home visiting program.

Results from the EHSRE Project found that children and parents who participated in EHS home visiting had many favorable outcomes as compared to families who did not participate in EHS home visiting services. Parents who participated were more likely to create a better home learning environment and had more knowledge of child development when their children were toddlers (Love et al., 2001). They were also more likely to promote language and literacy activities in the home when their children were preschool age (Chazan-Cohen et al., 2013). Parents were also more likely to use more positive and stimulating parenting behaviors by the end of the program (ACF, 2002). The study also found that parents who participated in EHS home visiting were more engaged while playing with their children at age three (ACF, 2002). Participating children were also more likely to be rated as having positive approaches to learning and fewer behavioral problems in preschool (Chazan-Cohen et al., 2013). Researchers have also explored the idea that much of the change in children's development as a result of EHS home visiting is the result of more positive parenting practices (Raikes et al., 2014).

The EHSRE Project also found that EHS home visiting had many positive impacts on parents' education and employment opportunities. Compared to the control group, parents who participated in EHS home visiting were more likely to participate in high school, vocational programs, or ESL classes (ACF, 2002). They also spent more hours per week involved in educational or job training activities when their children were toddlers, and were more likely to be employed or enrolled in educational programs (ACF, 2002). Consequently, parents who participated in EHS home visiting reported higher incomes when their children were preschool age (Chazan-Cohen, et al., 2013). Parents also reported being better connected to community services and receiving help with identification and services for a child's disability (Love et al., 2001).

Individual EHS home visiting programs have also reported that home visiting is associated with improved attachment relationships between parents and toddlers, as well as increased child cognitive development and less use of physical punishment in preschool (Roggman et al., 2009; Roggman & Cook, 2010). Most EHS parents are mothers, but for one program that had particularly high father participation, the program was structured specifically to focus on father-toddler play and father involvement (Roggman et al., 2004). Researchers found that when the program was structured this way, there was success in improving their social play.

It is important to note that most of the statistical effects of EHS home visiting described above are small to moderate. There are also many instances in which research has demonstrated no effect of the program (ACF, 2018b). According to the HomVEE database, as of 2016, there is no rigorous research that demonstrates the program's ability to improve child health (e.g., doctor visits, immunizations) or maternal health (e.g., subsequent pregnancies, mental health) (ACF, 2018b). This may sound discouraging, but is actually quite typical of research on most home visiting programs (Gomby et al., 1999). Because of this, researchers also spend considerable efforts trying to understand *under which conditions* programs are most effective (Raikes et al., 2006).

When is EHS Home Visiting Most Effective?

Home visiting programs are costly to execute, so programs are interested in maximizing their efforts to the greatest benefit. Research that focuses on the conditions under which home visiting is more effective helps EHS programs make evidence-based decisions on how to best serve their families.

Program involvement. Program involvement is key in understanding when EHS home visiting is most effective. Involvement is "the process of the parent connecting with and using the services of a program to the best of the client's and the program's ability" (Korfmacher et al., 2008, p. 171). The concept of involvement is multifaceted and includes participation quantity, such as the number of home visits families participate in, or the family's duration of time spent in the program. Involvement also includes engagement, meaning the family's dedication and emotional investment in the program (Korfmacher et al., 2008). Program involvement is essential because families that are more involved are less likely to drop out of the program (Roggman et al., 2008). Families who drop out of the program tend to have more risks and stress in their lives, such as residential instability, teen and/or single mothers, no high school degree, language barriers, or children with diagnosed special needs (Peterson et al., 2012; Roggman et al., 2008). It is important that home visiting programs understand how best to foster program involvement, especially for the most vulnerable families.

Better program involvement is also associated with better family and child outcomes at the end of the program. In the EHSRE study, Raikes and colleagues (2006) found a positive correlation between the number of months families participated in EHS home visiting and the quality of home language and literacy environments they provided for their children when they were preschool age. Consistent and intensive participation in EHS home visiting was also associated with better child development and school readiness outcomes at the preschool and 5th grade follow-ups (Peterson et al., 2012). These families had better teacher–child and teacher–parent relationships in 5th grade as well (Peterson et al., 2012).

Process quality. Process quality, meaning the interactions that occur between the home visitor and family, is also important in understanding when EHS home visiting is most effective. Quality interactions between parents and home visitors help build trusting relationships that serve as the foundation for collaboration during the home visiting program. Home visitors cultivate quality relationships by interacting with families from a strengths-based perspective, meaning that the home visitor provides support and collaboration versus trying to "fix" the family. When EHS parents report that home visitors build on existing family strengths, they also report feeling more empowered, competent, and that they provide better home learning environments for their children (Green et al., 2004). Some evidence suggests that the home visitor–parent relationship is more important to program involvement than overall satisfaction with the EHS program (Korfmacher et al., 2007).

Roggman and colleagues (2016a) completed an in-depth examination of EHS home visiting process quality. The researchers observed how responsive the home visitor was to the family's strengths and cultural practices, the quality of the parent–provider relationship, the home visitor's ability to facilitate parent–child interactions, the degree of collaboration with families, and the overall engagement of everyone participating in the visit. Families who participated in home visits characterized by better process quality were more involved in the EHS program. These families also reported more positive experiences during the program and more favorable child development and parenting outcomes at the end of the program (Roggman et al., 2016b). Research such as this highlights that there is something special about the family-provider relationship that helps keep families involved in EHS home visiting and leads to more favorable outcomes.

Home visitor qualifications. As outlined in the HSPPS, home visiting professionals may have a range of professional qualifications, with the minimum requirement as a CDA credential. Most current research on EHS home visiting was conducted before this minimal educational requirement was added to the HSPPS (e.g., Avellar et al., 2016). In 2010, according to the Early Head Start Family and Child Experiences Survey, 51% of EHS home visitors held a bachelor's degree or higher, and 59% were trained in the areas of early childhood education or child development with at least an associate's degree (Vogel et al., 2015). Some evidence suggests that when home visitors are more focused on the child (as a home visitor trained as a CDA would), children show better cognitive and language scores, and are in better home learning environments at age three (Raikes et al., 2006). However, the two-generation nature of EHS is important to keep in mind. Professional training that provides a more holistic view of the family unit may help programs better address complex family needs.

Structure and content of the home visit. The HSPPS also provide considerable flexibility in the structure and content of EHS home visits. This allows individual communities to tailor EHS programs to the needs of their families; however, it also leads to considerable variation across programs and the lack of a consistent, evidence-based model (Gomby et al., 1999; Korfmacher et al., 2007; Petkus, 2015). According to HomVEE, EHS home visiting is one of the few evidence-based home visiting models that does not specify certain structure and content across all programs (Avellar et al., 2016). Many EHS programs utilize packaged curricula such as Parents as Teachers (PAT). PAT has approximately 182 affiliates in the United States that offer Early Head Start services (PAT, 2015), and focuses on improving multiple dimensions of parent–child interactions, increasing parental efficacy (i.e., feelings that one can parent effectively), informing knowledge of child development, and helping parents develop everyday learning opportunities in the home (Hebbeler & Gerlach-Downie, 2002).

There is some evidence that EHS home visiting is more effective when a focused intervention or philosophy is integrated to guide home visitor training and the structure of the home visit. For example, one EHS program integrated an infant mental health framework, meaning a focus on infant-parent relationships and infant emotional experiences from a psychotherapeutic perspective (McKelvey et al., 2015). Home visitors were social work professionals and encouraged parents' reflections on their own childhood experiences. In this experiment, the infant mental health program reported more positive family relationships and coping skills, and less parenting stress than the "business as usual" EHS home visiting group (McKelvey et al., 2015). Other EHS programs have also achieved more favorable outcomes by including interventions that focus on targeted aspects of development, such as attachment or language and literacy development (Manz et al., 2017; West et al., 2017).

Interventions that specifically operate from a strengths-based perspective have also been successfully incorporated within EHS home visiting. For example, Knoche and colleagues (2012) integrated the Getting Ready intervention within an EHS home visiting program (to a random selection of families). The intervention focused on building a sensitive, responsive parent–child relationship through a collaborative parent–home visitor relationship. Parents that participated in the intervention displayed more warm, sensitive, and supporting behaviors towards their children at the end of the program than the families who received regular EHS home visiting services (Knoche et al., 2012).

Summary

Research demonstrates that the EHS home visiting program model is effective at improving child and family wellbeing. Nevertheless, effects tend to be small to moderate in size, and sometime insignificant. Factors such as parental involvement in the program, the quality of the family–home visitor relationship, the professional qualifications of the home visitor and the structure and content of the home visit, likely all play a role in just how effective EHS actually is. Much of this simply speaks to the complexities of family life and the fact that creating meaningful change in families' interactions and circumstances is complicated. However, the current research offers insight into the ways in which family life education might offer a unique role in EHS home visiting program philosophy, professional preparation, training, and program development. The following chapter introduces FLE as a new philosophy or perspective that has the potential to increase the effectiveness of EHS home visiting. We suggest that alignment with the strengths-based family life education (FLE) methodology and/or employing Certified Family Life Educators (CFLE) as home visitors would bring more consistency to EHS home visiting.

Key Concepts

- Child Development Associate
- Early Head Start Research and Evaluation Project (EHSRE)
- Evidence-based
- Federal poverty level
- Head Start Project
- Home Visiting Evidence of Effectiveness (HomVEE)
- Maternal, Infant, and Early Childhood Home Visiting (MIECHV)
- Process quality
- Randomized experiment
- Two-generation program
- Vulnerable families

Recommended Readings

Administration for Children and Families. (2015). *The faces of Early Head Start: A national picture of Early Head Start programs and the children and families they serve.* OPRE Report #2015-29, Washington, DC: Office of Planning, Research, and Evaluation, Administration for Children and Families, U.S. Department of Health and Human Services.

Sama-Miller, E., Akers, L., Mraz-Esposito, A., Zukiewicz, M., Avellar, S., Paulsell, D., & Del Grosso, P. (2018). *Home visiting evidence of effectiveness review: Executive summary*. Office of Planning, Research and Evaluation, Administration for Children and Families, US Department of Health and Human Services. Washington, DC. Retrieved from https://homvee.acf.hhs.gov/Publications/9/Publications/55/

References

Administration for Children and Families (ACF). (2002). *Making a difference in the lives of infants and toddlers and their families: The impacts of Early Head Start*. Washington, DC: Office of Planning, Research, and Evaluation, U.S. Department of Health and Human Services.

Administration for Children and Families(ACF). (2004). *The role of Early Head Start programs in addressing the child care needs of low-income families with infants and toddlers: Influences on child care use and quality*. Washington, DC: Office of Planning, Research, and Evaluation, U.S. Department of Health and Human Services.

Administration for Children and Families (ACF). (2015). *The faces of Early Head Start: A national picture of Early Head Start programs and the children and families they serve*. OPRE Report #2015-29, Washington, DC: Office of Planning, Research, and Evaluation, Administration for Children and Families, U.S. Department of Health and Human Services.

Administration for Children and Families (ACF). (2016). *Head Start program performance standards*. Retrieved from: https://eclkc.ohs.acf.hhs.gov/policy/45-cfr-chap-xiii

Administration for Children and Families (ACF). (2018a). *DHHS criteria for evidence-based program models*. Retrieved from: https://homvee.acf.hhs.gov/document.aspx?rid=4&sid=19&mid=6. U.S. Department of Health and Human Services.

Administration for Children and Families (ACF). (2018b). *Head Start timeline*. Retrieved from: https://eclkc.ohs.acf.hhs.gov/about-us/news/head-start-timeline. U.S. Department of Health and Human Services.

Avellar, S., Paulsell, D., Sama-Miller, E., Del Grosso, P., Akers, L., & Kleinman, R. (2016). *Home visiting evidence of effectiveness review: Executive summary*. Washington, DC: Office of Planning, Research and Evaluation, Administration for Children and Families, U.S. Department of Health and Human Services.

Azzi-Lessing, L. (2013). Serving highly vulnerable families in home-visitation programs. *Infant Mental Health Journal, 34*(5), 376–390.

Bradley, R., & Corwyn, R. (2002). Socioeconomic status and child development. *Annual Review of Psychology, 53*, 371–399.

Chazan-Cohen, R., Raikes, H.H., Vogel, C. & Klute, M.M. (2013). Program subgroups: Patterns of impacts for home-based, center-based, and mixed-approach programs. *Monographs of the Society for Research in Child Development, 78*(1), 93–109.

Council for Professional Recognition (CPR). (2017). *About the Child Development Associate (CDA) credential*. Retrieved https://www.cdacouncil.org/about/cda-credential.

Evans, G. W. (2004). The environment of childhood poverty. *American Psychologist, 59* (2), 77–92.

Evans, G. W., & Cassells, R. C. (2014). Childhood poverty, cumulative risk exposure, and mental health in emerging adults. *Clinical Psychological Science, 2*(3), 287–296.

Green, B. L., McAllister, C. A., & Tarte, J. (2004). The strengths-based practices inventory: A measure of strengths-based practices for social service programs. *Families in Society, 85,* 326–335.

Gomby, D. S., Culross, P. L., Behrman, R. E. (1999). Home visiting: Recent program evaluations—analysis and recommendations. *The Future of Children, 9,* 4–26.

Hebbeler, K. M., & Gerlach-Downie, S. G. (2002). Inside the black box of home visiting: A qualitative analysis of why intended outcomes were not achieved. *Early Childhood Research Quarterly, 17,* 28–51. doi:10.1016/S0885-2006(02)00128-X

Knoche, L. L., Edwards, C. P., Sheridan, S. M., Kupzyk, K. A., Marvin, C. A., Cline, K. D., & Clarke, B. L. (2012). Getting ready: Results of a randomized trial of a relationship-focused intervention on the parent–infant relationship in rural Early Head Start. *Infant Mental Health Journal, 33,* 439–458.

Korfmacher, J., Green, B., Spellmann, M., & Thornburg, K. R. (2007). The helping relationship and program participation in early childhood home visiting. *Infant Mental Health Journal, 28,* 459–480.

Korfmacher, J., Green, B., Staerkel, F., Peterson, C., Cook, G., Roggman, L., Faldowski, R. A. (2008). Parent involvement in early childhood home visiting. *Child Youth Care Forum, 37,* 171–196.

Love, J., Kisker, E., Ross, C., Schochet, P., Brooks-Gunn, J., Boller, K., et al.(2001). *Building their futures: How Early Head Start programs are enhancing the lives of infants and toddlers in low-income families. Summary report.* Report to Commissioner's Office of Research and Evaluation, Head Start Bureau, Administration on Children, Youth and Families, and Department of Health and Human Services. Princeton, NJ: Mathematica Policy Research.

Manz, P. H., Eisenberg, R., Gernhart, A., Faison, J., Laracy, S., Ridgard, T., & Pinho, T. (2017). Engaging Early Head Start parents in a collaborative inquiry: The co-construction of Little Talks. *Early Child Development and Care, 187*(8), 1311–1334.

McKelvey, L., Schiffman, R. F., Brophy-Herb, H. E., Bocknek, E. L., Fitzgerald, H. E., Reischel, T. M., Hawver, S., & Deluca, M. C. (2015). Examining long-term effects of an infant mental health home-based Early Head Start program on family strengths. *Infant Mental Health Journal, 36,* 353–365.

Miller, G. E., & Chen, E. (2013). The biological residue of childhood poverty. *Child Development Perspectives, 7,* 67–73.

Parents as Teachers (PAT). (2015). *2016–2017 Affiliate performance report, summary.* Retrieved from https://static1.squarespace.com/static/56be46a6b6aa60dbb45e41a5/t/5a37eca0085229e36d170e8e/1513614498107/APR_2pgr_2016-2017.pdf

Peterson, C. A., Luze, G. J., Eshbaugh, E. M., Jeon, H. J., & Kantz, K. R. (2007). Enhancing parent-child interactions through home visiting: Promising practice or unfulfilled promise? *Journal of Early Intervention, 29,* 119–140. doi: 10.1177/105381510702900205

Peterson, C. A., Zhang, D., Roggman, L., Green, B., Chazan Cohen, R., Atwater, J. B. McKelvey, L., & Korfmacher, J. (2012). Family participation and involvement in Early Head Start Home Visiting services: Relations with longitudinal outcomes executive summary. *Human Development and Family Studies Reports, 1.* http://lib.dr.iastate.edu/hdfs_reports/1

Petkus, J. (2015). A first-hand account of implementing a Family Life Education model: Intentionality in Head Start home visiting. In M. J. Walcheski, & J. S. Reinke (Eds.), *Family life education: The practice of family science* (pp. 325–331). Minneapolis, MN: National Council on Family Relations.

Raikes, H. H., & Love, J. M. (2002). Early Head Start: A dynamic new program for infants and toddlers and their families. *Infant Mental Health Journal, 23*, 1–13.

Raikes, H., Green, B. L., Atwater, J., Kisker, E., Constantine, J., & Chazan-Cohen, R. (2006). Involvement in Early Head Start home visiting services: Demographic predictors and relations to child and parent outcomes. *Early Childhood Research Quarterly, 21*, 2–24.

Raikes, H., Roggman, L. A., Peterson, C. A., Brooks-Gunn, J., Chazan-Cohen, R., Zhang, X., & Schiffman, R. F. (2014). Theories of change and outcomes in home-based Early Head Start programs. *Early Childhood Research Quarterly, 29*, 574–585.

Rodrigue, E., & Reeves, R. V. (2015). *Home visiting programs: An early test for the 114th Congress.* Brookings https://www.brookings.edu/research/home-visiting-programs-an-early-test-for-the-114th-congress/

Roggman, L. A., Boyce, L. K., Cook, G. A., Christiansen, K., & Jones, D. (2004). Playing with daddy and toys: Father-toddler social toy play, developmental outcomes, and Early Head Start. *Fathering: A Journal of Theory, Research, and Practice about Men as Fathers, 2*, 83–108.

Roggman, L. A., Cook, G. A., Peterson, C. A., & Raikes, H. H. (2008) Who drops out of Early Head Start home visiting programs?, *Early Education and Development, 19*, 574–599, DOI: 10.1080/10409280701681870

Roggman, L., Boyce, L. K., & Cook, G. (2009). Keeping kids on track: Impacts of a parenting-focused Early Head Start program on attachment security and cognitive development. *Early Education & Development, 20*(6), 920–941.

Roggman, L. A., & Cook, G. A. (2010). Attachment, aggression, and family risk in a low-income sample. *Family Science, 1*(3), 191–204. doi:10.1080/19424620.2010.567829

Roggman, L. A., Peterson, C. A., Chazan-Cohen, R., Ispa, J., Decker, K., Hughes-Belding, K., Cook, G. A., & Vallotton, C. D. (2016a). Preparing home visitors to partner with families of infants and toddlers. *Journal of Early Childhood Teacher Education, 37*, 301–313. doi: 10.1080/10901027.2016.1241965

Roggman, L. A., Cook, G. A., Innocenti, M. S., Jump Norman, V., Boyce, L. K., Christiansen, K., & Peterson, C. A. (2016b). Home visit quality variations in two Early Head Start programs in relation to parenting and child vocabulary outcomes. *Infant Mental Health Journal, 37*, 193–207.

Sama-Miller, E., Akers, L. Mraz-Esposito, A., Zukiewicz, M., Avellar, S., Paulsell, D., & Del Grosso, P. (2017). *Home visiting evidence of effectiveness review: Executive summary.* Office of Planning, Research and Evaluation, Administration for Children and Families, U.S. Department of Health and Human Services. Washington, DC.

U.S. Department of Health and Human Services. (2019). *Poverty guidelines.* Retrieved from https://aspe.hhs.gov/poverty-guidelines

Vogel, C. A., Caronongan, P., Thomas, J., Bandel, E., Xue, Y., Henke, J., Aikens, N., Boller, K., & Murphy, L. (2015). *Administration for children and families. Toddlers in Early Head Start: A portrait of 2-year-olds, their families, and the programs serving them.* OPRE Report #2015-10, Washington, DC: Office of Planning, Research, and Evaluation, Administration for Children and Families, U.S. Department of Health and Human Services.

West, A. L., Aparicio, E. M., Berlin, L. J., & Jones Harden, B. (2017). Implementing an attachment-based parenting intervention within home-based Early Head Start: Home visitors' perceptions and experiences. *Infant Mental Health Journal*, *38*(4), 514–522.

Zigler, E., & Muenchow, S. (1992). *Head Start: The inside story of America's most successful educational experiment*. New York, NY: Basic Books.

3 Family Life Education
A Foundation for Early Head Start Home Visiting

Despite a history of research in the home visiting field, there is still much to learn about how to actively engage families in home visiting activities and processes (Hughes, Moni, Joslyn, & Younts, 2018; Paulsell, Del Grosso, Supplee, 2014). A family-centered approach to home visiting is important for promoting family engagement (Hughes et al., 2018). Family life education (FLE) is the practice of family science (Darling, Cassidy, & Rehm, 2017) and is an exemplary family-centered approach. Problems—such as unemployment, substance abuse, and domestic violence—are addressed through a systems perspective and these problems can be mitigated through prevention, education, a strengths-based approach, and skill-building (Darling et al., 2017). This chapter describes the foundational and operational principles central to FLE, which can serve as a metaframework for many home visiting models (e.g., EHS-HBO).

Certified Family Life Educators (CFLEs) are credentialed family life educators and hold a four-year degree or a graduate degree (see Chapter 1 and Appendix D). Recall that CFLEs have to take coursework in ten FLE content areas in a CFLE approved program or pass a national exam. After success with one of these paths, provisional CFLEs need to document work experience in the ten FLE content areas to earn full CFLE certification. To maintain certification, continuing education credits and experience must be documented every five years (see NCFR, 2018). CFLE is a nationally recognized credential, not a license (Darling & Cassidy, 2014). Nonetheless, CFLEs, as well as social workers, nurses, ECE professionals, and infant mental health certified professionals, are in a unique position to support families. CFLEs tend to have degrees in family science, but this credential has also been obtained by professionals with degrees in fields such as social work or education (Darling, Fleming, & Cassidy, 2009). CFLEs play an essential role in EHS-HBO to promote outcomes including building parental efficacy in parent-child interactions (Walsh, 2017a, 2019). We suggest that alignment of FLE principles and/or employing CFLEs as home visitors would bring more consistency to this important component of EHS services.

Why FLE is a Good Fit for EHS Home Visiting

Early Head Start includes collaborating with parents and families in their performance standards but it is unclear as to the dosage of FLE that actually

30   *Family Life Education*

occurs during home visiting (Palm & Cooke, 2018). Nonetheless, Early Head Start has a clear focus on parents, especially how to educate and support them (Palm & Cooke, 2018). FLE focuses on the whole family and shares that emphasis with Early Head Start (Palm & Cooke, 2018; Walsh, Mortensen, Edwards, & Cassidy, in press), especially given that EHS HV emphasizes family self-sufficiency and wellbeing (Roggman, Cook, Peterson, & Raikes, 2008) as does FLE (Darling et al., 2017).

EHS-HV and FLE share important theoretical assumptions and position families' individual needs and concerns at the forefront of programming. The following nine features of EHS-HV (HomVEE, 2016) align directly with FLE principles. The references in parentheses identify FLE sources that align with the EHS-HV features in HomVEE.

1. Commitment to high-quality service through qualified professionals (Arcus, Schvaneveldt, & Moss, 1993)
2. Identification and addressing of atypical and typical development (Leventhal, 2015)
3. Importance of parenting, parent education, and parent as child's first teacher (Darling & Cassidy, 2014; Jacobson, 2015)
4. Provision of opportunities for parents to share educational goals and practices, actively shape the program, and view themselves as members of their community and world (Arcus et al., 1993; Duncan & Goddard, 2017; Doherty, Erickson, & Cutting, 2015)
5. Inclusion of and support for children with unique developmental trajectories and medical or other special needs (Jacobson, 2015)
6. Demonstration of cross-cultural competence and respecting different values (Allen & Blaisure, 2015; Arcus et al., 1993; Ballard & Taylor, 2012)
7. A basis in needs of individuals and families, and offering in many different settings according to life situation demands (Arcus et al., 1993)
8. Responsiveness to developmental transitions through ages and stages (Leventhal, 2015) and other life transitions (Arcus et al., 1993; Duncan & Goddard, 2017)
9. Encouragement of professional collaboration to build strong, healthy families (Myers-Walls, Ballard, Darling, & Myers-Bowman, 2011)
    Source: Walsh (2017a, p. 8 and p. 9); Permission to reprint was granted by the National Council on Family Relations

A Closer Look at FLE as a Foundation for EHS Home Visiting

Home visitors with a background in FLE would be expected to understand the foundational principles of education, prevention, and strengths-based approaches, and have a strong understanding of theory and research. Home visiting and FLE both value these principles. A foundation in FLE also necessarily includes operational components of culture, contexts, content, and practice (see Darling et al., 2017; Darling, Cassidy, & Rehm, 2019). The following sections identify and explain this FLE foundation and discuss how they complement aims and practices of EHS–HBO.

Education

The centerpiece of the foundational principle of education is that techniques and approaches set the stage to empower families to build skills and maintain or promote their functioning (Darling et al., 2017). FLE has similarities and distinctions from other domains of family practice, such as family therapy (FT) and family case management or FCM (Myers-Walls et al., 2011). It is important to understand these boundaries to truly know the role of FLE. Understanding evidence-based approaches, program evaluation, and the importance of relationships is also key to this principle. FLEs have also posited that the relationship between the professional and the family and the process of learning may be more important than the educational content (Duncan & Goddard, 2017). In its current state, FLE content delivery occurs increasingly in individual settings, including coaching (Darling et al., 2017) and home visiting (Darling & Cassidy, 2014; Petkus, 2015).

EHS Home Visiting (EHS HV). The home visitor primarily operates in the education domain of family practice as compared to the FT and FCM domains (Petkus, 2015). Families can find the experience of home visiting to be therapeutic without it being therapy. Home visitors without a license in therapy should not practice therapy. Practicing in all three domains (FLE, FT, and FCM) leads to undefined boundaries and mixed expectations of the home visitor (Petkus, 2015) and supports mission-creeping that encourages home visitors to do additional work that is not central to their home visiting positions.

EHS home visitors can promote parenting skills and education (Wasik & Bryant, 2001). Social support is often helpful to families learning new skills (Wasik & Bryant, 2001). EHS socialization experiences are an opportunity beyond the home visit for further skill building and socialization experiences for children and parents. At socialization events further parenting education and skills can be developed in a planned manner (e.g., formally teaching nutrition education to a group through small group activities) or in a more organic way (e.g., a group picnic at a park). As mentioned in Chapter 2, there should be a minimum of 22 group socialization opportunities throughout the entire program year (HSPPS § 1302.22; Administration for Children and Families, 2016).

As of 2016, EHS sites also have to employ evidence-based approaches to their services (Administration for Children and Families, 2016). FLE's strengths as an evidence-based approach make it a strong fit for meeting this recent call for EHS sites to incorporate more evidence and evaluation. Perhaps a long-term goal is to conduct research on the practice of family life education and home visiting to undergo a Home Visiting Evidence of Effectiveness (HomVEE) review to determine if there is enough evidence for FLE to meet criteria for an evidence-based early childhood home visiting model (Walsh & Peterson, 2019). Program evaluation and

32 *Family Life Education*

the empirical examination of families are also crucial to FLE (Darling et al., 2017), further demonstrating the powerful overlap of these programs and approaches.

In EHS home visiting, the client and the professional each affect the relationship and processes of the visit and help the field understand why some families do not fully engage in the home visiting program (Brookes, Summers, Thornburg, Ispa, & Lane, 2006). Engagement in home visiting is complex because different agencies use different ways of measuring it (National Home Visiting Resource Center, 2017). Nonetheless, a close and collaborative bond between the home visitor and family is essential for family engagement in the home visiting program (Brookes et al., 2006; Hughes et al., 2018; Petkus, 2015). However, home visitors should be mindful that simply forming relationships is not sufficient and should not be at the expense of supporting child development (Peterson et al., 2013). Professionals who wish to support positive outcomes for young children must also establish a relationship with caregivers and other professionals (Sosinsky, Ruprecht, Horn, Kriener-Althen, Vogel, & Halle, 2016) and perhaps find ways to occasionally incorporate them into the home visit as needed.

Prevention

FLE embraces primary, secondary, and tertiary prevention (Darling et al., 2017). Primary prevention protects families before something occurs and secondary prevention aims to slow down the problem in its nascent stages (Darling et al., 2017). Tertiary prevention helps people deal with long-term problems and to prevent further damage (Darling & Cassidy, 2014; Darling et al., 2017). FLE may focus on risk and protective factors (Duncan & Goddard, 2017). Effective FLEs proactively work to mitigate risks and increase protection (Duncan & Goddard, 2017).

EHS Home Visiting. Home visiting services can be a preventive approach (Slaughter-Defoe, 1993) and voluntary. Primary prevention, such as skill training, can target individuals and families before something happens (Espelage et al., 2013; Myers-Walls et al., 2011). EHS home visitors employ a myriad of techniques to help the parents and the children in areas such as child development (e.g., cognitive and language development) and family development (e.g., financial management). Education and support in these areas can help minimize problems and promote how the family works (Darling et al., 2017).

As secondary prevention, home visiting may counter some of the negative effects of living in poverty (Walsh, 2017a). When we are talking about families with risk factors, we are talking about secondary prevention (Walsh, 2017b). While much FLE literature focuses on primary and secondary prevention (e.g., Myers-Walls et al., 2011), it is often appropriate to use FLE as tertiary prevention to help people handle complicated and chronic problems (Darling & Cassidy, 2014; Darling et al., 2017) that may be characteristic of the Early

Head Start population. Nonetheless, rather than responding to problems such as abuse or neglect and existing to monitor those problems, home visiting is best positioned for establishing prevention methods or as a method of treatment (Slaughter-Defoe, 1993).

In terms of early childhood development outcomes, risk factors include maternal depression and lack of cognitive stimulation, and examples of protective factors include breastfeeding and maternal education (Walker et al., 2011). Home visitors are confronted in their daily work with the vulnerabilities of families and particularly with Adverse Childhood Experiences (ACEs) (Counts, Gillam, Perico, & Eggers, 2017). ACEs include adversity, such as emotional, psychological, physical and sexual abuse, parental separation/divorce, parental mental illness, and many other examples (Felitti et al., 1998). Home visitors cannot prevent most major adversities from happening but they can support how trauma is handled and teach skills and provide education to prevent further trauma. Lemonade for Life provides information for home visitors to help build resilience in families and it can be integrated into evidence-based home visiting programs as an add-on support to provide home visitors with ACEs training (Counts et al., 2017).

Strengths-based Approach

A goal of FLE is to help families use their strengths (Myers-Walls et al., 2011). DeFrain and Asay (2007) present several family strengths characteristics. For example, they argue that "all families have strengths" and "it's not about structure, it's about function" (DeFrain & Asay, 2007, p. 5).A strengths base approach can include strategies such as each participant stating what is going well at the beginning of each session (Ballard, Tyndall, Baugh, Bergeson, & Littlewood, 2016). This can also include the professional reframing negative statements made by participants into positive remarks (Ballard et al., 2016).

EHS Home Visiting. Early Head Start home visitors must help families build on positive and daily aspects of family life to promote child development, and families need support and encouragement from home visitors to engage in developmentally appropriate practice (Roggman et al., 2016a). To support families and to understand them, EHS home visitors can practice *being with* families rather than *doing for* families (Petkus, 2015). Through FLE, a home visitor can become an important part of the home visitor, parent, and child triad (Walsh, 2017a) by observing (Duncan & Goddard, 2017; Hughes-Belding, Rowe, Peterson, Clucas, Fan, Wang, & Dooley, 2017) and narrating (Hughes-Belding et al., 2017; Petkus, 2015), modeling for families (Hughes-Belding et al., 2017), coaching (Allen, 2016; Petkus, 2015), and collaborating with families (Darling & Cassidy, 2014; Darling et al., 2017). Allowing parents the opportunity to own and to demonstrate their skills in an organic manner during the visit diminishes overreliance on the home visitor and potentially promotes families' greater self-sustainability (Petkus, 2015).

34   *Family Life Education*

Home visitors who can support family strengths play a crucial role in supporting families with young children. Home visitors look for strengths and acknowledge challenges during the visit. Home visitors administer home visiting assessments as part of their profession and home visitors operating in FLE will work with families to find out their felt needs as well. Felt needs are the needs that families identify themselves and about which families are motivated to learn coping and problem-solving skills (Myers-Walls et al., 2011). Home visitors may help families see a vision for themselves and create goals and action plans to work toward that vision. Home visitors should work with families to reflect on family strengths and how they help families meet their goals.

Foundation in research and theory

FLE is research-based and includes evidence-based programs, practices, and evaluation (Darling & Cassidy, 2014). Theories, such as ecological systems theory and family systems theory, are important to the design and implementation of FLE programs and activities (Darling et al., 2017; Duncan & Goddard, 2017). Theories of change are also important to FLE and can be depicted via logic models.

EHS Home Visiting. EHS home visitors have to follow the guidelines of their program and carry out home visiting with fidelity (Howard & Brooks-Gunn, 2009). In other words, to achieve fidelity, the home visitor would obtain correspondence between the EHS program's outcome goals and the way in which they are implemented (e.g., activities, processes) in their daily work with families. An EHS–HBO site employing Parents as Teachers (PAT) as the model would be expected to apply the goals, objectives, and strategies of PAT. Home visitors also have to be flexible to respond to diverse goals and groups, such as African American mothers in low-income groups (Woolfolk & Unger, 2009) and to negotiate the goals of EHS, PAT, and the families. Home visitors need to recognize the essential elements of home visiting to create positive outcomes in families. It is important to distinguish between objective and subjective information, recognizing which practices are supported by robust evidence and what are lived experience. The skilled CFLE and home visitor should recognize both worlds and integrate them. Best practices in FLE are methods that have evidence of effectiveness and include individual program hallmarks and features, but are susceptible to adaptation while maintaining program fidelity (Ballard & Taylor, 2012; Ballard et al., 2016).

Similar to FLE, the ecological systems framework (see Bronfenbrenner, 1961) undergirds home visiting programs (Wasik & Bryant, 2001) and home visiting research (e.g., Sharp, Ispa, Thornburg, & Lane, 2003). Ecological systems theory takes into account the exchange, factors, and bi-directional relationships surrounding a developing person (Bronfenbrenner, 2001). An excellent support service for families would have small to no effect if it was not available at a time and location convenient for families or did not make attempts to engage families (Asmussen, 2011).

Another organizing framework for home visitors is family systems theory. A common metaphor to describe family systems theory is likening the family to a mobile, meaning that when one piece or one or more members of the family move, all other parts or family members are subsequently moved (Turnbull, Turnbull, Erwin, Soodak, & Shogren, 2011). For example, with family systems theory in mind, a home visitor would make an attempt to involve siblings or other family members in the home during the visit (Petkus, 2015).

Other theories about human development, parenting education, and family dynamics also give direction to practice and research in home visiting. We also need theories from other disciplines, micro-theories, and learning theories, to understand and effectively work with families.

A theory of change relates theoretical underpinnings to its inputs (resources, skills of professionals), outputs (i.e., objectives), and outcomes or impacts. Theories of change in EHS-HV may be based on the assumption that working with parents in their homes leads to positive child outcomes, albeit indirectly (Raikes et al., 2014). Ideally, a theory of change for EHS–HV would include high specificity regarding outcomes/impacts for parents and children; the inputs and outputs need to reach the outcomes (Raikes et al., 2014). A theory of change can be visually depicted by a logic model. To obtain outcomes, professional development, coaching, reflective supervision, and technical assistance are often helpful.

Operational Components of FLE

Operational components of culture, context, content, and practice work in tandem with the aforementioned foundational principles of education, prevention, and strengths-based approaches, and have a strong foundation in theory and research. Darling et al. (2017) stated:

> These components include *culture* to better recognize the characteristics, needs, issues, and values of learners and teachers involved in FLE; *context* to better understand the environmental conditions; *content* to address the relevant topics in daily family life; and *practice* to incorporate the best possible methodology to facilitate participants' learning experiences.
>
> (p. 743)

Next, we start to consider these four operational components of FLE— culture, context, content, and practice—in light of home visiting.

Culture

Cultural competence is a process of development that can help family life educators work with a variety of families (Allen & Blaisure, 2015). Individuals can develop knowledge, skills, and attitudes to effectively collaborate with

36   Family Life Education

families (Allen & Blaisure, 2015). For example, one activity to promote awareness of cultural differences and similarities is to engage in reflexivity (Allen & Blaisure, 2015; Taylor & Ballard, 2012). Consider that reflexivity is a process that helps professionals become aware of their own culture and how this affects their relationships with families (Taylor & Ballard, 2012).

In thinking and in practice, it is important to acknowledge both risk and protective factors (see "Strengths-based Approach" in this chapter) and that reacting to minority families by focusing only on risks promotes a deficit approach (García-Coll et al., 1996). Differences are simply differences and family life educators should not make judgements across cultures (Darling et al., 2017). Developmental scholars expect young children to view the world in terms of good or bad, whereas adults are expected to view characteristics as relative and complex.

Exploring assumptions and goals surrounding cultural competence and finding out families' beliefs and goals can bridge gaps between the professional and families (Slaughter-Defoe, 1993). Scholars in home visiting (e.g., Slaughter-Defoe, 1993) and family life education (e.g., Ballard & Taylor, 2012) both concur that identifying characteristics of families and thinking about how to incorporate these into services is crucial to effective programs.

Culture: Before and After Home Visits. Home visitors need to have the knowledge, attitudes, and skills to be responsive to diverse families' needs and to provide quality home visiting (Azzi-Lessing, 2011; Wasik & Bryant, 2001). In-service home visitors may develop cultural competence during reflective supervision, coaching, and professional development opportunities. The Intercultural Development Inventory (IDI) helps individuals reflect on their goals surrounding cultural competence (Intercultural Development Inventory, 2018).

Being a culturally responsive home visitor requires intentional work, which includes learning about the cultural background, practice, and beliefs of families (Mead, 2018). This requires home visitors to be aware of their own cultural beliefs and identities and reflecting on how biases and assumptions can interact with relationship building with families (Mead, 2018).

It is important to withhold preconceived judgment when working with all families, particularly when meeting families that are new to a home visitor's caseload (Guardado, 2019). For example, an in-take form may reveal that a family is Mexican. A Hispanic Latina home visitor is not from the same country as the family and home visitors need to be aware of differences in origin before meeting the family (Guardado, 2019).

Culture: During Home Visits. The culturally competent home visitor considers families' needs and strengths in an *ongoing dialogue*. For example, upon arriving to the home visit, the professional realizes that an immigrant family who used an outdoor cooking area in their home country now needs help adapting to an indoor stove and oven (Walsh, 2017a). The professional would be interested in what cooking was like in the home country and how it is similar to and different from cooking in the United States (Walsh, 2017a). The family could generate ideas on how to get utensils and ingredients. The home visitor can be with the family as they cook a meal (Petkus, 2015; Walsh, 2017a). Once these goals are met, the family could set additional goals. Home visiting often occurs in conditions of disparate resources and this may be evident in different approaches to visits (Lombardi, Korfmacher, Araujo, Powell, & Rubio-Codina, 2018). Home visiting outside of the United States is often focused on nutrition and health services (Lombardi et al., 2018). Global awareness and cultural responsiveness are necessities for today's professionals (Darling & Cassidy, 2014; Lombardi et al., 2018) and there is no one solution to global enhancements of family wellbeing (Darling & Turkki, 2009).

Context

Context is a multidimensional construct and has been operationalized in a variety of ways. In order to understand anything, it is important to consider multiple contributing factors or contexts (Bronfenbrenner, 2001). There is a need to better understand contexts and processes of individuals and families. For example, one standardized measure of school readiness may not tell families and professionals everything about the child's potential for school. FLE emphasizes understanding characteristics of families as well as conditions in which something occurs (Darling et al., 2017). In addition to understanding the conditions in which the standardized measure was administered, observations, policies, culture, talking in depth with parents and professionals, and other measures will help professionals understand the potential and risks for positive adaptation.

Context can be a protective factor or a risk factor. Media as a context can promote connectivity and learning. For example, a pregnant woman who works part-time and is enrolled in EHS home visiting might visit social media to learn about socialization events in order to connect with other pregnant women in the program. Alternatively, media can be negative when the woman does not see other women working while pregnant or if she sees examples of prejudice against pregnant women.

Poverty is situated in social contexts (Niemietz, 2010) and is a societal concern that family life educators must address (Arcus & Thomas, 1993; Walsh, 2017a). EHS home visitors operating in a FLE paradigm set the stage to empower all families to create change through many factors, such as the home visitor and family relationship.

Context: Before and After Home Visits. The needs and challenges of families in poverty can be large, and professionals that understand this are needed as we prepare the next generation of home visitors. Indeed, infants and children with parents in poverty have contextual risks to development but also opportunities for meaning-making and resilience that home visitors should

38   *Family Life Education*

promote (Halpern, 1993). Contextual theories can guide work with families and many such theories are used by FLEs.

For example, Bronfenbrenner's bioecological model (1977) helps to identify factors that may promote positive development. This theory helps home visitors recognize resources and influences in addition to interactions at the microsystem level. Home visitors cannot fix problems of income, health, or housing, but they can understand the contexts of their families and provide supportive services to help families get resources and to better understand themselves, their needs, and their strengths (Halpern, 1993).

Context: During Home Visits. It is important to look deeply at a context through listening and observing. The family itself can be a context that can be comprised of many factors that are thought to affect outcomes. For example, if positive parenting practices are taught then we should expect good outcomes. The family is a context in which parenting styles, family stress, or emotional climate of the unit may moderate the association between treatment and outcome (Kitzmann, Dalton, & Busceni, 2008). Home visiting researchers suggest that it is important to examine under which conditions home visiting is most effective and promotes favorable family and child outcomes (Raikes et al., 2006). Understanding family characteristics, as well as individual characteristics within the family, helps the home visitor to individualize home visiting services and to meet each individual and each family where they are at present (Wasik & Bryant, 2001).

Content

FLE training emphasizes knowing the families you work with and tailoring the organization of content to meet their needs and strengths (Darling et al., 2017). This hallmark of FLE, as well as the fact that best practices are still evolving in family life education, characterizes FLE as flexible. FLEs should understand that they have content knowledge in FLE but that they also collaborate with families and that families are the child's first teacher.

There are ten FLE content areas and each content area has specific competencies. When home visitors have a Certified Family Life Educator (CFLE) credential, they assure EHS and local hiring agencies that they are trained to be competent in the following content areas:

- families and individuals in societal contexts
- internal dynamics of families
- human growth and development across the lifespan
- human sexuality across the lifespan
- interpersonal relationships
- family resource management
- parenting education and guidance

- professional ethics and practice
- family law and public policy
- and FLE methodology.

(Walcheski & Reinke, 2015; NCFR, 2014)

CFLEs have strengthened and acknowledged content area knowledge, skills, and attitudes. To reiterate, there are two ways to demonstrate content knowledge. One pathway is to earn a passing score on a national exam that assesses FLE content area knowledge and applications. The other pathway is to complete coursework and meet criteria in the FLE content areas in an NCFR approved program. Regardless of the pathway, CFLEs will need to then complete a work experience summary form and have an employer assess their work in the content areas.

Content: Before and After Home Visits. Content knowledge does not diminish the necessity of attitudes and skills such as observing families, narrating for them, meeting them where they are, and valuing families' perspectives. In other words, knowledge, skills, and attitudes are all important for home visitors (Roggman et al., 2016b), and these are highlighted in Appendix B. Competencies and a certificate in infant mental health (Weatherston, Kaplan-Estrin, & Goldberg, 2009; Michigan Association for Infant Mental Health, 2018) and other home visiting credentials value similar content to FLE. Because EHS values the whole family and an intergenerational approach, CFLE may be more appropriate for EHS home visitors than an endorsement in infant mental health and research is warranted to explore this area. The field also needs conclusive evidence about home visitor training and qualifications in regards to competencies such as the National Family Support Competency Framework (Institute for the Advancement of Family Support Professionals, 2018) with consideration to program goals, family characteristics, and family outcomes.

CFLEs can expand their content knowledge while earn continuing education credits through a variety of options, such as Achieve OnDemand™ through the Ounce of Prevention Fund's (Ounce) innovative online training program. Also, the Institute for the Advancement of Family Support Professionals features free modules on a variety of home visiting topics. See Chapter 16 for the importance of online modules to promote home visitor content knowledge and growth.

Content: During Home Visits. The home visiting field recognizes the need to individualize services to families while adhering to program goals and missions in order to promote positive family outcomes and to achieve model fidelity. Content knowledge in human growth and development across the lifespan, particularly child development, and content knowledge in parenting education and guidance, particularly parent–child interactions and parenting that supports children's early development, is crucial. When working with families and individualizing services, it is important to keep this knowledge and accompanying skills in mind.

40 *Family Life Education*

A home visitor with a CFLE credential has knowledge and skills in parenting education and guidance and knows that parental resilience is an important protective factor for families (Guardado, 2019). Because of this knowledge, in practice she observed that two children on a home visit coped well with a problem. For example, the younger child took the older child's blocks. The older brother started to cry and so the younger child returned the blocks. The home visitor stated to the mother, "Learning to share at your child's age is hard but you seem to have been teaching your children effectively to notice when others are upset. Could you tell me more about what you have been doing?" (Guardado, 2019, p. 22).

Practice

The professional with expertise in FLE methodology, professional practice and ethics, and family law and public policy is key to practice (Darling et al., 2017). The professional implementing evidence-based practices is crucial to the program's success (Ballard et al., 2016; Wasik & Bryant, 2001).

In practice, the content area of FLE methodology prepares a CFLE to do the following:

a. Employ a variety of strategies to identify and meet the needs of different audiences
b. Employ techniques and technologies to promote application of information in the learner's environment
c. Create learning environments that are respectful of individual vulnerabilities, needs, and learning styles
d. Demonstrate group process and facilitation skills
e. Demonstrate sensitivity to diversity and community needs, concerns, and interests
f. Develop culturally competent educational materials and learning experiences
g. Identify appropriate sources for evidence-based information
h. Implement evidence-based programs
i. Design educational experiences:

1. Needs assessment
2. Goals and objectives
3. Content development
4. Implementation
5. Evaluation/outcome measures

j. Promote and market educational programs
k. and Implement adult educational principles into work with individuals, parents, and families.

(Source: NCFR (2015, p. 5); Permission to reprint was granted by the National Council on Family Relations)

In addition to service planning and delivery skills, FLEs have training in professional ethics and practice. FLEs are trained in principles of FLE (Arcus & Thomas, 1993), values of FLE (Palm, 2009), and relational ethics (MNCFR, 2009). One of the 36 ethical principles in the Family Life Educators Code of Ethics is, "I will create data privacy and confidentiality guidelines respectful of family members and protective of their legal rights" (NCFR, 2016). Family law and public policy in practice emphasize educating families, politicians, or legislators, promoting evidence based programs, and engaging in policy efforts (Bogenschneider, 2014; Darling et al., 2017).

Practice: Before and After Home Visits. The best way to serve families in the home is not always clear and it takes preparation to do so (Wasik & Bryant, 2001). The National Family Support Competency Framework includes professional practice as a domain, which includes dimensions, such as ethical and legal practice, as well as professional boundaries (Institute for the Advancement of Family Support Professionals, 2018). For example, one component of ethical and legal practice is confidentiality (Institute for the Advancement of Family Support Professionals, 2018). There are federal laws, state laws, and regulations that need to be considered in confidentiality and it is important to consider client protection and wellbeing when deciding on whether or not to release information (Selby, 2018). Training in professional ethics and practice is necessary for home visitors to provide quality services to families and for home visitors to avoid burnout that can be due to not knowing how to handle ethical challenges (Wasik & Bryant, 2001). Families need to know that you are a mandated reporter and if you do not explain your role as a mandated reporter you might find yourself in ethical dilemmas (Selby, 2018).

Practice: During Home Visits. The home visitor should respond to the immediate needs of their families, and promote the families' and program's goals (Wasik & Bryant, 2001). Roggman et al. (2016a) stated:

> Four key home-visiting practices effectively increase parents' developmental support for their infants and young children: (a) establishing a positive relationship with the parent, child, and other participating family members; (b) responding to each family's unique strengths and culture; (c) facilitating developmentally supportive parent–child interactions; and (d) establishing a collaborative partnership with the parent to support the child's ongoing development.
>
> (p. 195)

A variety of strategies, gleaned from FLE content areas as well as other professional training, will be needed to accomplish the aforementioned practices. Home visiting measures, such as the Home Visiting Rating Scales or HOVRS (Roggman, Cook, Jump Norman, Christiansen, Boyce, & Innocenti, 2008) and the Parenting Interactions with Children: Checklist of Observations

42   *Family Life Education*

Linked to Outcomes or PICCOLO (Roggman, Cook, Innocenti, Jump Norman, & Christiansen, 2013) will help determine the quality of the practice.

Keep in mind that working with families is a process and the content area of professional practice and ethics should undergird each visit. As a home visitor there may be times when you work with a parent with mental health issues who becomes unstable and after deliberation it may be necessary to contact Child Protective Services (CPS) and to work with a guardian ad litem (Palm, Cooke, & Alden, 2019). When ethical issues arise during a visit, it is important to seriously consider them, and this may include working with a team of professionals and supervisor after the visit that the issue arises. Home visitors can resolve ethical issues through a concrete process (see Minnesota Council on Family Relations, 2016) and ethical principles for family life educators (Palm, 2018).

Conclusion

FLE and home visiting principles share substantial common ground. Understanding FLE foundational and operational principles, and how they are germane to EHS-HV, solidifies the work of a subset of current CFLEs and potentially stimulates how FLE and EHS-HV can be integrated into coursework and training for home visitors. Family life educators are well-suited to deliver home visiting and understand the need to build relationships that put families first in high-quality services (Walsh, 2017a, 2019). CFLEs are well versed not only in the knowledge of the content areas, but also in the application of such skills as developmental guidance, building and maintaining relationships, professional ethics and practice, money and other resource management, family-centered practice, and many more. CFLEs understand the foundational principles and operational principles discussed in this chapter and, equally important, they are trained in FLE methodology (see Darling et al., 2017).

Summary

FLE, the practice of family science, is an exemplary family-centered approach to collaborating with families. Certified Family Life Educators (CFLEs), or credentialed FLEs, play an important role in bringing more consistency to obtaining outcomes in EHS-HV. FLE and EHS-HV share nine important theoretical assumptions and position families' individual needs and concerns at the forefront of programming.

Home visitors with a background in FLE would expect to have knowledge, skills, and attitudes that reflect FLE foundational and operational principles. Foundational principles include *education* to promote skills and techniques in a group or individual setting within the domain of FLE as opposed to FT or FCM. Evidence-based approaches, program evaluation, and similar concepts are also essential to the practice of FLE. Relationships between the FLE and families facilitate the planning and delivery of educational content. *Prevention* is another foundational principle and includes primary, secondary, and tertiary prevention. Understanding and assessment of risk and protective factors are also key to prevention. A *strengths-based approach* is important to working with and for families. There are several strengths-based approaches in the family field to ground practice. As also mentioned in the foundational principle of education, FLE is *research-based* and includes evidence-based programs, practices, and evaluation. *Theories*, such as ecological systems theory and family systems theory, are important to the design and implementation of FLE programs and activities. *Theories of change* are important to organizing theory, research, and practice in a manner that specifies inputs, outputs, and outcomes for parents and children. Operational components of *culture, context, content*, and *practice* work in tandem with the aforementioned foundational principles of education, prevention, strengths-based approaches, and a foundation in theory and research.

Key Concepts

- Content
- Context
- Culture
- Education
- Evidence-based
- Fidelity
- Foundational principles
- Inputs
- Ongoing dialogue
- Operational principles
- Outcomes
- Outputs
- Practice
- Prevention
- Research-based
- Strengths-based approach
- Theory of change

Recommended Reading

Henry, C. S., & Struckmeyer, K. M. (2017). Research update for practitioners: Family resilience. *CFLE Network, 29.2*, 19–21.

McCawley, P. F. (n.d.). *The logic model for program planning and evaluation. University of Idaho*. Retrieved from https://www.cals.uidaho.edu/edcomm/pdf/CIS/CIS1097.pdf

44 Family Life Education

Moore, K. A., Chalk, R., Scarpa, J., & Vandivere, S. (2002). *Family strengths: Often overlooked, but real*. Retrieved from http://www.childtrends.org/publications/family-strengths-often-overlooked-but-real/

U.S. Department of Health and Human Services and Administration for Children and Families (n.d.). *Home visiting evidence of effectiveness*. Retrieved https://homvee.acf.hhs.gov/

References

Administration for Children and Families (2016). *Head Start program performance standards*. Retrieved from: https://eclkc.ohs.acf.hhs.gov/policy/45-cfr-chap-xiii

Allen, K. (2016). *Theory, research, and practical guidelines for family life coaching*. Switzerland: Springer.

Allen, W. D., & Blaisure, K. R. (2015). Family life education and the practice of cross-cultural competence. In M. J. Walcheski, & J. S. Reinke (Eds.), *Family life education: The practice of family science* (pp. 27–37). Minneapolis, MN: National Council on Family Relations.

Arcus, M. E., & Thomas, J. (1993). The nature and practice of family life education. In M. E. Arcus, J. D. Schvaneveldt, & J. J. Moss (Eds.), *Handbook of family life education: The practice of family life education* (pp. 1–32). Newbury Park, CA: Sage.

Arcus, M. E., Schvaneveldt, J. D. & Moss, J. J. (Eds.) (1993). *Handbook of family life education: The practice of family life education*. Newbury Park, CA: Sage.

Asmussen, K. (2011). *The evidence-based parenting practitioner's handbook*. New York: Routledge.

Azzi-Lessing, L. (2011). Home visitation programs: Critical issues and future directions. *Early Childhood Research Quarterly, 26*, 387–398. doi: 10.1016/j.ecresq.2011.03.005

Ballard, S. M., & Taylor, A. C. (2012). Best practices in family life education. In S. M. Ballard & A. C. Taylor (Eds.). *Family life education with diverse populations* (pp. 1–18). Thousand Oaks, CA: Sage.

Ballard, S. M., Tyndall, L. E., Baugh, E., Bergeson, C. B., & Littlewood, K. (2016). Framework for best practices in family life education: A case example. *Family Relations, 65*, 393–406. doi: 10.1111/fare.12200

Bogenschneider, K. (2014). *Family policy matters: How policymaking affects families and what professionals can do* (3rd ed.). New York: Taylor & Francis.

Bronfenbrenner, U. (1961). Toward a theoretical model for the analysis of parent–child relationships in a social context. In J. C. Glidewell (Ed.), *Parental attitudes and child behavior* (pp. 90–109). Springfield, IL: Charles C. Thomas.

Bronfenbrenner, U. (1977). Toward an experimental ecology of human development. *American Psychology, 32*, 513–531.

Bronfenbrenner, U. (2001). Growing chaos in the lives of children, youth and families: How can we turn it around? In J. C. Westman (Ed.), *Parenthood in America: Under-valued, underpaid, under siege* (pp. 197–210). Madison, WI: University of Wisconsin Press.

Brookes, S. J., Summers, J. A., Thornburg, K. R., Ispa, J. M., & Lane, V. J. (2006). Building successful home visitor–mother relationships and reaching program goals in two Early Head Start programs: A qualitative look at contributing factors. *Early Childhood Research Quarterly, 21*, 25–45. doi: 10.1016/j.ecresq.2006.01.005

Counts, J. M., Gillam, R. J., Perico, S., & Eggers, K. L. (2017). Lemonade for life—A pilot study on a hope-infused, trauma-informed approach to help families understand their past and focus on the future. *Children and Youth Services Review, 79,* 228–234. doi: 10.1016/j.childyouth.2017.05.036

Darling, C. A., & Cassidy, D. (2014). *Family life education: Working with families across the lifespan* (3rd ed.). Long Grove, IL: Waveland.

Darling, C. A., Cassidy, D., & Rehm, M. (2017). Family life education: Translational family science in action. *Family Relations, 66,* 741–752. doi: 10.1111/fare.12286

Darling, C. A., Cassidy, D., & Rehm, M. (2019). The foundations of family life education model: Understanding the field. Family Relations. Advance online publication. doi: 10.1111/fare.12372

Darling, C. A., Fleming, W. M., & Cassidy, D. (2009). Professionalization of family life education: Defining the field. *Family Relations, 58,* 330–345.

Darling, C. A., & Turkki, K. (2009). Global family concerns and the role of family life education: An ecosystemic analysis. *Family Relations, 58,* 14–27.

DeFrain, J., & Asay, S. M. (2007). Strong families around the world. *Marriage & Family Review, 41,* 1–10. doi: 10.1300/J002v41n01_01

Doherty, W. J., Erickson, J. J., & Cutting, B. (2015). Community engaged parent education: Strengthening civic engagement among parents and parent educators. In M. J. Walcheski & J. S. Reinke (Eds.), *Family life education: The practice of family science* (pp. 73–84). Minneapolis, MN: National Council on Family Relations.

Duncan, S. F., & Goddard, H. W. (2017). *Family life education: Principles and practices for effective outreach* (3rd ed.). Thousand Oaks, CA: Sage.

Espelage, D.. Anderman, E. M., Brown, B. E., Jones, A., Lane, K. L., McMahon, S. D., … Reynolds, C. R. (2013). Understanding and preventing violence directed against teachers: Recommendations for a national research, practice, and policy agenda. *American Psychologist, 68,* 75–87.

Felitti, V. J., Anda, R. F., Nordenberg, D., Williamson, D., Spitz, A., Edwards, V., Koss, M., & Marks, J. (1998). Relationship of childhood abuse and household dysfunction to many of the leading causes of death in adults. The adverse childhood experiences (ACE) study. *American Journal of Preventive Medicine, 14,* 245–258.

García-Coll, C., Lamberty, G., Jenkins, R., McAdoo, H., Crnic, K., & Wasik, B. (1996). An integrative model for the study of developmental competencies in minority children. *Child Development, 67,* 1891–1914.

Guardado, M. D. (2019). Family life education within an Early Head Start home-based program. *CFLE Network, 32,* 22–23.

Halpern, R. (1993). The societal context of home visiting and related services for families in poverty. *The Future of Children, 3,* 158–171.

Home Visiting Evidence of Effectiveness (HomVEE). (2016). *Early Head Start—Home visiting: Program model overview.* Retrieved from https://homvee.acf.hhs.gov/Model/1/Early-Head-Start-%20Home-Visiting-%28EHS-HV%29/8/2

Howard, K. S., & Brooks-Gunn, J. (2009). The role of home visiting programs in preventing child abuse and neglect. *The Future of Children, 19,* 119–146.

Hughes, M., Moni, Y., Joslyn, A., & Younts, C. W. (2018, January). Maximizing impact through intentional collaboration. Collaborative Science of Home Visiting Meeting, Washington, DC.

46 Family Life Education

Hughes-Belding, K., Rowe, N., Peterson, C., Clucas, M., Fan, L., Wang, W., & Dooley, L. (2017, April). *Triadic interactions in home visiting: Setting the stage for quality.* Poster session at the meeting for the Society for Research in Child Development, Austin, TX.

Intercultural Development Inventory (2018). *The Intercultural Development Inventory (IDI).* Retrieved https://idiinventory.com/products/the-intercultural-development-inventory-idi/

Institute for the Advancement of Family Support Professionals. (2018). *National Family Support Competency Framework.* Retrieved from https://institutefsp.org/compasses/4

Jacobson, A. L. (2015). Parenting education and guidance. In M. J. Walcheski & J. S. Reinke (Eds.), *Family life education: The practice of family science* (pp. 213–222). Minneapolis, MN: National Council on Family Relations.

Kitzmann, K. M., Dalton, W. T., & Buscemi, J. (2008). Beyond parenting practices: Family context and the treatment of pediatric obesity. *Family Relations, 57,* 13–23.

Leventhal, J. (2015). Human growth and development across the lifespan. In M. J. Walcheski, & J. S. Reinke (Eds.), *Family life education: The practice of family science* (pp. 167–176). Minneapolis, MN: National Council on Family Relations.

Lombardi, J., Korfmacher, J., Araujo, M. C., Powell, C., & Rubio-Codina, M. (2018). Home visiting from program to scale: A global perspective. Seventh National Summit on Quality in Home Visiting Programs. Washington, D.C.

Mead, E. (2018). Just ask! One CFLEs lesson in becoming a culturally responsive home visitors. *CFLE Network, 32,* 9–10.

Michigan Association for Infant Mental Health. (2018). *Endorsement®.* Retrieved http://mi-aimh.org/endorsement/faqs/endorsement/

Minnesota Council on Family Relations (MNCFR). (2009). Ethical thinking and practice for parent and family life educators. In D. Bredehoft & M. Walcheski (Eds.), *Family life education: Integrating theory and practice* (pp. 233–239). Minneapolis, MN: National Council on Family Relations.

Minnesota Council on Family Relations (MNCFR). (2016). *Ethical thinking and practice for parent and family life education.* Minneapolis, MN: Ethics Committee, Parent and Family Education Section. Retrieved from https://mn.ncfr.org/resources/

Myers-Walls, J. A., Ballard, S. M., Darling, C. A., & Myers-Bowman, K. S. (2011). Reconceptualizing the domain and boundaries of family life education. *Family Relations, 60,* 357–372. doi: 10.1111/j.1741-3729.2011.00659.x

National Council on Family Relations (NCFR) (2014). *Family life education content areas.* Retrieved from https://www.ncfr.org/sites/default/files/fle_content_areas_2014_0.pdf

National Council on Family Relations (NCFR) (2015). *Family life education content areas Content and practice guidelines.* Retrieved from https://www.ncfr.org/sites/default/files/2017-01/fle_content_and_practice_guidelines_2015_0.pdf

National Council on Family Relations (NCFR) (2016). *Family life education code of ethics.* Retrieved from https://www.ncfr.org/sites/default/files/cfle_code_of_ethics_2.pdf

National Council on Family Relations (NCFR) (2018). *Maintain your certification.* Retrieved from https://www.ncfr.org/cfle-certification/maintain-your-certification

National Home Visiting Resource Center. (2017, December). Promoting family engagement in home visiting: An overview of innovative efforts. Issue Brief.

Niemietz, K. (2010). Measuring poverty: Context specific but not relative. *Journal of Public Policy, 30,* 241–262.

Palm, G. (2018). Professional ethics and practice in family life education. In: *Tools for ethical thinking and practice in family life education* (4th ed., pp. 1–10). Minneapolis, MN: National Council on Family Relations.

Palm, G. (2009). Professional ethics and practice. In D. J. Bredehoft & M. Walcheski (Eds.), *Family life education: Integrating theory and practice* (2nd ed., pp. 191–197). Minneapolis, MN: National Council on Family Relations.

Palm, G., & Cooke, B. (2018). *Parent education and family life education: A critical link in early childhood education policy. National Council on Family Relations Policy Brief.* Retrieved from https://www.ncfr.org/sites/default/files/2018-07/Policy%20Brief%20July%202018.pdf

Palm, G., Cooke, B., & Alden, A. (2019). Case study: Parent with mental health issues. *CFLE Network, 32*, 25–27.

Paulsell, D., Grosso, P. D., & Supplee, L. (2014). Supporting replication and scale-up evidence-based home visiting programs: Assessing the implementation knowledge base. *American Journal of Public Health, 104*, 1624–1632.

Peterson, C.A., Roggman, L.A., Green, B., Chazan-Cohen, R., Korfmacher, J., McKelvey, L. et al. (2013). Home visiting processes: Relations with family characteristics and outcomes. *Zero to Three, 33*(3), 39–44.

Petkus, J. (2015). A first-hand account of implementing a Family Life Education model: Intentionality in Head Start home visiting. In M. J. Walcheski, & J. S. Reinke (Eds.), *Family life education: The practice of family science* (pp. 325–331). Minneapolis, MN: National Council on Family Relations.

Raikes, H., Green, B. L., Atwater, J., Kisker, E., Constantine, J., & Chazan-Cohen, R. (2006). Involvement in Early Head Start home visiting services: Demographic predictors and relations to child and parent outcomes. *Early Childhood Research Quarterly, 21*, 2–24.

Raikes, H., Roggman, L. A., Peterson, C. A., Brooks-Gunn, J., Chazan-Cohen, R., Zhang, X., & Schiffman, R. F. (2014). Theories of change and outcomes in home-based Early Head Start programs. *Early Childhood Research Quarterly, 29*, 574–585.

Roggman, L. A., Cook, G. A., Jump Norman, V. K., Christiansen, K., Boyce, L. K., & Innocenti, M. S. (2008). Home Visiting Rating Scales (HOVRS). In L. A. Roggman, L. K. Boyce, & M. S. Innocenti (Eds.), *Developmental parenting: A guide for early childhood practitioners* (pp. 209–217). Baltimore: Brookes.

Roggman, L. A., Cook, G. A., Innocenti, M. S., Jump Norman, V., & Christiansen, K. (2013). Parenting Interactions with Children: Checklist of Observations Linked to Outcomes (PICCOLO) in diverse ethnic groups. *Infant Mental Health Journal, 34*, 290–306. doi: 10.1002/imhj.21389

Roggman, L. A., Cook, G. A., Innocenti, M. S., Jump Norman, V., Boyce, L. K., Christiansen, K., & Peterson, C. A. (2016a). Home visit quality variations in two Early Head Start programs in relation to parenting and child vocabulary outcomes. *Infant Mental Health Journal, 37*, 193–207.

Roggman, L. A., Cook, G. A., Peterson, C. A., & Raikes, H. H. (2008). Who drops out of Early Head Start home visiting programs? *Early Education and Development, 19*, 574–599. doi: 10.1080/10409280701681870

Roggman, L. A., Peterson, C. A., Chazan-Cohen, R., Ispa, J., Decker, K., Hughes-Belding, K., Cook, G. A., & Vallotton, C. D. (2016b). Preparing home visitors to partner with families of infants and toddlers. *Journal of Early Childhood Teacher Education, 37*, 301–313. doi: 10.1080/10901027.2016.1241965

48 *Family Life Education*

Selby, J. (2018). *Ethics and boundaries in home visiting.* Nevada Home Visiting Statewide Meeting, Reno, NV.

Sharp, E. A., Ispa, J. M., Thornburg, K. R., & Lane, V. (2003). Relations among mother and home visitor personality, relationship quality, and amount of time spent in home visits. *Journal of Community Psychology, 31*, 591–606. doi: 10.1002/jcop.10070

Slaughter-Defoe, D. T. (1993). Home visiting with families in poverty: Introducing the concept of culture. *The Future of Children, 3*, 172–183.

Sosinsky, L., Ruprecht, K., Horn, D., Kriener-Althen, K., Vogel, C., & Halle, T. (2016). *Including relationship-based care practices in infant–toddler care: Implications for practice and policy.* Brief prepared for the Office of Planning, Research and Evaluation, Administration for Children and Families, U.S. Department of Health and Human Services. Retrieved from https://www.acf.hhs.gov/opre/resource/including-relationship-based-care-practices-infant-toddler-care-implications-practice-and-policy

Taylor, A. C., & Ballard, S. M. (2012). Preparing family life educators to work with diverse populations. In S. M. Ballard & A. C. Taylor (Eds.). *Family life education with diverse populations* (pp. 285–302). Thousand Oaks, CA: Sage.

Turnbull, A., Turnbull, R., Erwin, E.J., Soodak, L.C., & Shogren, K.A. (2011). *Families, professionals, and exceptionality: Positive outcomes through partnerships and trust.* (6th ed.). Upper Saddle River, NJ: Pearson Education Inc.

Walcheski, M. J. & Reinke, J. S. (2015). *Family life education: The practice of family science.* Minneapolis, MN: National Council on Family Relations.

Walker, S. P., Wachs, T. D., Grantham-McGregor, S., Black, M. M., Nelson, C. A., Huffman, S. L., Richter, L. (2011). Inequality in early childhood: Risk and protective factors for early childhood development. *The Lancet, 378*, 1325–1338. doi: 10.1016/S0140-6736(11)60555-2

Walsh, B. A. (2017a). Setting the stage for families in poverty as catalysts: A family life education approach to Early Head Start Home Visiting. *Family Focus, 73*, 8–10.

Walsh, B. A. (2017b). Calling an ACE an ACE with ideas and examples from integrating prevention science and efforts. *National Council on Family Relations CFLE Network, 29.3*, 12–14.

Walsh, B. A. (2019). The interface of FLE and EHS home-based services: Past, present, and future. *CFLE Network, 32*, 11–13.

Walsh, B. A., Mortensen, J. A., Edwards, A. L., & Cassidy, D. (in press). The practice of family life education within Early Head Start home visiting. *Family Relations.*

Walsh, B. A., & Peterson, C. A. (2019, September 26). Linkages between family life education and early childhood home visiting [Webinar]. In *NCFR on-demand webinars.* Retrieved from https://www.ncfr.org/events/past-webinars

Wasik, B. H., & Bryant, D. M. (2001). *Home visiting: Procedures for helping families* (2nd ed.). Thousand Oaks, CA: Sage.

Weatherston, D. J., Kaplan-Estrin, M., & Goldberg, S. (2009). Strengthening and recognizing knowledge, skills, and reflective practice: The Michigan Association for the Infant Mental Health competency guidelines and endorsement process. *Infant Mental Health Journal, 30*, 648–663. doi: 10.1002/imhj.20234

Woolfolk, T. N., & Unger, D. G. (2009). Relationships between low-income African American mothers and their home visitors: A parents as teachers program. *Family Relations, 58*, 188–200.

4 Family Life Education Approach to Home Visiting
A Qualitative Study

Home Visiting (HV) includes many different models, and many home visiting programs were initiated to support families living in conditions of poverty (Wasik & Bryant, 2001). One example of a home visiting program is the Early Head Start–Home-Based Option (EHS-HBO), which commenced in 1995 with the intent to serve low-income pregnant women and families with infants and children up to age three (Wasik & Bryant, 2001). Some EHS programs are home-based and mainly deliver program services through weekly home visits and twice-monthly group socialization activities. Early Head Start is one of the five largest programs serving families and young children via home visits (Raikes, Green, Atwater, Kisker, Constantine, & Chazan-Cohen, 2006). EHS-HBO had 55,735 funded enrollment slots in the 2017–2018 fiscal year (Office of Head Start, 2017–2018).

Despite the number of families it serves, the EHS-HBO model does not specify certain content and activities across all of its programs and the home visitors have varying educational backgrounds and experiences (Avellar, Paulsell, Sama-Miller, Del Grosso, Akers, & Kleinman, 2016). Individual programs have flexibility in the content they choose as long as they meet guidelines set by the Office of Head Start (ACF, 2000). Some existing EHS-HBO programs take a child-centered approach, while others take a family-centered approach, but more research is needed to elucidate these differences and outcomes associated with different approaches (Jeon, Peterson, Roggman, Luze, & Mortensen, 2016).

One EHS-HBO program that now takes a family-centered approach has aligned their HV practices and philosophy with the strengths-based methodology of family life education (FLE) (Petkus, 2015). No empirical research has explored a program's efforts to identify FLE as their approach to EHS home visiting. The purpose of this qualitative study was to explore how the FLE approach was implemented at an EHS home visiting site, which transitioned from a child-centered toy approach to a FLE approach.

Importance of the Study

This study contributes to the FLE literature and home visiting literature in a few key ways. First, a traditional child-centered approach in which home visitors bring toys to the home to promote parent–child interaction is ineffective (Scarr & McCartney, 1988; Wasik & Bryant, 2001). This study captures perspectives about transitioning from a toy approach to a FLE approach and may provide valuable insight for others wanting to make a shift. Second, EHS-HBO programs are difficult to replicate (Avellar et al., 2016) and there is increasing contemporary interest in innovations for evidence-based practice. For example, Maternal, Infant, Early Childhood Home Visiting (MIECHV) Grants have the intent of supporting high-quality, evidence-based practices. It is the priority of home-visiting researchers to build a foundation for evidence-based models and approaches to EHS home visiting with high implementation fidelity (Home Visiting Research Network, 2013). Finally, the door is open for family life educators with a bachelor's degree and/or a CFLE credential to have the training as required by an EHS-HBO program that takes a FLE approach. The National Council on Family Relations (NCFR) is encouraged by the fact that the Head Start Performance Standards now include recognition of a "credential or certification in social work, human services, family services, counseling, or a related field" as that opens the door for family science graduates and CFLEs (D. Cassidy, personal communication, November 18, 2016). A family science degree or CFLE credential will meet the Head Start Performance Standards and CFLEs have access to additional training for EHS-HBO.

A Family Life Education Approach to EHS-HBO

Petkus (2015) argued that a FLE approach to EHS-HBO encompasses several tenets. Petkus, a former EHS HV supervisor, used Myers-Walls, Ballard, Darling, and Myers-Bowman's (2011) domains of family practice model and applied it to EHS HV (see Appendices A and B). He asserted that before this model, the home visitors operated in the three domains of FLE, family therapy, and family case management, which created uncertainty and ill-defined roles for the home visitors and the expectations families had of them (Petkus, 2015). He asserted that the goal is to promote "sustainable, self-sufficient, and empowered parents" (Petkus, 2015, p. 327). Similarly, Myers-Walls et al. (2011) suggested that the purpose is "strong, healthy families" (p. 362). FLE focuses on the present and the future (Myers-Walls et al., 2011; Petkus, 2015). To achieve this goal and to keep families focused on the present and the future, Petkus (2015) noted that home visitors take a *being with* approach rather than a *doing for* approach.

Petkus (2015) initiated the transition from a toy approach to a FLE approach, which encourages parents to maintain their normal activities with the child and enables the home visitor to empower the parent. He purported that the relational dyad of a home visit has the goal of focusing on the parent–child relationship (Petkus, 2015). Finally, he suggested that Roggman et al.'s (2008) Home Visiting Rating Scale is a way to measure the emphasis on the parent–child relationship with the parent as the first teacher and primary attachment figure (see Appendix C at the end of this chapter).

Method

Because the FLE approach to EHS home visiting is a new area of inquiry, an inductive, qualitative approach seemed essential. Along this line, no a priori hypotheses guided this study. We aimed to understand how the FLE was adopted at an EHS home visiting site.

Context

The context of the present study included one host site, located in the Midwestern United States, which mostly identified with a FLE approach to EHS home visiting. Petkus (2015) illustrates how a FLE approach shifted the practices of this EHS-HBO program by altering the entire program philosophy. Prior to this, home visitors were previously viewed as the experts, tasked with *fixing* the family but now value a strengths-based approach to *being with* families (Petkus, 2015). The core tenets of FLE, prevention, education, and collaboration, were integrated through trainings and changes in practices. After the shift, home visitors stopped bringing special toys and instead had parents and children interact as they normally would in their home, with the materials they would typically use (Petkus, 2015). The site also subscribes to tenets within routines-based early intervention, such as shared goal setting between the family and HV (see McWilliam, 2010).

Participants

To our knowledge, this is the only EHS HV program that at the time of data collection identified with a FLE approach; therefore, this was a purposeful sample. Seventeen EHS leaders and home visitors participated, all of the home visitors were employed by the host site, in one focus group. It is possible to have a focus group size of 15 to 20 participants and to maintain appropriate involvement from all (Morgan, 1997). Focus group participants received an electronic link to a PsychData survey about participant characteristics (see Table 4.1). The survey included 10 questions and the response rate was 14 out of 17 participants (82%).

Procedure

Approval from the Institutional Review Board at the researcher's institution was obtained. This included getting permission from the host site. The host site provided the space for data collection via a focus group. The focus group approach is useful for exploration and brainstorming, particularly when there is a dearth of information on a topic (Dekel, Goldblatt, Keidar, Solomon, & Polliack, 2005).

52 FLE Approach to Home Visiting

The focus group was semi-structured, in order to have a climate that had structure and informality (Flick, 2006). The focus group included 17 participants and it lasted one hour and 15 minutes. There were seven planned questions, which were inspired from Petkus' model of a FLE approach to EHS home visiting. Examples of the types of questions asked were: (a) What is your philosophy to home visiting?, (b) How have your home visits changed or stayed the same from before you shifted to a FLE approach to home visiting and now?, and (c) What would you need to help you earn the credential of Certified Family Life Educator (CFLE) from the National Council on Family Relations (NCFR)? Probes and follow-up questions were used to help guide the discussion. The first author audiotaped and transcribed verbatim the focus group with no personal information included.

Rigor of Study

Researcher reflections, memos, linkages to published literature on EHS HV with a FLE approach (e.g., Petkus, 2015), inter-rater reliability, and member checking all promoted the rigor of this qualitative study. The researcher recorded preconceptions about the FLE approach to EHS home visiting by writing a one-page typed reflection statement. Reflection by the researcher is a practice that promotes sincerity in qualitative research (Tracy, 2010). The researcher's journal from shadowing four home visits done by the hosting site also informed her reflection.

Memos created by the researcher were entered into Computer Assisted Qualitative Data Analysis Software (CAQDAS) used for this study. The researcher noted any concepts in that data that linked to Petkus' (2015) article. A second coder independently coded the data and inter-rater reliability is reported (see Table 4.2). Member checking was done by sharing a draft of the findings with an expert in the FLE approach to home visiting to obtain feedback on the codes and themes (Glesne, 2006). Additionally, themes and focused codes were sent to all of the focus group participants to elicit any for feedback. The site informed the researcher that they approved of the codes and themes and the presentation of them.

Data Analysis

The focus group was audiotaped and transcribed verbatim with no personal information included. The CAQDAS program MAXQDA Analytics Pro 12 was used to manage and analyze the data for this study (Saldaña, 2011).

The researcher read the transcript multiple times before coding and importing it to MAXQDA Analytics Pro 12. There were three coding phases: initial, focused, and themes.

Initial coding was completed by line-by-line coding. Initial coding included descriptive codes (Saldaña, 2011) and in vivo codes (Charmaz, 2006). There were 365 initial codes, with the range of initial codes appearing from 1 to 11 times.

The researcher transitioned to focused coding by considering codes with the greatest frequency and codes that grouped together by topic; "Focused coding means using the most significant and/or frequent earlier codes to sift through large amounts of data" (Charmaz, 2006, p. 57). The second coder was given a list of focused codes and independently coded the data by assigning focused codes. Twelve focused codes were identified and inter-rater reliability is reported, see Table 4.2.

Three major themes emerged that best explained how the FLE approach transformed an EHS HV program. The major themes that emerged were: (a) "paradigm shift to FLE" (b) "professionals with knowledge and experience in developmental and family science" and (c) "intentionality and empowerment in EHS home visiting is FLE." MAXQDA Analytics Pro 12 was also used to calculate inter-rater reliability (see Table 4.2).

Table 4.1 Participant Characteristics

		N	%
Gender			
	Female	13	92.9
	Male	1	7.1
Ethnicity			
	Caucasian	14	100.0
	Other (please specify)	0	0.0
Education level			
	Associate's degree	0	0.0
	Bachelor's degree	6	42.9
	Master's degree	8	57.1
Family science degree			
	Yes	3	21.4
	No	11	78.6
CFLE?			
	Yes	1	7.1
	No	13	92.9
Licensed			
	Yes	7	50.0
	No	7	50.0
Position			
	Home visitor	7	50.0
	Supervisor	1	7.1
	Manager	1	7.1
	Other (please specify)	5	35.7
Years at EHS			
	0 to 1	3	21.4
	1 to 2	8	57.1

(*Continued*)

54   *FLE Approach to Home Visiting*

Table 4.1   (Cont.)

		N	%
	2 to 3	2	14.3
	7 to 8	1	7.1
	8 to 9	0	0.0
	10 +	0	0.0
Age			
	Mean	28.93	
	Standard deviation	5.99	
	Min	23	
	Max	44	
Years at EHS			
	Mean	2.36	
	Standard deviation	1.74	
	Min	1	
	Max	8	

Findings

Paradigm Shift to FLE

The theme, Paradigm Shift to FLE, captured the home visiting paradigm shift in philosophy and practice. In the old model, home visitors would bring a bag of toys to the home visits and the child's interaction with the toys would be the center of the visit. In the current model, the home visitors no longer bring a bag of toys to the home visits and the site's approach aligns with a FLE model in theory and in practice. From coding and analysis, it was apparent that there was resistance and challenges associated with changing from a toy-based and child-focused approach to a FLE approach, which did not include toys. Supervisors and managers emphasized that the paradigm shift was difficult for both home visitors and families. During this paradigm shift, there was 100% turnover rate in the home visitors and the home visiting leadership reported that families expressed an acute longing for the toys.

A focus group interview question prompted the EHS leadership and home visitors to share the training they engaged in to undertake this shift. The training ran the gamut from PowerPoint presentations with small group discussions to bringing in national speakers.

The home visitors were aware that professionals subscribing to a FLE approach in theory and in practice may earn the CFLE credential. Fully embracing the shift to FLE was one matter but earning a CFLE credential proved to be another matter. The home visitors' perspectives reflected concerns about the paths to become a CFLE, the lack of recognition of

CFLE, and balancing this credential with other credentials (e.g., Certified Child Life Specialist [CCLS], Licensed Social Worker [LSW]). To reiterate, while the site as a whole embraced tenets of FLE, most of the home visitors asserted that pursuing CFLE as an individual professional was not worthy of their investment at present due to the abundance of real and perceived challenges they shared. The theme, Paradigm Shift to FLE, emerged from focused coding, which included (a) challenge of transition from toys to FLE, (b) agency preparation for FLE approach, and (c) challenges to obtaining CFLE.

Challenge of Transition from Toys to FLE. Six participants (35%) discussed the challenge of the transition from toys to FLE with two participants mentioning the challenges multiple times throughout the focus group. Participants reported that the transition from toys to the FLE approach was "drastic" and "uncomfortable" and it created uncertainty for home visitors and families. There was 100% turnover in the department when the switch occurred, meaning that most of the participants in the focus group started working during the transition or after it. One participant mentioned "I was fortunate to come to the agency when the toys were already gone." Two participants' perspectives on why the transition was challenging was due to the belief that change in general is challenging. One participant thought that the toys were home visitor-centric by being a "comfort zone" and "safety net" for the home visitors. Leadership reflected that home visitors reported having difficulty meeting the one hour and 30 minute allotted time for home visits when toys were the main approach to home visits. Home visitors asserted that the FLE approach is right for families and is a more organic approach that puts the focus on what really matters for the parent–child relationship by using materials that are already in the home.

Agency Preparation for FLE Approach. Three participants discussed the efforts to prepare for the FLE approach to EHS home visiting. Some home visitors and staff attended a conference where such topics as the family-centered approach and meeting families where they are were the focus. FLE training also included watching a NCFR webinar on FLE. The materials presented by leadership are also included in the following Appendices: (D) philosophy, mission, goals, values, purpose statements, (E) program goals, (F) empowering preschool parents (presented as a PowerPoint presentation), (G) home visiting paradigm shift (also a PowerPoint presentation), and (H) home visiting next steps planning form. The agency brought in experts to discuss a strengths-based developmental parenting approach and the Home Visiting Rating Scales (see Appendix C).

Agencies in the area of the host site collaborated to bring in Robin McWilliam (see McWilliam, 2010) to train on the family-centered approach to home visiting and the next steps home visiting planning form (see Appendix H). Participants' responses revealed that this training reiterated that toy bags are not effective, which made many people from other sites uncomfortable by the mere thought

56 FLE Approach to Home Visiting

of switching from toy bags to another approach. Leadership from the target site suggested that it was an "impactful" training.

Challenges to Obtaining CFLE. Consistent with previous research (Walsh et al., in press), nine participants (53%) discussed that the current pathways to becoming a CFLE present challenges. The abbreviated application process for completed CFLE coursework timeline of applying within two years of graduation from where they took the CFLE courses was reported as a challenge. They mentioned that often there is not a clear path from graduating from a family science program and immediately securing a job and that providing an expanded timeline for the abbreviated application process would be helpful. The other certification pathway, or the CFLE exam, also had perceived challenges. These included: expense of exam, anxiety of taking exam, time commitment of preparing for and taking exam, and once it is earned keeping up with the work experience. Several participants expressed that maintaining other credentials, such as CCLS and LSW, along with earning the CFLE credential, seemed like a lot to ask of home visitors. Leadership expressed that because the program already experienced 100% turnover, the fear was that requiring the CFLE would create more turnover. There were also concerns that home visiting may be thought of as an entry level position and that the CFLE does not appear in most job advertisements, meaning that it is not widely recognized in the HV field and beyond it. One participant stated that "If it is not a requirement for you to have this job then it is not going to get paid for." Similar to Walsh et al.'s (in press) study, participants expressed concern that EHS has an interesting stance on the flexibility in qualifications of home visitors and that if EHS were to take an explicit stance that CFLE was important, then it would create a demand for it.

Knowledge and Experience in Developmental Science and Family Science

The theme, Knowledge and Experience in Developmental Science and Family Science, captured participants' expressions on a variety of topics, such as child socio-emotional development, holistic child development, parenting attitudes, attachment, trust, and insight about families in poverty. Although participants were not directly asked about their developmental and family knowledge and experiences, the interview protocol seemed to spark participants' perspective sharing on human development and families. Participants connected their knowledge and experiences to the topics of FLE and what home visits were like for them as professionals. This theme emerged from focused coding, which included (a) knowledge and insight about families and (b) perspectives about infant and child development.

Knowledge and Insight about Families. Nine participants (53%) shared content knowledge about family life as well as insights gleaned from working with families in the context of home visiting. Two home visitors discussed some of the challenges for families in poverty, such as not having resources and having struggles that some of the home visitors from a middle-class socioeconomic status have not experienced. Participants also discussed individual differences of families. For example, one home visitor stated "Whereas other families I visit might be in crisis, and they can't even really focus on their child, they have other issues on their mind." One participant suggested that individual differences in families create different levels of family engagement and comfort during the home visit. Three participants' concurred with one home visitor statement that "a family's trust is a big thing" and that trust levels vary across families. They elaborated that when families trust the home visitor, they are more open to working with specialists. A specialist stated, "When the parent really, really trusts the home visitor, it is easy for me to come into that home, it feels differently."

Perspectives about Infant and Child Development. Although knowledge and insight about families were shared more often, perspectives about infant and child development were also shared. Three participants shared their perspectives about infant and child development. Two participants discussed how not bringing toys into the home allows the home visitor to learn what the family perceives as the greatest child development needs. One specialist stated "If you are coming into the home with different toys and activities, you don't really know what the family wants to work on. Their kid's teeth can be rotting out of their mouth. That's more important to them at present than if their kid can stack blocks." Two participants also emphasized that social-emotional skills in infancy and early childhood take priority over cognitive development and academic skills.

Empowerment and Intentionality of EHS Home Visiting: Family Life Education

The theme, Empowerment and Intentionality of EHS Home Visiting: Family Life Education, captured participants' understanding and perspectives of the FLE approach to EHS HV. Participants expressed ways their current work and thinking aligned with the model espoused by Petkus (2015). Although participants did not explicitly state that they were making expansions to Petkus' work, they did suggest considerations that Petkus (2015) did not capture in his original book chapter. Participants' descriptions in essence advance Petkus's model and thus the practice of family science and HV. The theme, Empowerment and Intentionality of EHS Home Visiting: Family Life Education, emerged from focused coding, which included (a) relational dyad and triad of home visit, (b) orientation of home visiting is present and future, (c) hallmarks of FLE approach to home visiting, (d) roles of home visitor, (e) reflective supervision, (f) value of CFLE, and (g) other.

Relational Dyad and Triad of Home Visit. Consistent with Petkus' (2015) FLE approach to EHS HV, seven participants (41%) discussed the relational dyad of the home visit. The parent and child relationship was a common focal point of home visits. Language included: "parent and child attachment," "it is all about the parent and child interaction," and "parent is the foremost and most important teacher to the child." Participants also mentioned that home visits are "a triad of home visitor, parent, and child" expanding upon Petkus' (2015) notion of the relational dyad as key.

Orientation of Home Visiting is Present and Future. Five participants (29%) expressed that the focus of FLE is on family strengths in the present and the future (Myers-Walls et al., 2011; Petkus, 2015). One home visitor said "Giving them skills that they need and confidence that they need so that they can advocate for their kids in the future without a home visitor is a big thing." One participant from leadership emphasized that "the family should be setting the goals for the present and the future and the home visitor should not be directing the goals."

Hallmarks of FLE Approach to Home Visiting. In addition to the relational dyad and triad of the home visit as well as the orientation on the present and the future, nine participants (53%) shared other hallmarks of FLE Approach to HV. Participants expressed that it is a balance of *being with* families rather than *doing for*, consistent with Petkus' (2015) hallmark. One participant noted that this balance creates tension. Specifically, a home visitor stated "I need to be willing to let the family take the lead. Sometimes that is really hard for me because I'm like, 'I'm the professional.'" Participants emphasized that it is important to the FLE approach to use materials that are already in the family's home to make the home visit as organic as possible and to focus on the parent–child interaction. Participants also emphasized that hallmarks of this approach include: "skill-building" and "confidence building." They also emphasized components of relationship-based care as essential to FLE, including: (a) continuity of care between HV and families, (b) HV is finding out about families, including their issues and strengths, and (c) family engagement in the home visit. One participant noted that Head Start's goal of school readiness is able to be achieved through a FLE approach, particularly by focusing on the whole child and not favoring one developmental domain (e.g., cognitive) over the others. Shared goal setting with families was also noted as important using a form, such as the one in Appendix H.

Two participants mentioned that one disposition that is important to the FLE approach in the context of HV is to have an open mind in order to consider what works best for families and to empower families. Another disposition noted was humility and that the work of HVs is often an art. Specifically, the participant stated

> You have to be really tactful in the way you deliver the information, also making sure that it is the right time. It is almost like an art of making it be appropriate. It does not need to come from a haughty place rather a humble place, which requires tact and humility to get parents the information that is needed.

Finally, two participants expressed that the agency believes in the FLE approach and that it is a right approach for families. They also discussed how there should also be evidence that the families are satisfied with the services. One participant cited results from a parent satisfaction survey, which included 11 forced choice items (yes vs. no) with the opportunity for respondents to provide open-ended comments for each question. There was one open-ended question that asked how the site could increase satisfaction as a participant in the program. See Appendix I.

Roles of Home Visitor. Thirteen participants (76%) discussed the roles of home visitors, with 11 participants expressing this topic more than once throughout the focus group. Some participants were certain that a home visitor is a FLE and suggested that being an FLE provides a professional identify. Other participants were not so sure. For example, one participant questioned "Is the role of HV becoming a FLE?" and one participant questioned "What is my role sometimes?"

Participants made statements that demonstrated awareness of a FLE philosophy and what it should look like in practice. In addition to describing a HV as a FLE, which was the most frequent description, they also used such descriptions as: "coach," "mentor," "facilitator," and "a link to resources for families." They also mentioned that central to the role of HV is possessing skills and using different approaches, such as: "scaffolding," "reinforcing the positives," "relationship building," "asking critical questions," "building communication skills," "listening to families," and "meeting families where they are." One participant emphasized that it is important to create a safe environment for families and to keep in mind that home visitors are mandated reporters but they are not from CPS.

Additionally, home visitors viewed their role as that of a collaborator, which is one of the main tenets of FLE (see Darling & Cassidy, 2014; Myers-Walls et al., 2011). They viewed themselves as collaborators with families, with each other, and with specialists. Along this line, they viewed themselves as part of a system with specialists. One participant mentioned that it takes a team approach to do an IEP or IFSP and it takes communications with specialists, who make mental health referrals.

Parental empowerment was also expressed as central to the role of a home visitor, which is consistent with Petkus' (2015) expression. One participant mentioned "Something we talk a lot about is empowering the parents. That is a big push for us."

60 FLE Approach to Home Visiting

Reflective Supervision. Five participants (29%) discussed supports that they had. Reflective supervision was seen as a way to prevent HV burnout and to establish appropriate boundaries with families. One participant stated "we have a ton of people to help us for things that are just too big to handle by ourselves."

Value of CFLE. Three participants (18%) expressed that they perceived CFLE to be of value. One participant found it of value because they earned CFLE provisional status. Another participant mentioned that they were in a meeting with community supports and they were asking about the CFLE as a credential for home visitors. This participant stated that the community supports "were really excited about the CFLE, it would great." Another participant mentioned that it was of value to her academic home. They stated "our professors have a CFLE plus degrees."

Other. During the transition from initial to focused coding, there were five statements across four participants coded as "other," given that they did not fit. One participant stated, "They are not going to learn that in an hour and a half, number one." One participant posed questions that were challenging to code, these were: (a) "If I were to change things and it would benefit the family, isn't that what I'm supposed to do so why not give it a try?" and (b) "Whatever the model they are using now, I assume it might be the infamous toy bag. Who is that working for?" Another participant noted, "Child life specialists used to be called play therapists and then they would take the certification exam and then become a CCLS." Another participant stated, "I'm coming from a MSW and the staff we have here, which is relatively a group of young people."

Table 4.2 Coding Analysis

Themes			
Focused codes	*Cohen's Kappa*	*Percentage Agreement*	*Exemplary quotes*
Paradigm Shift to FLE			
Challenge of Transition from Toys to FLE	.89	91.95%	"The switch of taking away the toy bag was like punching people in the face. It was personal, they thought I was from Mars. What are you talking about? What are we going to talk about with families?" (Leadership)
Agency Preparation for FLE Approach	.73	80.00%	"When we had a previous supervisor here, we had like PowerPoints and staff meetings or we talked about family life education … We watched a webinar on

(Continued)

Table 4.2 (Cont.)

Themes			
Focused codes	*Cohen's Kappa*	*Percentage Agreement*	*Exemplary quotes*
			that. We are all well aware of the philosophy change. What was it before what it is supposed to look like now." (Home Visitor)
Challenges to Obtaining CFLE	.94	95.56%	"I just want to say that I think even the work experience and training are not as big of a deal as the exam is for me. A lot of us here have taken boards before and they are expensive and they are hard and they are time consuming. Getting training times or work experience is a lot easier than taking a board exam. Or just like the anxiety of going into a board exam is difficult." (Home Visitor)
Knowledge and Experience in Developmental Science and Family Science			
Knowledge and Insight about Families	.82	86.27%	"I think for a lot of our families trust is a big thing. We have a lot of refugee families. They were in camps, you know they've been burned before. We have a lot of foster care families. They don't trust the system a lot." (Home Visitor)
Perspectives about Infant and Child Development	.78	83.33%	"I think for zero to 3, and I think you all would agree, that social emotional domain is the most important. Yes, cognitive development is and we do focus on that too but skills, such as interacting with others are huge." (Leadership)
Empowerment and Intentionality of EHS HV: FLE			
Relational Dyad and Triad of Home Visit	.79	84.44%	"It is like a triad where they are all working together. Primarily the child wants to be with the parent and that is what we want. The home visitors are

(*Continued*)

Table 4.2 (Cont.)

Themes			
Focused codes	*Cohen's Kappa*	*Percentage Agreement*	*Exemplary quotes*
Orientation of Home Visiting is Present and Future	.79	84.62%	there to support that, the attachment that is taking place. I see the home visitors and if the child is constantly wanting to come to them, they redirect the child back to the parent." (Leadership) "It is good to think about how will this approach affect my family and make it a long-term effect or benefits that the family can get out of it. You always have to be thinking, what happens when there is no more home visiting? What can the family take from this? How is this going to benefit them more when I'm not there? What can I give, what can I educate on, or offer advice to on now in the current moment? What is the family going to get out of it that will help them in the future?" (Home Visitor)
Hallmarks of FLE Approach to Home Visiting	.83	87.50%	"We believe that the approach that is more in line with FLE was right for our program and our families." (Leadership)
Roles of Home Visitor	.82	86.27%	"For me it is about this balance between being an educator and following up on what the family might see as a concern and what the HV might see as a concern." (Home Visitor)
Reflective Supervision	.86	89.66%	"Being able to come back and talk to other people about boundaries and we do share family struggles, confidentially, because otherwise you are holding onto it yourself." (Leadership)
Value of CFLE	.67	75.00%	"I think it is of value. I have my CFLE provisional." (Home Visitor)

Discussion

We aimed to understand how FLE transformed and is transforming an EHS home visiting site. The present findings help in growing the FLE model for EHS home visiting by describing what tends to be the most salient parts of this model and which areas of it need to grow for philosophical and practical purposes.

Relationships to Previous Literature

The consensus by study participants that a home visiting approach that brings toys into the families' homes is ineffective is concordant with previous literature (Petkus, 2015; Scarr & McCartney, 1988; Wasik & Bryant, 2001). Abandoning this approach for a FLE approach had a range of challenges, including that a toy-centric approach was a comfort zone for HVs, change is hard in general, and the 100% turnover rate demonstrated that perhaps not all home visitors are comfortable with transitioning to a more organic home visiting approach.

The agency took great effort in providing training for the transition to FLE, which seemed to be mostly knowledge and discussion-based. However, because HVs have varying educational backgrounds and life experiences (Avellar et al., 2016), it may be helpful to include training that covers knowledge formation and discussion but also parity in demonstration of core tenets of FLE and practicing the FLE approach, along with reflective supervision that provides feedback and guidance about the FLE approach. Hands-on and applied experiences may promote more consistency between program goals and prescribed philosophy and practice. The HVs valued reflective supervision, particularly as important to avoiding burn-out and to promoting professionalism (Finello, 2016). We propose that going forward it would be helpful to identify key elements of the reflective supervision process that mirror the FLE approach (i.e., what is being provided to families), as well as including supervisors and HVs tools that provide feedback and guidance to the HV about their work with the FLE approach. Once the FLE approach to EHS HV becomes solidified as well as develops supportive measures, such as training that focuses on knowledge and application, and reflection supervision elements that match the FLE approach, participants may be more interested in seeking out ways for the site to wholeheartedly embrace FLE as well as the credential or CFLE, which accompanies it. Perhaps until there are more supports, HVs will remain somewhat skeptical not about the value of CFLE but rather its utility for HVs (Walsh et al., in press).

The findings within the theme, Empowerment and Intentionality of EHS Home Visiting: Family Life Education, which included: (a) relational dyad and triad of home visit, (b) orientation of home visiting is present and future, (c) hallmarks of FLE approach to home visiting, (d) roles of home visitor, (e) reflective supervision, and (f) value of CFLE, demonstrated that the home

64   FLE Approach to Home Visiting

visitors described similarities to Petkus' (2015) model as well as modifications to it. Petkus (2015) proposed that the relational dyad (i.e. parent–child) is of high importance during the home visit. This focus group acknowledged this dyad but believes that the home visitor, parent, and child are a triad and that this is an important part of the visit. It is possible that identifying a triad in addition to the parent–child dyad is appropriate given the concern of retention of home visitors and home visitors' uncertainty in their role.

Our findings suggest variability in home visitors' understanding of their role in working with their clients or families. Some participants were certain that a HV is a FLE and suggested that being an FLE provides a professional identity (Petkus, 2015). Participants concurred with FLE's views that collaboration and parental empowerment are important (Darling & Cassidy, 2014; Petkus, 2015). Our findings suggest that further delineation of the role of a HV in the FLE approach is needed especially since most home visitors expressed interest in family life education as an approach to EHS HV.

Strengths and Limitations

To our knowledge, this is the first study to focus on home visitors' perspectives about a FLE approach to EHS HV. Because this was the only site in the country that declared employing the FLE approach to EHS HV at the time of data collection, it was not possible to include other sites. The analysis and conclusions would potentially be enhanced by including more data from several sites. Another strength of our study was that our qualitative approach was rigorous.

The researcher worked on establishing rapport with HVs and leadership prior to the focus group. Nonetheless, one limitation is that participants may have provided socially desirable responses rather than candid responses to the questions. The heterogeneity of the focus group (leadership and home visitors) was preferred by the target site. The researchers think that this was important to make sure that individual opinions were individual opinions in a realistic manner and to increase the dynamic of different perspectives (Flick, 2006). The size of the focus group was orderly (Morgan, 1997) but some might consider it large. Given the site's preference to have everyone together and to have the focus group as part of their regular meetings, it was the most practical approach.

Implications

Home visiting programs need more specificity on what the FLE approach should look like and what home visitors' roles and responsibilities are within the FLE approach to EHS HV. Receiving training that includes applications of the FLE approach to HV seems essential. Reflective supervision seems essential not only to prevent HV burnout but also to provide a parallel FLE process to HV and an opportunity to provide further guidance and feedback on the FLE approach.

The FLE model to EHS HV (Petkus, 2015) needs to be expanded. This site was trained by Petkus and others to adopt an approach that resembled this model; however, the participants discussed some deviations from this model, which, based on their day-to-day experiences, serve them better. Once the model is refined and expanded upon and training is further developed, it needs to be determined if FLE holds up in practice over time with families and if it used effectively. It will also be helpful to determine if certain characteristics (e.g., having a CFLE) influence how this model is used and perceived. We also recommend developing FLE tools that could be used in reflective supervision to set the stage for home visitor empowerment.

Summary

This qualitative research was conducted to understand how the FLE approach transformed the work of an EHS home visiting site, which transitioned from a child-centered toy approach to a FLE approach. One focus group was conducted with 17 home visitors and leadership from one site. Three major themes emerged: Paradigm Shift to FLE, Knowledge and Experience in Developmental Science and Family Science, and Empowerment and Intentionality of EHS Home Visiting: Family Life Education. The themes captured participants' views about the challenges of transition from a child-centered to FLE approach, the challenges to obtaining a CFLE, insight to working with families in poverty, and their perspectives of child development. Participants also discussed their conceptualization of a parent–child–home visitor triad and the role of the home visitor as a collaborator with the family, which has important implications for expanding Petkus' (2015) current framework. The results of this study suggest that although this agency took great effort in providing training for the transition to FLE, training that focuses on direct application and reflective supervision of implementing the FLE approach during home visits might be an important way for home visitors to wholeheartedly embrace FLE.

Key Concepts

- Being with rather than doing for
- Collaborators
- Domains of family practice
- Early Head Start home visiting
- Family Life Education approach to EHS HV
- Home visiting paradigm shift
- Home Visiting Rating Scale or HOVRS
- Maternal, Infant, Early Childhood Home Visiting (MIECHV) Grants

66 *FLE Approach to Home Visiting*

- Orientation of services: Present and future
- Parental empowerment
- Relational dyad and triad of home visit
- Reflective supervision

Recommended Reading

Goddard, W., & Marshall, J. P. (2015). The art of family life education: Getting our hearts right. In M. J. Walcheski & J. S. Reinke (Eds.), *Family life education: The practice of family science* (pp. 9–16). Minneapolis, MN: National Council on Family Relations.

Sosinsky, L., Ruprecht, K., Horn, D., Kriener-Althen, K., Vogel, C., & Halle, T. (2016). *Including relationship-based care practices in infant-toddler care: Implications for practice and policy.* Brief prepared for the Office of Planning, Research and Evaluation, Administration for Children and Families, U.S. Department of Health and Human Services. Retrieved from https://www.acf.hhs.gov/opre/resource/including-relationship-based-care-practices-infant-toddler-care-implications-practice-and-policy

References

Administration for Children and Families (ACF). (2000). *Child development services during home visits and socializations in the Early Head Start home-based program option.* Retrieved from http://eclkc.ohs.acf.hhs.gov/policy/im

Administration for Children and Families (ACF). (2008). Home based program option. Head Start Program Performance Standards and Other Regulations Source: 61 FR 57210, November 5, 1996; Amended 73 FR 1285, January 8, 2008. 1306.33.

Anderson, D., & Howard, S. (2015). Human sexuality across the lifespan. In M. J. Walcheski, & J. S. Reinke (Eds.), *Family life education: The practice of family science* (pp. 177–188). Minneapolis, MN: National Council on Family Relations.

Avellar, S., Paulsell, D., Sama-Miller, E., Del Grosso, P. Akers, L., & Kleinman, R. (2016). *Home visiting evidence of effectiveness review: Executive summary.* Washington, DC: Office of Planning Research and Evaluation, Administration for Children and Families, U.S. Department of Health and Human Services.

Bogenschneider, K. (2015). Family law and public policy. In M. J. Walcheski, & J. S. Reinke (Eds.), *Family life education: The practice of family science* (pp. 223–234). Minneapolis, MN: National Council on Family Relations.

Charmaz, K. (2006). *Constructing grounded theory: A practical guide through qualitative analysis.* Thousand Oaks, CA: Sage.

Covey, M. (2015). Family life education methodology. In M. J. Walcheski, & J. S. Reinke (Eds.), *Family life education: The practice of family science* (pp. 243–251). Minneapolis, MN: National Council on Family Relations.

Darling, C. A., & Cassidy, D. (2014). *Family life education: Working with families across the lifespan* (3rd ed.). Long Grove, IL: Waveland.

Dekel, R., Goldblatt, H., Keidar, M., Solomon, Z., & Polliack, M. (2005). Being a wife of a veteran with posttraumatic stress disorder. *Family Relations, 54,* 24–36. doi: 10.1111/j.0197-6664.2005.00003.x

Duncan, S. F., & Goddard, H. W. (2017). *Family life education: Principles and practices for effective outreach* (3rd ed.). Thousand Oaks, CA: Sage.

Finello, K. M. (2016). *Building the capacity of reflective supervisors to respond to complexities in home visiting*. Poster presentation at the Home Visiting Applied Research Collaborative, Arlington, VA.

Flick, U. (2006). *An introduction to qualitative research* (3rd ed.). Thousand Oaks, CA: Sage.

Glesne, C. (2006). *Becoming qualitative researchers: An introduction* (3rd ed.). New York: Pearson.

Glotzer, R. (2015). Interpersonal relationships. In M. J. Walcheski, & J. S. Reinke (Eds.), *Family life education: The practice of family science* (pp. 189–203). Minneapolis, MN: National Council on Family Relations.

Home Visiting Research Network (2013, October 29). *National home visiting research agenda*. Retrieved from http://www.hvrn.org/uploads/3/4/5/0/34508506/home_visiting_research_agenda_2013_10_29_final.pdf

Jacobson, A. L. (2015). Parenting education and guidance. In M. J. Walcheski, & J. S. Reinke (Eds.), *Family life education: The practice of family science* (pp. 213–222). Minneapolis, MN: National Council on Family Relations.

Jeon, H. J., Peterson, C. A., Roggman, L., Luze, G., & Mortensen, J. A. (2016). *Early Head Start home visiting program: Home visiting process and child and family outcomes at age 5*. Poster presentation at the Home Visiting Applied Research Collaborative, Arlington, VA.

Leventhal, J. (2015). Human growth and development across the lifespan. In M. J. Walcheski, & J. S. Reinke (Eds.), *Family life education: The practice of family science* (pp. 167–176). Minneapolis, MN: National Council on Family Relations.

MacDermid Wadsworth, S. M., Roy, K. M., & Watkins, N. (2015). Interpersonal relationships. In M. J. Walcheski, & J. S. Reinke (Eds.), *Family life education: The practice of family science* (pp. 147–155). Minneapolis, MN: National Council on Family Relations.

McWilliam, R. A. (2010). *Routines-based early intervention: Supporting young children and their families*. Baltimore, MD: Paul H. Brookes.

Morgan, D. L. (1997). *Focus groups as qualitative research* (2nd ed.). Thousand Oaks, CA: Sage.

Moore, T. J., & Asay, S. M. (2015). Family resource management. In M. J. Walcheski, & J. S. Reinke (Eds.), *Family life education: The practice of family science* (pp. 205–212). Minneapolis, MN: National Council on Family Relations.

Myers-Walls, J., Ballard, S., Darling, C., & Myers-Bowman, K. (2011). Reconceptualizing the domains and boundaries of family life education. *Family Relations, 60*, 357–372.

Office of Head Start. (2017–2018). Early Head Start Services Snapshot. Retrieved from https://eclkc.ohs.acf.hhs.gov/sites/default/files/pdf/no-search/service-snapshot-ehs-2017-2018.pdf

Palm, G. F. (2015). Professional ethics and practice. In M. J. Walcheski, & J. S. Reinke (Eds.), *Family life education: The practice of family science* (pp. 235–240). Minneapolis, MN: National Council on Family Relations.

Petkus, J. (2015). A first-hand account of implementing a Family Life Education model: Intentionality in Head Start home visiting. In M. J. Walcheski, & J. S. Reinke (Eds.),

Family life education: The practice of family science (pp. 325–331). Minneapolis, MN: National Council on Family Relations.

Raikes, H., Green, B. L., Atwater, J., Kisker, E., Constantine, J., & Chazan-Cohen, R. (2006). Involvement in Early Head Start home visiting services: Demographic predictors and relations to child and parent outcomes. *Early Childhood Research Quarterly, 21*, 2–24. doi: 10.1016/j.ecresq.2006.01.006

Reinke, J. S., & Walcheski, M. J. (2015). Internal dynamics of families. In M. J. Walcheski, & J. S. Reinke (Eds.), *Family life education: The practice of family science* (pp. 157–166). Minneapolis, MN: National Council on Family Relations.

Roggman, L. A., Cook, G. A., Jump Norman, V. K., Christiansen, K., Boyce, L. K., & Innocenti, M. S. (2008). Home Visiting Rating Scales (HOVRS). In L. A. Roggman, L. K. Boyce, & M. S. Innocenti (Eds.), *Developmental parenting: A guide for early childhood practitioners* (pp. 209–217). Baltimore, MD: Brookes.

Saldaña, J. (2011). *Fundamentals of qualitative research: Understanding qualitative research.* New York: Oxford.

Scarr, S., & McCartney, K. (1988). Far from home: An experimental evaluation of the mother-child home program in Bermuda. *Child Development, 59*, 531–543. doi: 10.2307/1130555

Tracy, S. J. (2010). Qualitative quality: Eight 'Big-Tent' criteria for excellent qualitative research. *Qualitative Inquiry, 16*, 837–851. doi: 10.1177/1077800410383121

Walsh, B. A., Mortensen, J. A., Edwards, A. L., & Cassidy, D. (in press). The practice of family life education within Early Head Start home visiting. *Family Relations.*

Wasik, B. H., & Bryant, D. M. (2001). *Home visiting: Procedures for helping families* (2nd ed.).Thousand Oaks, CA: Sage.

Appendix A Multidisciplinary Family Service Approaches

Goal: How can the agency as a whole continue offering services from the middle to ensure family needs are met, without the home visitor doing it all?

Why: To be intentional in the home visiting role and purpose, operate within our scope of practice, and to avoid burn not.

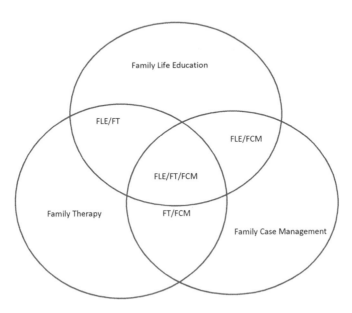

FLE

- FLE methodology
- Normal, healthy functioning
- Broad, inclusive knowledge base
- Education/prevention

FT

- Therapeutic intervention
- Assessment and diagnosis
- Psychotherapy

FCM

- Coordination of services
- Family advocacy
- Focus on meeting family needs

FLE/FT

- Quantitative research
- Healthy sexual functioning
- Life course perspective

FLE/FCM

- Family resource management
- Family policy

FT/FCM

- Focus on family problems
- Intervention techniques
- Treatment goals/methods
- Management of client records
- Closure of cases

(Continued)

Appendix A (Cont.)

FLE/FT/FCM

- Family Systems theory
- Sensitivity to diversity
- Research-based practice
- Ecological context
- Values and ethics

Let's Identify Who is Doing Each Piece:

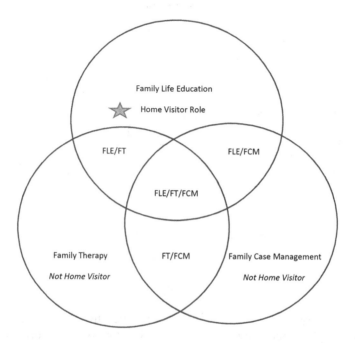

Family Life Education (prevention, education, and coach):

- Home visitors
- Joint problem solving
- Collaborative planning approach
- Parent demonstration of learned skills
- Family Systems theory, sibling involvement
- Adverting later problems, through empowering self-sustainability
- Parent education through focus on attachment
- Parent meetings

Family Therapy (assessment/screening and diagnosis):

- Mental Health Specialist consulting
- Special Needs Specialist consulting

(Continued)

Appendix A (Cont.)

- Referrals
- Edinburgh, prenatal and postnatal
- ASQ
- Home visiting advisor

Family Case Management (coordination of services);
- Home visitor (case) meetings with LMSW, CFLE, CCLS, and Special Needs Specialist
- Social Services Department Resources/FSW
- IFSP

★ In the past model, the home visitor was the primary person operating in each approach. Essentially, the home visitors were attempting to practice three disciplines at once.

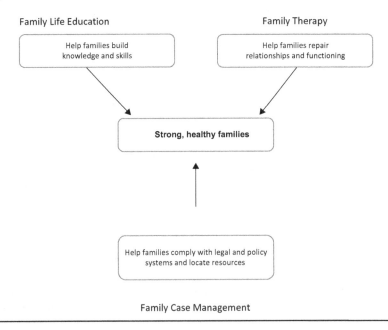

Appendix B Hallmarks of Effective vs. Ineffective Home Visits

Red Flags of Ineffective Visits		Green Flags of Effective Visits	
STOP	Parents leave the room or go in and out during a home visit.	GO	Parent and child interact during most of the visit.
STOP	Child races to greet home visitor and rummages through bag.	GO	Child exceedingly turns to the parent when you arrive, expecting fun together.
STOP	More time spent on family problems than on child development.	GO	You comment on positive interactions that you observe.
STOP	Not much gets done when other family members are present.	GO	Other family members are involved in the activities.
STOP	Parent says, "Oh, you are so good with children!"	GO	Parent says, "We enjoy doing these things together."

Provided by Head Start for Kent County (October 2014)

Appendix C Home Visiting Rating Scale (HOVRS)

Measuring Tool	HOVRS (Home Visiting Rating Scale)
Purpose	Evidence based way to ensure deliverance of high quality sustainable parenting skill development in home visits.
From the Authors	"HOVRS emphasizes a developmental parenting support approach that respects each family's strengths and culture. The HOVRS measures were developed with input from practitioners and supervisors in home visiting programs and rate aspects of home visiting quality that are supported by the research literature on various home visiting programs. HOVRS measures have been used to provide feedback to practitioners and supervisors for program improvement."
Scale 1: Home Visitor Responsiveness to Family	This scale assesses the extent to which the home visitor is (1) prepared for the home visit, (2) attempts to get needed information from the

(Continued)

Appendix C (Cont.)

Measuring Tool	HOVRS (Home Visiting Rating Scale)
	parent, (3) observes and responds to the parent and child during the home visit, and (4) elicits input on the content and activities of the home visit from the parent. A high rating on this scale suggests that the home visitor is frequently engaging in responsive behaviors during the home visit.
Scale 2: Home Visitor Family Relationship	This scale examines the nature of the relationship between the home visitor and the family, as observed during the home visit it focuses on (1) warmth between home visitor and parent, (2) parent comfort with the home visitor, (3) positive interactions of the home visitor with the child and other members of the family, and (4) the home visitor's respect and understanding of the family as a whole. A high rating on this scale suggests that the home visitor and family are frequently engaging in warm, positive behaviors during the home visit.
Scale 3: Home Visitor Facilitation of Parent Child Interaction	This scale assesses the effectiveness of the home visitor at facilitating and promoting positive parent–child interactions during the home visit. It reflects how much the home visitor (1) encourages the parents' leadership when guiding parent–child interactions, (2) involves and responds to both the parent and the child during interactions, and (3) uses materials available in the home for promoting parent–child interactions. A high rating on this scale suggests that the home visitor is frequently engaging in facilitative behaviors during the home visit.
Scale 4: Home Visitor Non-Intrusiveness/Collaboration with Family	This scale focuses on the lack of intrusiveness by the home visitor on parent behavior and parent–child interactions during the visit. It assesses (1) home visitor control and (2) home visitor flexibility and responsiveness. A high rating on this scale suggests that the home visitor rarely engages in intrusive behaviors during the home visit and that he or she uses effective

(Continued)

Appendix C (Cont.)

Measuring Tool	*HOVRS (Home Visiting Rating Scale)*
	strategies to collaborate with the parent. A high rating on this scale means the home visitor is non-intrusive in a manner that promotes collaboration with the parent as a partner supporting the child's development.
Scale 5: Parent–Child Interaction during Home Visit	This scale examines the nature of the parent–child relationship, as observed during the home visit. It assesses (1) parent–child warmth and physical closeness, (2) parent attentiveness to the child, (3) parent responsiveness to the child, and (4) parent–child joint attention. A high rating on this scale suggests that the parent and child are frequently engaging in warm, positive behaviors during the home visit.
Scale 6: Parent Engagement during Home Visit	This scale examines the engagement of the parent and the activities of the home visit. It focuses on (1) parent interest, (2) parent involvement and initiative, and (3) the parent's physical closeness to the home visitor and child. A high rating on this scale suggests that the parent is frequently displaying behaviors that indicate interest and engagement in the home visit activities and discussion.
Scale 7: Child Engagement during Home Visit	This scale focuses on the child's engagement in the activities of the home visit. It focuses on (1) child involvement and (2) child interest. A high rating on this scale suggests that the child is frequently displaying behaviors that indicate engagement and interest in the home visit.

Provided by Head Start for Kent County (October 2014)

Appendix D Philosophy, Mission, Goals, Values, and Purpose Statements

Mission–Values–Purpose	*Key Points or Description*
Mission of Head Start for Kent County	"Head Start for Kent County's mission is to deliver comprehensive services to low income children five and under and their families promoting their well-being and development."
Mission of the Home Visiting Department	"Ensure best practice family life education principles are utilized in Head Start for Kent County home visits in order to provide children and families an enriched family life through a strength based prevention, education, and collaborative approach."
Purpose of the Home Visit	"The purpose of the home visit is to help parents improve their parenting skills and to assist them in the use of the home as the child's primary learning environment. The home visitor must work with parents to help them provide learning opportunities that enhance their child's growth and development." *Sec 1306.33 (1) Head Start Performance Standards and Other Regulations*
Our Core Values	"Professionalism–Respectfulness–Integrity–Competence–Commitment–Humanitarianism"
Philosophical Basis What is Family Life Education?	**Key Points or Description** ◊ Educational approach ◊ Build strengths ◊ Commonalities with family therapy or social work but a distinct area ◊ Prevention
Home Visitors as Family Life Educators	◊ Home visitor as family life educator ◊ Home visitor as coach ◊ Encouragement through narration of the parent–child interaction ◊ Promote parental understanding of child development ◊ Promote parental responsiveness to child ◊ Encourage long-term self-confidence and skill building in parents ◊ Discourage reliance on service provider ◊ Promote attachment ◊ Guide parents to understanding child health, safety, and nutritional needs and provide avenues to make sure child's needs are met

Provided by Head Start for Kent County (October 2014)

Appendix E Program Goals

Goals emphasize:	◊ Parent–child attachment ◊ School readiness ◊ Health, nutrition, and similar
Goals are positioned within Family Life Education:	◊ Based on research and best practice for individuals and families ◊ Build strengths and work to prevent problems ◊ Family life education provides skills to develop, maintain, and evaluate programs ◊ Overlap and distinctions with other professions ◊ Appreciation and active participation in continuing education and other opportunities to develop and to maintain skills
Different approaches to reach goals:	◊ Expert (see Duncan & Goddard, 2017) ◊ Facilitator (see Duncan & Goddard, 2017) ◊ Critical Inquirer (see Duncan & Goddard, 2017) ◊ Collaborator (see Duncan & Goddard, 2017) ◊ Interventionist (see Duncan & Goddard, 2017) ◊ Eclectic (see Duncan & Goddard, 2017)
Knowledge and practice needed to reach goals:	◊ Families and individuals in societal contexts (MacDermid Wadsworth, Roy, & Watkins, 2015) ◊ Internal dynamics of families (Reinke & Walcheski, 2015) ◊ Human growth and development across the lifespan (Leventhal, 2015) ◊ Human sexuality across the lifespan (Anderson & Howard, 2015) ◊ Interpersonal relationships (Glotzer, 2015) ◊ Family resource management (Moore & Asay, 2015) ◊ Parent education and guidance (Jacobson, 2015) ◊ Family law and public policy (Bogenschneider, 2015) ◊ Professional ethics and practice (Palm, 2015) ◊ Family life education methodology (Covey, 2015)

Provided by Head Start for Kent County (October 2014)

Appendix F Empowering Preschool Parents

Components	Key Points or Description
Birth to five continuity of development	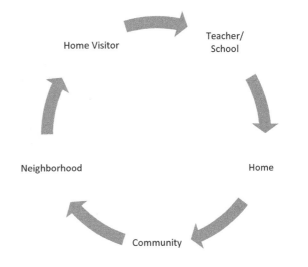
What do home visitors do? Why?	**Home Visiting Objective.** Ensure best practice principles are utilized in home visits in order to provide children and families an enriched family life through a strength based prevention, education, and collaborative approach. **Home Visit Purpose.** Head Start Performance Standards 1306.33: "The purpose of the home visit is to help parents improve their parenting skills and to assist them in the use of the home as the child's primary learning environment. The home visitor must work with parents to help them provide learning opportunities that enhance their child's growth and development." (ACF, 2008) **Approach.** (a) Use of Self = Observer. Home visitor acts as narrator of parent–child interaction. (b) Primary Source of Knowledge = Caregiver. Empowering primary caregiver. Building their confidence. (c) Main Focus = Encourage parent–child attachment. (d) Toys = None. Extend existing natural experiences. (e) Additional Family Members = Include in experiences. (f) Visits = Family Planning. (g) Planning = Ask questions to empower. Joint problem solving.

(Continued)

Appendix F (Cont.)

Components	Key Points or Description
	Extended sustainable learning and demonstration of skill development.
	Explaining to Families. (a) "We want to help you identify your skills and creativity, and build your confidence to support you in being your child's first teacher." (b) "We collaborate on finding what items and environments are already in your home that can be used for playing with your child, rather than bringing toys to you each week." (c) "Your child is learning most when I leave your home and you continue to play and talk with her." (d) "When at your home, you can expect me to observe as you play and talk with your child. I will provide explanation of how the play and words you use are supporting your child's development."
What we will discover?	◊ Opportunities to enhance parent–child relationship (attachment). ◊ Opportunities to empower parents as child's first teacher. ◊ Opportunities to strengthen parent–teacher relationship. ◊ Opportunities to extend classroom learning experiences in the home.
How are you promoting this now? Staff examples.	◊ Child drew a picture and home visitor showed excitement for what the parent taught the child to draw. ◊ Stroke the ego of the parent.
Brainstorm.	Within a small group, discuss and write at least two examples for: enhance, empower, strengthen, extend. Share with the large group via posters. Display posters at site.

Provided by Head Start for Kent County (October 2014)

Appendix G Home Visiting Paradigm Shift

Nine Dimensions of Home Visiting	*Characteristics of Old Model*	*Characteristics of FLE Model*
Use of Self	▫ as a model	▫ as crucial observer ▫ as narrator of parent-child interaction
Primary Source of Knowledge	▫ home visitor	▫ primary caregiver ▫ home visitor empowers primary caregiver to build their confidence to see child's progressing development
Main Focus	▫ home visitor to child interaction	▫ encourage parent–child attachment
Toys	▫ brought on every visit by home visitor	▫ no toys brought (i.e., point is to extend existing natural experiences)
Additional Family Members	▫ ignored to slightly acknowledged	▫ include in experiences
Visits	▫ according to home visitors agenda	▫ family planning ▫ parents agenda
Planning	▫ based on curriculum	▫ home visitor asks thoughtful questions to empower ▫ home visitor and parent engage in joint problem solving ▫ extended and sustainable learning ▫ demonstration of skill development
Methodology	▫ infant mental health/family case management/family therapy	▫ family life education/family therapy/family case management
Monitoring	▫ non-evidence based subjective approach	▫ Home Visitor Rating Scale (HOVRS)

Provided by Head Start for Kent County

Appendix H Home Visiting Next Steps Planning Form

Child's name: _____

What we did today...

_____
_____
_____
_____

What we will do before the next visit...

Parent: _____

_____
_____

Home visitor: _____

_____
_____

What we will do on the next visit... _____

_____
_____

Family updates: _____

_____
_____

Next visit (date and time):

_____

Parent/guardian signature: _____ Date: _____

Staff signature: _____Date: _____

Provided by Head Start for Kent County

Appendix I Home Visitor Service Satisfaction Survey and Results

		n
1. Is your home visitor regularly on time for scheduled visits?		
	Yes	9
	No	0

(Continued)

Appendix I (Cont.)

2. Are your home visits scheduled for the same day and time each week? (If not, is this your choice?)

Yes	9
No	0

3. Is your home visitor friendly/positive and professional during the visit? (If not, what occurred?)

Yes	9
No	0

4. Have you established a relationship with your home visitor in which you feel comfortable sharing information regarding your family? (Why not?)

Yes	9
No	0

5. Does your home visitor listen to your concerns or questions, if any? (What did you ask?)

Yes	9
No	0

6. Does your home visitor describe the next developmental milestones your child will reach as well as activities you can do to support your child in reaching those milestones?

Yes	9
No	0

7. Does your home visitor relate your day-to-day activities/ interactions with your child to school readiness?

Yes	9
No	0

8. Does your home visitor remind you about needed health events for your child? Are you supported in obtaining these health services?

Yes	9
No	0

9. Does your home visitor bring snacks at least once per month?

Yes	9
No	0

10. Does your home visitor provide you with resources you request? What resources?

Yes	8
No	1

11. Does your home visitor provide parenting information and support you in dealing with any challenging behaviors your child may present?

Yes	8
No	1

5 Reflective Practice

Home visitors in EHS-HBO programs have a simple yet complex goal: support families. Each family is comprised of unique individuals with their own strengths, challenges, and life experiences. Home visitors are faced with the diversity of family life but must find ways to spur change and growth in everyone. This is no simple task. A first important step in this professional journey is understanding and engaging in reflective practice. Simply stated, reflective practice is the ability to "hold others' minds in mind" (Luyten, Nijssens, Fonagy, & Mayes, 2017, p. 175). This chapter will explore the CUPID Competency **Reflective Practice** (Roggman et al., 2016; CUPID, 2017).

Competency	Pausing to think about (i.e., reflect upon) immediate or past experiences with children or parents, to consider each person's role in the interaction, and reasons for each person's responses. Using such reflections to consider whether alternative responses would be productive, and to guide changes in practices
Knowledge	Expanded knowledge of cultural, emotional, and experiential influences on parenting and the role of reflection in parenting, social support, and collaborative relationships
Skills	Skills for guiding parents' reflections on parenting and children's development and wellbeing, reflecting on one's own personal reactions to parenting and family life, and sharing reflections appropriately
Attitudes	Attitudes that support parallel processes for supporting social-emotional development and accepting families as they are

The FLE Content Areas that help expand this competency include:

Human growth and development across the lifespan	Understanding of the developmental changes (both typical and atypical) of individuals in families across the lifespan with an emphasis on knowledge of developmental domains

(Continued)

Reflective Practice   83

(Cont.)

Parenting education and guidance	How parents teach, guide, and influence as the dynamic context of the parent–child relationship
Families and individuals in societal contexts	Understand families in regard to other institutions
Professional ethics and practice	Understanding the character and quality of human social conduct and critically examine ethical questions and issues as they relate to professional practice
FLE methodology	Understand principles of FLE in tandem with planning and delivery of programs
Internal dynamics of families	Understanding of family strengths and weaknesses and how family members relate to each other

Note: Permission to reprint was granted from the National Council on Family Relations.

Knowledge

In order to engage in reflective practice with parents and children, home visitors in EHS-HBO must have knowledge on how family life is shaped by experiences, as well as the role reflection actually plays in home visiting. CUPID summarizes this knowledge as:

> Expanded knowledge of cultural, emotional, and experiential influences on parenting and the role of reflection in parenting, social support, and collaborative relationships.
>
> (CUPID, 2017)

Influences on Parenting

The science is clear that human biology interacts with culture to shape beliefs and behaviors (Li, 2003). As such, beliefs, attitudes, and mindsets about parenting do not develop randomly—they are embedded in the cultural values and experiences of each individual (Bornstein & Cheah, 2006). The daily interactions between parents and children are all shaped by culture. Thus, what feels "normal" to one family may feel completely unnatural to another. Parenting is influenced by: (1) settings (e.g., home, school, communities), (2) activities that take place within these settings (e.g., guidance and discipline strategies, communication patterns, opportunities for play), and (3) cultural values assigned to these settings and activities (e.g., *independence* in white families; *familism* in Latino families) (Bornstein & Cheah, 2006).

84   *Reflective Practice*

For families that experience marginalization (based on race, ethnicity, social class, etc.), their outlook on the world is also shaped by adaptive culture, which is "a social system defined by sets of goals, values, and attitudes that differs from the dominant culture" (García Coll, Crnic, Lamberty, Wasik, Jenkins, Garcia, & McAdoo, 1996, p. 1896). Adaptive culture includes a family's cultural traditions, economic and political histories, migration, acculturation, and current demands the family is facing (e.g., immigration issues) (García Coll et al., 1996). All of these experiences work together to impact parenting and family life.

Parenting practices and family ways of life are passed down from generation to generation. Adults bring their childhood cultural and emotional experiences with them when they become parents themselves. Attachment theory (discussed in more detail in Chapter 6) examines the ways in which early life experiences with parents (and other caregivers) shapes one's internal thoughts about the self and relationships with others (Bowlby, 1969/1982). From this perspective, ideas about parenting come naturally, but only in the ways that one was treated as a child. These memories are thought of as "ghosts in the nursery," subconsciously influencing how adults approach caring for their own infants when they become parents (Fraiberg, Adelson, & Shaprio, 1975). Experiences of safety, nurturing, and security as an infant will translate in to sensitive and responsive parenting behaviors, whereas issues stemming from inconsistent caregiving and trauma or loss may persist in to the next generation (Siegel & Hartzell, 2013).

The Role of Reflection

Home visitors can think about reflective practice in two important ways: 1) how reflective practices shape parenting and 2) how reflective practice inform the home visitor's own professional work.

To the first point, the ability to consider the self and others' underlying mental states is the basis for all social relationships (Fonagy, Gergely, Jurist, & Target, 2002), and thus affects all aspects of interpersonal family life. From an attachment perspective, the manner in which parents think about their own childhood has a major impact on how they parent their children (Siegel & Hartzell, 2013). This idea developed out of attachment research, in which early parental experiences shape who one becomes and how one interacts with others across the lifespan. The ability to articulate organized and coherent stories about one's own childhood is critical for creating healthy parent–child relationships in the future (van IJzendoorn, 1995). Researchers suspect that this ability is a good indicator that a parent will be sensitive and responsive towards his/her infant, which will increase the quality of their attachment bond (van IJzendoorn, 1995). Parents should be encouraged to reflect on their own childhood experiences as a way to organize and understand their own responses as a parent. Even parents who experienced negative or traumatic childhood events can reflect on their experiences in ways that promote healthy parent–child relationships. Siegel and Hartzell (2013) state why such reflection is helpful:

> A deeper self-understanding changes who you are. Making sense of your life enables you to understand others more fully and gives you the possibility of choosing your behaviors and opening your mind to a fuller range of experiences. The changes that come with self-understanding enable you to have a way of being, a way of communicating with your children, that promotes their security of attachment.
>
> (p. 134)

Similarly, "parental reflective functioning" is when parents reflect on their children's mental states (Luyten et al., 2017). This includes how parents' own mental states affect (and are affected by) interactions with their children. Parents with negative, inconsistent, or traumatic childhood experiences may have trouble "entering the internal world" of their infant. This limits their ability to understand how the infant sees the world. These parents are more likely to make assumptions that their infant is acting with malicious intent (e.g., "My baby is crying because he hates me") (Luyten et al., 2017). This is important to address in the context of home visiting because parental reflective functioning is directly linked to the quality of the parent–child infant attachment relationship (Slade, Grienenberger, Bernbach, Levy, & Locker, 2005a).

Second, home visitors must also be aware of the role reflection plays in their own professional practice. Reflection is a key element to building supportive and collaborative relationships with families. Reflective functioning, or the ability to "hold others' minds in mind" (Luyten et al., 2017, p. 175) also applies to the relationships home visitors cultivate with families. A competent home visiting professional has the knowledge to "look at oneself from the outside and at others from the inside" (Luyten et al., 2017, p. 175). For example, research with early childhood educators suggests that professionals can become more culturally responsive educators when they engage in reflection and self-study regarding their own ideas about human differences (Chen, Nimmo, & Fraser, 2009). When building relationships with families that have a variety of social and cultural experiences, the home visitor's ability to engage in reflective functioning will help her be mindful of her own thoughts and experiences in an objective manner, while also putting herself in the family's shoes to truly understand their experiences from the inside.

In a similar vein, reflective practice regarding the structure and content of the home visit with professional colleagues is also important (Keilty, 2008). A reflective approach to home visiting situates the home visit in a meaningful context for families, considers how to actively engage the child and parent(s) in meaningful interactions, and continually evaluates parental confidence and competence (Keilty, 2008).

FLE Content Area Knowledge and Knowledge of Reflective Practice

Human growth and development. *Understanding of the developmental changes (both typical and atypical) of individuals in families across the lifespan with an emphasis on knowledge of developmental domains.*

Home visitors in EHS-HBO can use their knowledge of human growth and development, particularly emotional and cultural theories, to understand how parents' own early experiences influence them as adults. Given an attachment perspective (Bowlby, 1969/1982), parents' emotional wellbeing and ability to reflect upon their own childhood in a coherent manner, are directly linked with the quality of caregiving experiences from their own childhood. Some parents in EHS-HBO may have had nurturing, warm caregiving experiences, whereas others had inconsistent, harsh, and punitive experiences. According to Siegel and Hartzell (2013), "nurturing relationships support our growth by helping us to make sense of our lives and to develop the more reflective, integrative functioning that emerges from secure attachments" (p. 136). Parents who did not experience nurturing relationships as children may need more guidance in making sense of their own childhoods and how it affects their behaviors as a parent.

Home visitors can also incorporate their knowledge about the interactions between human development and culture to inform their own understanding of how parents view and interpret their own lived experiences. García Coll and her colleagues (1996) proposed an integrative model of development that accounts for a variety of socio-cultural factors that influence how humans grow and learn within the family. Social position variables such as race/ethnicity and social class influence development, particularly the prejudice and discrimination experienced by families of color or families of low social class (García Coll et al., 1996). These factors, combined with experiences within neighborhoods, communities, and the family's adaptive culture, to affect social, cognitive, and emotional development (García Coll et al., 1996). Knowledge of this provides a more comprehensive understanding for why parents think and behave in certain ways. Home visitors need this understanding to effectively guide parenting practices.

Parenting education and guidance. *How parents teach, guide, and influence as the dynamic context of the parent–child relationship.*

Home visitors can use knowledge of parenting education and guidance as they work with parents to enhance reflective practice. Research suggests that enhancing parents' abilities to keep their own and their infant's mental state in mind is an effective way to improve the quality of parent–child relationships (e.g., Slade, Sadler, De Dios-Kenn, Webb, Currier-Ezepchick, & Mayes, 2005b). Parents who engage in reflective practice are better at understanding human behavior in terms of one's internal motives and intentions (Slade et al., 2005b). Thus, home visitors can use this in their parenting education work to help families better understand the process of parenting and to promote healthy parenting behaviors.

Table 5.1 Family Life Education Concepts and Resources that Align with Reflective Practices

FLE Content Area: Human Growth and Development	Resources
Emotional, experiential influences on parenting Culture[2]; Emotional development[1,2]; Parenting[2]; Reflective judgment[2]	[1]Leventhal, J. (2015). Human growth and development across the lifespan. In M. J. Walcheski, & J. S. Reinke (Eds.), *Family life education: The practice of family science* (pp. 167–176). Minneapolis, MN: National Council on Family Relations. [2]Boyd, D., & Bee, H. (2015). Lifespan development (7th ed.). Upper Saddle River, NJ: Pearson.

Reflective practice can be included as an important component of parenting education and guidance. As one example, parents can be educated about the role of self-reflection in the parenting process. Siegel and Hartzell (2013) suggest starting with the acronym COAL: be curious, open, accepting, and loving. This approach puts parents in the right mindset for using reflective practice. During activities such as pretend play or storytelling, home visitors can have parents develop mindsight, "the ability to perceive the internal experience of another person and make sense of that imagined experience" (Siegel & Hartzell, 2013, p. 258) by asking them to reflect on how they perceive their children's experiences during the interactions. When parents are frustrated by their children's behavior, home visitors can encourage parents to pause and think about how and why their child may be acting the way they are before responding. Developing mindsight may enable parents to offer more compassionate responses in challenging situations (Siegel & Hartzell, 2013).

Families and individuals in societal contexts. *Understand families in regard to other institutions.*

Home visitors should use their knowledge of how families and individuals are embedded in societal contexts to fully appreciate how cultural, emotional, and experiential influences shape parenting. Most families in EHS-HBO are living in poverty. Poverty brings major challenges to family life such as increased risk for parental depression/anxiety, family violence, food insecurity, and generalized feelings of stress (Evans & Kim, 2007). Poverty also affects families' interactions with important social institutions such as education, health care, and the labor market. Local, state, and federal policy decisions also directly affect families in poverty (e.g., expanding funding for Medicaid, funding for TANF, etc.). As home visitors work with families to engage in reflective practice, they need to keep these

88   *Reflective Practice*

Table 5.2 Family Life Education Concepts and Resources that Align with Reflective Practices

FLE Content Area: Parenting Education and Guidance	Resources
Emotional, experiential influences on parenting Identify sources of support for parenting, such as family, neighborhood, community[1]; parenting as a process[2]; influences on parenting[2]; supports for parents[2]; collaborative family atmosphere[2]	[1]Jacobson, A. L. (2015). Parenting education and guidance. In M. J. Walcheski, & J. S. Reinke (Eds.), *Family life education: The practice of family science* (pp. 213–222). Minneapolis, MN: National Council on Family Relations. [2]Brooks, J. B. (2013). *The process of parenting* (9th ed.). New York: McGraw Hill.

issues in mind to help understand parents' perspectives on family life and the goals they have for their children. For example, Annette Lareau (2011) interviewed and observed families from different socioeconomic backgrounds for multiple decades. She found that because poor families must spend so much time figuring out how to meet basic necessities, they place less importance on teaching their children how to navigate the ins and outs of social institutions. Consequently, their interactions with schools, health care, among others, can be strained and create a climate of distrust (Lareau, 2011). This example illustrates how the social context of living in poverty shapes how parents reflect on their own lived experiences. Home visitors will have a hard time supporting change and growth in families unless they have a complete picture of how each family's life is situated within and interacts with this context.

Professional ethics and practice. *Understanding the character and quality of human social conduct and critically examine ethical questions and issues as they relate to professional practice.*

Knowledge of professional ethics and practice is highly relevant to reflective practices, primarily in terms of the home visitor's own work. While much of this chapter has focused on helping parents with their own self-reflection, home visitors can also use their own reflective practice to enhance the quality of the home visiting experience. Keilty (2008) suggested that home visitors routinely reflect on the context of the home visit, child and caregiver engagement, and caregiver competence and confidence:

- How are the family's routine activities used as the setting for home visits?
- How does the home visit support active child participation in the family's routine activities to promote child learning?

Table 5.3 Family Life Education Concepts and Resources that Align with Reflective Practices

FLE Content Area: Families and individuals in societal contexts	Resources
Emotional, experiential influences on parenting Ecological perspective[1,2]; life course perspective[1]; interrelationship of families, work, and society[1]; supportive networks[1,2]; family systems and family strengths[2]; cultural competence[2]	[1]Wadsworth, S. M. M., Roy, K. M., & Watkins, N. (2015). Families and individuals in societal contexts. In M. J. Walcheski & J. S. Reinke (Eds.), *Family life education: The practice of family science* (pp. 147–155). Minneapolis, MN: National Council on Family Relations. [2]Olson, D. H., DeFrain, J., & Skogrand, L. (2014). *Marriages and families: Intimacy, diversity, and strengths* (8th ed.). New York: McGraw Hill.

- How is the caregiver actively participating so that she or he can learn specific intervention strategies?
- How does the home visit ensure the caregiver can accurately utilize the intervention strategies?

(Keilty, 2008, The Home Visiting Principles Checklist)

All of this reflective work on the part of the home visitor sets the stage for a high-quality relationship to develop with the family, which is essential if parents are to engage in their own reflective work (Slade et al., 2005b).

It is also critical that the home visitor uses reflective practice as a professional development tool. Mindfulness and reflective practice are increasingly being considered as an important (and even necessary) component to a competent home visiting workforce (e.g., Brophy-Herb et al., 2018). According to Brophy-Herb and colleagues (2018), mindfulness may help professionals' "recognition of their emotional reactions without judgement allowing them to accept their feelings but also regulate their reactions to respond with intention and empathy" (p. 1) towards others. Derman-Sparks and Edwards (2010) state that early childhood professionals should spend time reflecting on their own ideas about family, relationships, values, and biases. Social identities denote "membership in groups that are defined by society, are shared with many other people, and have societal advantages and disadvantages attached to them. These identities include gender, economic class, racial identity, heritage, religion, age group, and so on" (Derman-Sparks & Edwards, 2010, p. xiii). A reflective professional

90 Reflective Practice

should spend time thinking about their own social identities, how they perceive others, and how these identities inform their values and ideas about family life (specific exercises are in Skills).

FLE methodology. *Understand principles of FLE in tandem with planning and delivery of programs.*

A cornerstone of FLE methodology is developing collaborative relationships with families (Darling & Cassidy, 2014). Collaborative relationships create an environment in which families are working in partnership with home visitors, rather than the home visitor serving as a voice of authority for what the family *should* do. Reflective practice asks each party to consider each person's role in the interaction and reasons for each person's responses. This is inherently at the base of collaborative relationships. As home visitors guide parents' reflections (as well as engage in their own professional reflections), this collaborative relationship can develop. This relationship can then be used as the base for transformative learning, another important component of FLE methodology (Covey, 2015). Transformative learning is concerned with how people take new information and move from previously held positions to new ways of thinking that are based on informed decisions and reflective thought (Covey, 2015). The ultimate goals of EHS-HBO is to support families in ways that bolster family wellbeing and children's developmental outcomes. Transformative learning by way of collaborative relationships aids these goals.

Internal dynamics of families. *Understanding of family strengths and weaknesses and how family members relate to each other.*

As home visitors collaborate with EHS families, they can use their knowledge of the internal dynamics of families to inform how they guide parents through their own reflections. The system and ecological characteristics of families are important to consider here. Individual family members work together to impact the functioning of the entire family system – all members and relationships are interdependent (Segrin & Flora, 2005). Likewise, ecological weaknesses (e.g., housing instability, neighborhood danger) and strengths (e.g.,

Table 5.4 Family Life Education Concepts and Resources that Align with Reflective Practices

FLE Content Area: Professional Ethics and Practice	Resources
Emotional, experiential influences on parenting Make decisions based on reflection and consultation[1]; Assist others in the formation of ethical concepts and behavior[1]	[1]Palm, G. F. (2015). Professional ethics and practice. In M. J. Walcheski, & J. S. Reinke (Eds.), *Family life education: The practice of family science* (pp. 235–241). Minneapolis, MN: National Council on Family Relations.

Table 5.5 Family Life Education Concepts and Resources that Align with reflective Practices

FLE Content Area: FLE Methodology	Resources
Emotional, experiential influences on parenting Transformative learning[1]; reflective thought[1]; problems in families and prevention of problems in families[1]; collaborations[2,3]; collaborative partnerships[3]; social support[3]; reflective practice[2]	[1]Covey, M. (2015). Family life education methodology. In M. J. Walcheski, & J. S. Reinke (Eds.), *Family life education: The practice of family science* (pp. 243–251). Minneapolis, MN: National Council on Family Relations. [2]Darling, C. A., & Cassidy, D. (2014). Family life education: Working with families across the lifespan (3rd). Long Grove, IL: Waveland. [3]Duncan, S. F., & Goddard, H. W. (2017). *Family life education: Principles and practices for effective outreach* (3rd ed.). Thousand Oaks, CA: Sage.

community resources, social support) relevant to the EHS population must be understood as they relate to the overall functioning of the family system. While these issues may seem unrelated to reflective practice, they inform the home visitor's understanding of how the family actually operates, which is essential if the home visitor is going to guide parents through reflections on their parenting behaviors, childhood experiences, and understanding their child's development. As one example, stress and trauma have a major impact on the internal dynamics of families. Trauma leftover from parents' own experiences shape the adults they become and affects how parents approach their own parenting (Siegel & Hartzell, 2013). Reflective practice can be particularly helpful for stressed and traumatized families (Slade et al., 2005b) because it helps families make sense of their experiences, creating opportunity for growth. However, severe trauma can interfere with an individual's ability to be reflective (Fonagy et al., 2002).

Skills

The CUPID HV expanded competency for Skills related to Reflective Practice include:

> Skills for guiding parents' reflections on parenting and child's development and well-being, reflecting on one's own personal reactions to parenting and family life, and sharing reflections appropriately.
>
> (CUPID, 2017)

92 Reflective Practice

Table 5.6 Family Life Education Concepts and Resources that Align with Reflective Practices

FLE Content Area: Internal Dynamics of Families	Resources
Emotional, experiential influences on parenting Family systems theory[1,2]; ecological theory[1,2]; family strengths and families as sources of support[1,2]; cultural competence[2]; family interaction patterns (e.g., cultural, social)[1]	[1]Reinke, J. S., & Walcheski, M. J. (2015). Internal dynamics of families. In M. J. Walcheski, & J. S. Reinke (Eds.), *Family life education: The practice of family science* (pp. 157–166). Minneapolis, MN: National Council on Family Relations. [2]Olson, D. H., DeFrain, J., & Skogrand, L. (2014). *Marriages and families: Intimacy, diversity, and strengths* (8th ed.). New York: McGraw Hill.

Human Growth and Development

- Guide practice using developmental theories

  - Understand how developmental theories, such as attachment, explain why parents early caregiving experiences shape who they are and how they approach parenting their own children.
  - Understand how ecological/cultural theories help explain why cultural and social experiences and histories of families provide a context for family life and parenting practices.

Parenting Education and Guidance

- Promote healthy parenting from systems and lifespan perspectives

  - Encourage parents to reflect on their own parenting experiences from their family of origin to make connections between these experiences and their current family system.

- Promote healthy parenting from a child's and parent's developmental perspective

  - Encourage parents to develop mindsight compassion and engage in reflective dialogues (Siegel & Hartzell, 2013) to improve the quality of the attachment relationship with their child.

- Identify parenting styles and their related child outcomes

- Observe parent behaviors and identify connections with infant/toddler outcomes.
- Help parents identify connections between their behaviors and infant/toddler outcomes and guide them in reflections about these connections.

- Evaluate various parenting strategies

- Observe parenting strategies and look for opportunities to pause and reflect with parents to help them understand why they engaged in the strategy they did.
- Ask parents to engage in reflective practice when they use parenting strategies that are harsh, punitive, or harmful for children.

- Identify strategies to support children in various settings.

- Guide parents in reflection on the goals they have for their children when they enter formal schooling.
- Help parents make connections between their behavior in the home and their children's behaviors in school or other settings outside the home.

Families and Individuals in Societal Contexts

- Identify the influence of local and global systems on individuals and families.

- Analyze the role of economic disadvantage (and related issues that stem from living in poverty) in shaping parents' beliefs, behaviors, and experiences.

- Identify contemporary and historical factors that influence individuals and families

- Learn about the cultural histories, values, and practices that are important to the family and how they shape parents' beliefs, behaviors, and experiences.

- Identify social and cultural influences on family composition and family life.

- Talk with families to identify the specific economic and cultural factors that support (or hinder) daily family life.

- Recognize reciprocal interactions between individuals, families, and systems

- Understand how individuals and families in EHS-HBO are affected by (and have an effect on) economic and cultural forces.

94   *Reflective Practice*

- Assess the impact of demographics (e.g., class) on families
  - ○ Analyze how aspects of living in poverty uniquely affect each family.
  - ○ Analyze how race/ethnicity and the broader family culture uniquely affect each family.

Professional Ethics and Practice

- Demonstrate professional attitudes, values, behaviors, and responsibilities to clients and the broader community that are reflective of ethical standards and practices: (1) Understand the domains and scope of practice for family life educators and the role of collaboration, (2) Establish and maintain appropriate personal and professional boundaries, (3) Create a personal ethics plan to support/reflect the standards of the profession

  - ○ Integrate reflective practice as an important part of professional development.
  - ○ Work with colleagues and supervisors to reflect on the context of the home visit, engagement of the family during the home visit, and the competencies being developed during the home visit.
  - ○ Engage in self-reflection to gain better insight into your own ideas about family, relationships, values, and biases.

- Identify and apply appropriate strategies to deal with conflicting values and demonstrate respect for diverse cultural values

  - ○ Use mindfulness techniques to pay attention, without judgement, to conflicting values with families.
  - ○ Reflect on your own social identities and how they inform your understanding of family life. Examples from their book, *Anti-Bias Education* (Derman-Sparks & Edwards, 2010) include:
    - □ "What is your earliest memory of realizing that some people were different from you and/or your family? (Differences of economics, religion, racial identity, language, disability?)" (p. 15)
    - □ "What stereotypes or negative messages did you learn from home, school, religious setting, and/or media about people whose identities were different in some way from yours?" (p. 15)
    - □ "What childhood experiences did you have with peers or adults who were different from you in some way (racial identity, culture/ethnicity, family structure, economic class, religion, gender role, sexual orientation)? Were these experiences comfortable? Why or why not?" (p. 23)
    - □ "Think about your interactions with various social institutions such as school, health care, transportation, media, law, employment and the like. In what ways did your social identities ease or hamper your access to these institutions?" (p. 25)

FLE Methodology

- Employ strategies to meet the needs of different audiences; create learning environments that support individual differences

    - Reflect with parents on the goals they have for themselves, their children, and their family. Use this as a starting point for building a collaborative relationship that places the family's interests at the center of the relationship.
    - Be with families as support, rather than do things for them.

- Develop culturally competent materials and experiences

    - Incorporate knowledge about attachment and cultural theories to understand how parents lived experiences as children play a role in their current reflective practices.

- Implement adult education principles in work with individuals, parents, and families

    - View individuals as capable of making meaningful change through transformative learning (Covey, 2015).
    - Develop clear objectives for the home visit that are based on the program and family goals and identify activities that will achieve these goals.
    - Use parental reflections as an adult education tool to build collaborative relationships, identify family goals, and refine activities that will help achieve these goals.

Internal Dynamics of Families

- Recognize and define healthy and unhealthy characteristics pertaining to family relationships and family development

    - Identify family strengths and weaknesses and how these characteristics influence how the family approaches child development, parenting, and family interactions.

- Analyze family functioning using various theories

    - Use ideas from systems and ecological theories to guide reflective practices with parents.
    - Analyze how parents' emotional experiences as children influence how they reflect on their current family life (attachment theory).
    - Analyze how race/ethnicity and social class (particularly marginalization and discrimination) shape parents' reflections on their current family life (socio-cultural theory).

96   *Reflective Practice*

- Assess family dynamics from a systems perspective

  - When pausing to reflect on past experiences with parents, use family systems ideas to help parents understand how their past experiences affect the rest of the family system.
  - When engaging in your own professional reflections, conceptualize family interactions as occurring within a family system in which all interactions affect all family members—avoid thinking about family members as distinct individuals that have no effect on others.

- Analyze family dynamics in response to stressors, stress, crises, and trauma

  - Analyze how stressors common to EHS families (food insecurity, housing quality, unemployment, etc.) shape parents' reflections about their children and family interactions.
  - Take time to understand past or current crises and trauma family members have experienced (or are currently experiencing). Analyze how families define and make sense of these events. Use this information to help analyze how crisis and/or trauma shapes parents' reflections about their current family life.

- Facilitate and strengthen communication processes, conflict-management, and problem-solving skills; Develop, recognize, and reinforce strategies that help families function effectively

  - Encourage parents to pause and think about specific behaviors that occur during the home visit such as a child's misbehavior, a parent's reaction towards the child, or other family interactions.
  - Model reflective practices to help parents to think about their children's behavior. For example, "I wonder how your child was feeling when … ?"
  - Model reflective practices for parents to consider their own behaviors towards their children. For example, "You seem frustrated with your baby today. How do you feel when your baby cries?"
  - Use reflections to help parents decide on the best course of action to change parenting practices.

Attitudes

According to CUPID, the expanded home visiting competency for attitudes related to Reflective Practice is stated as:

Attitudes that support parallel processes for supporting social-emotional development and accepting families as they are.

(CUPID, 2017)

Working with families in a reflective manner requires a commitment to understanding and supporting the cultural and emotional experiences parents and children have undergone in the present and the past. Important values related to this are reflected in the CFLE Code of Ethics: "I will respect cultural beliefs, backgrounds and differences and engage in practice that is sensitive to the diversity of child-rearing values and goals" and "I will strive to understand children and youth in the context of their families" (NCFR, n.d.). These values help anchor the home visitor's own reflective practices in a space that respects the cultural and emotional experiences of the family, especially when they diverge substantially from the home visitor's own lived experiences. This also relates to the importance of accepting families as they are—FLE encourages professionals to be systematic and objective when examining the values that guide each family (Palm, 2009). Accepting families as they are is the cornerstone of strengths-based work with families.

Box 5.1 CDA Home Visitor Competencies

The CDA Subject Areas and Competency Standards are national standards for Home Visitors. The subject areas that are most relevant to this chapter include **CDA Subject Area 3: Promoting parents' use of positive ways to support children's social and emotional development** and **CDA Subject Area 6: Maintaining an effective home visitor program operation.** Each competency standard is comprised of competency goals, functional areas, items, indicators, and examples. The competency goals that are most relevant to this chapter are "To support social and emotional development and provide positive guidance", "To establish positive and productive partnerships with families" and "To maintain a commitment to professionalism" (Council for Professional Recognition, 2016).

Competency Goal	Functional Area	Example Items	Example Indicators
III. To support social and emotional development and provide positive guidance	**8 Self**: Home visitor helps parents develop a warm, positive, supportive, and responsive relationship with each of their children, and helps parents and children	**Item 8.2**: Help parents to value their own self-worth and to know, accept, and appreciate each child and adult family member as an individual.	Use words and actions that parents can interpret as demonstrations of respect and trust. Asks parents to discuss the personal qualities

(Continued)

98   *Reflective Practice*

(Cont.)

Competency Goal	Functional Area	Example Items	Example Indicators
	learn about and take pride in their individual and cultural identity.	**Item 8.3:** Demonstrates sensitivity to differing cultural values and expectations concerning independence, autonomy, and expression of feelings.	that they value in their children. Helps parents and children feel proud of themselves.
IV. To establish positive and productive partnerships with families	**11 Families:** Home visitor establishes a positive, responsive, and cooperative relationships with each family, engages in two-way communication with families, encourages the parents to take leadership in personal and family education, and supports the relationship of the families with their children.	**Item 11.2:** Help parents recognize that they are the center of the program.	Implements a family centered-responsive home visitor practice.
VI: To maintain a commitment to professionalism	**13 Professionalism:** Home visitor makes decisions based on knowledge of research-based early childhood practices and adult learning, promotes high quality childcare	**Item 13.2:** Continues to seek new knowledge and deeper understanding of the home visitation field. **Item 13.3:** Identifies and recognizes areas of own professional	Seeks professional development opportunities (a "lifelong learner", seeks feedback, Finds ways to meet his or her own needs and maintain energy and enthusiasm.

(Continued)

Reflective Practice 99

(Cont.)

Competency Goal	Functional Area	Example Items	Example Indicators
	services, and takes advantage of opportunities to improve knowledge and competence, both for personal and professional growth and for the benefit of children and families.	growth and gains the needed skills to provide high quality home visits.	

Permission to reprint from the Council for Professional Recognition, 2019

Box 5.2 National Family Support Competency Framework for Family Support Professionals

The National Family Support Competency Framework for Family Support Professionals are competencies that include ten domains that are further clarified by dimensions (Institute for the Advancement of Family Support Professionals, 2018). There is one domain that is relevant to this chapter: (a) Professional Practice. Professional Practice includes five dimensions: ethical and legal practice, reflective practice, professional development, professional boundaries, and quality improvement.

Domain 10	Dimension 35	Component a.	Levels of Competency
Professional Practice	**Reflective practice**	**Critical reflection**	**1-Recognizing.** Understands key elements of critical reflection
			3-Applying. Supports parents by utilizing critical reflection to examine thoughts, feelings, strengths, and identify areas for growth
			5-Extending. Coaches parents in using critical reflection to examine thoughts, feelings, strengths, and identify areas for growth

Permission to reprint from the Institute for the Advancement of Family Support Professionals.

Summary

Reflective practice is an important tool for the home visitor to engage with parents as a means to understand how parents' past emotional and cultural experiences influence their parenting practices. Home visitors can also use reflective practices to enhance their own professional work by considering their own values and biases. Reflective practices can be deepened when home visitors incorporate knowledge of human development, particularly attachment and culture into their understanding of family processes. Home visitors can use reflective practices as an important component of parenting education. They can also build reflective practices within their own professional ethics and practices. Reflective practices are also connected to important components of FLE methodology, such as building collaborative relationships with families, and understanding the strengths and weaknesses that shape family wellbeing.

Key Concepts

- Adaptive culture
- Attachment
- Collaborative relationships
- Parental reflective functioning
- Reflective practice
- Social identities
- Transformative learning

Recommended Reading

García Coll, C. G., Crnic, K., Lamberty, G., Wasik, B. H., Jenkins, R., García, H. V., & McAdoo, H. P. (1996). An integrative model for the study of developmental competencies in minority children. *Child Development, 67,* 1891–1914.

Lareau, A. (2011). *Unequal childhoods: Class, race, and family life.* Oakland, CA: University of California Press.

Siegel, D. & Hartzell, M. (2013). *Parenting from the inside out.* New York, NY: Tarcher and Perigee.

References

Bornstein, M. H. & Cheah, C.S.L. (2006). The place of "culture and parenting" in the ecological contextual perspective on developmental science. In K.H. Rubin & O. Boon Chung (Eds.) *Parental Beliefs, Parenting, and Child Development in Cross-Cultural Perspective* (pp. 3–33). London, UK: Psychology Press.

Bowlby, J. (1969/1982). *Attachment and loss: Vol. 1. Attachment.* (2nd ed). New York: Basic Books.

Boyd, D., & Bee, H. (2015). *Lifespan development* (7th ed.). Upper Saddle River, NJ: Pearson.

Brooks, J. B. (2013). *The process of parenting* (9th ed.). New York: McGraw Hill.

Brophy-Herb, H., Williamson, A. C., Cook, G. A., Torquarti, J., Decker, K. B., Vu, J., Vallotton, C. D., Duncan, L. G., The Collaborative for Understanding the Pedagogy of Infant/Toddler Development. (2018). Preservice students' dispositional mindfulness and developmentally supportive practices with infants and toddlers. *Mindfulness*, 1–10.

Chen, D. W., Nimmo, J., & Fraser, H. (2009). Becoming a culturally responsive early childhood educator: A tool to support reflection by teachers embarking on the anti-bias journey. *Multicultural Perspectives*, *11*(2), 101–106.

Collaborative for Understanding the Pedagogy of Infant/toddler Development (CUPID) (2017). *Comprehensive competencies for educators of infants and toddlers in group care and home visiting settings*. Unpublished.

Council for Professional Recognition. (2016). *The Child Development Associate National Credentialing Program and CDA Competency Standards, home visitor edition*. Washington DC: Council for Professional Recognition.

Covey, M. (2015). Family life education methodology. In M. Walcheski & J. Reinke (Eds.) *Family life education: The practice of family science* (pp. 243–251). Minneapolis, MN: National Council on Family Relations.

Darling, C. A., & Cassidy, D. (2014). *Family life education: Working with families across the lifespan*. Long Grove, IL: Waveland Press.

Derman-Sparks, L., & Edwards, J. O. (2010). *Anti-bias education for young children and ourselves*. Washington, DC: National Association for the Education of Young Children.

Duncan, S. F., & Goddard, H. W. (2017). *Family life education: Principles and practices for effective outreach* (3rd ed.). Thousand Oaks, CA: Sage.

Evans, G. W., & Kim, P. (2007). Childhood poverty and health: cumulative risk exposure and stress dysregulation. *Psychological Science*, *18*, 953–957.

Fonagy P., Gergely, G., Jurist, E., & Target, M. (2002). *Affect regulation, mentalization, and the development of the self*. New York: Other Books.

Fraiberg, S., Adelson, E., & Shaprio, V. (1975). Ghosts in the nursery: A psychoanalytic approach to the problems of impaired infant–mother relationships. *Journal of the American Academy of Child Psychiatry*, *14*, 387–421.

García Coll, C. G., Crnic, K., Lamberty, G., Wasik, B. H., Jenkins, R., García, H. V., & McAdoo, H. P. (1996). An integrative model for the study of developmental competencies in minority children. *Child Development*, *67*, 1891–1914.

Institute for the Advancement of Family Support Professionals. (2018). *National Family Support Competency Framework for Family Support Professionals*. Retrieved from: https://cppr-institute-prod.s3.amazonaws.com/modules/Approved%20National%20Family%20Support%20Competency%20Framework_FINAL_7_18_2018.pdf.

Jacobson, A. L. (2015). Parenting education and guidance. In M. J. Walcheski, & J. S. Reinke (Eds.), *Family life education: The practice of family science* (pp. 213–222). Minneapolis, MN: National Council on Family Relations.

Keilty, B. (2008). Early intervention home-visiting principles in practice: A reflective approach. *Young Exceptional Children*, *11*, 29–40.

Lareau, A. (2011). *Unequal childhoods: Class, race, and family life*. Oakland, CA: University of California Press.

Leventhal, J. (2015). Human growth and development across the lifespan. In M. J. Walcheski, & J. S. Reinke (Eds.), *Family life education: The practice of family science* (pp. 167–176). Minneapolis, MN: National Council on Family Relations.

102 *Reflective Practice*

Li, S. C. (2003). Biocultural orchestration of developmental plasticity across levels: The interplay of biology and culture in shaping the mind and behavior across the life span. *Psychological Bulletin, 129,* 171.

Luyten, P., Nijssens, L., Fonagy, P., & Mayes, L. C. (2017). Parental reflective functioning: Theory, research and clinical applications. *The Psychoanalytic Study of the Child, 70,* 174–199.

NCFR. (n.d.). *Family life educators code of ethics.* Retrieved https://www.ncfr.org/sites/default/files/cfle_code_of_ethics_2.pdf

Olson, D. H., DeFrain, J., & Skogrand, L. (2014). *Marriages and families: Intimacy, diversity, and strengths* (8th ed.). New York: McGraw Hill.

Palm, G. (2009). Professional ethics and practice. In D. J. Bredehoft & M. Walcheski (Eds.), *Family life education: Integrating theory and practice* (2nd ed., pp. 191–197). Minneapolis, MN: National Council on Family Relations.

Palm, G. (2015). Professional ethics and practice. In M. J. Walcheski, & J. S. Reinke (Eds.), *Family life education: The practice of family science* (pp. 235–241). Minneapolis, MN: National Council on Family Relations.

Reinke, J. S., & Walcheski, M. J. (2015). Internal dynamics of families. In M. J. Walcheski, & J. S. Reinke (Eds.), *Family life education: The practice of family science* (pp. 157–166). Minneapolis, MN: National Council on Family Relations.

Roggman, L., Peterson, C., Cohen, R. C., Ispa, J., Decker, K. B., Hughes-Belding, K., Cook, G., & Vallotton, C. D. (2016). Preparing home visitors to partner with families of infants and toddlers. *Journal of Early Childhood Teacher Education, 37,* 301–313. http://dx.doi.org/10.1080/10901027.2017.1298369

Segrin, C., & Flora, J. (2005). *Family communication.* Mahwah, NJ: Lawrence Erlbaum Associates.

Siegel, D. J., & Hartzell, M. (2013). *Parenting from the inside out: How a deeper self-understanding can help you raise children who thrive.* New York, NY: Tarcher/Perigee.

Slade, A., Grienenberger, J., Bernbach, E., Levy, D., & Locker, A. (2005a). Maternal reflective functioning, attachment, and the transmission gap: A preliminary study. *Attachment & Human Development, 7,* 283–298.

Slade, A., Sadler, L., De Dios-Kenn, C., Webb, D., Currier-Ezepchick, J., & Mayes, L. (2005b). Minding the baby. *The Psychoanalytic Study of the Child, 60,* 74–100.

van IJzendoorn, M. H. (1995). Adult attachment representations, parental responsiveness, and infant attachment: A meta-analysis on the predictive validity of the Adult Attachment Interview. *Psychological Bulletin, 117,* 387–403.

Wadsworth, S. M. M., Roy, K. M., & Watkins, N. (2015). Families and individuals in societal contexts. In M. J. Walcheski & J. S. Reinke (Eds.), *Family life education: The practice of family science* (pp. 147–155). Minneapolis, MN: National Council on Family Relations

6 Building and Supporting Relationships

Building and supporting healthy relationships is the cornerstone of home visiting practices for many reasons. First, relationships are essential for healthy child development. Second, healthy family relationships contribute to the overall wellbeing of the family system. Finally, the family's relationship with the home visitor plays a major role in whether or not home visiting is successful (Korfmacher, Green, Spellmann, & Thornburg, 2007). As such, it is important that home visitors in EHS-HBO demonstrate the capacity for understanding, building, and supporting relationships. This chapter will explore the CUPID Competency **Building and Supporting Relationships** (CUPID, 2017; Roggman et al., 2016b):

Competency	Engaging in warm and responsive interactions with children, families, and colleagues to foster a positive network of relationships over time. Creating opportunities for the child and families to contribute to reciprocal relationships
Knowledge	Expanded knowledge of the importance of secure attachment, the centrality of parent–child relationships for children's development, and the co-constructed nature of family relationships and systems
Skills	Skills for supporting high-quality and sustained home visitor–family relationships, explaining attachment to parents, guiding parents to establish secure attachment relationships with their children, and facilitating warm, sensitive, responsive, respectful, co-constructed parent–child interactions
Attitudes	Attitudes that respect the primacy of the family in the child's development, value the child's relationships with parents and other family members, and respect parents' competencies and contributions

See full alignment in Appendix B.

104   *Building and Supporting Relationships*

The FLE Content Areas that help expand this competency include:

Human growth and development across the lifespan	Understanding of the developmental changes (both typical and atypical) of individuals in families across the lifespan with an emphasis on knowledge of developmental domains
Parenting education and guidance	How parents teach, guide, and influence as the dynamic context of the parent–child relationship
Families and individuals in societal contexts	Understand families in regard to other institutions
Professional ethics and practice	Understanding the character and quality of human social conduct and critically examine ethical questions and issues as they relate to professional practice
Interpersonal relationships	Understand the development and maintenance of interpersonal relationships
Internal dynamics of families	Understanding of family strengths and weaknesses and how family members relate to each other

Note: Permission to reprint was granted from the National Council on Family Relations.

Knowledge

According to CUPID, home visitors should possess:

> Expanded knowledge of the importance of secure attachment, the centrality of parent–child relationships for children's development, and the co-constructed nature of family relationships and systems.
>
> (CUPID, 2017)

Secure Attachment

Attachment is the special bond between parents and their children that has lifelong implications for how children grow to see themselves, as well as what they expect from other people. Theorist John Bowlby (1969/1982) proposed that attachment develops over the first few years of life. Infants use specific behaviors to get parents to respond to them and keep them close by (e.g., cries, gazes, smiles, crawling, reaching). At the end of the first year, infants start to be much more selective about which adults they interact with, and "stranger anxiety" is common. By about 24 months of age, toddlers can use their new cognitive and language skills to think and talk about attachment.

Researcher Mary Ainsworth (1979) studied infants in the U.S. and Uganda to develop four patterns that describe the attachment bond of most parent–child relationships. Secure attachment is characterized by patterns of interactions in which the child uses his parent as a safe haven when he is upset, but then also uses the parent as a secure base from which to explore his world. This cyclical pattern of safety and security is known as the circle of security (Powell, Cooper, Hoffman, & Marvin, 2014). Parents build the circle of security when they respond to their infant's needs in a sensitive and responsive manner (McElwain & Booth-LaForce, 2006). In contrast, insecure attachment is characterized by a disruption in the circle of security. The child may have received the message that his caregiver is not a reliable safe haven when upset (insecure avoidant) or is anxious about using his parent as a secure base to explore elsewhere (insecure ambivalent). Insecure attachment bonds develop when parents are unresponsive to signals that their infant is in distress or are unpredictable in their caregiving behaviors. Disorganized attachment is outside the realm of "typical" experiences for infants and is a complete breakdown in the circle of security. These children have usually experienced maltreatment or other traumas that have prevented them from developing an attachment bond with a caregiver.

Attachment lays an important foundation for future development and relationships. Bowlby proposed that attachment builds children's internal working model, a cognitive structure that shapes how the child thinks about herself, as well as what she expects from other people (Bretherton & Munholland, 2008). Children with secure attachment bonds tend to see themselves as capable, worthy, and expect that others will treat them as such. Children with insecure bonds are more likely to be mistrusting of others (insecure avoidant) or feel that others are reluctant to get too close to them (insecure ambivalent) (Hazen & Shaver, 1987). Children with disorganized attachment may have trouble regulating stress, show increased aggression, and may even dissociate (i.e., detach) from reality (Van Ijzendoorn et al., 1999). It's easy to see how these differences can lead to relationships and experiences of varying quality as children get older and form peer and romantic relationships later in life.

Parent–Child Relationships

There are other elements of the parent–child relationship that are a central force in children's development. The actual back-and-forth interactions between parents and their children provide the setting within which child development takes place. In other words, child development occurs within the context of relationships. For example, gross motor skills mature naturally (e.g., crawl, cruise, walk, run, etc.), but these skills do not develop by themselves – they develop in combination with the social interactions children have with their parents as they hold them, talk with them, help them take their first

106 Building and Supporting Relationships

steps, cheer them on, comfort them when they stumble and so on. Infants and toddlers are extremely vulnerable, both physically and emotionally. As such, they are completely reliant on caregivers for comfort and survival, making the interactions that occur during the first three years critical for development.

Parent–child interactions are usually thought of as bidirectional. This means that children and parents affect each other in mutual fashion. The behaviors parents use towards children are (at least partially) dependent on the child's own behaviors (Paschall & Mastergeorge, 2016). For example, infants who are cheerful and smiley elicit different types of reactions than infants who are negative and fussy. However, adults have more emotional and cognitive maturity, which means they are able to monitor and modify their own behavior to best meet the needs of the child (Cole, 2003). For example, a fussy infant may be unpleasant to deal with, but a parent can take a deep breath and decide to keep soothing the infant in a sensitive manner while working to figure out why the infant is upset.

To examine parent–child relationships, researchers video-recorded Early Head Start mothers and their toddlers playing together to see how different parenting behaviors influence toddler behaviors. Children with mothers who displayed positive emotions, responded to their needs, and stimulated cognitive development during play were more likely to be positive and engaged with their mother when they were older (ACF, 2002). In contrast, children with mothers who interrupted and showed disregard for their efforts during play were more negative and less engaged when they were older (Ispa et al., 2004).

Family Relationships and Systems

The parent–child relationship is important for the overall family system because the interactions that occur within one relationship reverberate to all other parts of the system (Segrin & Flora, 2005). Some researchers refer to this as "spillover," meaning that the quality of interactions in one relationship spill over to other aspects of family life (Cummings & Davies, 2002). For example, happiness in a romantic relationship will spill over to affect happiness as a parent. Research with mothers has shown that conflict and instability with a romantic partner can reduce her mental health and stress (Cummings & Davies, 2002; Osborne & McLanahan, 2007). In contrast, positive and stable romantic relationships had long-lasting psychological benefits to parents (Kamp Dush, Taylor, & Kroeger, 2008), serving as a source of support and strength for the family system.

The co-parenting relationship is also important to the family system. Co-parenting is how adults relate "to each other in the role of parent" (Feinberg, 2003, p. 96). Co-parenting involves negotiating shared childrearing responsibilities and the degree to which adults are able to support and coordinate duties

(Feinberg, 2003). In two-parent households, co-parenting is separate from the romantic relationship. For first-time parents, developing a co-parenting relationship is a big adjustment for the family system. It is critical that parents with a new infant realize this new aspect of their relationship and learn to work together to manage their new roles and responsibilities. Cooperative and collaborative co-parenting relationships are associated with positive effects on children's development (Favez, Frascarolo, Carneiro, Montfort, Corboz-Warney, & Fivaz-Depeursinge, 2006). Co-parenting relationships endure even when romantic relationships end – divorced parents still have to co-parent. Co-parenting is also not limited to biological parents. It can include any adults working together to raise a child. For example, mother-grandmother co-parenting is very common (McHale, Kuersten-Hogan, & Rao, 2004).

Family and Home Visitor Relationships

The relationship between the family and home visitor is also important. Research suggests that even after accounting for parents' overall satisfaction with the EHS-HBO program, the quality of the helping relationship between the parent and the home visitor affected the parents' continual participation in the program (Korfmacher et al., 2007). This is important because families who are more engaged in EHS-HBO are less likely to drop out (Roggman et al., 2008). The Home Visit Rating Scale – Adapted and Extended to Excellence (HOVRS-A+; Roggman et al., 2010) defines a quality relationship between the home visitor and parent along four dimensions: responsiveness to the family, relationship with the family, the ability to facilitate parent–child interactions, and collaboration with the family (Roggman et al., 2010). Using these dimensions, a high-quality relationship starts with a home visitor who is prepared, observes and responds to family members appropriately, and elicits necessary information from the family. The relationship is characterized by warmth, positive interactions, respect, and home visitors minimize overly controlling or intrusive actions (Roggman et al., 2010). Relationships that score high on these dimensions have been associated with improvements in the home environment and children's development (e.g., Roggman, Cook, Innocenti, Jump Norman, Boyce, Christiansen, & Peterson, 2016a).

FLE Content Area Knowledge and Knowledge of Building and Supporting Relationships

Human growth and development. *Understanding of the developmental changes (both typical and atypical) of individuals in families across the lifespan with an emphasis on knowledge of developmental domains*

Knowledge in human growth and development assists the home visitor in understanding the role of attachment in child development. If child development occurs within the context of relationships, then home visitors must have the knowledge base to recognize how parents and infants work together to establish a secure bond. The newborn brain requires attachment to develop in a healthy manner and the brain "expects" that parents (or other caregivers) will be available to reliably meet its needs. The ability of parents to reliably meet their infants' needs is referred to as sensitivity and is the foundation of creating a secure attachment bond (Gross, 2019).

Home visitors can use their knowledge of human growth and development to recognize when parents may need help learning to read their baby's cues, which will increase sensitivity. Knowledge in this area also helps the home visitor tune in to the back-and-forth interactions that will help develop secure attachment. For example, infants/toddlers who use their parents as a safe place to retreat to when upset or nervous are demonstrating that their parents are a haven of safety. Likewise, infants and toddlers who are confident to explore their environment when their parents are close by (with checking in from time to time) are demonstrating that they feel secure when their parent is nearby. For children living in poverty, secure attachment with parents (or other caregivers) is an important protective factor (Werner, 2000). Unfortunately, rates of disorganized attachment tend to be higher for families living in poverty, teen parents, and parents with substance issues (Gross, 2019), making this an important intervention point for EHS home visitors.

Knowledge in this area also prepares the home visitor to recognize other attachment-related issues. Attachment styles are often passed down through families across generations (Klein Velderman et al., 2006). Parents interact with their infants in ways that feel "natural" to them, which is informed by their own childrearing experiences. For example, a mother with an insecure attachment bond with her own mother may respond to and interact with her infant in ways that continue a cycle of insecurity, because it is what feels natural to her. Parents who experienced trauma as children may not have any template for creating a secure bond with their infant. Moreover, EHS home visitors must be able to recognize and understand the issues facing children who have experienced their own trauma (e.g., maltreatment). These children have the highest rates of disorganized attachment (Gross, 2019) which can manifest as atypical psychological issues (Van Ijzendoorn et al., 1999). While these behaviors may be frustrating to parents and home visitors, it is critical to understand that they are the direct result of a disorganized attachment pattern that hinders the child's ability to make organized responses about himself or others.

An important point to mention here is that EHS home visitors need to recognize that severely disrupted attachment relationships within families should be monitored and counseled by an infant mental health specialist or family therapist and referrals should be provided as necessary.

Building and Supporting Relationships   109

Table 6.1   Family Life Education Concepts and Resources that Align with Building and
Supporting Relationships

FLE Content Area: Human Growth and Development	Resources
Parent–child bonds[1]; Secure attachment[2]; family system[1]; reciprocal influences[1]; how parenting styles affect children's development[2]	[1]Leventhal, J. (2015). Human growth and development across the lifespan. In M. J. Walcheski, & J. S. Reinke (Eds.), *Family life education: The practice of family science* (pp. 167–176). Minneapolis, MN: National Council on Family Relations. [2]Boyd, D., & Bee, H. (2015). *Lifespan development* (7th ed.). Upper Saddle River, NJ: Pearson.

Parenting education and guidance. *How parents teach, guide, and influence as the dynamic context of the parent–child relationship.*

The home visitor needs to be aware of research-based practices on supporting attachment, parent–child interactions, and family dynamics as they work with parents to develop and maintain healthy relationships. Home visitors can use their knowledge of human development to help parents understand how their parenting behaviors are connected to infant development. Decades of research support the idea that parents (and other caregivers) literally shape the neural connections in the developing brain (Shonkoff & Phillips, 2000). The home visitor's knowledge about attachment and the bidirectional nature of parent–child interactions should be incorporated in discussions of family relationships so parents are armed with the knowledge of how their actions towards their infants are connected to future development.

Although parents and children elicit reactions from each other in a bidirectional manner, they are not equal parties (Cole, 2003). Adults hold much more power in the situation—they are older, wiser, and the only one capable of modulating their own emotions and behaviors to better meet the needs of the other party. When issues arise, home visitors can help parents "tune in" to times when they need to stop, reflect, and make a new plan of action. Research on attachment-based home visiting programs support this as effective way to boost attachment security in at-risk populations. For example, Klein Velderman and colleagues (2006) found that video-taped recordings of mothers interacting with their infants during a home visit could be used to discuss the quality of the interactions

110 *Building and Supporting Relationships*

Table 6.2 Family Life Education Concepts and Resources that Align with Building and Supporting Relationships

FLE Content Area: Parenting education and guidance	Resources
Parenting processes to support children's growth and development[1,2]; responsibilities of parent–child relationship[1]; parental guidance across the lifespan[1]; secure attachment[2]; family system[2]; nested systems and a process-person-context-time[2] framework	[1]Jacobson, A. L. (2015). Parenting education and guidance. In M. J. Walcheski, & J. S. Reinke (Eds.), *Family life education: The practice of family science* (pp. 213–222). Minneapolis, MN: National Council on Family Relations. [2]Brooks, J. B. (2013). *The process of parenting* (9th ed.). New York: McGraw Hill.

and as teachable moments to increase maternal sensitivity. This was especially effective when the home visitor worked with the mother to reflect on her own attachment experiences. Other attachment-based interventions, such as the Circle of Security use the mantra "Be bigger, stronger, wiser, kind" to help adults remember the power they hold during these interactions (Powell et al., 2014).

Families and individuals in societal contexts. *Understand families in regard to other institutions*

Subject matter in this content area helps the home visitor understand how parent–child and family relationships are situated within various contexts in society. Given an ecological perspective (e.g., Bronfenbrenner & Morris, 2006), family relationships interact with the contexts within which they are nestled—neighborhoods, communities, educational and health care institutions, state and federal policies, and more. Most families in Early Head Start are living in poverty, which can be thought of as a "social address" that represents a common set of experiences and conditions (Huston & Bentley, 2010). Knowledge in this area helps the home visitor understand family relationships within this context. For example, food insecurity, low wage employment, and housing instability are stressful, and can strain family relationships (Huston & Bentley, 2010). Home visitors must be sensitive to these issues.

A strengths-based approach is important here as well. Familiy relationships are sources of great support for Early Head Start families. In research with Early Head Start mothers, positive and stimulating parenting behaviors were observed with much greater frequency than intrusive, negative, and detached behaviors (ACF, 2002). Families can pull strength from cultural values and/or spirituality, a positive outlook on life, spending time together,

Table 6.3 Family Life Education Concepts and Resources that Align with Building and Supporting Relationships

FLE Content Area: Families and individuals in societal contexts	Resources
Ecological perspective and bi-directional effects in parent–child relationship[1,2]; interrelationship of families, work, and society[1]; secure attachment[2]; family systems perspective[2]	[1]Wadsworth, S. M. M., Roy, K. M., & Watkins, N. (2015). Families and individuals in societal contexts. In M. J. Walcheski & J. S. Reinke (Eds.), *Family life education: The practice of family science* (pp. 147–155). Minneapolis, MN: National Council on Family Relations [2]Olson, D. H., DeFrain, J., & Skogrand, L. (2014). *Marriages and families: Intimacy, diversity, and strengths* (8th ed.). New York: McGraw Hill.

and community supports (Black & Lobo, 2008). Moreover, most children living in poverty develop secure attachment relationships with a parent (Gross, 2019). Quality family relationships can even help counteract the negative effects of poverty on child development (Werner, 2000).

As such, home visitors can use their knowledge of families and individuals in societal contexts to understand that while the context of poverty may strain family relationships, strong and supportive relationships within the family are protective for infants and toddlers. The home visitor should have a comprehensive understanding of the contextual realities facing the families on their caseload in terms of housing, employment, and neighborhood quality. They also must be able to identify resources in the community context that support healthy relationship development. This may include school family engagement programs, marriage and family therapy, or infant mental health programs.

Professional ethics and practice. *Understanding the character and quality of human social conduct and critically examine ethical questions and issues as they relate to professional practice*

In terms of collaborating with families to build and support healthy relationships, it is critical for the home visitor to use their knowledge of professional ethics and practice to recognize when a family needs help managing or treating a relationship issue that is beyond the scope of their training. The primary function of FLE is to provide prevention, education, and support (Darling & Cassidy, 2014). Family therapy may be required to provide secondary or tertiary intervention to improve relationships. Professionals such as marriage and family therapists and infant mental health specialists are

112 Building and Supporting Relationships

Table 6.4 Family Life Education Concepts and Resources that Align with Building and Supporting Relationships

FLE Content Area: Professional ethics and practices	Resources
Ethical philosophy of life[1]; balance personal autonomy and social responsibility[1]; interrelationship of rights and responsibilities[1]	[1]Palm, G. F. (2015). Professional ethics and practice. In M. J. Walcheski, & J. S. Reinke (Eds.), *Family life education: The practice of family science* (pp. 235–241). Minneapolis, MN: National Council on Family Relations.

trained to counsel families with young children through therapy-focused philosophies and methodologies. Relationship issues that stem from traumatic events need to be approached carefully and by a professional trained in trauma-informed approaches (Substance Abuse and Mental Health Services Administration [SAMHSA], 2018). Children who have been maltreated may need specialized behavior services and interventions by working with a developmental specialist (a licensed professional trained to provide clinical emotional and behavioral support services), or a counselor trained in parent–infant psychotherapy. These services are beyond the scope of home visiting and knowledge of professional ethics and practice should guide the home visitor's approach to referring families for such services.

Additionally, professional ethics and practice must also guide the home visitor's relationship with each family. It is the home visitor's responsibility to set appropriate boundaries. Working with families on the most intimate aspects of their lives is emotionally challenging work. The home visitor needs to engage in reflective practices (see Chapter 5) and self-care practices that give them time and space to recharge and reduce burnout. One cannot be a competent professional when the emotional toll of working with at-risk families becomes too burdensome to handle. Reflection and mindfulness exercises are two evidence-based techniques that help social service professionals manage burnout and fatigue at work by balancing care for families with care for the self (Shapiro, Brown, & Biegel, 2007; Skovholt & Trotter-Mathison, 2014).

Interpersonal relationships. *Understand the development and maintenance of interpersonal relationships*

As discussed above, quality parent–child and family relationships can be protective for families living in poverty. Home visitors can use their knowledge of interpersonal relationships to help cultivate these relationships in ways that support the entire family. Attachment has already been discussed extensively, but it bears repeating that home visitors should use knowledge of human

Table 6.5 Family Life Education Concepts and Resources that Align with Building and Supporting Relationships

FLE Content Area: Interpersonal relationships	Resources
Attachment[1,2]; parents with infants and young children[1]; marriage and relationships[1]; parenting styles and outcomes for children and strong families[2]	[1]Leventhal, J. (2015). Human growth and development across the lifespan. In M. J. Walcheski, & J. S. Reinke (Eds.), *Family life education: The practice of family science* (pp. 167–176). Minneapolis, MN: National Council on Family Relations.
	[2]Hanna, S. L., Suggett, R., & Radtke, D. (2008). *Person to person: Positive relationships don't just happen* (5th ed.). Upper Saddle River, NJ: Pearson.

development to place the parent–child relationship as a centerpiece of the family system to support infant development.

For families facing challenging behavior issues with their toddlers, home visitors can use their knowledge of interpersonal relationships to halt the development of coercive cycles of interaction. Coercive cycles occur when the child's negativity and subsequent parental hostility traps the family in a cycle of harsh and negative interactions (Scaramella & Leve, 2004). Home visitors can also target the family's communication and problem-solving abilities as a means of developing family strengths (Orthner et al., 2004). The co-parenting interpersonal relationship is also the strongest when adults cooperate instead of being disengaged or having conflict (Waller, 2012). This can be harder for unmarried couples, or when fathers are unemployed or facing other stressors (Waller, 2012). Nevertheless, the home visitor needs to be "in tune" with the interpersonal relationships within the family as a way to build strengths within the family system.

Internal dynamics of families. *Understanding of family strengths and weaknesses and how family members relate to each other*

Strengths and weaknesses within the family system affect how family members develop and maintain relationships. For families in EHS-HBO, strengths that support healthy relationships may derive from the family's cultural values, religion/spirituality, quality time spent together, and support from other families or services in the local community (Black & Lobo, 2008). The home visitor can use knowledge of the internal workings of families to help each family identify and capitalize on these strengths in ways that support parent–infant attachment and other family relationships. This will increase the likelihood for sensitive parent–child interactions,

114   *Building and Supporting Relationships*

Table 6.6 Family Life Education Concepts and Resources that Align with Building and Supporting Relationships

FLE Content Area: Internal dynamics of families	Resources
Family systems theory[1]; circumplex model of marital and family systems[1,2]; human ecology theory[1]; family development theory[1]; secure attachment[2]; bi-directional effects in parent–child relationship[2]	[1]Reinke, J. S., & Walcheski, M. J. (2015). Internal dynamics of families. In M. J. Walcheski, & J. S. Reinke (Eds.), *Family life education: The practice of family science* (pp. 157–166). Minneapolis, MN: National Council on Family Relations.
	[2]Olson, D. H., DeFrain, J., & Skogrand, L. (2014). *Marriages and families: Intimacy, diversity, and strengths* (8th ed.). New York: McGraw Hill.

which will have a positive impact on child development and the overall family system (Werner, 2000). Likewise, weaknesses within the family system can also strain relationships. Stress, crises, and trauma are chronic issues for some Early Head Start families. Home visitors can use knowledge of the internal workings of families to recognize how these issues affect the development of attachment, parent–child interactions, and other family relationships.

Skills

The CUPID HV expanded competency for Skills related to Building and Supporting Relationships include:

> Skills for supporting high-quality and sustained home visitor-family relationships, explaining attachment to parents, guiding parents to establish secure attachment relationships with their children, and facilitating warm, sensitive, responsive, respectful, co-constructed parent–child interactions.
>
> (CUPID, 2017)

Human Growth and Development

- Identify developmental stages and contexts
  - Recognize infancy as a developmental stage that relies on relationships for healthy development.
  - Recognize that developing attachment with parents (and other caregivers) is a major developmental task of infancy.

- Identify reciprocal influences on development

Building and Supporting Relationships **115**

- Recognize that child development occurs within the context of relationships.
- Recognize that parent–child interactions are bidirectional in nature.

- Assist families with developmental transitions.

  - Help parents learn to read their infants' cues so they can respond to their infants in a sensitive-responsive manner.
  - Help parents make the connection between sensitive caregiving and the development of a secure attachment bond.
  - Help parents adjust their expectations for what parental sensitivity looks like as their infants strive for more independence as toddlers.

- Guide practice using developmental theories

  - Use principles of attachment theory (e.g., secure base, safe haven) to help parents reflect on their relationships with their infants.

- Recognize socio-ecological influences on human development (e.g., trauma)

  - Understand the connection between trauma (or other stressful conditions) and disorganized attachment.
  - Recognize how the stress associated with living in poverty affects parent–child and other family relationships.
  - Support relationships within the family that are positive so that they are sources of strength for the family system.

Parenting Education and Guidance

- Promote healthy parenting from systems and lifespan perspectives

  - Recognize that the parent–child relationship is an important part of the family system.
  - Recognize that the parent–child relationship evolves over time to meet the ever-changing developmental needs of the child.
  - Help parents understand how their relationships with their infants affect (and are affected by) the rest of the family system.

- Promote healthy parenting from a child's and parent's developmental perspective

  - Support parents' understanding of the centrality of relationships to healthy infant development.

- Apply strategies based on child's age and stage and unique characteristics to support development

  - Encourage parents to reflect on and modify their own feelings and behaviors to better meet the needs of their infant.

116 *Building and Supporting Relationships*

- ○ Help parents recognize the "back and forth" interactions they use with their infants.
- ○ Facilitate parental sensitivity by helping parents read their infants' cues and meet their needs in a responsive manner.

- Identify parenting styles and their related child outcomes

  - ○ Help parents evaluate their degree of parental sensitivity and how it is related to their relationship with their infant and the quality of their attachment bond.

- Evaluate various parenting strategies

  - ○ Watch for "teachable moments" when parents are interacting with their infants to help them tune in to their infants cues as a way of boosting parental sensitivity.

- Recognize various parenting roles and their impact on families

  - ○ Talk with parents about their co-parenting partners. Co-parents may be the child's biological parent, step/adoptive/foster parents, the parent's romantic partner, the parent's own mother/father, or other unrelated adults.

- Identify strategies to support children in various settings

  - ○ Work with parents to identify simple phrases that parents can remind themselves of when they are feeling frustrated and need to modify their own behavior when they are with their child in various settings. For example, the Circle of Security intervention uses the mantra, "Be bigger, stronger, wiser, kind" (Powell et al., 2014).

Families and Individuals in Societal Contexts

- Identify contemporary and historical factors that influence individuals and families

  - ○ Recognize the ecological context of poverty and how it affects the development of family relationships at micro and macro levels.

- Identify social and cultural influences on family composition and family life

  - ○ Recognize that the relationships that develop within families are affected by food insecurity, low wage employment, housing instability, and other stressors common for families living in poverty.
  - ○ Recognize the many strengths that that families living in poverty possess in terms of positive parenting practices, values, and community supports.
  - ○ Connect families with community and mental health resources that promote healthy family relationships and parent–child attachment.

Building and Supporting Relationships   117

- Recognize reciprocal interactions between individuals, families, and systems
  - Understand that families are embedded within neighborhoods, communities, and the larger values of the macro culture, and the relationships that develop within the family interact with these different systems.
  - Recognize the systemic barriers economically disadvantaged families face in receiving community and mental health services to improve family relationships, particularly for families of color.

Professional Ethics and Practice

- Demonstrate professional attitudes, values, behaviors, and responsibilities to clients, colleagues, and the broader community, that are reflective of ethical standards and practice: (1) Understand the domains and scope of practice for family life educators and the role of collaboration, (2) Establish and maintain appropriate personal and professional boundaries, (3) Create a personal ethics plan to support/reflect the standards of the profession, (4) Maintain current knowledge and skills in the field
  - Recognize the professional limitations of home visiting in terms of providing secondary and tertiary intervention for family relationship issues.
  - Recognize that children dealing with attachment and/or other relationship issues that stem from trauma or maltreatment may need specialized behavior and emotional services that are beyond the scope of home visiting or family life education.
  - Have knowledge of counseling and infant mental health professionals available in the community (including how low income families can access such services) that can help families with relationship issues.
  - Take the time to reflect with supervisors and colleagues about the emotionally challenging aspects of home visiting work.
  - Take initiative to engage in mindfulness stress reduction techniques and reflection with supervisors to maintain appropriate boundaries with families and reduce professional burnout and fatigue.

- Identify and apply appropriate strategies to deal with conflicting values
  - Take time to reflect on your own values regarding parent–child relationships. A competent professional must have a solid understanding of their own values before understanding families with values that differ from their own.
  - Recognize that parents may have approaches to building and maintaining relationships with their infants that conflicts with the home visitor's values.

118   *Building and Supporting Relationships*

- ○ When differences in values regarding parent–child relationships are apparent, meet the family where they are and first work to understand their perspective.

- Demonstrate respect for diverse cultural values

  - ○ Work with families to identify their values around parent–child relationships, sensitivity, attachment, and their understanding of healthy family relationships.
  - ○ Express respect for families' values around parent–child relationships in conversation.
  - ○ Work with families to identify cultural values that are strengths to building healthy family relationships.

Interpersonal Relationships

- Recognize the impact of personality and communication styles

  - ○ Help parents understand how their own behaviors and communication styles shape the quality of interactions with their infants.
  - ○ Help parents recognize that they are responsible for adjusting their behavior to better meet the needs of their young children.

- Recognize the developmental stages of relationships

  - ○ Help parents understand how parent–child attachment develops and becomes more established over time.
  - ○ Help parents recognize when they need to adjust their own behaviors as children's needs change, to continue to foster a positive relationship.

- Analyze interpersonal relationships using various theoretical perspectives

  - ○ Help parents understand their behaviors towards their infants are related to the development of attachment.
  - ○ Help parents understand that their infant's behavior (e.g., secure base and safe haven behaviors) is related to the development of attachment.
  - ○ Use systems and ecological perspectives to help parents understand how events, resources, and other environmental elements affect parent–child and other relationships within the family.

- Develop and implement relationship enhancement and enrichment strategies

  - ○ Observe parent–infant interactions and identify "teachable moments" to help increase parental sensitivity.

Building and Supporting Relationships 119

  - ○ Observe and identify elements of the co-parenting relationship that are strengths to the family.

- Develop and implement effective communication, problem solving, and anger and conflict management strategies.

  - ○ Develop a plan with parents to identify when they are in a coercive cycle with their toddler, and strategies for breaking this cycle of toddler emotions and parental hostility. For example, parents can develop a simple message (e.g., "Be bigger, stronger, wiser, kind"; Powell et al., 2014) when they are stressed out dealing with their infant/toddler. This will give them a moment to reduce stress/hostility before continuing the interaction.

- Recognize the impact of violence and coercion in interpersonal relationships.

  - ○ Recognize when family relationships are being affected by violence and coercion and provide referrals and resources as necessary.
  - ○ For parents in violent romantic relationships, recognize the ways in which this relationship spillover to the parent–child relationship, attachment, and co-parenting.

- Recognize the influence of unhealthy coping strategies (e.g., substance abuse) on interpersonal relationships

  - ○ Recognize the ways in which a parent's own unhealthy coping strategy is limiting their ability to be sensitive and responsive with their infant, hindering the development of secure attachment.
  - ○ Recognize the ways in which the stress of another family/household member's unhealthy coping strategy is spilling over to the parent, affecting the parent–child relationship.

Internal Dynamics of Families

- Recognize and define healthy and unhealthy characteristics pertaining to family relationships and family development

  - ○ Recognize strengths within the family system that foster the development of healthy family relationships.
  - ○ Recognize weaknesses within the family system that hinder healthy relationship development.
  - ○ Help families define and discuss these strengths and weaknesses.

- Analyze family functioning using various theories

  - ○ Use family systems theory to understand how strengths/weaknesses in one area of the system affect the whole system's functioning.

120 *Building and Supporting Relationships*

- ○ Use systems and attachment theories to understand how secure parent–child attachment bonds strengthen the family system.

- Assess family dynamics from a systems perspective

  - ○ Observe how attachment and parent–child interactions are affected by forces within the family system, as well as how open the family is to elements outside of the family system.
  - ○ Observe how family relationships within the system affect the development of parent–child attachment. For example, look for ways that the co-parenting relationship either enhances or hinders parental sensitivity.

- Analyze family dynamics in response to stressors, stress, crises, and trauma

  - ○ Watch how family relationships, particularly parent–child attachment, are affected by stress, crisis, and trauma.
  - ○ Watch for instances when infants/toddlers have limited or no ability to use their parent(s) as a secure base or safe haven. Recognize when referral to an infant mental health specialist, marriage and family therapist, or developmental specialist is warranted.

- Facilitate and strengthen communication processes, conflict-management, and problem solving skills

  - ○ Model for parents sensitive and responsive caregiving towards infants.
  - ○ Strengthen parents' ability to recognize when they are headed towards a coercive cycle with their toddler.
  - ○ Work with co-parents together to identify and address parenting issues/responsibilities that are a continual source of conflict.
  - ○ For co-parents who are also romantic partners, work with the couple to identify the co-parenting aspects of their relationship that are separate from their romantic relationship.

- Develop, recognize, and reinforce strategies that help families function effectively

  - ○ Identify family strengths such as cultural values, religion/spirituality, quality family time, and community supports. Help parents recognize and reinforce their use of these strengths as a means to improve family relationships and parent–child attachment.

Attitudes

According to CUPID, the expanded home visiting competency for Attitudes related to Supporting Development and Learning are stated as:

Building and Supporting Relationships 121

Attitudes that respect the primacy of the family in the child's development, value the child's relationships with parents and other family members, and respect parents' competencies and contributions.

(CUPID, 2017)

The manner in which parents "should" interact with their children to develop healthy relationships is informed by one's own values and family experiences. How one understands healthy family relationships in general also originates from one's deeply held values. In working with families, especially families that may have very different experiences from the home visitor, it is critical that the home visitor brings certain attitudes to his/her professional work. For example, the FLE Code of Ethics states that the professional "will respect cultural beliefs, backgrounds and differences and engage in practice that is sensitive to the diversity of child-rearing values and goals" (NCFR, n.d.). When observing bidirectional parent–child interactions it is important that the home visitor understands these behaviors in context of the parents' goals for their children. The home visitor has a responsibility to examine family value systems objectively (Palm, 2009), which allows them to use their theoretical and methodological knowledge to understand and value the child's relationships with parents and other family members. When it comes to something as personal and intimate as parent–child interactions, the home visitor must respect parents' contributions to these interactions, holding to the FLE Code of Ethics statement "I will strive to understand families as complex, interactive systems where parents have the primary responsibility as educators, nurturers and limit-setters for their children" (NCFR, n.d.).

Box 6.1 CDA Home Visitor Competencies

The CDA Subject Areas and Competency Standards are national standards for Home Visitors. The subject area that is most relevant to this chapter includes **CDA Subject Area 3: Promoting parents' use of positive ways to support children's social and emotional development.** Each competency standard comprises competency goals, functional areas, items, indicators, and examples. The competency goals that are most relevant to this chapter are "To support social and emotional development and provide positive guidance" with the functional areas "self" and "social" (Council for Professional Recognition, 2016).

Competency Goal	Functional Area	Example Items	Example Indicators
III. To support social and	**8 Self:** Home visitor helps	**Item 8.2:** Help parents to value	Use words and actions that

(Continued)

122 *Building and Supporting Relationships*

(Cont.)

Competency Goal	Functional Area	Example Items	Example Indicators
emotional development and provide positive guidance	parents develop a warm, positive, supportive, and responsive relationship with each of their children, and helps parents and children learn about and take pride in their individual and cultural identity.	their own self-worth and to know, accept, and appreciate each child and adult family member as an individual. **Item 8.3:** Demonstrates sensitivity to differing cultural values and expectations concerning independence, autonomy, and expression of feelings.	parents can interpret as demonstrations of respect and trust. Asks parents to discuss the personal qualities that they value in their children. Helps parents and children feel proud of themselves.
	9 Social: Home visitor helps parents to ensure that each child functions effectively in the family, learns to express feelings, acquires social skills, and makes friends, and helps parents promote mutual respect among children and adults in their lives.	**Item 9.1:** The home environment provides opportunities for children to experience collaboration. **Item 9.4:** Helps parents to understand and promote feelings of empathy and respect for others.	Materials, equipment, and activities provided help children experience working and playing in harmony with other siblings and/or adults in the home. Uses empathy and respect for others in all interactions with families.

Permission to reprint from the Council for Professional Recognition, 2019

Box 6.2 National Family Support Competency Framework for Family Support Professionals

The National Family Support Competency Framework for Family Support Professionals are competencies that include ten domains that are further clarified by dimensions (Institute for the Advancement of Family Support Professionals, 2018). There are two domains that are relevant to this chapter: (a) Parent–Child Interactions and (b) Relationship-Based Family Partnerships. Parent–Child Interactions includes three dimensions: influences on parenting, parent–child relationship, and developmentally appropriate guidance. Relationship-Based Family Partnerships includes three dimensions: respect and responsiveness, positive communication, and collaboration

Domain 3	Dimension 12	Component a.	Levels of Competency
Parent–Child Interactions	**Parent–child relationship**	Attachment	**1-Recognizing.** Understands the terms "attachment" and "secure base"
			3-Applying. Supports parents' understanding of the importance of sensitive, responsive, and consistent caregiving in ensuring the development of trust and a secure attachment
			5-Extending. Coaches parents in sensitively responding to infant cues to develop a secure attachment between parents and their infant

Domain 7	Dimension 25	Component b.	Levels of Competency
Relationship-based family partnerships	**Respect and responsiveness**	Relationship building	**1-Recognizing.** Understands how relationships are the key element of successful home visiting

(Continued)

124 *Building and Supporting Relationships*

(Cont.)

Domain 3	Dimension 12	Component a.	Levels of Competency
			3-Applying. Supports parents by building rapport to develop a trusting, mutually respectful relationship
			5-Extending. Coaches parents to look for and engage in meaningful decision-making opportunities for their child

Permission to reprint from the Institute for the Advancement of Family Support Professionals.

Summary

Building and supporting relationships is a cornerstone of home visiting practices for so many reasons. Secure attachment and sensitive parent–child interactions are the heart of healthy child development, so home visitor knowledge in these areas is critical. Relationships between other family members, including the relationships with the home visitor are also essential to wellbeing (and home visiting program success). FLE content knowledge enhances the home visitor's understanding of attachment and parent–child relationships from a developmental perspective, as well as how to incorporate these ideas within parenting education. FLE content knowledge also underscores the importance of situating family relationships within the context of poverty and other issues common to EHS families. Home visitors can use this knowledge to meet parents where they in terms of their competencies and contributions, strengthening attachment and important family relationships.

Key Concepts

- Bidirectional
- Circle of security
- Coercive cycles
- Co-parenting
- Disorganized attachment
- Home Visit Rating Scales (HOVRS)
- Insecure ambivalent
- Insecure avoidant

- Internal working model
- Safe haven
- Secure attachment
- Secure base
- Sensitivity
- Spillover

Recommended Readings

Powell, B., Cooper, G., Hoffman, K., & Marvin, B. (2014). *The Circle of Security intervention*. New York: The Guilford Press.

Skovholt, T., & Trotter-Mathison, M. (2014). *The resilient practitioner: Burnout prevention and self-care strategies for counselors, therapists, teachers, and health professionals*. New York, NY: Routledge.

References

Administration for Children and Families (ACF). (2002). *Making a difference in the lives of infants and toddlers and their families: The impacts of Early Head Start: Vol. 1. Final technical report*. Washington, DC: U.S. Department of Health and Human Services.

Ainsworth, M. S. (1979). Infant–mother attachment. *American Psychologist, 34*(10), 932.

Black, K., & Lobo, M. (2008). A conceptual review of family resilience factors. *Journal of Family Nursing, 14*(1), 33–55.

Bowlby, J. (1969/1982). *Attachment and loss: Vol. 1. Attachment*. ed(2nd). New York: Basic Books.

Boyd, D., & Bee, H. (2015). *Lifespan development* (7th ed.). Upper Saddle River, NJ: Pearson.

Bretherton, I., & Munholland, K. A. (2008). Internal working models in attachment relationships: Elaborating a central construct in attachment theory. In J. Cassidy & P. R. Shaver (Eds.), *Handbook of attachment: Theory, research, and clinical applications* (pp. 102–127). New York, NY, US: Guilford Press.

Bronfenbrenner, U., & Morris, P. A. (2006). The bioecological model of human development. In R. M. Learner & W. Damon (Eds.) *Handbook of child psychology* (pp. 793–828). Hoboken, NJ: John Wiley & Sons Inc.

Brooks, J. B. (2013). *The process of parenting* (9th ed.). New York: McGraw Hill.

Cole, P. M. (2003). The developmental course from child effects to child effectiveness. In A. C. Crouter & A. Booth (Eds.), *Children's influence on family dynamics: The neglected side of family relationships* (pp. 109–118). Hillsdale, NJ: Erlbaum.

Council for Professional Recognition. (2016). The Child Development Associate National Credentialing Program and CDA Competency Standards, Home Visitor Edition. Washington DC: Council for Professional Recognition.

Collaborative for Understanding the Pedagogy of Infant/toddler Development (CUPID). (2017). *Comprehensive competencies for educators of infants and toddlers in group care and home visiting settings*. Unpublished.

126 Building and Supporting Relationships

Cummings, E. M., & Davies, P. T. (2002). Effects of marital conflict on children: Recent advances and emerging themes in process-oriented research. *Journal of Child Psychology and Psychiatry, 43*(1), 31–63.

Darling, C. A., & Cassidy, D. (2014). *Family life education: Working with families across the lifespan.* Long Grove, IL: Waveland Press.

Favez, N., Frascarolo, F., Carneiro, C., Montfort, V., Corboz-Warnery, A., & Fivaz-Depeursinge, E. (2006). The development of the family alliance from pregnancy to toddlerhood and children outcomes at 18 months. *Infant and Child Development, 15* (1), 59–73.

Feinberg, M. E. (2003). The internal structure and ecological context of coparenting: A framework for research and intervention. *Parenting: Science and Practice, 3*(2), 95–131.

Gross, D. (2019). *Infancy: Development from birth to age 3* (3rd ed.). Lanham, MD: Roman & Littlefield.

Hanna, S. L., Suggett, R., & Radtke, D. (2008). *Person to person: Positive relationships don't just happen* (5th ed.). Upper Saddle River, NJ: Pearson.

Hazen, C., & Shaver, P. R. (1987). Romantic love conceptualized as an attachment process. *Journal of Personality and Social Psychology, 59,* 270–280.

Huston, A. C., & Bentley, A. C. (2010). Human development in societal context. *Annual Review of Psychology, 61,* 411–437.

Institute for the Advancement of Family Support Professionals. (2018). *National Family Support Competency Framework for Family Support Professionals.* Retrieved from: https://cppr-institute-prod.s3.amazonaws.com/modules/Approved%20National%20Family%20Support%20Competency%20Framework_FINAL_7_18_2018.pdf.

Ispa, J. M., Fine, M. a, Halgunseth, L. C., Harper, S., Robinson, J., Boyce, L., … Brady-Smith, C. (2004). Maternal intrusiveness, maternal warmth, and mother–toddler relationship outcomes: Variations across low-income ethnic and acculturation groups. *Child Development, 75*(6), 1613–1631. http://doi.org/10.1111/j.1467-8624.2004.00806.x

Jacobson, A. L. (2015). Parenting education and guidance. In M. J. Walcheski, & J. S. Reinke (Eds.), *Family life education: The practice of family science* (pp. 213–222). Minneapolis, MN: National Council on Family Relations.

Kamp Dush, C. M., Taylor, M. G., & Kroeger, R. A. (2008). Marital happiness and psychological well-being across the life course. *Family Relations, 57*(2), 211–226.

Klein Velderman, M., Bakermans-Kranenburg, M. J., Juffer, F., & Van Ijzendoorn, M. H. (2006). Effects of attachment-based interventions on maternal sensitivity and infant attachment: differential susceptibility of highly reactive infants. *Journal of Family Psychology, 20*(2), 266.

Korfmacher, J., Green, B., Spellmann, M., & Thornburg, K. R. (2007). The helping relationship and program participation in early childhood home visiting. *Infant Mental Health Journal: Official Publication of The World Association for Infant Mental Health, 28*(5), 459–480.

Leventhal, J. (2015). Human growth and development across the lifespan. In M. J. Walcheski, & J. S. Reinke (Eds.), *Family life education: The practice of family science* (pp. 167–176). Minneapolis, MN: National Council on Family Relations.

McHale, J. P., Kuersten-Hogan, R., & Rao, N. (2004). Growing points for coparenting theory and research. *Journal of Adult Development, 11*(3), 221–234.

McElwain, N. L., & Booth-LaForce, C. (2006). Maternal sensitivity to infant distress and nondistress as predictors of infant–mother attachment security. *Journal of Family Psychology, 20*(2), 247.

NCFR. (n.d.). *Family life educators code of ethics.* Retrieved https://www.ncfr.org/sites/default/files/cfle_code_of_ethics_2.pdf

Olson, D. H., DeFrain, J., & Skogrand, L. (2014). *Marriages and families: Intimacy, diversity, and strengths* (8th ed.). New York: McGraw Hill.

Orthner, D. K., Jones-Sanpei, H., & Williamson, S. (2004). The resilience and strengths of low-income families. *Family Relations, 53*(2), 159–167.

Osborne, C., & McLanahan, S. (2007). Partnership instability and child well-being. *Journal of Marriage and Family, 69*(4), 1065–1083.

Palm, G. (2009). Professional ethics and practice. In D. J. Bredehoft & M. Walcheski (Eds.), *Family life education: Integrating theory and practice* ed(2nd., pp. 191–197). Minneapolis, MN: National Council on Family Relations.

Palm, G. F. (2015). Professional ethics and practice. In M. J. Walcheski, & J. S. Reinke (Eds.), *Family life education: The practice of family science* (pp. 235–241). Minneapolis, MN: National Council on Family Relations.

Paschall, K. W., & Mastergeorge, A. M. (2016). A review of 25 years of research in bidirectionality in parent–child relationships: An examination of methodological approaches. *International Journal of Behavioral Development, 40*(5), 442–451.

Powell, B., Cooper, G., Hoffman, K., & Marvin, B. (2014). *The Circle of Security intervention.* New York: The Guilford Press.

Reinke, J. S., & Walcheski, M. J. (2015). Internal dynamics of families. In M. J. Walcheski, & J. S. Reinke (Eds.), *Family life education: The practice of family science* (pp. 157–166). Minneapolis, MN: National Council on Family Relations.

Roggman, L. A., Cook, G. A., Peterson, C. A., & Raikes, H. H. (2008). Who drops out of Early Head Start home visiting programs? *Early Education and Development, 19*, 574–599. doi:10.1080/10409280701681870

Roggman, L. A., Cook, G. A., Innocenti, M. S., Jump Norman, V. K., Christiansen, K., Boyce, L. K., Aikens, N., Boller, K., Paulsell, D., & Hallgren, K. (2010). Home Visit Rating Scales—Adapted and Extended (HOVRS-A+) version 2. Adapted from Roggman, L. A., et al. (2008). Home Visit Rating Scales. In L. Roggman, L. Boyce, and M. Innocenti, *Developmental Parenting* (pp. 209–217). Baltimore: Paul H. Brookes Publishing.

Roggman, L. A., Cook, G. A., Innocenti, M. S., Jump Norman, V., Boyce, L. K., Christiansen, K., & Peterson, C. A. (2016a). Home visit quality variations in two early head start programs in relation to parenting and child vocabulary outcomes. *Infant Mental Health Journal, 37*(3), 193–207.

Roggman, L., Peterson, C., Cohen, R. C., Ispa, J., Decker, K. B., Hughes-Belding, K., Cook, G., & Vallotton, C. D. (2016b). Preparing home visitors to partner with families of infants and toddlers. *Journal of Early Childhood Teacher Education, 37*, 301–313. http://dx.doi.org/10.1080/10901027.2017.1298369

Scaramella, L. V., & Leve, L. D. (2004). Clarifying parent–child reciprocities during early childhood: The early childhood coercion model. *Clinical Child and Family Psychology Review, 7*(2), 89–107.

Segrin, C., & Flora, J. (2005). *Family communication.* Mahwah, NJ: Lawrence Erlbaum Associates.

128 *Building and Supporting Relationships*

Shapiro, S. L., Brown, K. W., & Biegel, G. M. (2007). Teaching self-care to caregivers: Effects of mindfulness-based stress reduction on the mental health of therapists in training. *Training and Education in Professional Psychology, 1*(2), 105–115.

Shonkoff, J. P., & Phillips, D. A. (2000). *From neurons to neighborhoods: The science of early childhood development*. Washington DC: National Academy Press.

Skovholt, T., & Trotter-Mathison, M. (2014). *The resilient practitioner: Burnout prevention and self-care strategies for counselors, therapists, teachers, and health professionals.* New York, NY: Routledge.

Substance Abuse and Mental Health Services Administration. (2018). *Trauma-informed approach and trauma-specific interventions*. Retrieved from: https://www.samhsa.gov /nctic/trauma-interventions

Van Ijzendoorn, M. H., Schuengel, C., & Bakermans–Kranenburg, M. J. (1999). Disorganized attachment in early childhood: Meta-analysis of precursors, concomitants, and sequelae. *Development and Psychopathology, 11*(2), 225–250.

Wadsworth, S. M. M., Roy, K. M., & Watkins, N. (2015). Families and individuals in societal contexts. In M. J. Walcheski & J. S. Reinke (Eds.), *Family life education: The practice of family science* (pp. 147–155). Minneapolis, MN: National Council on Family Relations

Waller, M. R. (2012). Cooperation, conflict, or disengagement? Coparenting styles and father involvement in fragile families. *Family Process, 51*(3), 325–342.

Werner, E. E. (2000). Protective factors and individual resilience. In J. P. Shonkoff & S. J. Meisels (Eds.), *Handbook of early childhood intervention* (pp. 115–132). New York, NY: Cambridge University Press.

7 Supporting Development and Learning

Infants and toddlers develop and learn through interactions and experiences with their environment. This includes interactions with materials, toys, and everyday activities and routines. This also includes interactions and experiences with important caregivers in young children's lives. Parents and caregivers support development and learning when they are mindful of the unique needs of each child and adapt their behaviors accordingly (Cole, 2003).

Infant/toddler development and learning occurs in multiple domains. Physical development includes gross motor (sitting, crawling, walking, running, etc.) and fine motor (hand and finger movements) skills. Cognitive development includes all mental process such as attention, memory, executive function skills, and other skills that lay the foundation for success in school. Infancy is a major sensitive period for the development of language—babies go from babbling, to one- and two-word sentences by age two. Social and emotional skills also develop over the first three years, with toddlers gaining increasing control over their emotions and behaviors, and developing social relationships with parents, peers, and others. All of these aspects of development are a major concern for EHS-HBO. Children in EHS-HBO are already at risk for poorer developmental outcomes because of the stressors that accompany living in poverty (Conger, Conger & Martin, 2010). As such, supporting development and learning—and more importantly, supporting parents in supporting their children's development and learning—is a critical part of EHS-HBO. The CUPID competency **Supporting Development and Learning** (Roggman et al., 2016; CUPID, 2017) includes:

Competency	Structuring the physical environment and daily routines with the intention to promote engagement, exploration, and communication that supports learning and development across domains. Individualizing interactions to be responsive to children's interests, needs, and developmental skills
Knowledge	Expanded knowledge of how learning is embedded in family routines, of individuality in child development pace and processes, of curriculum resources for parents and of the range of home, family, and community resources available for parents to use to support their child's development

(Continued)

130 *Supporting Development and Learning*

(Cont.)

Skills	Skills to help parents observe and enjoy their children's development, understand their child's individual developmental trajectory and pace, and actively support their children's learning
Attitudes	Attitudes reflecting compassion and understanding for the challenges of adult life, the difficulty of parenting when experiencing depression or anxiety, and the influence of a parent's earlier life experiences

See full alignment in Appendix B.
Note: Permission to reprint was granted from the National Council on Family Relations.

The FLE Content Areas that align with this competency include:

Human growth and development across the lifespan	Understanding of the developmental changes (both typical and atypical) of individuals in families across the lifespan with an emphasis on knowledge of developmental domains
Parenting education and guidance	How parents teach, guide, and influence as the dynamic context of the parent–child relationship
FLE methodology	Understand principles of FLE in tandem with planning and delivery of programs
Interpersonal relationships	Understand the development and maintenance of interpersonal relationships
Internal dynamics of families	Understanding of family strengths and weaknesses and how family members relate to each other
Families and individuals in societal contexts	Understand families and their relationships to other institutions, such as the educational, governmental, religious, health care, and occupational institutions in society.

Knowledge

According to CUPID, the expanded knowledge for home visitors related to supporting development and learning is stated as:

Expanded knowledge of how learning is embedded in family routines, of individuality in child development pace and processes, of curriculum resources for parents and of the range of home, family, and community resources available for parents to use to support their child's development.

(CUPID, 2017)

Supporting Development and Learning   131

Learning within the Family

For infants and toddlers, learning is embedded in the everyday activities and routines of family life. From an ecological perspective, individuals are nested in microsystems, which are defined as proximal (i.e., close) environments that the individual interacts within frequently (Bronfenbrenner & Morris, 2006). Infants and young children are nested in the home microsystem. Thus, the activities, routines, and interactions that occur within the home microsystem play an important role in development and learning. The home microsystem "sets the stage" for development in all domains. Likewise, from a family systems perspective, the interactions that occur in one part of the system, affect all parts of the system (Segrin & Flora, 2005). This means that all aspects of family life impact infants' and toddlers' development and learning, even if they are not directly involved. For example, parental mental health issues (e.g., anxiety, depression) directly impacts parental wellbeing, but also has an indirect effect on development because of the toll it takes on parents' warm and sensitive behaviors (e.g., Jones Harden, Denmark, Holmes, & Duchene, 2014).

Culture plays a critical role in determining what occurs within the family by shaping the "developmental niche" within which the infant develops (Super & Harkness, 2002). Cultural and familial experiences are passed down from generation to generation, including norms and values about parenting and young children. Culture shapes beliefs and values about child development, the physical and social spaces parents expose infants to, and the parenting practices they actually use (Super & Harkness, 2002). Each infant has a unique "niche" that shapes what the family does, where they go, what they value, and how they interact with each other, all of which provides a unique setting for development and learning.

Individuality in Child Development

A complete understanding of how children learn and grow, means understanding (and respecting) the wide variation and individuality in child development. Child development in all domains (physical, cognitive, language, social, and emotional) is usually discussed in terms of milestones that infants and toddlers reach at certain ages. For example, infants typically start sitting up at 6 months, crawling at 8 months, and walking at 12 months (Gross, 2019). Milestones are typically presented as sequential and predictable—meaning that they happen in the same order at around the same time, for all infants (Gross, 2019). This is important, but it's only half the story. There is wide variation in when infants achieve certain milestones—for example, it is typical for infants to start walking anywhere from 9 to 18 months. It is important for adults to realize that there is a wide range of what is considered "normal," and infants and toddlers reach developmental milestones in their own time.

132   Supporting Development and Learning

Infants are unique individuals from day one, as is readily seen in their temperament. Temperament refers to biologically based differences in motor activity, biological rhythms (e.g., eating, sleeping), mood, adaptability, and more (Thomas & Chess, 1977). Each infant has an individual "style" of temperament. Some are happy and easygoing, while others are fussy and easily upset in new situations. Infants vary in their emotional and social behaviors as infants get older as well. Some toddlers are extremely social, while others are fearful and shy. Some toddlers enjoy getting dirty during sensory play (e.g., sand, water, clay), while other toddlers cringe at these activities. All toddlers need help learning to manage their emotions (Cole, Martin & Dennis, 2004), but some may need more physical touch, transitional objects (i.e., stuffed animals, blankets, etc.), or space to let out a tantrum to calm down. As toddlers' language development becomes more complex, some may have the words to express how they are feeling, while others need more help from adults.

The examples of individuality in child development across all domains of development are endless. The pace and process of development is different for each infant. Children approach learning in different ways, enjoy different types of interactions, elicit different types of reactions from others, and enjoy participating with the environment in different ways. Parents and caregivers must "tune in" to their child by observing them and getting to know them as individuals. When adults learn about and respect the unique attributes of their infant/toddler, they can modify their own behaviors to best support their child's development and learning (Cole, 2003).

Resources for Parents

Supporting parents is one of the best ways to support child development and learning (Shonkoff & Phillips, 2000). Parents rarely function completely on their own—they usually rely on a myriad of resources within the home and the community for support. This is reflected in the EHS-HBO program philosophy. EHS-HBO is a "two-generation" program, meaning that the program supports parents in addition to infants/toddlers (ACF, 2002). Many EHS-HBO programs utilize the Parents as Teachers curriculum (PAT, 2015), which supports parents in developing their own skills as their child's first and most important teacher. Other evidence-based curricula resources to help parents in supporting their child's development include Incredible Years (Webster-Stratton, Rinaldi, & Reid, 2011) and The Triple P-Positive Parenting Program (Sanders, 2008). These curricula share the common goal of improving child development by enhancing parents' knowledge and abilities to interact with their children in ways that improve learning.

Parents feel happier and healthier when they have social, emotional, and child-rearing support from others. When parents feel supported, they are better able to care for their infants and toddlers in ways that support development and learning. Within the home, parents may draw on romantic relationships and kin relationships (Barnett, Scaramella, Neppl, Ontai, & Conger, 2010; Kamp Dush et al., 2008) for strength, meaning that adults need support from other adults to thrive as parents. This leads to decreased parental stress and more positive parenting behavior (Cummings & Davies, 2002; Slykerman et al., 2005).

Communities also provide valuable resources for parents that help their children thrive. Community supports for families helps parents build links with other individuals and important institutions such as schools (Hutchings & Webster-Stratton, 2004). Informal support may come from neighbors in the form of social support, help with childcare, food in times of need, and more (Keene & Geronimus, 2011). Formal programs exist to help new parents across the transition into parenthood in terms of childbirth and newborn education, new parent support groups, and more. One of the main functions of EHS-HBO is to provide support in all of these areas mentioned, as well as help parents connect with others and agencies that can be of further use (ACF, 2002). Home visitors play an important role in teaching families how to identify and access beneficial supports around them. Research demonstrates that networks of informal and formal supports are critical for mental health, parenting, and ultimately children's development (Armstrong, Birnie-Lefcovitch, & Ungar, 2005; Balaji et al., 2007).

For economically disadvantaged families, state and federal supports for food (including infant formula), housing, and health care are critical resources for parents. For example, approximately 17 million families struggle with food insecurity (Coleman-Jensen, Rabbitt, Gregory, & Singh, 2017), meaning that they cannot count on having enough food to feed their family. This affects young children directly by affecting their nutrition, but it also impacts them indirectly by the stress and strain it places on parents. Food assistance programs such as the Supplemental Nutrition Assistance Program (SNAP), the Special Supplemental Nutrition Program for Women, Infants, and Children (WIC), plus local charities and food banks help children meet the nutritional requirements they need to grow and thrive and reduces stress and strain on parents which allows them to have more meaningful interactions with their children. Programs such as these are discussed in more details below.

FLE Content Area Knowledge and Knowledge of Supporting Development and Learning

FLE content area of human growth and development. *Understanding of the developmental changes (both typical and atypical) of individuals in families across the lifespan with an emphasis on knowledge of developmental domains.*

FLE content knowledge on human growth and development enhances knowledge of supporting development and learning in multiple ways. First is by understanding the critical role families play in child development. As discussed above, family systems (Segrin & Flora, 2005) and ecological

134 Supporting Development and Learning

systems (Bronfenbrenner & Morris, 2006) theories both place the individual child as nested within the family. It's the interactions that occur within the family that create the context within which all development actually occurs. In Chapter 6 we reviewed how the bidirectional interactions between parents and children contribute to development.

For infants and toddlers, other aspects of family life such as routines and the structure of daily activities play an important role in shaping development and learning. Household chaos is when day-to-day home life is characterized by instability in settings, routines, and activities, as well as disorder (e.g., noisy, crowded, cluttered, unstructured) (Evans & Wachs, 2010; Sameroff, 2010). Research suggests that household chaos is associated with poorer early language development (Vernon-Feagans, Garrett-Peters, Willoughby, Mills-Koonce, & Family Life Project Key Investigators, 2012), delayed gratification and attention problems, and higher aggression (Martin, Razza, & Brooks-Gunn, 2012). Unfortunately, household chaos is more prevalent in low-income families due to instability in employment, work hours, transportation, and childcare (Evans, Gonnella, Marcynyszyn, Gentile, & Salpeker, 2005). Other ways in which child behavior, particularly misbehavior, is affected by family life is discussed in more detail in Chapter 10.

Home visitors must also use their knowledge in this content area to deepen their understanding of and respect for the wide variation in the pace and process of children's learning. Some developmental researchers use the metaphor of orchids and dandelions to understand individual differences (Kennedy, 2013). As flowers, orchids are challenging to care for and require very particular amounts of sunlight and water; however, when cared for correctly, they are beautiful. In contrast, dandelions are robust to different amounts of water and sunlight and flourish in a variety of conditions. In line with this metaphor, infants and toddlers also vary in how "sensitive" they are to their environment, particularly changes in their environment. Just as with orchids, some children are more fussy, reactive, and just simply more challenging to care for; whereas with dandelions, some children are more resilient and less reactive to variations in their environment. "Orchid" children are more "sensitive" to changes in their environment (Ellis, Boyce, Belsky, Bakermans-Kranenburg, & Van IJzendoorn, 2011) and thus require parents and caregivers to be amenable and flexible if they are to meet their needs appropriately. But, just as with orchids, the investment is worth it in the long run. In fact, challenging infants and toddlers who do not get the sensitive care they need when they are young (e.g., parents react harshly to their challenging behaviors) are at risk for poor social and academic outcomes when they get to kindergarten (Ellis et al., 2011).

Finally, knowledge of human growth and development is also critical for understanding why resources such as nutrition services, health care, and mental health services for parents are essential to support development and learning. In terms of nutrition, "infants require the greatest amount of energy per pound of body weight, and children under the age of 2 years need more fat in their diets than any other age group" (Gross, 2019, p. 153). Infants under 6 months of age should get all of their nutritional requirements from breastmilk or infant formula. It is critical that parents have access to lactation resources and/or access to formula if infants are to develop in a healthy manner. Malnutrition during infancy is more damaging than any other point in the lifespan (Martins et al., 2011). Once solid foods are introduced, and infants become less reliant on breastmilk/formula, they require nutritious carbohydrates, proteins, and especially fats. Infants and toddlers require high fat diets because of their fast-growing brains. Neurons (brain cells) are becoming increasingly connected and streamlined over the first few years of life. Fat in their diet facilitates myelination. Myelin (i.e., fat) covers parts of the neuron to speed up communication between brain cells and is essential for healthy brain development, laying the foundation for all other cognitive, language, physical, and social processes (Konner, 1991). Physical health is another important foundation for development. Regular well-baby checks with a pediatrician are opportunities for monitoring nutrition, sleep, health, developmental milestones, and screening for atypical developmental issues. Medical professionals are also encouraged to screen and identify families experiencing toxic levels of stress as ways to improve young children health outcomes (Garner et al., 2012). From an ecological systems perspective, these exosystem (i.e., community-level) nutrition and health care supports improve infant/toddler development because they provide an environment in which families have access to the services they need to keep children on a healthy developmental trajectory.

Table 7.1 Family Life Education Concepts and Resources that Align with Supporting Development and Learning

FLE Content Area: Human Growth and Development	Resources
How Learning is Part of Family Life Families as influential on early childhood learning and development[2] **Individual Differences in Development** Individual differences in development, which is multi-faced and involves gains and losses[1, 2] **Resources that Support** Nutrition[2]; healthcare[2]; mental health[2]	[1]Leventhal, J. (2015). Human growth and development across the lifespan. In M. J. Walcheski, & J. S. Reinke (Eds.), *Family life education: The practice of family science* (pp. 167–176). Minneapolis, MN: National Council on Family Relations. [2]Boyd, D., & Bee, H. (2015). *Lifespan development* (7th ed.). Upper Saddle River, NJ: Pearson.

136 *Supporting Development and Learning*

FLE content area parenting education and guidance. *How parents teach, guide, and influence as the dynamic context of the parent–child relationship*

Knowledge of parenting education and guidance should be used to help families establish daily routines and activities that support children's growth and development. Parents will want to focus on guidance and discipline strategies (discussed in more detail in Chapter 10), but home visitors should work with parents to see how infant/toddler development and learning is integrated within daily home life. Home visitors can take a systems-oriented approach to help parents see how daily family life contributes to their child's wellbeing. The home learning environment is a crucial part of parenting education and guidance in addition to specific strategies for managing misbehaviors. The home learning environment comprises all the daily activities and routines the child is part of, including the materials they are exposed to (e.g., books, puzzles) and interactions with important people within the family (e.g., parents, siblings, extended family). Seemingly small routines, such as playing on the floor with toys or reading books together each night, have a big impact on children's language and early literacy skills (Karrass & Braungart-Rieker, 2005). Shared family mealtimes are opportunities for conversation, family connectedness, and offer teachable moments for children; however, families report that shared mealtimes can be challenging because of parents' work schedules and finding time/resources to cook (Quick, Fiese, Anderson, Koester & Marlin, 2011). For many families in Early Head Start, establishing routines and predictability can be challenging given the many stressors that go along with living in poverty. Home visitors should involve parents as collaborative partners in determining routines that are suitable and feasible for each family (Jacobson, 2015).

Table 7.2 Family Life Education Concepts and Resources that Align with Supporting Development and Learning

FLE Content Area: Parenting education and guidance	Resources
How Learning is Part of Family Life Family routines as supporting children's growth and development[2]; bioecological theory and family systems[2] **Individual Differences in Development** Developmentally and individually appropriate activities for children[1] **Resources that Support** Community as support[2]	[1]Jacobson, A. L. (2015). Parenting education and guidance. In M. J. Walcheski, & J. S. Reinke (Eds.), *Family life education: The practice of family science* (pp. 213–222). Minneapolis, MN: National Council on Family Relations. [2]Brooks, J. B. (2013). *The process of parenting* (9th ed.). New York: McGraw Hill.

Part of parenting education and guidance also involves helping parents tune in to appreciate the pace and process of their infant or toddler's development. This can help parents and home visitors work together to decide on not only age-appropriate activities, but also activities that support the individual needs of each child. "Tuning in" to infants and toddlers requires parents to observe and interpret their infants' cues. For example, a parent may notice that their four-month-old always turns his head away when a toy is shaken in his face, and may take that to mean that he feels overstimulated during those types of interactions. When parents are playing with their infants they can maintain engagement with mutual attention, turn-taking, and matching the infant or toddler's activity level (Harrist & Waugh, 2002). The "burden" of tuning in matching the child's rhythm and pace of play falls on the caregiver (Harrist & Waugh, 2002).

FLE content area FLE methodology. *Understand principles of FLE in tandem with planning and delivery of programs.*

Core components of FLE methodology can guide the home visitor in working with parents to support their children's development and learning. Much of the knowledge and strategies discussed in this chapter are indirectly related to the child—that is, they involve parent and family-level changes as means of supporting children's development. As such, to support child development, home visitors can facilitate experiential learning experiences for parents (Darling & Cassidy, 2014). For example, rather than simply telling parents how to support their children, exercises that ask parents to *feel, watch, think*, and *do* are more meaningful (Kolb, 1984). For example, home visitors can introduce a few important pieces of information regarding toddler emotion development (e.g., tantrums, emotion regulation, etc.), then have parents practice with each other how they would respond to situations in which their toddler is having a tantrum. This gives parents a chance to feel, watch, think, and do (i.e., experiment) with the information rather than just listen (Darling & Cassidy, 2014).

Additionally, ecological systems theory (e.g., Bronfenbrenner & Morris, 2006) is critical here because it provides a framework for thinking about the individual child nested within the home microsystem, with all the interactions that occur within it critical to child development and learning. It also situates the home within exo- and macro-level contexts, helping the home visitor see why community-level resources, state and national policies, and cultural values play a role in child development and learning. An understanding of individual and family development is also central to FLE (Darling & Cassidy, 2014). While the focus of this chapter is on individual children's development and learning, this cannot be separated from the daily life and interactions of the family. This broader conceptualization of child development is critical for the home visiting field and two-generation programs such as EHS-HBO because real change and improvement in children's wellbeing has to be sustained by changes to the

138   *Supporting Development and Learning*

Table 7.3 Family Life Education Concepts and Resources that Align with Supporting
Development and Learning

FLE Content Area: FLE methodology	Resources
How Learning is Part of Family Life Learning theories, activities, and contexts[2,3]; ecological systems[2,3] **Individual Differences in Development** Variety of age-appropriate practices[1]; individual and family development theory[2]; understand child development[2] **Resources that Support** Community-based social services[3]	[1]Covey, M. (2015). Family life education methodology. In M. J. Walcheski, & J. S. Reinke (Eds.), *Family life education: The practice of family science* (pp. 243–251). Minneapolis, MN: National Council on Family Relations. [2]Darling, C. A., & Cassidy, D. (2014). *Family life education: Working with families across the lifespan* (3rd.). Long Grove, IL: Waveland. [3]Duncan, S. F., & Goddard, H. W. (2017). *Family life education: Principles and practices for effective outreach* (3rd ed.). Thousand Oaks, CA: Sage.

whole family system (Conger, Conger, & Martin, 2010). Finally, FLE methodology also emphasizes the importance of community-level family support as a preventative and collaborative approach to enhancing child development and learning (Hutchings & Webster-Stratton, 2004). While EHS-HBO is a community support in itself, helping families create linkages in the community to other resources that support child nutrition, health care, and parenting expands their support networks and works as another layer of prevention. Home visitors have a responsibility to teach families how to identify and access appropriate resources, so families have the tools to seek continued support after the EHS-HBO program ends.

FLE content area interpersonal relationships. *Understand the development and maintenance of interpersonal relationships.*

As discussed earlier, child development and learning occur within the context of family relationships. Knowledge of interpersonal relationships within the family will ultimately serve to support child development and learning. Relationships between parents and children (and others in the family) are dynamic, meaning that they are constantly changing and taking new shape over time (Glotzer, 2015). As infants turn to toddlers, their developmental needs change completely. As such, parents have to keep up with supporting development and learning in new ways. As just one example, a toddler's ever-increasing need for autonomy (i.e., doing things for herself) changes the nature of the interaction with the parent. It creates new struggles, as well as new opportunities for learning. It is important that the parent–child relationship is flexible enough to allow for these new changes and growth.

Supporting Development and Learning 139

Table 7.4 Family Life Education Concepts and Resources that Align with Supporting Development and Learning

FLE Content Area: Interpersonal relationships	Resources
How Learning is Part of Family Life Learning as strengthening families[2]; importance of relationships and social environments[1]	[1]Glotzer, R. (2015). Interpersonal relationships. In M. J. Walcheski, & J. S. Reinke (Eds.), *Family life education: The practice of family science* (pp. 189–202). Minneapolis, MN: National Council on Family Relations.
Individual Differences in Development Appreciate diverse individuals[1] **Resources that Support** Support groups[2]	[2]Hanna, S. L., Suggett, R., & Radtke, D. (2008). *Person to person: Positive relationships don't just happen* (5th ed.). Upper Saddle River, NJ: Pearson.

Infants' and toddlers' individual differences also play a key role in the interpersonal relationships that develop with parents and other family members. The concept of goodness-of-fit proposes that children's characteristics "fit" with some environments better than others (Lerner & Lerner, 1983). For example, a parent may have demands and expectations for her infant that are incompatible with the infant's inborn temperament. A parent who is active, loud, and constantly on the go may find it challenging to have an infant that needs quiet routines at home to eat and sleep regularly. Conversely, a parent with a low activity level and low emotional reactivity may feel challenged by a toddler who is very physically active and has intense reactions. Home visitors can observe for potential mismatches and help parents understand and adjust their behaviors to best meet the developmental and learning needs of their child.

FLE content area internal dynamics of families. *Understanding of family strengths and weaknesses and how family members relate to each other.*

Knowledge of the internal dynamics of families involves knowledge on both theories and the social processes that drive family life (Reinke & Walcheski, 2015). Ecological and family systems perspectives of family dynamics, which have been discussed extensively in the sections above, lay the foundation for conceptualizing child development and learning as situated within the networks of relationships and interactions that occur not only between parents and children, but across the entire family as well. Part of the knowledge in this content area is understanding "normative and non-normative family stresses and crises" (Reinke & Walcheski, 2015, p. 157), including the unique challenges for families in particular circumstances. For families in EHS-HBO, the stressors that come along with living in poverty

140 *Supporting Development and Learning*

can be particularly troublesome for children's development and learning. Conger and Donnellan (2007) describe the various ways in which economic disadvantage negatively impacts children's development and learning. The "family stress model" proposes that living in poverty places daily stressors on parents in the form of housing issues, food insecurity, unstable employment, long work hours, and more. These stressors have a negative impact on parents' mental health, which then leads to the types of harsh, negative, and putative parenting behaviors that are associated with poor child development and learning outcomes. The "family investment model" proposes that families living in poverty do not have the same resources to invest in their children's learning (both in terms of time investments and material investments) as families with higher incomes, leading to disparities in the home learning environment, especially once children reach school age (Conger & Donnellan, 2007).

These models help explain some of the internal challenges for families living in poverty, but supportive resources must be considered as well. Sensitive behaviors from parents and strong family relationships are protective for children's development and learning in the context of poverty (Evans & Kim, 2013). Family programs such as EHS-HBO impact child development because of the social support provided to parents and increased positive parent–child interactions (Morris, Robinson, Hays-Grudo, Claussen, Hartwig, & Treat, 2017). In this vein, other community resources available to parents ranging from childbirth education to childcare to counseling services, are also sources of support for the family system.

Table 7.5 Family Life Education Concepts and Resources that Align with Supporting Development and Learning

FLE Content Area: Internal Dynamics of Families	Resources
How Learning is Part of Family Life Learners and learning theories[2]; family strengths[2]; family dynamics[2]; ecological theory[1,2]; family systems theory[1,2] **Individual Differences in Development** Individual differences in well-being[2] **Resources that Support** Child care[2]; child support[2]; childbirth education[2]; child abuse hotline[2]; counseling[2]; community resources and strengths[2]	[1]Reinke, J. S., & Walcheski, M. J. (2015). Internal dynamics of families. In M. J. Walcheski, & J. S. Reinke (Eds.), *Family life education: The practice of family science* (pp. 157–166). Minneapolis, MN: National Council on Family Relations. [2]Olson, D. H., DeFrain, J., & Skogrand, L. (2014). *Marriages and families: Intimacy, diversity, and strengths* (8th ed.). New York: McGraw Hill.

Supporting Development and Learning   141

FLE content area families and individuals in societal contexts.
Understand families and their relationships to other institutions.

For most families in EHS-HBO programs, poverty is a major contextual force shaping their lives. As discussed above, living with all of the stressors that accompany economic disadvantage, affects child development by straining parents and the family system. The effect of the physical community environment is influential as well. For example, neighborhood social disorder (e.g., drug dealing, loitering, gang activity, disorderly behavior) has been shown to have a negative impact on parenting stress for families with infants and toddlers (Franco, Pottick, & Huang, 2010). In contrast, the same study found that social cohesion (e.g., neighbors getting along, trusting, helping, sharing values) was associated with reduced parenting stress, operating as an important protective factor. Poor housing quality for children in low-income urban neighborhoods has been linked to worse emotional, behavior, and cognitive skills, with these associations partially accounted for by mothers' worse mental health (Coley, Leventhal, Lynch, & Kull, 2012). Other aspects of the physical environment such as toxins (e.g. lead exposure), noise, and crowding can also take a direct toll on the social and academic skills children need to be successful in school (Evans, 2006).

Community programs and resources are another important part of the societal context families live within. Community resources play an important role in child development and learning because of the information and support

Table 7.6 Family Life Education Concepts and Resources that Align with Supporting Development and Learning

FLE Content Area: Families and Individuals in Societal Contexts	Resources
How Learning is Part of Family Life Learners and learning theories[2]; family strengths[2]; family dynamics[2]; ecological theory[1,2]; family systems theory[1,2] **Individual Differences in Development** Bi-directional effects on child development[2] **Resources that Support** Child care[2]; child support[2]; childbirth education[2]; child abuse hotline[2]; counseling[2]; community resources (and support services) and strengths[1,2]; supportive networks[1]	[1]Wadsworth, S. M. M., Roy, K. M., & Watkins, N. (2015). Families and individuals in societal contexts. In M. J. Walcheski & J. S. Reinke (Eds.), *Family life education: The practice of family science* (pp. 147–155). Minneapolis, MN: National Council on Family Relations [2]Olson, D. H., DeFrain, J., & Skogrand, L. (2014). *Marriages and families: Intimacy, diversity, and strengths* (8th ed.). New York: McGraw Hill.

142 *Supporting Development and Learning*

they provide to parents (Morris et al., 2017). Community programs such as childcare, childbirth education, child abuse prevention services, counseling, and parental support networks can be thought of as public services that help families be healthy, taking somewhat of a public health approach to family wellbeing (Hutchings & Webster-Stratton, 2004). Moreover, state and federal policies regarding EHS-HBO, food and housing assistance, and health care provide a macro-context for child development and learning. These decisions do not directly involve infants and toddlers, but they do shape the societal contexts they develop within—in other words, they impact the resources, opportunities, and supports parents have access to, affecting family decisions, parental wellbeing, which trickles down to opportunities (material, educational, and social) for children's development and learning (Huston & Bentley, 2010). Again, it is not enough to simply give families referrals to services, but instead teach families how to identify and access appropriate resources.

Skills

Skills home visitors need to support children's development and learning include:

> Skills to help parents observe and enjoy their children's development, understand their child's individual developmental trajectory and pace, and actively support their children's learning.
>
> (CUPID, 2017)

Human Growth and Development

- Identify developmental stages and contexts

  - Identify the developmental and learning needs in infancy and toddlerhood.
  - Identify the nutritional and health care needs that are unique to infancy and toddlerhood, and how they impact learning and development.
  - Identify the unique aspects of each infant/toddler's physical, cognitive, and social needs. Help parents tune in to these unique aspects of their child's development and identify ways in which parents can meet their needs, particularly if parents find the behavior challenging/frustrating.
  - Identify the unique aspects of each infant/toddler's development that bring joy to parents.

- Identify reciprocal influences on development

  - Identify the how family routines can be adapted to better align with the developmental stage of the child.
  - Watch for infants/toddlers who are particularly sensitive to changes in the environment, routines, or caregiving practices. Help parents tune

in to what makes their own child unique and discuss why adapting their behaviors to meet these unique needs supports their overall learning and development.

- ○ Identify nutrition and health care needs for each family.

- Apply appropriate practices based on theories

  - ○ Establish routines and daily activities that support their children's development (in parallel with the family's needs as a unit). Work with the family to build an understanding that the interactions that occur within the home microsystem impact their child's learning and development.
  - ○ Analyze the family system for changes and adaptations (that are feasible and realistic) that can be made to improve the functioning of the whole system in ways that will benefit the child's learning and development.

- Recognize socio-ecological influences on human development (e.g., trauma)

  - ○ Recognize the importance of nutrition and health during infancy as the foundation for all development and learning.
  - ○ Recognize the role of nutrition and health care services available in the family's community in helping parents support their child's development.

Parenting Education and Guidance

- Promote healthy parenting from systems and lifespan perspectives

  - ○ Help the family establish routines and daily activities that support the child's development and learning but also fit with the realities and demands of family life.

- Promote healthy parenting from a child's and parent's developmental perspective

  - ○ Help parents "tune in" to their child's cues and signals during play. Point out what the infant/toddler is trying to "tell" the parent with their actions and gestures.
  - ○ Help parents extend back-and-forth interactions by modeling how to take turns and extend attention and interactions (particularly with young infants).
  - ○ Have parents identify the aspects of their children's development they find interesting or bring them joy. Marvel at these moments or when children learn something new.

- Apply strategies based on child's age and stage and unique characteristics to support development

144 *Supporting Development and Learning*

- o Work with parents to identify routines such as playing on the floor, reading books, or conversation during mealtime, that they can incorporate in daily family life.
- o As their child gets older, help parents identify new skills their infant has gained, and new areas h/she needs support – help parents modify family routines and daily activities as the child gets older so that they better meet his/her developmental needs.
- o When parents and children are interacting together, coach the parent to show interest in what the child is involved with (i.e., mutual attention).
- o Coach the parent to match their child's activity level—for example, if a young infant is turning his head away and tense when the parent is shaking a rattle in his face, encourage the parent to step back and hold the toy in a calm manner.

- Identify parenting styles and their related child outcomes

  - o Identify when parents are out of sync with their child's cues, pace of play, and individual developmental needs. Work with parents to help them understand how being more "in tune" will support development and learning.
  - o Identify ways that parents use materials in their home to support development and learning. Help parents maximize the resources available to them.

- Evaluate various parenting strategies

  - o Observe how parents approach their children during the home visit and use these examples as teachable moments for improving how they support development and learning.
  - o Have parents set small goals for their children that align with their age and individual needs. Monitor and evaluate how parents are working to achieve that goal.

- Recognize various parenting roles and their impact on families

  - o Recognize how the demands and realities of parents' lives, particularly for those living in poverty, affect children's learning opportunities within the home.
  - o Help parents identify the aspects of their children they find joyous and interesting.

- Recognize the impact of societal trends and cultural differences

  - o Have parents identify routines and daily activities that are sources of cultural strengths for the family system. Use these as a basis for brainstorming ways to support child development and learning in the home.

- Identify strategies to support children in various settings

Supporting Development and Learning 145

- ○ Identify community parenting education or support programs that are available to the EHS-HBO families in your area.
- ○ Help parents develop the skills to identify and access support programs they need, so they are able to access services after the EHS-HBO program ends.

FLE Methodology

- Employ strategies to meet the needs of different audiences

  - ○ Use experiential learning techniques to give the family the opportunity to feel, watch, think about, and experiment with information presented about young children's development and learning.

- Employ techniques to help the learner do hands-on learning

  - ○ Parents and adults can role-play, act out techniques with the home visitor, or manipulate toys and items in the house to brainstorm how they might support their child's learning.

- Create learning environments that support individual differences

  - ○ Structure home visits with different types of activities (i.e., avoid just talking with parents). Be sure parents have opportunities to have concrete learning experiences, reflective observations, visualization, and active experimentation (Kolb, 1984).

- Demonstrate sensitivity to diversity and community needs and interests

  - ○ Collaborate with parents to determine family routines and activities that are culturally relevant and important to their family.
  - ○ Collaborate with parents to determine which aspects of child development and learning are important to them.

- Develop culturally competent materials and experiences

  - ○ Guided by an ecological system understanding of the family, ensure that the goals and activities for supporting child development and learning are aligned with the individual family's values and culture.

- Design educational experiences from start to finish (needs assessment to outcome measures)

  - ○ In line with EHS-HBO standards and regulations, implement evidenced-based curricula that supports parents in supporting their child's development and learning (e.g., Parents as Teachers, Incredible Years). Use assessments and tools to assess fidelity and effectiveness of all curricula implemented.

146 *Supporting Development and Learning*

Interpersonal Relationships

- Recognize the impact of personality and communication styles

  - Identify areas in which parental demands and expectations for their child are incompatible with the unique aspects of their child's personality or temperament.

- Recognize the developmental stages of relationships

  - Recognize how the parent–child relationship needs to grow and change from infancy to toddlerhood as the child's physical, cognitive, social, and emotional capabilities change.
  - Support parents in modifying their behaviors towards their child to make room for their child's new developmental needs.

- Analyze interpersonal relationships using various theoretical perspectives

  - Recognize the interpersonal relationships the child has with parents and individual family members as "setting the stage" for all learning and development. Work with family members to nurture these relationships as a way of supporting child wellbeing.
  - Recognize ways in which interactions in other areas of the family system affect the interpersonal relationships between the child and family members.

- Develop and implement relationship enhancement and enrichment strategies

  - Help parents identify individual characteristics about their infant or toddler that feel unfamiliar to them or do not "fit" within their typical family life. Ask parents to put themselves in their child's shoes and brainstorm what the child might be feeling, thinking, and needing. Help the parent identify solutions to adjust their behavior/family life accordingly.

- Develop and implement effective communication, problem solving, and anger and conflict management strategies

  - Help parents "tune in" to the unique aspects of their infant/toddler's personality or temperament by asking them to "get to know" their infant. Have parents identify their child's likes, dislikes, interests, and unique quirks (even for young infants). If anger and frustrations related to parenting arise, have parents draw on this knowledge to brainstorm how to meet their child's needs in ways that will support their developing relationship.

Internal Dynamics of Families

- Recognize and define healthy and unhealthy characteristics pertaining to family relationships and family development

Supporting Development and Learning 147

- o For each family, recognize what are normative vs. nonnormative stresses and crises. How the family defines the stress/crisis will impact how it impacts the internal functioning of the family.
- o Recognize and help families define all the ways the internal workings of the family currently impact child development and learning.

- Analyze family functioning using various theories

  - o Use family systems and ecological perspectives to understand how child development and learning is affected by living in poverty (or other unique family circumstances).
  - o Analyze how family dynamics are impacting child development and learning with family stress and family resource models (to identify necessary resources and supports)

- Assess family dynamics from a systems perspective

  - o Assess how the family invests time and resources into their child's development and learning within the home.
  - o Assess how parent–child interactions may be strained by stressors and challenges that are unique to each family.
  - o Work with the family to identify the necessary resources and referrals that support the family's efforts to invest in their children's development and learning.

- Facilitate and strengthen communication processes, conflict-management, and problem-solving skills

  - o Model, coach and facilitate supportive parent–child interactions.

- Develop, recognize, and reinforce strategies that help families function effectively

  - o Provide connections and referrals to community supports ranging from childbirth education, to childcare, to counseling services.

Families and Individuals in Societal Contexts

- Identify the influence of local and global systems on individuals and families

  - o Have knowledge of current community, state, and federal assistance policies to help families access the housing, food, and health care assistance they need.
  - o Have knowledge of current local family support programs (e.g., childbirth education, childcare, etc.) to connect families with.

- Identify factors that influence individuals and families from contemporary and historical perspectives

148   *Supporting Development and Learning*

- Have knowledge of the local landscape of poverty and neighborhood life for families apart of the EHS-HBO program.

- Identify social and cultural influences on family composition and family life

  - Identify how neighborhood social disorder (e.g., drug dealing, loitering, gang activity, disorderly behavior) affects the family.
  - Identify aspects of neighborhood cohesion (e.g., neighbors getting along, trusting, helping, sharing values) that bring strengths to the family.

- Recognize reciprocal interactions between individuals, families, and systems

  - Recognize that child development and learning is directly impacted by important societal contexts (e.g., poverty for many EHS-HBO families), but also indirectly affected by these contexts via the impact they have on parents' stress and mental health.

Attitudes

Attitudes that home visitors must possess to effectively support development and learning are described as:

> Attitudes reflecting compassion and understanding for the challenges of adult life, the difficulty of parenting when experiencing depression or anxiety, and the influence of a parent's earlier life experiences.
>
> (CUPID, 2017)

Working to support child development and learning is no easy feat. On the surface it might seem simple to work one-on-one with a child using various activities that support development and learning. However, working to support child development within the context of parental mental health and wellbeing, family life (particularly challenges associated with living in poverty), adjusting for children's individual differences, and working within the resources offered by the community, it suddenly becomes a much more complicated task. The values and ethics of family life education can help guide the home visitor through this process. The CFLE code of ethics (NCFR, 2016) emphasize that parents (and other family members) must be respected for who they are and their circumstances. This is critical if home visitors are going to work with parents to change the ways in which parents go about supporting their child's development—they have to meet parents where they are and be mindful of the challenges that parents face, particularly if they are living in disadvantaged circumstances. This includes meeting children where they are developmentally, respecting the individual pace and process of each child's growth. A strengths-based perspective also values the goals parents have for

Supporting Development and Learning 149

their children's learning, even if they diverge with the home visitor's goals (NCFR, 2016). Moreover, home visitors must hold the attitude that they will support how families decide to utilize resources in the community (NCFR, 2016). The home visitor plays an important role in being informed about programs and make appropriate referrals that would help parents support their children's learning (NCFR, 2016), but ultimately family members must decide how they use these resources to their benefit.

Box 7.1 CDA Home Visitor Competencies

The CDA Subject Areas and Competency Standards are national standards for Home Visitors. The subject areas that are most relevant to this chapter include **CDA Subject Area 2: Enhancing parents' skills to advance children's physical and intellectual development** and **CDA Subject Area 3: Promoting parents' use of positive ways to support children's social and emotional development.** The CDA Competency Standards are national standards for Home Visitors. Each standard comprises competency goals, functional areas, items, indicators, and examples. The competency goals that are most relevant to this chapter are "To advance physical and intellectual competence" and "To support social and emotional development and provide positive guidance" (Council for Professional Recognition, 2016).

Competency Goal	Functional Area	Example Items	Example Indicators
II. To advance physical and intellectual competence	**4 Physical:** Home visitor helps parents provide a variety of developmentally appropriate learning experiences and teaching strategies to promote physical development.	**Item 4.1** There are activities, materials, and equipment to encourage parents to promote children of varying abilities to develop their large muscles.	Gross/Fine motors skills are encouraged through developmentally appropriate materials and activities.
	5 Cognitive: Home visitor encourages parents to use a variety of developmental learning experiences and teaching strategies to promote	**Item 5.1:** There is evidence that activities offered by parents encourage curiosity, exploration, and discovery.	Activities involve developmentally appropriate, hands-on experiences.

(Continued)

150   *Supporting Development and Learning*

(Cont.)

curiosity, reasoning, and problems solving, and to lay the foundation for all later learning. Candidate educates parents in implementing curriculum that promotes children's learning of important mathematics, science, technology, social studies, and other content areas.

	Item 5.3: Assist parents to enhance their own problem-solving and exploration skills and to encourage their children's questioning, probing, exploring and problem solving skills	Models the use of problem solving and exploration skills and discusses with parents ways that adults can use these skills.
6 Communication: Home visitor helps parents to use a variety of developmentally appropriate learning experiences and teaching strategies to promote their children's language and early literacy learning, to help them communicate their thoughts and feelings verbally and nonverbally.	**Item 6.1:** There is evidence that materials in the home promote early literacy. **Item 6.2:** There is evidence that activities in the home promote language development. **Item 6.4** Helps parents to use developmentally appropriate language with young children.	Developmentally appropriate books are available Children are read to every day. Activities in the home support the needs of dual language learners. Models and encourages parents to talk with children about real things they are experiencing.

(*Continued*)

Supporting Development and Learning 151

(Cont.)

	Candidate helps parents promote dual language learning.	
	7 Creative: Home visitor helps parents use a variety of developmentally appropriate learning experiences and teaching strategies for their children to explore music, movement, and the visual arts, and to develop and express their individual creative abilities.	**Item 7.1:** There is evidence of activities and materials provided to parents so they can encourage children to express themselves through the visual arts. **Item 7.3:** there is evidence of activities and materials provided to parents so they can encourage children to develop their imaginations.	Art materials and activities are available for children daily. Dramatic play materials and activities are available for children daily.
III. To support social and emotional development and provide positive guidance	**8 Self:** Home visitor helps parents develop a warm, positive, supportive, and responsive relationship with each of their children, and helps parents and children learn about and take pride in their individual and cultural identity.	**Item 8.1:** The home environment supports children's development of positive self-concepts	Spaces and activities help each child develop a sense of self-identity/worth. Materials chosen provide children opportunities to experience success.
	9 Social: Home visitor helps parents to ensure that each child functions effectively in the family, learns to express feelings, acquires social skills, and makes friends,	**Item 9.3:** Helps parents understand that children learn appropriate social skills by observing how other people act with each other. **Item 9.4:** Helps parents to	Reinforces parents and other family members' positive, consistent, and sensitive social interactions. Helps parents understand typical social behaviors in

(Continued)

152 *Supporting Development and Learning*

(Cont.)

and helps parents promote mutual respect among children and adults in their lives.	understand and promote feelings of empathy and respect for others.	young children and how they express them so they can have appropriate expectations, avoiding "guessing" while promoting learning.

Permission to reprint from the Council for Professional Recognition, 2019

Box 7.2 National Family Support Competency Framework for Family Support Professionals

The National Family Support Competency Framework for Family Support Professionals are competencies that include ten domains that are further clarified by dimensions (Institute for the Advancement of Family Support Professionals, 2018). There is one domain that is relevant to this chapter: (a) Infant and Early Childhood Development and (b) Dynamics of Family Relationships. Infant and Early Childhood Development includes five dimensions: typical and atypical development, prenatal development, infant care, early language and communication, and early learning. Dynamics of Family Relationships includes three dimensions: healthy family functioning, influences on family wellbeing and fatherhood.

Domain 1	Dimension 5	Component a.	Levels of Competency
Infant and Early Childhood Development	**Early learning**	Routines and interactions	**1-Recognizing.** Understands how development and early learning occurs within the context of a secure relationship with a consistent caregiver
			3-Applying. Supports parents' understanding of learning and development that occurs through their daily routines and interactions with their child

(Continued)

(Cont.)

			5-Extending. Supports parents' understanding of learning and development that occurs through their daily routines and interactions with their child
Domain 4	*Dimension 25*	*Component d.*	*Levels of Competency*
Dynamics of Family Relationships	**Influences on family wellbeing**	Risks and stressors	**1-Recognizing.** Understands potential risks and stressors to family wellbeing such as parental incarceration, divorce, mental health issues, substance abuse, intimate partner violence, and trauma
			3-Applying. Supports parents' understanding of the impact of these stressors on individual family members, parenting, and child development
			5-Extending. Coaches parents on accessing formal and informal supports as needed and follows up to ensure family is supported

Permission to reprint from the Institute for the Advancement of Family Support Professionals.

Summary

A major goal of EHS-HBO is to support infant/toddler physical, cognitive, social, and emotional development and learning. Child development and learning is complex because it happens in the context of family life and parent–child interactions, there is great individual variation in how each child develops, and resources available to parents provide the context within which all of this occurs. FLE content knowledge expands these ideas that understand the family, individual, and societal processes inform child development and learning, including how the parent–child relationship, parental wellbeing, and the family system also must be nurtured to support child development and learning in the home.

Key Concepts

- Developmental niche
- Experiential learning
- Family investment model
- Family stress model
- Goodness of fit
- Home learning environment
- Household chaos
- Microsystem
- Milestones
- Myelination
- Norms
- Orchids and dandelions
- Temperament

Recommended Readings

Conger, R. D., Conger K. J., and Martin. M. J. (2010). Socioeconomic status, family processes, and individual development. *Journal of Marriage and Family, 72,* 685–704.

Evans, G. W., Gonnella, C., Marcynyszyn, L. A., Gentile, L., & Salpekar, N. (2005). The role of chaos in poverty and children's socioemotional adjustment. *Psychological Science, 16,* 560–565.

Kennedy, E. (2013). Orchids and dandelions: How some children are more susceptible to environmental influences for better or worse and the implications for child development. *Clinical Child Psychology and Psychiatry, 18,* 319–321.

References

Administration for Children and Families (ACF). (2002). *Making a difference in the lives of infants and toddlers and their families: The impacts of Early Head Start: Vol. 1. Final technical report.* Washington, DC: U.S. Department of Health and Human Services.

Armstrong, M. I., Birnie-Lefcovitch, S., & Ungar, M. T. (2005). Pathways between social support, family well being, quality of parenting, and child resilience: What we know. *Journal of Child and Family Studies, 14,* 269–281.

Balaji, A. B., Claussen, A. H., Smith, D. C., Visser, S. N., Morales, M. J., & Perou, R. (2007). Social support networks and maternal mental health and well-being. *Journal of Women's Health, 16,* 1386–1396.

Barnett, M. A., Scaramella, L. V., Neppl, T. K., Ontai, L. L., & Conger, R. D. (2010). Grandmother involvement as a protective factor for early childhood social adjustment. *Journal of Family Psychology, 24,* 635–645.

Boyd, D., & Bee, H. (2015). *Lifespan development* (7th ed.). Upper Saddle River, NJ: Pearson.

Bronfenbrenner, U., & Morris, P. A. (2006). The bioecological model of human development. In R. M. Learner & W. Damon (Eds.) *Handbook of child psychology* (pp. 793–828). Hoboken, NJ: John Wiley & Sons Inc.

Brooks, J. B. (2013). *The process of parenting* (9th ed.). New York: McGraw Hill.

Cole, P. M. (2003). The developmental course from child effects to child effectiveness. In A. C. Crouter & A. Booth (Eds.), *Children's influence on family dynamics: The neglected side of family relationships* (pp. 109–118). Hillsdale, NJ: Erlbaum.

Cole, P. M., Martin, S. E., & Dennis, T. A. (2004). Emotion regulation as a scientific construct: Methodological challenges and directions for child development research. *Child Development, 75*, 317–333.

Coleman-Jensen, A., Rabbitt, M., Gregory, C., & Singh, A. (2015). *Household food security in the United States in 2014*. USDA ERS. Retrieved from www.ers.usda.gov/publica tions/err-economic-research-report/err194.aspx.

Coley, R. L., Leventhal, T., Lynch, A. D., & Kull, M. (2012). Relations between housing characteristics and the well-being of low-income children and adolescents. *Developmental Psychology, 49*, 1775–1789.

Collaborative for Understanding the Pedagogy of Infant/toddler Development (CUPID) (2017). *Comprehensive competencies for educators of infants and toddlers in group care and home visiting settings*. Unpublished.

Conger, R. D., & Donnellan, M. B. (2007). An interactionist perspective on the socio-economic context of human development. *Annual Review of Psychology, 58*, 175–199.

Conger, R. D., Conger K. J., and Martin. M. J. (2010). Socioeconomic status, family processes, and individual development. *Journal of Marriage and Family, 72*, 685–704.

Council for Professional Recognition. (2016). *The Child Development Associate National Credentialing Program and CDA Competency Standards, Home Visitor Edition*. Washington DC: Council for Professional Recognition.

Covey, M. (2015). Family life education methodology. In M. J. Walcheski, & J. S. Reinke (Eds.), *Family life education: The practice of family science* (pp. 243–251). Minneapolis, MN: National Council on Family Relations.

Cummings, E. M., & Davies, P. T. (2002). Effects of marital conflict on children: Recent advances and emerging themes in process-oriented research. *Journal of Child Psychology and Psychiatry, 43*, 31–63.

Darling, C. A., & Cassidy, D. (2014). *Family life education: Working with families across the lifespan*. Long Grove, IL: Waveland Press.

Duncan, S. F., & Goddard, H. W. (2017). Family life education: Principles and practices for effective outreach (3rd ed.). Thousand Oaks, CA: Sage.

Ellis, B. J., Boyce, W. T., Belsky, J., Bakermans-Kranenburg, M. J., & Van IJzendoorn, M. H. (2011). Differential susceptibility to the environment: An evolutionary–neurodevelopmental theory. *Development and Psychopathology, 23*, 7–28.

Evans, G. W., Gonnella, C., Marcynyszyn, L. A., Gentile, L., & Salpekar, N. (2005). The role of chaos in poverty and children's socioemotional adjustment. *Psychological Science, 16*, 560–565.

Evans, G. W. (2006). Child development and the physical environment. *Annual Review of Psychology, 57*, 423–451.

Evans, G., & Wachs, T. (2010). *Chaos and its influence on children's development: An ecological perspective*. Washington, DC: American Psychological Association.

Evans, G. W., & Kim, P. (2013). Childhood poverty, chronic stress, self-regulation, and coping. *Child Development Perspectives, 7*, 43–48.

156 Supporting Development and Learning

Franco, L. M., Pottick, K. J., & Huang, C.-C. (2010). Early parenthood in a community context: Neighborhood conditions, race-ethnicity, and parenting stress. *Journal of Community Psychology, 38*, 574–590. http://doi.org/10.1002/jcop

Garner, A. S., Shonkoff, J. P., Siegel, B. S., Dobbins, M. I., Earls, M. F., McGuinn, L., ... & Committee on Early Childhood, Adoption, and Dependent Care. (2012). Early childhood adversity, toxic stress, and the role of the pediatrician: translating developmental science into lifelong health. *Pediatrics, 129*(1), e224–e231.

Glotzer, R. (2015). Interpersonal relationships. In M. J. Walcheski, & J. S. Reinke (Eds.), *Family life education: The practice of family science* (pp. 189–202). Minneapolis, MN: National Council on Family Relations.

Gross, D. (2019). *Infancy: Development from birth to age 3* (3rd ed.). Lanham, MD: Roman & Littlefield.

Hanna, S. L., Suggett, R., & Radtke, D. (2008). *Person to person: Positive relationships don't just happen* (5th ed.). Upper Saddle River, NJ: Pearson.

Harrist, A. W., & Waugh, R. M. (2002). Dyadic synchrony: Its structure and function in children's development. *Developmental Review, 22*, 555–592.

Huston, A. C., & Bentley, A. C. (2010). Human development in societal context. *Annual Review of Psychology, 61*, 411–437.

Hutchings, J., & Webster-Stratton, C. (2004). Community-based support for parents. In M. Hoghughi and N. Long (Eds.), *Handbook of parenting: Theory and research for practice* (pp. 334–351). London: Sage Publications.

Institute for the Advancement of Family Support Professionals. (2018). *National Family Support Competency Framework for Family Support Professionals.* Retrieved from: https://cppr-institute-prod.s3.amazonaws.com/modules/Approved%20National%20Family%20Support%20Competency%20Framework_FINAL_7_18_2018.pdf.

Jacobson, A. L. (2015). Parenting education and guidance. In M. J. Walcheski, & J. S. Reinke (Eds.), *Family life education: The practice of family science* (pp. 213–222). Minneapolis, MN: National Council on Family Relations.

Jones Harden, B., Denmark, N., Holmes, A., & Duchene, M. (2014). Detached parenting and toddler problem behavior in early head start families. *Infant Mental Health Journal, 35*, 529–543.

Kamp Dush, C. M., Taylor, M. G., & Kroeger, R. A. (2008). Marital happiness and psychological well-being across the life course. *Family relations, 57*, 211–226.

Keene, D. E., & Geronimus, A. T. (2011). Community-based support among African American public housing residents. *Journal of Urban Health, 88*, 41–53.

Kennedy, E. (2013). Orchids and dandelions: How some children are more susceptible to environmental influences for better or worse and the implications for child development. *Clinical Child Psychology and Psychiatry, 18*, 319–321.

Kolb, D. (1984). *Experiential learning: Experience as the source of learning and development.* Upper Saddle River, NJ: Prentice-Hall.

Konner, M. (1991). Universals of behavioral development in relation to brain myelination. *Brain maturation and cognitive development.* In K. R. Gibson, & A. C. Peterson (Eds.), *Comparative and cross-cultural perspectives* (pp. 181–223). New York, NY: Routledge.

Karrass, J., & Braungart-Rieker, J. M. (2005). Effects of shared parent–infant book reading on early language acquisition. *Journal of Applied Developmental Psychology, 26* (2), 133–148.

Lerner, J. V., & Lerner, R. M. (1983). Introduction. In *Temperament and adaptation across life: Theoretical and empirical issues* (Vol. 5, pp. 198–231): Academic Press.

Leventhal, J. (2015). Human growth and development across the lifespan. In M. J. Walcheski, & J. S. Reinke (Eds.), *Family life education: The practice of family science* (pp. 167–176). Minneapolis, MN: National Council on Family Relations.

Martin, A., Razza, R. A., & Brooks-Gunn, J. (2012). Specifying the links between household chaos and preschool children's development. *Early Child Development and Care, 182*, 1247–1263.

Martins, V. J., Toledo Florêncio, T. M., Grillo, L. P., Do Carmo, P. F., Martins, P. A., Clemente, A. P. G., ... & Sawaya, A. L. (2011). Long-lasting effects of undernutrition. *International journal of environmental research and public health, 8*(6), 1817–1846.

Morris, A. S., Robinson, L. R., Hays-Grudo, J., Claussen, A. H., Hartwig, S. A., & Treat, A. E. (2017). Targeting parenting in early childhood: A public health approach to improve outcomes for children living in poverty. *Child Development, 88*(2), 388–397.

National Council on Family Relations (NCFR). (2016). *Family life educators code of ethics*. National Council on Family Relations. Retrieved from: https://www.ncfr.org/cfle-certification/cfle-code-ethics

Olson, D. H., DeFrain, J., & Skogrand, L. (2014). *Marriages and families: Intimacy, diversity, and strengths* (8th ed.). New York: McGraw Hill.

Parents as Teachers (PAT). (2015). 2016–2017 *Affiliate performance report, summary*. Retrieved from https://static1.squarespace.com/static/56be46a6b6aa60dbb45e41a5/t/5a37eca0085229e36d170e8e/1513614498107/APR_2pgr_2016-2017.pdf

Quick, B. L., Fiese, B. H., Anderson, B., Koester, B. D., & Marlin, D. W. (2011). A formative evaluation of shared family mealtime for parents of toddlers and young children. *Health Communication, 26*(7), 656–666.

Reinke, J. S., & Walcheski, M. J. (2015). Internal dynamics of families. In M. J. Walcheski, & J. S. Reinke (Eds.), *Family life education: The practice of family science* (pp. 157–159). Minneapolis, MN: National Council on Family Relations.

Roggman, L., Peterson, C., Cohen, R. C., Ispa, J., Decker, K. B., Hughes-Belding, K., Cook, G., & Vallotton, C. D. (2016). Preparing home visitors to partner with families of infants and toddlers. *Journal of Early Childhood Teacher Education, 37*, 301–313. http://dx.doi.org/10.1080/10901027.2017.1298369

Sameroff, A. (2010). Dynamic developmental systems: Chaos and order. In G. Evans & T. Wachs (Eds.), *Chaos and its influence on children's development: An ecological perspective* (pp. 255–264). Washington DC: American Psychological Association.

Sanders, M. R. (2008). Triple P-Positive Parenting Program as a public health approach to strengthening parenting. *Journal of family psychology, 22*(4), 506.

Segrin, C., & Flora, J. (2005). *Family communication*. Mahwah, NJ: Lawrence Erlbaum Associates.

Shonkoff, J. P., & Phillips, D. A. (2000). *From neurons to neighborhoods: The science of early childhood development*. Washington DC: National Academy Press.

Slykerman, R. F., J. M. D. Thompson, J. E. Pryor, D. M. O. Becroft, E. Robinson, P. M. Clark, C. J. Wild, & E. A. Mitchell. (2005). Maternal stress, social support and preschool children's intelligence. *Early Human Development, 81*, 815–821.

158 *Supporting Development and Learning*

Super, C. M., & Harkness, S. (2002). Culture structures the environment for development. *Human Development, 45,* 270–274.

Thomas, A., & Chess, S. (1977). *Temperament and development.* New York: Brunner/Mazel.

Vernon-Feagans, L., Garrett-Peters, P., Willoughby, M., Mills-Koonce, R., & Family Life Project Key Investigators. (2012). Chaos, poverty, and parenting: Predictors of early language development. *Early Childhood Research Quarterly, 27,* 339–351.

Wadsworth, S. M. M., Roy, K. M., & Watkins, N. (2015). Families and individuals in societal contexts. In M. J. Walcheski & J. S. Reinke (Eds.), *Family life education: The practice of family science* (pp. 147–155). Minneapolis, MN: National Council on Family Relations

Webster-Stratton, C., Rinaldi, J., & Reid, J. M. (2011). Long-term outcomes of Incredible Years Parenting Program: Predictors of adolescent adjustment. *Child and Adolescent Mental Health, 16,* 38–46.

8 Health and Safety

One cornerstone of home visits is health and safety. EHS-HBO values providing caregivers with information and materials on topics, such as health and safety. It is also important for home visitors to secure their own personal safety and to know when to work with other professionals to ensure the health and safety of all.

The Collaborative for Understanding the Pedagogy of Infant/Toddler Development (CUPID) drafted a set of competencies for the Infant/Toddler Workforce that includes *supporting development and learning*. From this competency, which encompasses structuring the physical environment and routines to support learning and development across the domains (e.g., physical), arose the **Health and Safety** competency (CUPID, 2017; Roggman et al., 2016) discussed in the present chapter. The knowledge for the health and safety competency for home visitors includes prenatal/neonatal health and health education (CUPID, 2017; Roggman et al., 2016). The skills for this competency include guiding parents in teaching children about healthy behaviors (CUPID, 2017; Roggman et al., 2016). The attitudes for this competency include respecting personal beliefs about health (CUPID, 2017; Roggman et al., 2016).

FLE Content Areas that are most germane to this expanded competency for home visitors include:

Human growth and development across the lifespan	Understanding of the developmental changes (both typical and atypical) of individuals in families across the lifespan with an emphasis on knowledge of developmental domains
Parenting education and guidance	How parents teach, guide, and influence as the dynamic context of the parent–child relationship
Families and individuals in societal contexts	Understand families in regard to other institutions
Human sexuality	Understanding of the physiological, psychological, and social aspects of sexual development across the lifespan, so as to achieve healthy sexual adjustment.

(Continued)

160   *Health and Safety*

(Cont.)

| **FLE methodology** | Understanding of FLE principles in tandem with planning and delivery of programs. |
| **Internal dynamics of families** | Understanding of family strengths and weaknesses and how family members relate to each other |

See full alignment in Appendix B.
Note: Permission to reprint was granted from the National Council on Family Relations.

Knowledge

The detailed description of the knowledge that home visitors should possess regarding health and safety includes: CUPIDs Home Visitor Expansion of Competency: Detailed knowledge of health education and home health and safety (e.g., household safety, healthy practices, home first aid; care of sick infant/child; prenatal/neonatal health, breastfeeding, infant sleeping) (see CUPID, 2017 and Roggman et al., 2016).

Basics and Background

Prenatal and neonatal health. Fetal brain development begins shortly after conception (The Urban Child Institute, 2018) and therefore it is essential for the expectant woman to take good care of herself during all three trimesters by, for example, practicing good nutrition. Nutrition assessments that help the pregnant woman to track her weight gain are important. Nutritionists may be available to join the home visit and can provide specific assessments, promote folic acid consumption, and help create a plan of care that meets the woman's individual needs (e.g., a woman with high blood glucose levels during pregnancy). Pregnant women also need opportunities to engage in ongoing discussions about avoiding teratogens (i.e., any substance that causes birth defects). For example, diet pills ingested by the pregnant woman may result in abnormal fetal development and low birth weight. Home visitors need to have prenatal and neonatal health knowledge and should empower the pregnant woman to call a doctor if she feels something different during the pregnancy.

Once the neonate is born, it is important to support families in learning how to meet the newborn's needs. Some parents and caregivers may see some aspects of care as being unnecessary or as spoiling the baby and may therefore need to hear the information in terms of context and consequences, such as on brain development, in order to be convinced. For example, a child's adaptability and resilience are determined by their experiences with a responsive adult, and young children are especially vulnerable to negative experiences such as maltreatment (The Urban Child Institute, 2018). A caregiver can practice what is considered responsive parenting by accepting and promptly responding to an infant's signaled needs and interests (Ainsworth, Blehar, Waters, & Wall, 1978; Landry, Smith, & Swank, 2006). This helps the infant and caregiver form trust and a healthy bond (Ainsworth et al., 1978; Landry, Smith, & Swank, 2006). Home visitors may also want to bring an additional perspective to a home visit, such as a well-respected and well-known counselor in the community, to speak in favor of responsive parenting as useful for neonatal and maternal health, particularly for hard-to-reach families. Responsive parenting and promoting child development are essential to the healthy practices discussed in this chapter.

Breastfeeding

Breastfeeding has nutritional and other benefits for the infant and mother (American Academy of Pediatrics, 2012). Breastfeeding provides infants with protection against childhood obesity (American Academy of Pediatrics, 2018a). There are also benefits for the breastfeeding woman, such as a lower risk of breast cancer (American Academy of Pediatrics, 2018a). Ideally, it would be helpful to encourage the woman to breastfeed starting at birth with the production of colostrum and continuing to breastfeed exclusively for the first six months of life (American Academy of Pediatrics, 2018b). Infants can be introduced to solid foods, such as bananas, around six months of age and at this time it is important to promote self-feeding behaviors in the infant, such as holding a sippy cup (American Academy of Pediatrics, 2018b).

Home visitors may be encouraged to become certified lactation educators (CLE) through the Childbirth and Postpartum Professional Association (CAPPA). Home visitors who receive this training often report that it feels like taking a college course on breastfeeding and that they can confidently explain how to breastfeed and its benefits. They also feel that they can provide an appropriate amount of information to help parents decide what is best for their family. Earning the CLE credential does involve some fees and membership dues, so it might be helpful for a home visiting site to talk with professionals at Women, Infants, and Children (WIC) to determine if this is something they are able to sponsor.

The topic of breastfeeding can be a springboard for other topics. For example, a home visitor may want to work with the parent to discuss oral health, such as using a clean, damp washcloth to clean the newborn's gums after feeding (Casamassimo & Holt, 2016). Breastfeeding is also linked to the topics of infant sleeping. Breastfeeding correlates to a reduced risk of SIDS or sudden infant death syndrome (AAP Task Force on Sudden Infant Death Syndrome, 2016). The next section will discuss healthy sleep practices and SIDS prevention.

162   *Health and Safety*

Infant sleeping

The American Academy of Pediatrics (AAP) is an authoritative source for information and recommendations on safe sleep. The AAP Task Force on Sudden Infant Death Syndrome (2016) states recommendations for a safe sleeping environment. There are 19 recommendations including such topics as: (a) putting the infant to sleep in a supine (upward facing) position, (b) using a firm mattress or sleep surface, and (c) providing a pacifier for sleep time.

Organizations often base their recommendations on AAP statements. For example, approved safe sleep training will help home visitors understand safe sleep practices as recommended by the AAP and will encourage home visitors to discuss these practices with parents. This professional development requirement or training may vary by state. For example, some programs use safe sleep training that is offered by the Regional Emergency Medical Service Authority (REMSA) whereas other states may use ChildCareTraining.org.

Sudden Infant Death Syndrome (SIDS). It is imperative that home visitors always emphasize putting the infant *safe to sleep* or *back to sleep*, verbal cues that originated in 1994 as a result of empirical studies that demonstrated that the supine position reduces SIDS (U.S. Department of Health and Human Services, n.d.). Some researchers have postulated that there is a SIDS gene that predisposes an infant to SIDS (Opdal & Rognum, 2004). There are rich resources available to raise awareness about preventing SIDS.

For example, home visitors should become aware of national organizations, such as Cribs for Kids (see www.cribsforkids.org) that emphasize parent education, public safety initiatives, and provide safe cribs for families in need. Home visitors can also work with directors and managers of programs to help obtain resources for families in poverty that are served by your home visiting program.

Like many of the topics in this chapter, home visitors should work with families to help them know that discussions on these topics are ongoing. Expectant parents should be actively engaged in learning about all of the topics in this chapter. For example, a home visitor and pregnant woman can discuss the importance of decorating a room (or space) but not the crib, and during each prenatal visit the home visitor can ask how the infant's sleep space looks. This can also be part of an ongoing discussion on safe versus unsafe environments and actions. There are also nuances to this ongoing discussion. For example, a pregnant couple should know that skin-to-skin contact will be helpful to the newborn and mother after birth but it is also important to know that this is only helpful if the parent is awake. It is important for the infant to be placed supine until one year of age (AAP Task Force on Sudden Infant Death Syndrome, 2016).

Some home visitors find it helpful to talk about Shaken Baby Syndrome (SBS) after discussing SIDS with families given the emphasis on safe versus unsafe actions and environments. SBS is a result of the brain pushing against the skull due to outside forces and is a form of abuse that results in severe damage to the infant, such as hemorrhages and hematomas (Mian et al., 2015). Parent education is key to preventing SBS (Mian et al., 2015), and discussing with parents ways to manage their emotions and connecting potential abusers to counselors and to medical professionals are paramount. A home visitor may want to include statistics from their state or county into their discussions on child abuse, child neglect, and child maltreatment.

Care of sick infant/child

Many immunizations occur during the first year of life to prevent diseases. For example, the HepB vaccine, which prevents against hepatitis B, should be administered by a health professional during the first or second month after birth (Centers for Disease Control and Prevention, 2018a). One of the purposes of well-child visits is for the infant to receive immunizations to prevent illness (American Academy of Pediatrics, 2017). In addition to prevention, pediatricians offer help when the infant/child is sick.

Home visitors should receive training in communicable diseases (e.g., pink eye, influenza, viral hepatitis) and should encourage the family to contact the pediatrician if the infant/child is sick. Some sites will offer home visitors shots (e.g., for hepatitis) but despite precautions, home visitors should reschedule with a family if someone is sick regardless of the severity of the illness or disease. In other words, when the family enrolls in the program, a handbook or similar should emphasize that if a family member and/or a home visitor is sick that a visit should be rescheduled. As a home visitor, you may get to a family's home and find out they are sick, and it is okay for you to reschedule (particularly if vomiting or fevers are present but really if any symptom of illness is present). Let the family know that you have other families to see and remind them to let you know ahead of time if someone is sick.

It is also important for home visitors to be aware of rashes, lice, and bed bugs and to provide families with information and a medical contact when needed to help them best decide upon a treatment. Home visitors should engage in frequent hand washing, keep hand sanitizers in their car, and know of public bathrooms between their site and families' homes.

In some home visits, it is common for the home visitor to collaborate with the family to make a phone call to other professionals and resources in the community, particularly if the family is new to the country. It is important to make sure that the family knows the difference between a common and non-urgent illness (e.g., fever, minor cut, etc.) compared to an urgent situation, such as a severe burn. Families should have the contact information for a doctor's office as well as the emergency room and know when to use each one, ideally without home visitor assistance.

Home health and safety

Household safety. A household safety checklist is important. For examples, please consult with http://kidshealth.org/en/parents/household-checklist.html. Your home visiting agency will likely have checklists for home visitors that may have been developed as a result of collaboration with local housing authorities, health departments, social services, or other agencies. Checklists can help the home visitor work with the family to provide information on baby-proofing the house (ideally before the child is born).

When thinking about household safety, it is important to consider the world from the child's eye level to consider what they see. It is also important to consider milestones. For example, many children start to take their first steps around their first birthday and this will require further household safety needs, such as protecting children from falls and other accidents.

Home visits are not always conducted in the home. Some home visitors conduct visits in spaces such as those at Child Protective Services (CPS). Just because a visit is not in the home does not mean that home visitors are exempt from safety issues. For example, a child with epilepsy requires extra safety precautions no matter where the visit is conducted. The home visitor may want to go over the protocol at the start of every visit after talking with the parent about what they would feel most comfortable doing if the child has a seizure during the visit and what the home visitor should do if this happens. This kind of consistent reminder about the protocol might help the parent feel confident that they can handle a child's seizures when they happen outside of time spent with a helping professional.

The emotional environment of the home and the visit is as important as the physical environment. Toxic stress in a child can occur when the body's stress response system is frequently activated in the absence of a responsive or supportive adult (Shonkoff et al., 2012). Exposure to Adverse Childhood Experiences (ACEs), such as parental mental illness, emotional and physical neglect and others (see Felitti et al., 1998), can cause a toxic stress response in infants and children and can be the root of negative changes in the brain and later physical and mental illness (Shonkoff et al., 2012). Early toxic stress screenings are important for children facing multiple adversities (Walsh, 2017a).

Local health departments, community-based organizations, religious centers, and online resources such as statements about tenant rights and landlord responsibilities are all part of a collaborative process of making sure that families' homes are safe.

Household safety extends beyond the physical living space and can include cars, too. Dealerships and hospitals may be able to assist families with appropriately installing car seats to ensure that families have safe car seats for use from birth to age 5.

Keep in mind that the curriculum a site uses, such as PAT (Parents as Teachers), may have a safety unit as part of a foundational unit and that these topics should be part of an ongoing discussion rather than having a few visits dedicated to these topics. Current events and personal experiences are also ways to engage families in ongoing talk. For example, a recent topic in the media was laundry pods, and the home visitors used this as an opportunity to discuss with families why these are appealing to young children (beautiful colors and inviting textures) and used discussion of the dangers of young children playing with or exploring them as a bridge to a larger conversation on poison prevention. In the instance that a child ingested poison, tertiary prevention would be needed and calling Poison Help is an example of this type of prevention (1-800-222-1222).

Healthy practices. Home visitors need to secure their own personal safety to be effective in their work (Wasik & Bryant, 2001). Safety concerns vary by program and by home visitor. For example, a home visitor serving pregnant women in jail has different safety concerns than a home visitor serving families in a suburban area (Reyes-Vargas, Selby, & Walsh, 2019). Home visitor safety includes each visitor having their own individualized safety plan. This may include safe parking and safety when walking through a neighborhood and being aware of one's surroundings, which includes noticing your environment and listening to your instincts. Home visitors should request to families that pets are secured during visits. Home visiting sites should have a check-in system, which may include texting or calling someone at the site prior to and/or after the home visit. When the family has a unique living space (e.g., a motel or a shelter), reach out to other home visitors as they may have experiences to share about working in these spaces. For example, if an elevator at a motel is questionable, they can advise you to take the stairs. Home visitors should wear their site badge to visits, which may encourage others to respect the professional as they walk alone from the car to the family's living space. Home visitors have to protect themselves and have the right to be safe, and they also have the right to minimize secondary trauma and seek out other home visitors, a supervisor, or a coach when support is needed.

As mandated reporters, home visitors are always watching for things and events that cross the line from safe to unsafe. If a family is going through a crisis (e.g., violence in the home) that results in a home visitor feeling unsafe in the home, the professional can most likely suggest with the support of a supervisor that a home visit occurs at a different location (e.g., home visiting site) and the program may be able to provide transportation passes (or similar accommodations) to support families' transportation between the site and their living space.

When a home visitor contacts CPS or the Police Department (PD), it is usually after much consideration has been given to an issue. Families volunteer

166   *Health and Safety*

for home visiting and usually want home visitors there, which is different from other helping relationships (e.g., case manager). An ideal situation would be for the family and the home visitor to call CPS together. A situation that is clearly unsafe requires reporting the family to CPS. The family may lose the child, WIC support, or TANF (Temporary Assistance for Needy Families) support but this will ultimately be in the best interest of the child. Calling the PD is usually appropriate when the children are not in danger but you, as the home visitor, think the family could use a welfare check. The police can then decide if CPS should be involved and calling the police typically does not jeopardize anything for the family (e.g., loss of public housing). Home visitors should be able to talk though these issues with reflective supervisors to get validation for their plans or to get a different perspective.

Home first aid. Home visitors typically need to be certified in first aid and cardiopulmonary resuscitation (CPR) prior to commencing work as a home visitor. The American Heart Association or local registries in your state should help you find training centers and instructors. Talking with other home visitors and a supervisor about the skills you learn is important. For example, some home visitors may have performed the Heimlich maneuver and talking with them can further demystify how they put an infant on their back and used the heel of their hands to remove the obstruction.

Health education. Your role as a home visitor is to provide education and support to families. This can be accomplished by sharing information, activities, and resources to help families make their own choices. You could also make referrals and linkages when necessary. For example, a family may need assistance from WIC or Supplemental Nutrition Assistance Program (SNAP) or they may need a list of food pantries close to where they live.

Collaboration with other professionals that visit the family may be essential. For example, as a home visitor you may emphasize that electronic tablets should not be used with children under the age of 18 months, unless for video chatting purposes, such as to skype with a grandparent (see American Academy of Pediatrics, 2016). The speech language pathologist, who also regularly visits the home, may use a tablet with the family to show them a card game that can be played to promote speech. It might be helpful for the home visitor to work with this helping professional and the family to emphasize how playing the actual card game in real form rather than electronically is age appropriate for the young child.

Familiarity with the Child and Adult Care Food Program (CACFP) guidelines is key to knowing what to prepare for families and for modeling healthy snacks for families. Specifically, how home visitors prepare snacks for Early Head Start socialization (or sometimes affectionately called play group) events will be guided by CACFP guidelines. In sum, two food groups should be prepared by home visitors at the site and provided for snack at socialization events.

FLE Content Area Knowledge and Knowledge of Health and Safety

Six FLE content areas and the most relevant guideline(s) within these content areas were selected through the process described in Appendix B as aligning with CUPID's HV expanded competency. The FLE content areas include: (1) Human growth and development, (2) Parenting education and guidance, (3) Families and individuals in societal contexts, (4) Human sexuality, (5) FLE methodology, and (6) Internal dynamics of families.

Next, we consider the topics from CUPID's HV expanded competency on health and safety as aligning with content guidelines within these FLE content areas. We start with a brief explanation of the gist of each FLE content area and then discuss the most relevant knowledge in this content area to the health and safety HV expanded competency by CUPID that was fully described at the start of this chapter. The readings featured in the tables in this section are either included in the "Resource List for the Certified Family Life Educator (CFLE Exam)" see NCFR (2015) or are chapters in Walcheski and Reinke's (2015) "Family Life Education: The Practice of Family Science."

Human growth and development across the lifespan. *Understanding of the developmental changes (both typical and atypical) of individuals and families across the lifespan with an emphasis on knowledge of developmental domains.*

Knowledge in human growth and development will equip home visitors with a variety of information. For example, home visitors will recognize typical (e.g., sore breasts) and atypical (e.g., substantial bleeding) experiences of pregnancy during each trimester. Hospitals tend to post checklists of typical versus atypical changes and encourage the pregnant woman to call if a change is a concern (e.g., Stanford Children's Health, 2018). Within this FLE content area, understanding typical prenatal development (i.e., conception to birth) is also important (see Table 8.1).

Knowledge that is germane to this content area also includes information about good diets during pregnancy, eliminating teratogens, milestones of pregnancy, the common signs of pregnancy complications, and general information on preparing for labor, delivery, and newborn care (Wasik & Bryant, 2001). Helping the expectant woman to be informed is a major part of your role, but an EHS home visitor is not a medical professional. Open-ended questions or checklists can help the home visitor understand what the expectant woman knows and can set the stage for ongoing discussions and for recommending medical assistance when needed.

The pregnant woman on your visit may be a teenage mother, first-time mother, or a seasoned mother. Understanding that a teenage mother has different experiences as a result of her age and stage compared to a woman in adulthood is essential. A home visit with a pregnant woman may include four

168 *Health and Safety*

Table 8.1 Family Life Education Concepts and Resources that Align with Health and Safety

FLE Content Area: Human Growth and Development	Resources
Prenatal/neonatal and home health; Health education Personal and family health[1]; health and wellness in infants and toddlers, including nutrition, malnutrition, health care and immunizations, sleeping, breastfeeding, and more; prenatal development and development in infants, toddlers, and in early childhood[2]	[1]Leventhal, J. (2015). Human growth and development across the lifespan. In M. J. Walcheski, & J. S. Reinke (Eds.), *Family life education: The practice of family science* (pp. 167–176). Minneapolis, MN: National Council on Family Relations. [2]Boyd, D., & Bee, H. (2015). *Lifespan development* (7th ed.). Upper Saddle River, NJ: Pearson.

or more people, including: pregnant woman, baby in utero, home visitor, and people from the woman's social support system (e.g., relative, partner, friend). As a home visitor you may have certainties and uncertainties around pregnancy and it is best to maintain a neutral stance with the mother and her unborn child that conveys mutual respect and understanding (see Minnesota Council on Family Relations, 2009). This will allow the mother to engage in education with you about topics within human growth and development, such as pregnancy and the prenatal period in a manner that encourages her to seek the answers and to form opinions for herself. It is important to not only understand the age of mother and expected developmental changes and milestones within her age and stage but also to understand the interdependent nature of developmental domains (cognitive, emotional, and physical). For example, breastfeeding can engage all of the infant's senses (physical and cognitive) and promote building a bond between infant and parent (emotional).

Information about a safe environment for the neonate, including breastfeeding and sleeping, is also crucial to this content area, particularly for content knowledge within the physical domain. See Table 8.1 for NCFR endorsed resources that explicitly target content in the CUPIDs Home Visitor Expansion of Competency.

Parenting education and guidance. *How parents teach, guide, and influence as the dynamic context of the parent–child relationship.*

It is important for the home visitor to be aware of research-based practices on topics related to prenatal/neonatal development, home health, health education, and others discussed in this chapter as home visitors work with parents to prepare them to parent an infant. The body of knowledge in this content area should include evidence on health and safety practices within the goals of the family, their parental skills, and their preferences for care

(Middlemiss & Seddio, 2017). For example, existing studies, including a meta-analysis, reveal that pacifier use at bedtime and naptime can be protective against SIDS (AAP Task Force on Sudden Infant Death Syndrome, 2016). Mothers selecting this sleep practice should be informed that they are engaging in a research-based practice. The home visitor should find out what the family does at home regarding sleep practices and should share information about the research-based sleep practices that are safe and healthy so that parents are informed when making decisions (Middlemiss & Seddio, 2017). Parents of infants have concerns related to basic issues of protection and caregiving (Jacobson, 2015). The subject matter in this content area is designed to promote strong, healthy families.

Home visitors may be engaged in working with families in the nascent stages of family development (see Duvall & Miller, 1985). Parents as Teachers (PAT) is an evidence-based curriculum that has the goal of promoting parent knowledge of child development and encouraging positive parenting practices in childbearing families (Parents as Teachers National Center, 2018). Foundational visits in PAT address health and safety, which may be useful for novice home visitors. Nonetheless, PAT may not be enough to equip home visitors with the knowledge base to effectively address a wide range of family needs and strengths beyond the parent–child interaction (Walsh, Mortensen, Edwards, & Cassidy, in press). EHS HVs need to understand how to work with the entire family and this needs to be considered when planning visits. A skilled professional may set the stage for parents to find mentors in extended family members who can provide guidance on nurturing and protecting infants and young children. See Table 8.2 for NCFR-endorsed resources that explicitly target content in the CUPIDs Home Visitor Expansion of Competency.

Table 8.2 Family Life Education Concepts and Resources that Align with Health and Safety

FLE Content Area: Parenting Education and Guidance	Resources
Prenatal/neonatal and home health; Health education Demonstrate safety, health, and the feeding of children[1]; healthy lifestyles, safety, eating, ways to prevent accidents and injuries, sleep[2]	[1]Jacobson, A. L. (2015). Parenting education and guidance. In M. J. Walcheski, & J. S. Reinke (Eds.), *Family life education: The practice of family science* (pp. 213–222). Minneapolis, MN: National Council on Family Relations.
	[2]Brooks, J. B. (2013). *The process of parenting* (9th ed.). New York: McGraw Hill.

170　*Health and Safety*

Families and individuals in societal contexts. *Understand families in regard to other institutions (e.g., health care).*

Subject matter in this content area requires the professional to understand a variety of contexts and their interactions with families. For a family in poverty, a father's positive engagement in the child's development is a protective factor for the child's social-emotional development (Lee & Schoppe-Sullivan, 2017). When the father does not live with the child, this may present additional challenges to promoting the child's positive social-emotional development. When families face challenges, it is important to simultaneously consider the family itself and its interaction with social systems (Wadsworth, Roy, & Watkins, 2015). See Chapter 3 for information on contexts and on Bronfenbrenner's bioecological model.

It is important to identify and describe resources within the community that support children and families in poverty, such as resources to support maternal health. Knowledge of these resources is important because "home visiting is often thought of as a key entry point into a system of care" (Goldberg, Winestone, Fauth, Colon, & Mingo, 2018, p. 22). Home visitors can help families meet the challenges of applying for services, such as maternal health, housing, food/nutrition, behavioral health, and others (Goldberg et al., 2018). Home visitors can provide referrals to the aforementioned services and act as important conduits between families and other systems. One study found that approximately 20% of home visitor referrals resulted in an actual service connection (Goldberg et al., 2018) suggesting that service system coordination and referrals is an area that warrants further attention. Perhaps key to this area is promoting the flexibility of service institutions to meet the needs of families in the twenty-first century (Wadsworth et al., 2015).

See Table 8.3 for NCFR-endorsed resources that explicitly target content in the CUPIDs Home Visitor Expansion of Competency.

Table 8.3 Families And Individuals In Societal Contexts Concepts and Resources that Align with Health And Safety

FLE Content Area: Families and Individuals in Societal Contexts	Resources
Prenatal/neonatal and home health; Health education Understand how to nurture family members[1]; parenting and child rearing[2]	[1]Wadsworth, S. M. M., Roy, K. M., & Watkins, N. (2015). Families and individuals in societal contexts. In M. J. Walcheski & J. S. Reinke (Eds.), *Family life education: The practice of family science* (pp. 147–155).

(Continued)

Health and Safety 171

Table 8.3 (Cont.)

FLE Content Area: Families and Individuals in Societal Contexts	Resources
	Minneapolis, MN: National Council on Family Relations.
	[2]Olson, D. H., DeFrain, J., & Skogrand, L. (2014). *Marriages and families: Intimacy, diversity, and strengths* (8th ed.). New York: McGraw Hill.

Human sexuality. *Understanding of the physiological, psychological, and social aspects of sexual development across the lifespan, so as to achieve healthy sexual adjustment.*

This chapter focuses on health and safety and human sexuality is important to parents' health and wellbeing. The model of sexuality includes the influences of time (personal and historical), culture, gender, cognitive, psychological and physiological processes on health and wellbeing (Darling & Cassidy, 2014; Darling & Howard, 2015). This model can assist professionals in understanding sexuality. Health and wellbeing can include physical health, such as reproductive health, STIs, sexual functioning, and infertility (Darling & Howard, 2015). Psychological and emotional health are related to pleasure in sexuality and also issues, such as those that result from abusive or controlling relationships, trauma, violence, or fear (Hock, 2017; as cited in Darling & Howard, 2015). Along this line, home visitors should be aware of risks that jeopardize the health and wellbeing within the family system, such as intimate partner violence (IPV). The goal is to prevent IPV by promoting healthy and nonviolent relationships using strategies such as skill-building (Centers for Disease Control and Prevention, 2018b).

See Table 8.4 for NCFR-endorsed resources that explicitly target content in the CUPIDs Home Visitor Expansion of Competency.

Table 8.4 Family Life Education Concepts and Resources that Align with Health and Safety

FLE Content Area: Human Sexuality	Resources
Prenatal/neonatal and home health; Health education Health[1]; well-being[1]; sexual health[1]; physical health[1]; psychological/emotional health[1]; prevent	[1]Darling, C. A., & Howard, S. (2015). Human sexuality across the lifespan. In M. J. Walcheski, & J. S. Reinke (Eds.), *Family life education: The practice of family*

(Continued)

172 *Health and Safety*

Table 8.4 (Cont.)

FLE Content Area: Human Sexuality	Resources
sexual abuse[1]; reproductive health[1]; healthy practices[2]; prenatal period[2]; breastfeeding[2]; infants[2]	*science* (pp. 177–188). Minneapolis, MN: National Council on Family Relations. [2]Hyde, J. S., & Delamater, J. D. (2017). *Understanding human sexuality* (13th ed.). New York: McGraw Hill.

FLE methodology. *Understanding of FLE principles in tandem with planning and delivery of programs.*

There are several ways that FLE methodology aligns with the CUPID HV competency of health and safety. As explained in Chapter 3, there are four foundational principles of FLE, which are: prevention, education, a strengths-based approach, and a foundation in research and theory (see Darling, Cassidy, & Rehm, 2017). A strengths-based approach, for example, means that professionals work with and for families to minimize risk by cultivating strengths and supports within the family (Darling et al., 2017; Duncan & Goddard, 2017). FLE methodology, particularly the principle of a strengths-based approach reinforces *being with* the family (Petkus, 2015). Home visitors can use active questioning, coaching, narrating, observing, scaffolding, and other FLE techniques to promote families' active engagement in creating a healthy and safe environment for their children.

Also recall that there are four operational principles of FLE: culture, context, content, and practice (see Darling et al., 2017). Education and support of health and safety topics, such as nutrition, is important to the work of home visitors. It is important to teach about serving size, food groups, and exercise, and it is equally important to provide information and resources in an individualized manner to families to help them make their own choices. While many families in EHS may experience food insufficiency and need referrals to WIC and SNAP programs, it will be important to consider Darling et al.'s (2017) operational principles, such as culture and context, that undergird planning for and working with families. It may be helpful to find out the meanings and associations families have with food as well as how the family influences eating habits, and to ask questions to explore linkages between food and the family's cultural identity (Martinez, 2018). It is important to learn about meanings the family has around food and also what cooking is like for them (Walsh, 2017b). Practice *being with* the family as they prepare a meal in which the ingredients were purchased via food stamps. Once they meet the goal of cooking healthy meals, the family and home visitor could work together to generate other healthy meal ideas using the family's

Table 8.5 Family Life Education Concepts and Resources that Align with Health and Safety

FLE Content Area: FLE Methodology	Resources
Prenatal/neonatal and home health; health education Primary, secondary, and tertiary prevention[1,2]; health[1,2]; health care[1,2]; parenting education[1,2]	[1]Darling, C. A., & Cassidy, D. (2014). *Family life education: Working with families across the lifespan* (3rd ed.). Long Grove, IL: Waveland.
	[2]Duncan, S. F., & Goddard, H. W. (2017). *Family life education: Principles and practices for effective outreach* (3rd ed.). Thousand Oaks, CA: Sage.

available resources. When HV program goals align with families' strengths, wants, and needs, families are predicted to be engaged in the program and to remain in it (Osborne & Bobbitt, 2017).

See Table 8.5 for NCFR-endorsed resources that explicitly target content in the CUPIDs Home Visitor Expansion of Competency.

Internal dynamics of families. *Understanding of family strengths and weaknesses and how family members relate to each other.*

This content area encourages home visitors to consider families' health practices within the context of the family system and to promote family decision-making and goal-setting within this system. For example, a mother may engage in co-sleeping with her infant due to marital distress and spending time asleep with the infant may assuage a lack of intimacy with the mother's partner (Teti, 2017). Home visitors should equip families with information about healthy sleep practices. For instance, families are advised that infants sleep in the parents' room but on a separate surface designed for infants for at least the first six months (AAP Task Force on Sudden Infant Death Syndrome, 2016). While the mother may insist that bed sharing between mother and infant produces good sleep for the mother and the infant, a look at the family as a system may reveal that the mother's partner reports sleep deprivation because of this situation. It will be helpful for the adults in the family to talk about reducing stressors and to discuss their challenges. A home visitor could make a referral to a therapist and encourage the family to reach out to supportive family or fictive kin in their system for further support to find a solution that works for the whole family (Rodrigues, 2017). Home visitors can provide information about the risks of adults sleeping in the same bed as infants, such as suffocation, strangulation, and entrapment (AAP Task Force on Sudden Infant Death Syndrome, 2016). Home visitors can help the families make decisions and set goals about healthy sleep practices with the family system in mind. Home visitors can see Table 8.6 for NCFR-endorsed resources that explicitly target content in CUPIDs Home Visitor Expansion of Competency.

174   *Health and Safety*

Table 8.6 Family Life Education Concepts and Resources that Align with Health and
Safety

FLE Content Area: Internal Dynamics of Families	Resources
Prenatal/neonatal and home health; Health education Define individual and family roles[1]; understand responsibilities, rights, interdependence of family members[1]; consider family history[1]; parenting and child rearing[2]	[1]Reinke, J. S., & Walcheski, M. J. (2015). Internal dynamics of families. In M. J. Walcheski, & J. S. Reinke (Eds.), *Family life education: The practice of family science* (pp. 157–166). Minneapolis, MN: National Council on Family Relations.
	[2]Olson, D. H., DeFrain, J., & Skogrand, L. (2014). *Marriages and families: Intimacy, diversity, and strengths* (8th ed.). New York: McGraw Hill.

Skills

According to CUPID's Home Visitor Expansion of Competency, home visitors should have the following skills for supporting the health and safety of families:

> Skills to adapt health information for families who vary in practices, beliefs, and values and to effectively help parents understand and use reliable information to make decisions about healthy behaviors, modeling may be inappropriate.
>
> (CUPID, 2017)

As established at the start of this chapter, the FLE Content Areas that are most germane to this expanded competency for home visitors include: (a) Human growth and development, (b) Parenting education and guidance, (c) Families and individuals in societal contexts, (d) Human sexuality, (e) FLE methodology, and (f) Internal dynamics of families. These FLE Content Areas include tasks that should be done when planning for and working with families. Skills require taking the knowledge addressed in the first section of this chapter and applying it to practice.

FLE Practice within the Content Areas and EHS HV

Human Growth and Development

- Recognize the impact of individual health and wellness on families

This may include efforts to support individual health and wellness within the family:

Health and Safety 175

- Help parents be responsive to their infants and young children.
- Support parents in recognizing typical development and other concerns.
- Support parents in reducing exposure to negative stress.
- Set goals around attendance and completion of tasks related to well child visits.
- Support parents with safe sleep practices.
- Provide parents with resources on car seat safety and follow-up with parents.
- Support parents in household safety with an emphasis on prevention.
- Support parents with breastfeeding and transitions to solid foods at six months.
- Support parents with efforts to promote parental and child oral health.
- Collaborate with families to report abuse or related issues to CPS.
- Support parents in making safe choices compared to unsafe choices (e.g., work with parents to make sure they understand teratogens and how to avoid them during pregnancy).

- Guide practice using developmental theories

  This may include:

  - Encourage breastfeeding to support that babies will trust that their needs will be met (Erikson's psychosocial theory).
  - Encourage positive health and safety efforts to help infants trust that others care for them (Erikson's psychosocial theory).
  - Encourage parents to stay in close proximity to the infants/young children during immunizations to prevent white coat syndrome (Pavlov's classical conditioning).
  - When appropriate, bring additional experts (e.g., therapist, nutritionist) to the home visit to promote observation and imitation (Bandura's social learning theory).
  - Support parents in engaging their infant's senses (e.g., breastfeeding engages all of the senses) (Piaget's cognitive development theory).
  - Facilitate parents' learning of skills and knowledge that they are close to learning but that they need the home visitor's help to master (e.g., the use of a breast pump) (Vygotsky's sociocultural theory).
  - Brainstorm with the parents ways that they can support the infant's health and safety as part of a hierarchy: first their physiological needs (e.g., food), then their safety and security needs (e.g., being protected), and then their love and belonging needs (e.g., loved as part of a family) (Maslow's hierarchy of needs).

- Recognize socio-ecological influences on human development (e.g., trauma)

176 *Health and Safety*

This may include:

- o Recognizing when trauma incurred by a family may result in secondary trauma for the home visitor and seeking support when necessary
- o Support parents in connecting with friends, extended family, community members, or similar for parenting support for health and safety issues
- o Support parents in seeking medical and other attention for their family when needed
- o Support parents in forming positive relationships with their infant to mitigate the child's stress

Parenting Education and Guidance

- Promote healthy parenting from a child's and parent's developmental perspective Practices within this FLE guideline may include:
  - o Support families' goal setting and follow up with families.
  - o Consider the environment from the child's perspective (e.g., get at their eye level) and create a healthy home from that perspective.
  - o Redirect the child to the parent to promote a healthy parent–child relationship.
- Recognize various parenting roles and their impacts on families
  - o Engage the father in the home visit and socialization events.
- Recognize the impact of societal trends and cultural differences
  - o Support parents in identifying positive and negative contexts and cultures that influence the family.

Families and Individuals in Societal Contexts

- Identify the influence of local and global systems on individuals and families
  - o Support families in identifying systemic supports and barriers.
  - o Work with families to determine whether systems are meeting their goals and needs.
- Identify factors that influence individuals and families from contemporary and historical perspectives
  - o Discuss inequities that may persist across generations.
- Identify social and cultural influences on family composition and family life
  - o Support parents in exploring adverse childhood experiences and toxic stress that they experienced as a child and how to minimize ACEs and toxic stress for their own children.

Recognize reciprocal interactions between individuals, families, and systems

- Encourage parents to form healthy relationships within their families that emphasize routines.
- Encourage parents to form positive connections at family socialization and parent education events within EHS.
- Discuss with parents whether services within EHS and within the community are meeting their needs and strengths.

Assess the impact of demographics (e.g., class) on families

- Discuss poverty and support parents by providing education and information to support their job, home, and financial aspirations.

Human Sexuality

HV practice within this FLE practice guideline may include:

- Recognize the biological aspects of human sexuality (e.g., sexual functioning, reproductive health, family planning, sexually transmitted infections)

  - Support families in spacing pregnancies.
  - Support mothers' knowledge and practice of breastfeeding and the benefit of partial contraception.
  - Support families in understanding types of contraception.

- Address human sexuality from positions respectful of values

  - Support the family in using refusal skills in problematic situations that potentially harm the health and safety of the family (e.g., drugs/alcohol; situations that require pressure, such as a pregnant woman refusing to have sex without a condom).
  - Support screening and referral for intimate partner violence; support the formation of a safety plan.
  - Support the initial emotions that are associated with sexuality (e.g., teen parent) and link family to more comprehensive emotional services (e.g., therapist).

FLE Methodology

HV practice within this FLE practice guideline may include:

- Employ strategies to meet the needs of different audiences

  - Use strategies, such as coaching, narrating, and observing to understand families in order to provide them with information to make decisions.

178   *Health and Safety*

- ○ Actively engage in cultural practices that are important to home (e.g., taking shoes off at door).

- Employ techniques to help the learner do hands-on learning

  - ○ Work with the family to incorporate exercise into their routines.
  - ○ Support family in creating healthy home spaces by observing families engage in healthy practices.
  - ○ Engage in a cooking or nutrition activity during the home visit in consideration of nutritional recommendations for young children.

- Demonstrate sensitivity to diversity

  - ○ Ask parents about their way of life and how they like to live it at home.
  - ○ Understand one's own culture and tendencies.
  - ○ Support families by being *with them* to be flexible and responsive to all families.

- Develop culturally competent materials and experiences

  - ○ Collaborate with a translator or other resource when necessary.
  - ○ Use audio-visual materials for families with low literacy.
  - ○ Embrace materials in the home rather than bringing special toys and materials into the home for one hour and 30 minutes.

- Implement adult education principles in work with individuals, parents, and families; Create learning environments that support individual differences

  - ○ Plan home visits with principles of pedagogy and andragogy in mind that address individual styles and needs.
  - ○ Utilize a variety of FLE techniques (e.g., coaching) when working with families.

Internal Dynamics of Families

- Recognize and define healthy and unhealthy characteristics pertaining to family relationships and family development

  - ○ Promote families' strengths by providing meaningful educational experiences for families.
  - ○ Discuss healthy and unhealthy family functioning with families and encourage families to identify and discuss these characteristics and how they affect the family.
  - ○ Engage fathers (resident and nonresident when applicable) in home visits.

- Analyze family dynamics in response to stress, crises, and trauma

  - ○ Assist families with realizing the strengths they have to prevent crises.
  - ○ Assist families with access to services.

Develop, recognize, and reinforce strategies that help families function effectively

- Promote healthy communication and relationships skills in families.
- Work with families to set goals.

Box 8.1 CDA Home Visitor Competencies

The CDA Competency Standards are national standards for home visitors. The subject area that is most relevant to this chapter includes **CDA Subject Area 1: Promoting health and safety in the home environment**. Each standard comprises competency goals, functional areas, items, indicators, and examples. The competency goal that is most relevant to this chapter is "To establish and maintain a safe, healthy learning environment" and includes three functional areas: "safe," "healthy," and "learning environment" (Council for Professional Recognition, 2016, p. 40).

Competency Goal	Functional Area	Example Item	Example Indicator
III. To establish and maintain a safe healthy learning environment.	**1 Safe:** Home visitor helps parents provide a safe environment to prevent and reduce injuries.	**Item 1.1:** Home environments (indoor and outdoor) are safe for all children and adults.	Materials, toys, equipment and environments are safe.

Permission to reprint from the Council for Professional Recognition.

Box 8.2 National Family Support Competency Framework for Family Support Professionals

The National Family Support Competency Framework for Family Support Professionals are competencies that include ten domains that are further clarified by dimensions (Institute for the Advancement of Family Support Professionals, 2018). There are two domains that are relevant to this chapter, these are: (a) Child Health, Safety, and Nutrition, and (b) Family Health, Safety, and Nutrition. Child Health, Safety, and Nutrition includes five dimensions: infant mental health, child health and wellness, safe environments for young children, child nutrition, and child abuse, neglect, and maltreatment. Family Health, Safety, and Nutrition includes five

180 Health and Safety

dimensions: maternal health, mental health, physical health, environmental safety, and intimate partner violence.

Domain 2	Dimension 8	Component a.	Levels of Competency
Child Health, Safety, and Nutrition	**Safe environments for young children**	**Safe sleeping**	**1-Recognizing**. Understands common risk factors for SIDS and safe sleeping environments for infants
			3-Applying. Supports parents' understanding of "tummy to play and back to sleep" and emphasizes the importance of always placing infant to sleep on their backs
			5-Extending. Coaches parents to observe infant's sleep environment and facilitates access to a crib, bassinet, or portable play area with no toys or loose bedding

Domain 5	Dimension 17	Component e.	Levels of Competency
Family Health, Safety, and Nutrition	**Maternal health**	**Pregnancy risk factors**	**1-Recognizing**. Understands key risk factors in pregnancy, including high blood pressure, pre-eclampsia, substance use, and poor nutrition
			3-Applying. Supports parents' understanding of how these risk factors impact mother's health and the developing fetus
			5-Extending. Coaches parents to facilitate access to prenatal care in the community and follows up on completion of recommended care

Permission to reprint from the Institute for the Advancement of Family Support Professionals.

Attitudes

CUPIDs Home Visitor Expansion of Competency: Attitudes that respect personal beliefs and variations in cultural practices and health values.

Principles of FLE that align with CUPID attitudes. "Family life education should present and respect differing family values" (Arcus, Schvaneveldt, & Moss, 1993, p. 19). In the twenty-first century, the FLE operational principle of culture encompasses an ethno-relative approach to working with families (Darling et al., 2017). In other words, differences among families are viewed as differences through a non-judgmental framework and addressing the needs of the audience (regardless of differences) is paramount (Darling et al., 2017).

Virtues of FLE are also germane to this attitude. For example, one virtue is caring, or "a disposition to enhance the welfare of family members as agents in their own lives" (MNCFR, 2015, p. 304). This disposition sets the stage for families to engage in ethical practice when supporting families with their health and safety needs and strengths. Ethical issues can be guided through a series of steps (see MNCFR, 2016) for family life educators (Palm, 2018).

There were six FLE content areas addressed in this chapter:

- Human growth and development,
- Parenting education and guidance,
- Families and individuals in societal contexts,
- Human sexuality,
- FLE methodology, and
- Internal dynamics of families.

Family life educators practicing within EHS HV should adopt the principles, virtues, and relational ethics that are inherent within these content areas. Collectively, these four FLE sources (principles, virtues, relational ethics, and the understanding and practice of content areas) work to align with CUPIDs emphasis on respecting families' beliefs and differences in cultural practices and values germane to health and safety.

As we have seen, health and safety encompasses a myriad of topics. It is important to keep in mind issues that are within and beyond the scope of home visitors. For example, a parent with mental health issues that presents as anxious and unstable is beyond the scope of a home visitor. It will be important to work with a supervisor and team to identify possible solutions (Palm, Cooke, & Alden, 2019).

Summary

In this chapter, we have focused on various aspects of health and safety, including prenatal and neonatal health, breastfeeding, infant sleeping, SIDS,

182 Health and Safety

care of sick infant/child, household safety, healthy practices (e.g., home visitor personal safety), home first-aid, and health education. CUPID's home visitor expansion of competency on health and safety stems from their supporting development and learning competency. The knowledge, skills, and attitudes germane to health and safety align with six FLE content areas: human growth and development, parenting education and guidance, families and individuals in societal contexts, human sexuality, FLE methodology, and internal dynamics of families.

Key Concepts

- Adverse Childhood Experiences
- Breastfeeding
- Certified lactation educators
- Child and Adult Care Food Program
- Child Protective Services
- Communicable diseases
- Co-sleeping
- Household safety checklist
- Strengths-based approach
- Sudden Infant Death Syndrome
- Toxic stress

Recommended Reading

National Association for the Education of Young Children. (2004). Resources on health and safety for early childhood educators. *Young Children, 59*, 64–66.

Paradis, H. A., Belknap, A., O'Neill, K. M. G., Baggett, S., & Minkovitz, C. S. (2018). Coordination of early childhood home visiting and health care providers. *Children and Youth Services Review, 85*, 202–210. doi: 10.1016/j.childyouth.2017.12.029

References

AAP Task Force on Sudden Infant Death Syndrome. (2016). SIDS and other sleep-related infant deaths: Updated 2016 recommendations for a safe infant sleeping environment. *Pediatrics, 138*, 1–12. doi: 10.1542/peds.2016-2938

Ainsworth, M. D. S., Blehar, M., Waters, E., & Wall, S. (1978). *Patterns of attachment: A psychological study of the strange situation.* Hillsdale, NJ: Erlbaum.

American Academy of Pediatrics. (2012). Policy statement: Breastfeeding and the use of human milk. *Pediatrics, 129*, 827–841. doi: 10.1542/peds.2011-3552.

American Academy of Pediatrics. (2016). American Academy of Pediatrics announces new recommendations for children's media use. Retrieved https://www.aap.org /en-us/about-the-aap/aap-press-room/Pages/American-Academy-of-Pediatrics-Announces-New-Recommendations-for-Childrens-Media-Use.aspx

American Academy of Pediatrics. (2017). AAP schedule of well-child care visits. Retrieved https://www.healthychildren.org/English/family-life/health-management /Pages/Well-Child-Care-A-Check-Up-for-Success.aspx

American Academy of Pediatrics. (2018a). Breastfeeding. Retrieved https://www .aap.org/en-us/advocacy-and-policy/aap-health-initiatives/Breastfeeding/Pages/Bene fits-of-Breastfeeding.aspx

American Academy of Pediatrics. (2018b). Infant food and feeding. Retrieved https:// www.aap.org/en-us/advocacy-and-policy/aap-health-initiatives/HALF-Implementa tion-Guide/Age-Specific-Content/Pages/Infant-Food-and-Feeding.aspx/

Arcus, M. E., Schvaneveldt, J. D., & Moss, J. J. (1993). The nature of family life education. In M. E. Arcus, J. D. Schvaneveldt, & J. J. Moss (Eds.), *Handbook of family life education: Foundations of family life education* (pp. 1–25). Newbury Park, CA: Sage.

Boyd, D., & Bee, H. (2015). *Lifespan development* (7th ed.). Upper Saddle River, NJ: Pearson.

Brooks, J. B. (2013). *The process of parenting* (9th ed.). New York: McGraw Hill.

Casamassimo, P., & Holt, K. (2016). *Bright futures: Oral health—Pocket guide* (3rd ed.). Washington, DC: National Maternal and Child Oral Health Resource Center.

Centers for Disease Control and Prevention. (2018a). Immunization schedule for infants and children (birth through 6 years). Retrieved https://www.cdc.gov/vac cines/schedules/easy-to-read/child.html

Centers for Disease Control and Prevention. (2018b). Preventing intimate partner violence. Retrieved https://www.cdc.gov/violenceprevention/pdf/ipv-factsheet.pdf

Collaborative for Understanding the Pedagogy of Infant/toddler Development (CUPID). (2017). *Comprehensive competencies for educators of infants and toddlers in group care and home visiting settings*. Unpublished.

Council for Professional Recognition. (2016). *The Child Development Associate® National Credentialing Program and CDA® competency standards: Home visitor edition*. Washington, DC: Council for Professional Recognition.

Darling, C. A., & Cassidy, D. (2014). *Family life education: Working with families across the lifespan* (3rd ed.). Long Grove, IL: Waveland.

Darling, C. A., Cassidy, D., & Rehm, M. (2017). Family life education: Translational family science in action. *Family Relations, 66*, 741–752. doi: 10.1111/fare.12286

Darling, C. A., & Howard, S. (2015). Human sexuality across the lifespan. In M. J. Walcheski, & J. S. Reinke (Eds.), *Family life education: The practice of family science* (pp. 177–188). Minneapolis, MN: National Council on Family Relations.

Duncan, S. F., & Goddard, H. W. (2017). *Family life education: Principles and practices for effective outreach* (3rd ed.). Thousand Oaks, CA: Sage.

Duvall, E. M., & Miller, B. C. (1985). *Marriage and family development* (6th ed.). New York: Harper & Row.

Felitti, V. J., Anda, R. F., Norsenberg, D., Williamson, D., Spitz, A., Edwards, V., Koss, M., & Marks, J. (1998). Relationship of childhood abuse and household dysfunction to many of the leading causes of death in adults. The adverse childhood experiences (ACE) study. *American Journal of Preventive Medicine, 14*, 245–258.

Goldberg, J., Winestone, J. G., Fauth, R., Colón, M., & Mingo, M. V. (2018). Getting to the warm hand-off: A study of home visitor referral activates. *Maternal and Child Health Journal, 22*, 22–32. doi: 10.1007/s10995-018-2529-7

Hyde, J. S., & Delamater, J. D. (2017). *Understanding human sexuality* (13th ed.). New York: McGraw Hill.

Institute for the Advancement of Family Support Professionals. (2018). *National family support competency framework for family support professionals.* Retrieved from: https://cppr-institute-prod.s3.amazonaws.com/modules/Approved%20National%20Family%20Support%20Competency%20Framework_FINAL_7_18_2018.pdf.

Jacobson, A. L. (2015). Parenting education and guidance. In M. J. Walcheski, & J. S. Reinke (Eds.), *Family life education: The practice of family science* (pp. 213–222). Minneapolis, MN: National Council on Family Relations.

Landry, S. H., Smith, K. E., & Swank, P. R. (2006). Responsive parenting: Establishing early foundations for social, communication, and independent problem-solving skills. *Developmental Psychology, 42,* 627–642. doi: 10.1037/0012-1649.42.4.627

Lee, J. K., & Schoppe-Sullivan, S. J. (2017). Resident fathers' positive engagement, family poverty, and change in child behavior problems. *Family Relations, 66,* 484–496. doi: 10.1111/fare.12283

Leventhal, J. (2015). Human growth and development across the lifespan. In M. J. Walcheski, & J. S. Reinke (Eds.), *Family life education: The practice of family science* (pp. 167–176). Minneapolis, MN: National Council on Family Relations.

Martinez, K. (2018). Families and food: An extension perspective. *CFLE Network, 31*(2), 10–11.

Mian, M., Shah, J., Dalpiaz, A., Schwamb, R., Miao, Y., Warren, K., & Khan, S. (2015). Shaken Baby Syndrome: A review. *Fetal and Pediatric Pathology, 34,* 169–175. doi: 10.3109/15513815.2014.999394

Middlemiss, W., & Seddio, K. (2017). Empowerment and knowledge: Guiding parents in creating healthy infant sleep routines. *National Council on Family Relations Family Focus, 72,* 13–14.

Minnesota Council on Family Relations (MNCFR). (2009). Ethical thinking and practice for parent and family life educators. In D. Bredehoft & M. Walcheski (Eds.), *Family life education: Integrating theory and practice* (pp. 233–239). Minneapolis, MN: National Council on Family Relations.

Minnesota Council on Family Relations (MNCFR). (2015). Ethical thinking and practice for parent and family life educators. In M. J. Walcheski, & J. S. Reinke (Eds.), *Family life education: The practice of family science* (pp. 303–309). Minneapolis, MN: National Council on Family Relations.

Minnesota Council on Family Relations (MNCFR). (2016). Ethical thinking and practice for parent and family life education. Minneapolis, MN: Ethics Committee, Parent and Family Education Section. Retrieved from https://mn.ncfr.org/resources/

National Council on Family Relations (NCFR). (2015). *Resource list for the Certified Family Life Educator (CFLE) Exam.* Retrieved from https://www.ncfr.org/sites/default/files/2017-01/2015_cfle_exam_resources.pdf

Olson, D. H., DeFrain, J., & Skogrand, L. (2014). *Marriages and families: Intimacy, diversity, and strengths* (8th ed.). New York: McGraw Hill.

Opdal, S. H., & Rognum, T. O. (2004). The Sudden Infant Death Syndrome gene: Does it exist?. *Pediatrics, 114,* 506–512. doi: 10.1542/peds.2004-0683

Osborne, C., & Bobbitt, K. (2017, April). *Risk and retention in home visiting: Lessons from Texas*. Poster session at the meeting for the Society for Research in Child Development, Austin, TX.

Palm, G. F. (2018). Professional ethics and practice in family life education. In *Tools for ethical thinking and practice in family life education* (4th ed., pp. 1–10). Minneapolis, MN: National Council on Family Relations.

Palm, G., Cooke, B., & Alden, A. (2019). Case study: Parent with mental health issues. *CFLE Network, 32*, 25–27.

Parents as Teachers National Center. (2018). Evidence-based model. Retrieved from https://parentsasteachers.org/evidence-based-model/

Petkus, J. (2015). A first-hand account of implementing a Family Life Education model: Intentionality in Head Start home visiting. In M. J. Walcheski, & J. S. Reinke (Eds.), *Family life education: The practice of family science* (pp. 325–331). Minneapolis, MN: National Council on Family Relations.

Reyes-Vargas, M., Selby, J., & Walsh, B. A. (2019, January). *Home visiting for justice system involved parents*. The Ounce's National Home Visiting Summit, Washington, DC.

Rodrigues, N. D. (2017). Parents, children, and sleep deprivation. *National Council on Family Relations Family Focus, 72*, 22–24.

Roggman, L. A., Peterson, C. A., Chazan-Cohen, R., Ispa, J., Decker, K. B., Hughes-Belding, K., Cook, G. A., & Vallotton, C. D. (2016). Preparing home visitors to partner with families of infants and toddlers, *Journal of Early Childhood Teacher Education, 37*, 301–313.

Shonkoff, J. P., Garner, A. S., & The Committee on Psychosocial Aspects of Child and Family Health, Committee on Early Childhood Adoption, and Dependent Care, and Section on Developmental and Behavioral Pediatrics, Siegel, B. S., Dobbins, M. I., Earls, M. F., Garner, A. S., McGuinn, L., Pascoe, J., & Wood, D. L. (2012). The lifelong effects of early childhood adversity and toxic stress. *Pediatrics, 129*, 232–246. doi: 10.1542/peds.2011-2663

Stanford Children's Health. (2018). Pregnancy: What's normal … and what's not. Retrieved from http://www.stanfordchildrens.org/en/topic/default?id=pregnancy-whats-normal-and-whats-not-1-4076

Teti, D. M. (2017). Infant sleep arrangements and the family system. *National Council on Family Relations Family Focus, 72*, 8–9.

The Urban Child Institute. (2018). Baby's brain begins now: Conception to age 3. Retrieved from http://www.urbanchildinstitute.org/why-0-3/baby-and-brain

U.S. Department of Health and Human Services. (n.d.). Key moments in safe to sleep © history: 1994–2003. Retrieved from https://www1.nichd.nih.gov/sts/campaign/moments/Pages/1994-2003.aspx

Wadsworth, S. M. M., Roy, K. M., & Watkins, N. (2015). Families and individuals in societal contexts. In M. J. Walcheski & J. S. Reinke (Eds.), *Family life education: The practice of family science* (pp. 147–155). Minneapolis, MN: National Council on Family Relations.

Walcheski, M. J., & Reinke, J. S. (2015). *Family life education: The practice of family science*. Minneapolis, MN: National Council on Family Relations.

186 Health and Safety

Walsh, B. A. (2017a). Calling an ACE an ACE: Integrating prevention efforts. *CFLE Network, 29.3*, 12–14.

Walsh, B. A. (2017b). Setting the stage for families in poverty as catalysts: A family life education approach to Early Head Start Home Visiting. *Family Focus, 73*, 8–10.

Walsh, B. A., Mortensen, J. A., Edwards, A. L., & Cassidy, D. (in press). The practice of family life education within Early Head Start home visiting. *Family Relations.*

Wasik, B. H., & Bryant, D. M. (2001). *Home visiting: Procedures for helping families* (2nd ed.). Thousand Oaks, CA: Sage.

9   Observing Behavior, Development, and Environments

Observation and assessment provide vital information to home visitors about parents, children, and family life, as well as guide home visiting practices. Informal observations are useful, but home visitors also need systematic, unbiased, and valid formal assessments. According to the Head Start Act (ACF, 2007), EHS-HBO programs must

> (1) provide, either directly or through referral, early, continuous, intensive, and comprehensive child development and family support services that will enhance the physical, social, emotional, and intellectual development of participating children; (6) ensure that children with documented behavioral problems, including problems involving behavior related to prior or existing trauma, receive appropriate screening and referral.
>
> (Sec. 645A. [42 U.S.C. 9840A])

In addition to the program requirements for monitoring child development and behavior, home visitors need expanded knowledge in assessing parenting and the home environment. The CUPID competency for **Observing Behavior, Development and Environments** is as follows (CUPID, 2017; Roggman et al., 2016):

Competency	Observing and assessing children and families in order to adapt and individualize goals and practices, including supporting children's unique needs and cultural identities
Knowledge	Expanded knowledge of assessment of parenting and the quality of the home environment
Skills	Skills for helping parents assess child development; assessing home visiting practices and processes; and, assessing the program's learning environment for parents
Attitudes	Attitudes that support assessment as a collaborative process for positive purposes and respect parents' expertise on the child

For full alignment see Appendix B.

Behavior, Development, and Environments

The FLE Content Areas that extend this competency include:

Human growth and development	Understand the developmental changes (both typical and atypical) of individuals in families across the lifespan with an emphasis on knowledge of developmental domains
Parenting education and guidance	How parents teach, guide, and influence as the dynamic context of the parent–child relationship
Families and individuals in societal contexts	Understand families in regard to other institutions (e.g., healthcare)
FLE methodology	Understand principles of FLE in tandem with planning and delivery of programs
Internal dynamics of families	Understanding of family strengths and weaknesses and how family members relate to each other

Note: Permission to reprint was granted from the National Council on Family Relations.

Knowledge

Expanded knowledge for the home visitor related to observing behavior development and environments is stated as:

> Expanded knowledge of assessment of parenting and the quality of the home environment.
>
> (CUPID, 2017)

Even though much of the formal assessment in EHS-HBO is focused on child outcomes, a major premise of EHS-HBO (and most home visiting models) is that child development is improved by supporting healthy parenting practices and creating a supportive home environment (Korfmacher et al., 2008; Heaman et al., 2007; Roggman et al., 2016). This recognizes that although the home visitor can work one-on-one with the child to improve outcomes, results may be fleeting without sustained support from parenting and the home. As such, home visitors must be tuned in to observe and assess these aspects of family life (Roggman et al., 2016).

Observation and Assessment Basics

Watching and taking in information about family life is everyday practice for home visitors, and, as professionals, we probably like to think of ourselves as objective and unbiased. However, all humans are prone to flaws in their thinking, particularly when it comes to the topic of "family" – a topic that everyone has personal experiences, assumptions, biases, and values towards already. Without a guiding observation and assessment framework, home visitors run the risk of engaging in problematic behaviors. For example:

- Engaging in confirmation bias, meaning looking for favoring evidence that supports what one already believes to be true.
- Making decisions based on subjective (personal perspective) versus objective (factual) evidence.
- Experiencing fatigue from wasting time and energy piecing together poor quality or irrelevant information.

(Kirkman & Melrose, 2014)

To avoid these pitfalls, assessment offers a systematic way to gather information and make determinations about family life, defined as "a process for gathering information to make decisions ... The process is appropriate when it is systematic, multidisciplinary, and based on the everyday tasks of childhood [and families]. The best assessment system is comprehensive in nature" (Mindes, 2007, p. 10). Simple observation is the heart of assessment. In home visiting this involves observing the child, parent, or family "in action." Home visitors using informal observations strive for objectivity, meaning that the home visitor is only taking in observable facts rather than personal opinions.

The most basic form of assessment is informal observation, which in home visiting involves observing the child, parent, or family "in action" (Mindes, 2007). Informal observation is still objective (or at least strives to be), meaning that the information derived from the observation is based on observable evidence. In other words, "the watcher must have the capacity to separate judgement from watching" (Mindes, 2007, p. 12). As one might imagine, this is easier said than done when observing children and families with whom the home visitor has a close professional relationship. Assessment also includes formal methods, such as scientific measures with established reliability and validity. This simply means that these assessments consistently measure what they are supposed to measure. Assessments have reliability when they provide consistent results no matter who is administering the assessment or when it is administered (Babbie, 2007). For example, if five different home visitors use the same observation measure to assess a family's home learning environment, they should all derive similar scores. Assessments have validity when they truly measure what they are supposed to measure (Babbie, 2007). For example, if an assessment claims it measures the quality of the home learning environment, it should measure the quality of the home learning environment and not some other related concept (e.g., parenting practices).

According to the Head Start Performance Standards (ACF, 2016), all EHS-HBO programs are required to screen children's current developmental

190 Behavior, Development, and Environments

functioning in terms of behavior, motor skills, language, social, cognitive, and emotional skills. They must use research-based developmental tools as well as get input from parents and other adults familiar with the child's day-to-day behavior. Home visitors then use these assessments to make appropriate referrals to mental health or child development services if needs are identified (ACF, 2016). Individual programs decide which assessment tools work best for their staff and families. Common assessment screeners of child development include the Ages and Stages Questionnaire (ASQ; Squires & Bricker, 2009) and the ASQ Social Emotional (ASQ-SE; Squires, Bricker, & Twombly, 2002), Brigance (Brigance, 2013), and Teaching Strategies Gold (TSG; Teaching Strategies LLC, n.d.). The following sections examine informal and formal assessment strategies specific for parenting and the home environment.

Assessment of Parenting and the Home Environment

As discussed throughout this book, child development occurs within the context of parental relationships in the home environment (Shonkoff & Phillips, 2000). According to the Head Start Performance Standards, all EHS-HBO programs are required to use "strategies and activities that promote parents' ability to support the child's cognitive, social, emotional, language, literacy, and physical development" and "promotes the parent's role as the child's teacher through experiences focused on the parent–child relationship and, as appropriate, the family's traditions, culture, values, and beliefs" (ACF, 2016). As such, home visitors need ways to assess parenting and the home environment. Additionally, assessment should be used as an evaluative tool for the program, meaning that assessment of parenting and the home learning environment should provide home visiting programs with information on meeting families' needs and reaching program goals. To assist with this, the National Head Start Association (NHSA) developed the Parent Gauge tool to help professionals assess family needs in ways that align with the program's goals (NHSA, 2019). The tool includes a series of close-ended questionnaire questions and open-ended interview questions that are recorded and tracked over time. Information derived from this tool is useful to improve family engagement because it helps the home visitor know how the program is or is not meeting the family's needs. This also serves the program at large because it helps the program know how well they are meeting families' needs overall. This tool helps home visitors reflect on their own practices to ensure that families' concerns and goals are being addressed appropriately.

Home visitors may use a variety of other informal methods to systematically gather information about parenting and the home environment. Home visitors may be interested in parenting norms and values, how parents go about meeting their children's basic needs, parenting behaviors and skills, safety in the home, other family relationships, and many others (Holland, 2004). Home visitors can use a variety of methods to assess these topics. Parent questionnaires are compiled lists of questions that parents answer on a given topic. Parent interviews are structured questions the parent responds to on a particular topic. Interviews are most successful when they are structured with clear boundaries and follow a sequence of questions that allow for open-ended responses from parents (Mindes, 2007). An interview focused on family functioning should cover a variety of topics such as (1) the child's characteristics and special needs, (2) parent–child interactions, such as discipline and guidance methods, (3) family needs such as services or referrals, (4) important events unique to the family, such as an incarcerated family member or immigration status, and 5) family strengths such as supportive relationships (Lidz, 2003).

Home visitors may also use a variety of formal assessments to learn about parenting and the home environment. The Parenting Interactions with Children: Checklist of Observations Linked to Outcomes (PICCOLO; Roggman, Cook, Innocenti, Jump Norman & Christiansen, 2013) is widely used in EHS-HBO programs to assess the quality of parent–child interactions, specifically how developmentally appropriate parents are with their children. The assessment is a 29-item checklist that covers four areas: affection, responsiveness, encouragement, and teaching. It has been tested and validated with diverse groups of families (Roggman et al., 2013). The goal is to give home visitors information regarding what parents are doing to support their child's development, and areas that can be improved. The Infant Toddler-Home Observation for the Measurement of the Environment (IT-HOME) is another checklist that is used extensively in family science (Caldwell & Bradley, 2001). It comprises 45 items that the professional checks as Yes/No based on interviews with the parent and observation of the environment. The goal of the IT-HOME is to assess the quality of the home learning environment, meaning if the home environment is promotive for young children's development.

Home visitors may also use formal assessments that do not assess parent–child interactions directly, but rather aspects of wellbeing that influence parents' abilities to interact with their children effectively. For example, the Parent Health Questionnaire (PHQ-9) screens, diagnoses, and monitors depression (Kroenke, Spitzer, & Williams, 2001). Parents respond to a series of questions, asking how often they have been bothered by problems in the past two weeks such as "feeling tired or having little energy," "feeling down, depressed or hopeless," and "thoughts that you would be better off dead." Depending on the responses, the parent is categorized in one of six categories ranging from "minimal symptoms" to "major depression, severe" (Kroenke et al., 2001). This information is critical for the home visitor – it gives a sense of the parent's mental health, which will have a direct impact on their ability to parent effectively. It can then be used to refer to appropriate mental health services if needed. For pregnant and post-natal mothers, a specific post-

192 *Behavior, Development, and Environments*

partum depression scale, such as the Edinburgh Postnatal Depression Scale (Cox, Holden, & Sagovsky, 1987), should be used. Similarly, the Relationship Assessment Tool (Pope, Smith, Sanderson & Hussey, 2001) can be used to screen for the potential for intimate partner violence (IPV). It is a validated measure that "assesses for emotional abuse by measuring a woman's perceptions of her vulnerability to physical danger and loss of power and control in her relationship" (Coker et al., 2001, n.p.). Mothers indicate along a 6-point scale if they agree or disagree to statements such as "He makes me feel unsafe even in my own home", "I feel like he keeps me prisoner" and "I feel owned and controlled by him". Similar to a depression screener, this gives the home visitor fast and important information about the quality of the parenting and home environment.

All EHS-HBO programs must adopt a "research-based early childhood home-based curriculum" such as Baby TALK Newborn Encounters, Growing Great Kids, Love & Learn, Parents as Teachers (PAT), Partners for a Healthy Baby, Play and Learning Strategies (PALS) for Infants, Promoting First Relationships (ACF, 2018). Home visitors will also be tuned in to observing aspects of parenting and the environment as guided by the specific curriculum. For example, PAT uses visits, resources, and child screening to achieve their goals of increasing parental knowledge about child development, detect developmental delays, prevent child maltreatment, and support the child's school readiness (PAT National Center, 2019). Informal and formal assessment will be used in various forms and to gather a range of information so home visitors can make informed decisions when working with families.

FLE Content Area Knowledge and Knowledge of Observing Behavior, Development and Environment

Human growth and development. *Understand the developmental changes (both typical and atypical) of individuals in families across the lifespan with an emphasis on knowledge of developmental domains.*

A core principle of human growth and development is that there is great individual variation in how people grow and learn (Leventhal, 2015). Development is rapid over the first three years, with infants and toddlers quickly changing and acquiring new skills. Developmental milestones are typically discussed as norms. For example, the norm for independent walking is about 12 months old (Gross, 2019). However, a norm score is a just statistical average (i.e., mean score), meaning that it is comprised of a wide range of scores that fall higher and lower than the mean. Infant physical growth motor milestones illustrate this concept well. Gross motor (large muscle) and fine motor (small muscle) milestones are sequential and predictable across the first three years (Gross, 2019). This means that they usually occur in similar order (e.g., sitting, crawling, walking) and if you know what an infant's current skills, you can typically predict what their next big developmental gain will be. Across large populations of infants, researchers have estimated norms for when certain skills develop, but there is wide variation in when skills are considered within the range of typical development. For example, head control may develop anywhere from 3 weeks to 4 months, rolling over 2 to 7 months, independent sitting 5 to 9 months, crawling 5 to 11 months, and walking 9 to 17 months (Gross, 2019). Other developmental domains have similar wide individual variation. Parents often want to know if their child is "behind" on a certain skill. When observing infant/toddler development, home visitors need to be aware of the wide variation in developmental skills so they can guide parents appropriately. Moreover, knowing the wide range of "typical" development helps home visitors identify when infants may need referrals for services. Child development assessments commonly used in EHS-HBO programs such as the Ages and Stages Questionnaire (ASQ; Squires & Bricker, 2009) and the ASQ Social Emotional (ASQ-SE; Squires, Bricker, & Twombly, 2002), Brigance (Brigance, 2013), and Teaching Strategies Gold (TSG; Teaching Strategies LLC, n.d.), assess developmental domains with a wide range of scores. For example, ASQ scores in each developmental domain are placed on a continuum with a range of scores classified as the child being on schedule, a range of scores that indicate watching development closely and providing extra support, and a range of scores that indicate assessment with a professional (Squires & Bricker, 2009).

The interaction of nature and nurture is another important concept of human growth and development that influences how the home visitor observes child development. Nature refers to genetics and biological components of development (Kuther, 2017). From this perspective, development unfolds according to the genetic predispositions of the individual. Nurture is all environmental experiences, such as caregiving quality, nutrition, air pollution, and literally everything from the environment that touches the individual. From this perspective, nurture experiences shape and mold individual outcomes. In reality, nature and nurture are always interacting to influence human development (Kuther, 2017). For example, an infant may have a genetic predisposition to grow 6 feet tall, but chronic malnutrition in infancy may limit this potential. Individual variation in development also comes from these interactions. For example, a parent may be wondering why their infant is not crawling. The home visitor may notice that the infant spends very little time on her tummy, an environmental experience that is required to build the muscles to crawl. The caregiving practices and activities that parents engage in with their infants create the environmental context within which individual development takes shape. Moreover, all infants have unique temperament styles, personalities, and dispositions that contribute to variation in development (Gross, 2019). When parents and caregivers "get to know" the unique aspects to their infants, it helps develop a sense of

194 *Behavior, Development, and Environments*

Table 9.1 Family Life Education Concepts and Resources that Align with Observing
Behavior, Development, and Environments

FLE Content Area: Human growth and development	Resources
Development Individual differences in development, which is multi-faceted and involves gains and losses[1, 2]	[1]Leventhal, J. (2015). Human growth and development across the lifespan. In M. J. Walcheski, & J. S. Reinke (Eds.), *Family life education: The practice of family science* (pp. 167–176). Minneapolis, MN: National Council on Family Relations. [2]Boyd, D., & Bee, H. (2015). *Lifespan development* (7th ed.). Upper Saddle River, NJ: Pearson.

respect for their individual pace of development. Infant/toddler development occurs within the contexts of relationships, so the social interactions that occur between parents and their children provide an important setting for the environment to promote development.

Parenting education and guidance. *How parents teach, guide, and influence as the dynamic context of the parent–child relationship*

A core component of the FLE content area parenting education and guidance is that parents should be treated as collaborators (Jacobson, 2015). Parents are endlessly active learners when it comes to their children and their family. Parenting and family life is a process, meaning that parents, children, and all of the contexts of stress and support that surround families, all interact together (Brooks, 2013). In terms of assessment, this means that parents (and other important family members) should be incorporated in the assessment process because they make good assessment partners (Mindes, 2007). They can provide the home visitor with critical information about a range of behaviors, interaction patterns, and family needs. Parents and family members also make good partners because they are (obviously) heavily invested in the assessment process – it has direct implications for the wellbeing of their family system. Having a home visitor in one's home to observe and assess their parenting and home environment may feel intimidating or intrusive to some parents. It is important that adults are brought in to the assessment process by establishing constructive relationships with the home visitor (Holland, 2004). According to Holland (2004), cooperation and motivation on the part of the parent to be part of the process is helpful, as is being open and receptive to concerns the home visitor may have as a result of the assessment.

The home visitor's knowledge of parenting education and guidance can be used to guide how observation and assessment are integrated within the

Behavior, Development, and Environments   195

Table 9.2 Family Life Education Concepts and Resources that Align with Observing Behavior, Development, and Environments

FLE Content Area: Parenting education and guidance	Resources
Parenting Measures and Home Visiting Measures Parents as collaborators and active learners[1]; assessment, planning, discussion, and reflection[1]; assessment as a dynamic process[1]; healthy homes and lifestyles[2]	[1]Jacobson, A. L. (2015). Parenting education and guidance. In M. J. Walcheski, & J. S. Reinke (Eds.), *Family life education: The practice of family science* (pp. 213–222). Minneapolis, MN: National Council on Family Relations. [2]Brooks, J. B. (2013). *The process of parenting* (9th ed.). New York: McGraw Hill.

home visiting process. All assessment and observation that occurs within home visiting should be "nondiscriminatory, continuous, and must result in meaningful documentation of child [and family] progress" (Mindes, 2007, p. 10). As such, the information gained from observing parenting and the home environment should be purposeful and useful to the home visitor and family. Home visitors can discuss observation and assessment results with parents and use them to plan and reflect with families on their parenting goals. A reflective component to assessment is particularly important in a home visiting context because of the intense personal nature of the process. Reflective evaluation of observations and assessments means that the home visitor keeps an objective distance from the family, but also recognizes the in-depth knowledge they hold from working so closely together (Holland, 2004). This is not incompatible with a scientific view of observation and assessment, as Holland (2004) states, "in practice, whilst most strive for objectivity, many practitioners acknowledge that individual relationships, judgement and reflection play a central role in assessment" (p. 39). A main goal of FLE parenting education and guidance is creating healthy home and healthy lifestyles (Brooks, 2013) – assessments and observations of parenting and family should be useful in this endeavor.

Families and individuals in societal contexts. *Understand families in regard to other institutions (e.g., healthcare)*

Knowledge of families and individuals in societal contexts positions the home visitor to understand how child development is rooted in reciprocal interactions between individuals, families, and systems. An ecological perspective of human development (e.g., Bronfenbrenner & Morris, 2006), places the child at the center of a series of nested systems. The most proximal systems are those that include the child – such as the home, child care, or other caregiving settings.

196 *Behavior, Development, and Environments*

Table 9.3 Family Life Education Concepts and Resources that Align with Observing Behavior, Development, and Environments

FLE Content Area: Families and individuals in societal contexts	Resources
Individual Differences in Development Bi-directional effects on child development[1]	[1]Olson, D. H., DeFrain, J., & Skogrand, L. (2014). *Marriages and families: Intimacy, diversity, and strengths* (8th ed.). New York: McGraw Hill.

More distal systems include the neighborhood, parents' workplaces, community, politics, media, and culture. During infancy and toddlerhood, the home and child care proximal systems (i.e., microsystems) are comprised of interactions with family members and caregivers. These interactions are termed proximal processes and are bidirectional interactions that are the catalysts for development (Bronfenbrenner & Morris, 2006). For home visitors, the parent–child interactions, parent–home visitor interactions, and child-home visitor interactions are all proximal processes occurring in the home microsystem. The nature and quality of proximal processes provide a relational context for infant/toddler development. When observing and assessing child development, the home visitor must conceptualize development occurring as a product of the proximal processes occurring in the home.

FLE methodology. *Understand principles of FLE in tandem with planning and delivery of programs*

Content knowledge in FLE methodology provides guidance for incorporating observations and assessments in effective ways. Assessments and observations of parenting and the home environment obviously have direct application to the family and the home visitor's practices with the family, but they are also necessary for overall program evaluation. FLE methodology considers assessments, goals, implementation, evaluation, among other issues (Covey, 2015). Observation and assessment is one piece within the overall functioning of a program.

According to Covey (2015), the seven steps in program design are: beliefs, purpose, outcomes, design, implement, evaluate, and redesign (see The Planning Wheel, Clarke, 1998). Programs must establish goals and objectives (Duncan & Goddard, 2011). Goals are general statements about the overall purpose of the program. Objectives are specific intents of the program. Objectives are the elements of the program that are actually evaluated and monitored (Duncan & Goddard, 2011). Home visitors within EHS-HBO are obviously working within a program that has already been structured around the program's larger vision (beliefs and purpose as set forth in ACF, 2002), and has targeted outcomes they strive to meet.

The Head Start Early Learning Outcomes Framework describes the skills, behaviors, and knowledge that promote development and learning for all children (ACF, 2015). It focuses on children's approaches to learning, social-emotional development, language and literacy, cognition, and perceptual, motor and physical development. Within each of these domains, specific objectives are stated, along with indicators of what the objective looks like in practice. As such, observations and assessments of parenting and the home environment should serve a purpose in helping the home visitor help parents and children meet these outcomes. This is also done in partnership with the research-based curriculum individual programs select (as described above). Assessments and observations should reflect these goals and objectives, so that the information derived about families at the home visit is actually informing how well the program is doing what it is setting out to do (Duncan & Goddard, 2011). As Covey (2015) states, "the data gathered, whether through informal or formal means, not only can provide important information regarding the needs of the target population but also can inform the program designer about unique methods of delivery, program content, and approaches to implementation" (p. 245). Considerable thought must go in to determining which formal methods are used to assess parenting and the home learning environment. Individual EHS-HBO programs make these determinations in line with the Head Start Performance Standards. Home visitors also must decide how to hone their individual observation methods.

In FLE methodology, a needs assessment involves "discovering the needs of a target group" (Covey, 2015, p. 244). EHS-HBO is already designed for a specific population of families, but programs must conduct a needs assessment of individual families to discover what supports are already in place and what areas need assistance. For example, the Parent Gauge developed by the NHSA (2019), assesses family needs in the area of health, nutrition, and parent–child relationships. This information is vital for home visitors. It helps them identify family's current strengths. It also helps identify areas that need support. Home visitors will have a better sense of what resources and referrals are needed, as well as how to tailor their practices to best meet the needs of the family.

No matter the methods used, strong assessment practices are 1) guided by a theoretical framework, 2) identify needs and risks, 3) include clear steps for what to do next, 4) have clear objectives and consequences (i.e., what will happen as a result of an assessment), and 5) inform professional practice (Ofsted, 2014). Alternatively, weak assessment practices are 1) disconnected from program goals and objectives, 2) rely on a single method, 3) are not focused on truly understanding the family, and 4) are not clear about what steps to take with the information gathered (Ofsted, 2014). The methods the home visitor is going to use to observe the parent and the home environment must also be communicated clearly and transparently with families (Jones, Hindley, & Ramchandi, 2006). Home visitors must understand that they have a responsibility to comprehend the meaning and impact that assessments (and

198 Behavior, Development, and Environments

the resulting conclusions and decisions) can have on a family. Home visitors have an ethical responsibility to ensure that the process is as open as possible, and that parents have access to and clearly understand their assessment results (Mindes, 2007). Because home visitors are working with families from a variety of backgrounds and experiences, meeting the needs of different audiences in this area can be challenging. Parents have the right to be informed when assessments will take place, be assured that the assessments are unbiased, and that the assessment will be conducted in their native language (Mindes, 2007). Assessment results should be presented to families in a timely manner, and in a way that is easily understood by and meaningful to the family.

Home visitors can bring a reflective mindset to this work, meaning taking a critical and analytical look at the assumptions one holds about family life, particularly types of families and backgrounds (see Chapter 5). A reflective mindset also means spending time thinking through the entire observation and assessment process before it even starts – analysis, critical thinking, and critical reflection on the part of the program and the home visitor need to occur before the home visiting process even begins (Dalzell & Sawyer, 2016). This may involve talking through decisions, reflecting on why decisions are being made, and collaborating with the family and other program professionals (if appropriate). For all assessment and observation practices, moving through a step-by-step process is critical – relying on pure intuition is risky practice (Dalzell & Sawyer, 2016).

Table 9.4 Family Life Education Concepts and Resources that Align with Observing Behavior, Development, and Environments

FLE Content Area: FLE methodology	Resources
Parenting Measures and Home Visiting Measures Assessments[1, 2, 3]; conducting assessments[2]; assessment based interventions[3]; needs assessment[1]; assessment tools[A2]; goals[1]; quality assurance[1]; program design (and redesign), implementation, and evaluation[1]; knowledge as described through Bloom's taxonomy[1]; Prevention[1, 2, 3]; home environments[3]; parent development[2]; scholarly research, theoretical models, and instructional strategies[3]	[1]Covey, M. (2015). Family life education methodology. In M. J. Walcheski, & J. S. Reinke (Eds.), *Family life education: The practice of family science* (pp. 243–251). Minneapolis, MN: National Council on Family Relations. [2]Darling, C. A., & Cassidy, D. (2014). *Family life education: Working with families across the lifespan* (3rd ed.). Long Grove, IL: Waveland. [3]Duncan, S. F., & Goddard, H. W. (2017). *Family life education: Principles and practices for effective outreach* (3rd ed.). Thousand Oaks, CA: Sage.

Internal dynamics of families. *Understanding of family strengths and weaknesses and how family members relate to each other*

Content knowledge on the internal dynamics of families attunes the home visitor to strengths and weaknesses in the family system. In FLE, it is critical that observation is used to identify strengths in parents and the home environment, so they can be reinforced and capitalized on to support the family system, especially in times of crisis (Darling & Cassidy, 2014). Typical family routines are a good place to start. Observations and assessments of the family's daily activities helps paint a picture of typical life for the family. In terms of weaknesses, needs assessments help the home visitor identify what the family needs in terms of basics such as health and nutrition (NHSA, 2019). From a systems perspective, access to basic resources has a direct impact on children (e.g., access to healthy food, medical care), but also has an indirect effect on children's development via the impact it has on parents' own wellbeing (Huston & Bentley, 2010). Consequently, these types of assessments provide home visitors with useful information for supporting parenting practices and the home environment. Observations and assessments of parent–child interactions can also identify weaknesses in behaviors and skills. For example, home visitors need to know parents' knowledge of child development, if they promote children's development, if they read their infants' cues, if they meet their child's needs, and more.

Assessment and observations of parenting and the home environment can also help home visitors identify aspects of family life that are outside the bounds of healthy family functioning or stressors that some families face – such as family violence. In the U.S., the federal definition of child maltreatment is "any recent act or failure to act on the part of a parent or caretaker, which results in death, serious physical or emotional harm, sexual abuse, or exploitation, or an act or failure to act which presents an imminent risk of serious harm" (Child Abuse Prevention and Treatment Act [CAPTA], 2010). This includes all acts of physical, sexual, and psychological abuse. This also includes neglect which is "the failure of a parent or other person with responsibility for the child to provide needed food, clothing, shelter, medical care, or supervision to the degree that the child's health, safety, and well-being are threatened with harm" (Child Welfare Information Gateway, 2016, p. 2). From an ecological perspective, maltreatment is the "ultimate violation" of the caregiving environment young children need to develop (Cicchetti, Toth, & Maughan, 2000). As home visitors assess parenting and the home environment they need to be on high alert for signs of maltreatment and report suspicions in accordance with the mandating reporting policies of their program. For parents with infants and toddlers, the Child Welfare Information Gateway (2013) states that signs of maltreatment include (but are not limited to):

200 *Behavior, Development, and Environments*

- Parent does not provide adequate supervision
- Parent sees the child as bad, worthless, or burdensome or shows little concern
- Parent appears indifferent towards the child or is apathetic or depressed
- Child has unexplained burns, bites, bruises, broken bones, or black eyes and shrinks at the approach of adults
- Child is dirty or lacks appropriate clothing for the weather
- Child lacks proper medical attention, dental care, or immunizations (p. 6-7).

Intimate partner violence (IPV) is another element of family violence that the home visitor may observe in the household. As discussed above, some EHS-HBO programs may conduct a formal assessment of IPV, such as the Relationship Assessment Tool (Coker, et al., 2001). IPV can be defined as "extensive recurrent patterns of violence between adults, family members, partners, or extended family members. Such violence can take the form of physical, emotional, or sexual violence, and is often associated with living in a context of environmental stress" (Bentovim, Cox, Bingley Miller, & Pizzey, 2009, p. 14). The root of all IPV is power and control over another, but it can take various forms. Situational couple violence is violence between partners over everyday disagreements that heats up to the point of physical violence, and is the most common type of family violence (Williams, Sawyer, & Wahlstrom 2017). In contrast, intimate terrorism is controlling one's partner through intimidation and fear. It is usually patriarchal, meaning that men are typically the perpetrators controlling female victims (Williams et al., 2017). In addition to physical and/or sexual violence, perpetrators may also use coercion and threats, intimidation, emotional abuse, isolation, blaming, and economic abuse (i.e., no access to money) to maintain power and control over their victims (National Center on Domestic and Sexual Violence, 2019).

While observing parenting and the home environment, home visitors need to be on the lookout for signs of family violence so referrals and services can be provided appropriately. Family violence is incredibly stressful for young children. Maltreatment disrupts healthy patterns of care, resulting in direct trauma. IPV, while not experienced directly by the child, still contributes to an environment of stress and chaos that is absorbed by young children, even in infancy (Holmes, 2013). All family violence is "toxic stress" to young children's developing bodies and brains, having an overwhelming negative effect on their wellbeing (Shonkoff & Garner, 2012). As such, home visitors must be on high alert for these issues when observing parenting and the home environment. It should be recognized here that home visiting is emotionally laboring work, particularly when working with families dealing with trauma and crises. Home visiting and related helping professions have high burnout rates because there are often not the right social supports to help professionals

Table 9.5 Family Life Education Concepts and Resources that Align with Observing Behavior, Development, and Environments

FLE Content Area: Internal dynamics of families	Resources
Parenting Measures **Home Visiting Measures** Working with diverse parents and lower income parents[2]; maintaining a home[2]; human ecology theory[1]; family systems theory[1]; family development theory[1]	[1]Reinke, J. S., & Walcheski, M. J. (2015). Internal dynamics of families. In M. J. Walcheski, & J. S. Reinke (Eds.), *Family life education: The practice of family science* (pp. 157–166). Minneapolis, MN: National Council on Family Relations. [2]Olson, D. H., DeFrain, J., & Skogrand, L. (2014). *Marriages and families: Intimacy, diversity, and strengths* (8th ed.). New York: McGraw Hill.

working with families to process and deal with these emotions; professionals must be aware of their own emotions, feelings, because it will affect decision making (Dalzell & Sawyer, 2016).

Skills

The skills home visitors need to effectively observe behavior, development and environments include:

> Skills for helping parents assess child development; assessing home visiting practices and processes; and, assessing the program's learning environment for parents.
>
> (CUPID, 2017)

Human Growth and Development

Development

- Identify developmental stages and contexts
  - Identify developmental norms for infant/toddler development in multiple developmental domains: physical and motor, cognitive and language, social and emotional.
  - Understand the wide range of individual development within each domain.
  - Help parents understand "typical" development.
  - Help parents understand the unique aspects of their own infant/ toddler's development.

202   *Behavior, Development, and Environments*

- Identify reciprocal influences on development (individual development on families)

  - Identify nature and nurture components to infant/toddler development.
  - Help parents modify their caregiving behaviors to promote development, such as:

    - □ Ensuring that the infant gets enough awake "tummy time."
    - □ Talking to the infant and "taking turns" to promote language development.
    - □ Holding the infant's hands to help them take walking steps.
    - □ Ensuring that infants get the proper nutrition and health care.
    - □ Helping the toddler calm down when they are upset.
    - □ And more! The examples are endless.

Parenting Education and Guidance

Engaging Parents in Child Development and Observation

- Promote healthy parenting from systems and lifespan perspectives

  - Use a variety of informal observations and formal assessments to learn about parenting, including parental characteristics (e.g., depression) and aspects of the home environment (e.g., family needs, intimate partner violence) that affect healthy parenting abilities.
  - Integrate assessment and observation as part of supporting healthy homes and lifestyles.
  - Implement a needs assessment to identify what services/supports the family needs for their home and daily living.

- Promoting healthy parenting from a child's and parent's developmental perspective

  - Use a variety of informal observations and formal assessments (described above) to learn about parenting and the home environment as an indirect way to improve child wellbeing.
  - Use data from assessment and observations in the areas listed above as a starting point for supporting healthy parenting behaviors that support children's development.

- Apply strategies based on child's age and stage, and unique characteristics to support development

  - Use parents' expert knowledge on their child and family to support assessment practices.
  - Reflect on observations of child development with parents.

Behavior, Development, and Environments   203

- - Collaborate with parents on parenting strategies that support the unique needs of their child.
  - After applying strategies, assess again to ensure the strategies are promoting progress
- Identify parenting styles and their related outcomes and analyze various parenting programs, models, and principles
  - Observe parenting norms, values, skills, and behaviors.
  - Observe discipline, guidance, and punishment strategies.
  - Conduct formal assessments of parent–child interactions (e.g., PICCOLO).
  - Make connections between observed parenting values/behaviors/skills and infant/toddler behavior.
- Evaluate various parenting strategies
  - Analyze and reflect on observations and assessments of parenting and the home environment – are they working for the family? Are they supporting healthy child development?
- Recognize various parenting roles and their impact on families and recognize parenting issues within family structure
  - Observe and assess parent–child interactions.
  - Assess characteristics of parents that affect their ability to parent effectively:
    - ☐ depression, anxiety
    - ☐ family needs (e.g., food, clothing, housing, etc.)
    - ☐ intimate partner violence
    - ☐ social support
    - ☐ post-partum depression
- Recognize the impact of societal trends and cultural differences
  - Use formal assessments that are valid for use with various cultural backgrounds.
  - Be mindful of cultural or communication differences regarding discussing the home visitor's observation findings.
  - Use assessment and observation methods that reflect scientifically-accurate and developmentally appropriate information about parenting.
- Identify strategies to support children in various settings
  - Use assessments and observations to identify how parents support their child's development in the home (and areas that need to be improved).
  - After applying strategies in various settings, assess again to ensure the strategies are promoting progress

204   *Behavior, Development, and Environments*

Families and Individuals in Societal Contexts

Individual Differences in Development

- Recognize reciprocal interactions between individuals, families, and systems

  - Use ecological systems theory to understand child development (Bronfenbrenner & Morris, 2006).
  - Recognize that parent–child interactions, child–home visitor interactions and parent–home visitor interactions are proximal processes that shape child development.
  - Recognize that proximal processes that occur within the home microsystem are affected by more distal systems (e.g., community resources).

FLE Methodology

- Employ strategies to meet the needs of different audiences

  - Conduct assessments and observations with children, parents, and the home environment.

- Employ techniques to help the learner do hands-on learning

  - Actively incorporate parents and other important family members in the assessment and observation process.
  - Review observations with parents/family members.

- Create learning environments that support individual differences and develop culturally competent materials and experiences

  - Ensure that assessment and observations are unbiased.
  - Engage in reflective practices that take a critical and analytical look at biases and assumptions about family life.
  - Adopt research-based curricula that has been validated for use with diverse families.
  - Adopt assessment tools that have been validated for use with diverse groups of families.

- Identify sources of evidence-based information and implement evidence-based programs

  - Adopt evidence-based curricula and use fidelity tools to ensure that the program is being followed.
  - Adopt evidence-based assessment tools.

- Design educational experiences from start to finish (needs assessment to outcome measures)

Behavior, Development, and Environments   205

- ○ Work in tandem with the goals already founded by EHS-HBO.
- ○ Conduct needs assessments with children, parents, and the home environment (e.g., Parent Gauge; NHSA, 2019).
- ○ Use adopted research-based curriculum as a guide for planning educational experiences.
- ○ Conduct formal assessments and informal observations.
- ○ Work in tandem with the Head Start Early Learning Outcome Framework (ACF, 2015).

Internal Dynamics of Families

- Recognize and define healthy and unhealthy characteristics pertaining to family relationships and family development

  - ○ Use assessment and observation to clarify family strengths.
  - ○ Use assessment and observation to identify weaknesses that affect the child, parent, parent–child relationship, and other family relationships.
  - ○ Define child maltreatment including different types of abuse and neglect.
  - ○ Define intimate partner violence.

- Analyze family functioning using various theoretical perspectives

  - ○ From an ecological perspective, how do identified strengths and weaknesses contribute to the quality of the home microsystem, the interactions that occur between parents and children within the microsystem, and the child's individual development?
  - ○ Understand family violence as a microsystem that is failing to meet the needs of the child and is "toxic" to their development.

- Assess family dynamics from a "systems perspective" (NCFR, 2015, p. 2)

  - ○ From a systems perspective, how do identified strengths and weaknesses affect the functioning of the overall family system?
  - ○ Understand that family violence directly (e.g., abuse, neglect) or indirectly (e.g., intimate partner violence) impacts young children if it is occurring elsewhere in the family system (e.g., between adults).

- Analyze family dynamics in response to normative and non-normative stressors

  - ○ Use needs assessments to identify basic family needs (e.g., food, clothing, housing, medical care, etc.).
  - ○ Use assessments and observations to identify evidence of family violence.

- Analyze family dynamics in response to stress, crises, and trauma

206   *Behavior, Development, and Environments*

- o   Distinguish between physical, emotional or sexual abuse.
- o   Identify specific aspects of neglect (e.g., food, clothing, shelter, medical care, etc.).
- o   Distinguish situational couple violence and intimate terrorism.
- o   Identify different strategies perpetrators use to maintain power and control over victims.

- Facilitate and strengthen communication processes, conflict-management, and problem-solving skills

  - o   Be open and honest with families when conducting assessments, particularly when it comes to sensitive issues such as family violence.
  - o   Be open and honest if an observation or assessment is going to have specific consequences for the family (e.g., reporting suspected abuse or neglect).
  - o   Provide families with assessment results in a way they can easily understand and is meaningful to the family's daily life.
  - o   Refer families to appropriate resources to support consequences that may arise from assessment results.

- Develop, recognize, and reinforce strategies that help families function effectively

  - o   Use observation and assessment to identify strengths in:

    - □   Parent–child relationships
    - □   Mental health
    - □   Family resources
    - □   Adult relationships
    - □   Social support
    - □   Community support

Attitudes

The CUPID attitudes germane to observing behavior, development, and environments include:

> Attitudes that support assessment as a collaborative process for positive purposes and respect parents' expertise on the child.
>
> (CUPID, 2017)

The attitudes and values reflected here are a true appreciation for parents as collaborative partners in the home visiting process. The FLE code of ethics also reflects these values stating that relationships with parents and families must be based on a respect for parents as their child's primary "educators, nurturers and limit-setters for their children" and that they will "communicate openly and truthfully about the nature and extent of services provided" (NCFR, n.d.). Parents are experts on their children and family processes. A core FLE principle is "being with" families instead of "doing for" families (Petkus, 2015). Truly being with families means involving them in aspects of the home visiting process that initially seem to belong to the home visitor. While it is true that the assessment and observation process is very much driven by the EHS-HBO program, parents must still be brought in to the process. Observations and assessments of parenting and the home environment have real consequence for families, and home visitors have a duty to engage in an ethical decision-making process before launching straight into problem-solving mode (MCFR, 2009). This involves (1) identifying the important relationships involved in the issue, (2) identifying ethical principles (e.g., from the FLE code of ethics) that apply, (3) thinking through any tensions between the ethical principles, (4) brainstorming possible solutions with the family, keeping in mind all the information in steps 1–3, and (5) make an action plan rooted in the ethical principles (MCFR, 2009).

Box 9.1 CDA Home Visitor Competencies

The CDA Subject Areas and Competency Standards are national standards for Home Visitors. The subject area that is most relevant to this chapter includes **CDA Subject Area 5: Managing an effective home visitor program operation.** Each competency standard comprises competency goals, functional areas, items, indicators, and examples. The competency goals that are most relevant to this chapter are "to establish positive and productive partnerships with families" and "to ensure a well-run, coherent and purposeful program responsive to the needs of the families in his or her caseload." (Council for Professional Recognition, 2016).

Competency Goal	Functional Area	Example Items	Example Indicators
IV. To establish positive and productive partnerships with families	11 Families: Home visitor establishes a positive, responsive, and cooperative relationships with each family, engages in two-way communication with	Item 11.2: Help parents recognize that they are the center of the program.	Helps parents complete a family needs assessment Learns how to use assessment data and observations to help parents develop a family action plan to

(Continued)

208 *Behavior, Development, and Environments*

(Cont.)

Competency Goal	Functional Area	Example Items	Example Indicators
	families, encourages the parents to take leadership in personal and family education, and supports the relationship of the families with their children.		benefit the child and family members.

Permission to reprint from the Council on Professional Recognition, 2019

Box 9.2 National Family Support Competency Framework for Family Support Professionals

The National Family Support Competency Framework for Family Support Professionals are competencies that include ten domains that are further clarified by dimensions (Institute for the Advancement of Family Support Professionals, 2018). There is one domain that is relevant to this chapter: (a) Effective Home Visits, which includes three domains: assessment, planning, and data/documentation.

Domain 3	Dimension 31	Component d.	Levels of Competency
Effective Home Visits	**Assessment**	Observation	**1-Recognizing.** Understands the components of effective observation **3-Applying.** Supports parents by using observation to collect meaningful information in the home and family environment **5-Extending.** Coaches parents to utilize observations in interactions with their child

(Continued)

(Cont.)

Domain 3	Dimension 31	Component d.	Levels of Competency
	Dimension 32	**Component a.**	**Levels of Competency**
	Planning	Individualization to needs of each family	**1-Recognizing.** Understands specific needs and learning styles of each family **3-Applying.**
			Supports parents by adjusting learning approaches and activities to fit their learning styles **5-Extending.**
			Coaches parents by utilizing results from assessments and collaborative goal setting to individualize home visit activities for each family

Permission to reprint from the Institute for the Advancement of Family Support Professionals.

Summary

This chapter examined observation and assessment in home visiting, focusing specifically on observing parenting and the quality of the home environment (CUPID, 2017). The FLE content areas human growth and development, parenting education and guidance, families and individuals in societal contexts, FLE methodology, and internal dynamics of families align and expand content for the home visitor in terms of using observation and assessments to guide parenting education, incorporating assessment and observation effectively within programs, and using assessment and observations to identify and understand strengths and weaknesses within the family.

Key Concepts

- Assessment
- Confirmation bias
- Child maltreatment
- Goals
- Head Start Early Learning Outcomes Framework

210 *Behavior, Development, and Environments*

- Intimate partner violence
- Needs assessment
- Norms
- Objective
- Objectives
- Objectivity
- Observation
- Parent interviews
- Parent questionnaires
- Reflective evaluation
- Reflective mindset
- Reliability
- Subjective
- Toxic stress
- Validity

Recommended Readings

Administration for Children and Families. (2015). *Head Start Early Learning Outcomes Framework.* U.S. Department of Health and Human Services. Retrieved from https://eclkc.ohs.acf.hhs.gov/sites/default/files/pdf/elof-ohs-framework.pdf

Child Welfare Information Gateway. (2013). *What is child abuse and neglect? Recognizing the signs and symptoms.* Washington, DC: U.S. Department of Health and Human Services, Children's Bureau.

National Center on Domestic and Sexual Violence. (2019). *Power and control wheel.* Retrieved from http://www.ncdsv.org/images/PowerControlwheel NOSHADING.pdf

References

Administration for Children and Families (ACF). (2002). *Making a difference in the lives of infants and toddlers and their families: The impacts of Early Head Start: Vol. 1. Final technical report.* Washington, DC: U.S. Department of Health and Human Services.

Administration for Children and Families (ACF). (2007). *Head Start Act.* U.S. Department of Health and Human Services.

Administration for Children and Families (ACF). (2015). *Head Start Early Learning Outcomes Framework.* U.S. Department of Health and Human Services. Retrieved from https://eclkc.ohs.acf.hhs.gov/sites/default/files/pdf/elof-ohs-framework.pdf

Administration for Children and Families (ACF). (2016). *Head Start Performance Standards 45 CFR Chapter XIII September 2016.* U.S. Department of Health and Human Services.

Administration for Children and Families (ACF). (2018). *Parenting Curricula Review Databases.* U.S. Department of Health and Human Services. Retrieved from https://eclkc.ohs.acf.hhs.gov/parenting/article/parenting-curricula-review-databases

Behavior, Development, and Environments 211

Babbie, E. (2007). *The practice of social science research.* Belmont, CA: Thompson Wadsworth.

Bentovim, A., Cox, A., Bingley Miller, L., & Pizzey, S. (2009). *Safeguarding children living with trauma and family violence.* London: Jessica Kingsley Publishers.

Boyd, D., & Bee, H. (2015). *Lifespan development* (7th ed.). Upper Saddle River, NJ: Pearson.

Brigance, A. H. (2013). *Brigance inventory of early development – III (IED-III).* North Billerica, MA: Curriculum Associates, Inc.

Bronfenbrenner, U., & Morris, P. A. (2006). The bioecological model of human development. In R. M. Learner & W. Damon (Eds.) *Handbook of child psychology* (pp. 793–828). Hoboken, NJ: John Wiley & Sons Inc.

Brooks, J. (2013). *The process of parenting* (9th ed.). New York, NY: McGraw Hill.

Caldwell, B. M., & Bradley, R. H. (2001). *HOME inventory and administration manual* (3rd ed.). University of Arkansas for Medical Sciences and University of Arkansas at Little Rock.

Cicchetti, D., Toth, S. L., & Maughan, A. (2000). An ecological–transactional model of child maltreatment. In *Handbook of developmental psychopathology* (pp. 689–722). Boston, MA: Springer.

Child Abuse Prevention and Treatment Act. (2010). CAPTA Reauthorization Act of 2010 (P.L. 111–320), § 5101, Note (§ 3).

Child Welfare Information Gateway. (2013). *What is child abuse and neglect? Recognizing the signs and symptoms.* Washington, DC: U.S. Department of Health and Human Services, Children's Bureau.

Child Welfare Information Gateway. (2016). *Definitions of child abuse and neglect.* Washington, DC: U.S. Department of Health and Human Services, Children's Bureau.

Clarke, J. I. (1998). *Who, me lead a group?* Seattle, WA: Parenting Press, Inc.

Collaborative for Understanding the Pedagogy of Infant/toddler Development (CUPID) (2017). *Comprehensive competencies for educators of infants and toddlers in group care and home visiting settings.* Unpublished.

Coker, A.L., Pope, B.O., Smith, P.H., Sanderson, M., & Hussey, J.R. (2001). Assessment of clinical partner violence screening tools. *Journal of the American Medical Women's Association,* 19–23.

Council for Professional Recognition. (2016). The Child Development Associate National Credentialing Program and CDA Competency Standards, Home Visitor Edition. Washington DC: Council for Professional Recognition.

Covey, M. (2015). Family life education methodology. In M. Walcheski & J. Reinke (Eds.), *Family life education: The practice of family science* (pp. 243–251). Minneapolis, MN: National Council on Family Relations.

Cox, J. L., Holden, J. M., & Sagovsky, R. (1987). Detection of postnatal depression: Development of the 10-item Edinburgh Postnatal Depression Scale. *British Journal of Psychiatry 150,* 782–786.

Dalzell, R. & Sawyer, E. (2016). *Putting analysis in child and family assessment.* London, UK: National Children's Bureau.

Darling, C. A., & Cassidy, D. (2014). *Family life education: Working with families across the lifespan.* Long Grove, IL: Waveland Press.

212 *Behavior, Development, and Environments*

Duncan, S. F., & Goddard, H. W. (2011). *Family life education: Principles and practices for effective outreach.* Thousand Oaks, CA: Sage Publications.

Gross, D. (2019). *Infancy: Development from birth to age 3* (3rd ed.). Lanham, MD: Roman & Littlefield.

Heaman, M., Chalmers, K., Woodgate, R., & Brown, J. (2007). Relationship work in an early childhood home visiting program. *Journal of Pediatric Nursing, 22*(4), 319–330.

Holland, S. (2004). *Child and family assessment in social work practice.* Thousand Oaks, CA: Sage.

Holmes, M. R. (2013). The sleeper effect of intimate partner violence exposure: Long-term consequences on young children's aggressive behavior. *Journal of Child Psychology and Psychiatry, 54*(9), 986–995.

Huston, A. C., & Bentley, A. C. (2010). Human development in societal context. *Annual Review of Psychology, 61*, 411–437.

Institute for the Advancement of Family Support Professionals. (2018). *National Family Support Competency Framework for Family Support Professionals.* Retrieved from: https://cppr-institute-prod.s3.amazonaws.com/modules/Approved%20National%20Family%20Support%20Competency%20Framework_FINAL_7_18_2018.pdf

Kirkman, E. & Melrose, K. (2014). *Clinical judgment and decision-making in children's social work: An analysis of the Front Door System.* London: Department for Education.

Korfmacher, J., Green, B., Staerkel, F., Peterson, C., Cook, G., Roggman, L., Faldowski, R. A., & Schiffman, R. (2008). Parent involvement in early childhood home visiting. *Child & Youth Care Forum, 37,* 171–196.

Kroenke, K., Spitzer, R. L., & Williams, J. B. (2001). The PHQ-9: Validity of a brief depression severity measure. *Journal of General Internal Medicine, 16*(9), 606–613.

Kuther, T. L. (2017). *Lifespan development: Lives in context.* Thousand Oaks, CA: Sage Publications.

Leventhal, J. (2015). Human growth and development across the lifespan. In M. Walcheski & J. Reinke (Eds.) *Family life education: The practice of family science* (pp. 167–176). Minneapolis, MN: National Council on Family Relations.

Jacobson, A. L. (2015). Parenting education and guidance. In M. Walcheski & J. Reinke (Eds.) *Family life education: The practice of family science* (pp. 243–251). Minneapolis, MN: National Council on Family Relations.

Jones, D., Hindley, P. & Ramchandi, A. (2006). Making plans, assessment, intervention and evaluating outcomes. In J. Aldgate, W. Rose, & C. Jeffery (Eds.), *The Developing World of the Child.* London: Jessica Kingsley Publishers.

Lidz, C. S. (2003). *Early childhood assessments.* Hoboken, NJ: John Wiley & Sons.

Mindes, G. (2007). *Assessing young children.* Upper Saddle River, NJ: Pearson.

Minnesota Council on Family Relations (MCFR). (2009). *Ethical Thinking and Practice for Parent and Family Life Educators.* St. Paul, MN: Minnesota Council on Family Relations.

National Center on Domestic and Sexual Violence. (2019). *Power and control wheel.* Retrieved from http://www.ncdsv.org/images/PowerControlwheelNOSHADING.pdf

National Council on Family Relations (NCFR). (n.d.). *Family life educators code of ethics.* Retrieved https://www.ncfr.org/sites/default/files/cfle_code_of_ethics_2.pdf

National Council of Family Relations (NCFR). (2015). *Family life education content areas: Content and practice guidelines.* Retrieved from https://www.ncfr.org/sites/default/files/fle_content_and_practice_guidelines_2015_0.pdf

National Head Start Association (NHSA). (2019). *Engage, measure, act: Parent Gauge.* Retrieved from https://www.nhsa.org/our-work/initiative/parent-gauge

Ofsted. (2014). *The Help Care and Protection of Children. A Report of Ofsted's Inspection Findings in Relation to the Help Care and Protection of Children.* London: Oftsed.

Olson, D. H., DeFrain, J., & Skogrand, L. (2014). *Marriages and families: Intimacy, diversity, and strengths* (8th ed.). New York: McGraw Hill.

Parents as Teachers National Center. (2019). *Evidence-based model.* Retrieved from https://parentsasteachers.org/evidence-based-model

Petkus, J. (2015). A first-hand account of implementing a Family Life Education model: Intentionality in Head Start home visiting. In M. J. Walcheski, & J. S. Reinke (Eds.), *Family life education: The practice of family science* (pp. 325–331). Minneapolis, MN: National Council on Family Relations.

Reinke, J. S., & Walcheski, M. J. (2015). Internal dynamics of families. In M. J. Walcheski, & J. S. Reinke (Eds.), *Family life education: The practice of family science* (pp. 157–159). Minneapolis, MN: National Council on Family Relations.

Roggman, L. A., Cook, G. A., Innocenti, M. S., Jump Norman, V., & Christiansen, K. (2013). Parenting interactions with children: Checklist of observations linked to outcomes (PICCOLO) in diverse ethnic groups. *Infant Mental Health Journal, 34*(4), 290–306.

Roggman, L., Peterson, C., Cohen, R. C., Ispa, J., Decker, K. B., Hughes-Belding, K., Cook, G., & Vallotton, C. D. (2016). Preparing home visitors to partner with families of infants and toddlers. *Journal of Early Childhood Teacher Education, 37,* 301–313.

Shonkoff, J. P., & Phillips, D. A. (2000). *From neurons to neighborhoods: The science of early childhood development.* Washington DC: National Academy Press.

Shonkoff, J.P. & Garner, A.S. (2012). The lifelong effects of early childhood adversity and toxic stress. *Pediatrics, 129,* 232–246.

Squires, J., Bricker, D., & Twombly. E. (2002). *Ages and stages questionnaires: Social-emotional (ASQ: SE), A parent-completed, child-monitoring system for social-emotional behaviors.* Baltimore: Paul H. Brookes Publishing.

Squires, J., & Bricker, D. (2009). *Ages & stages questionnaires, third edition (ASQ-3).* Baltimore, MD: Brookes Publishing.

Teaching Strategies LLC. (n.d.) *Teaching strategies gold.* Washington, DC: Teaching Strategies LLC.

Williams, B. K., Sawyer, S. C., & Wahlstrom, C. M. (2017). *Marriage, families, & intimate relationships* (4th ed). New York, NY: Pearson.

10 Guidance of Infant/Toddler Behavior

Helping children learn new skills and socially acceptable ways to express and manage their emotions and behaviors is a critical part of parenthood. Infancy, particularly toddlerhood, is notorious for challenging behaviors and emotions. However, it is a critical time for parents to help their children develop skills that will benefit them when they enter kindergarten and beyond. It is critical that EHS-HBO home visitors have a comprehensive understanding of the basics of infant/toddler behavior as it occurs within the family, as well as be skilled in helping parents use appropriate guidance and discipline strategies. This chapter will examine the CUPID Competency **Guidance of Infant/ Toddler Behavior** (CUPID, 2017; Roggman et al., 2016):

Competency	Helping children meet behavioral expectations appropriate to their developmental level, by considering the child's needs, offering effective encouragement, scaffolding emotion regulation, stating behavior guidelines positively, and modeling desired behaviors, which, over time, supports self-regulation of emotion and behavior
Knowledge	Expanded knowledge of the role of family interaction patterns and adult mental health in child misbehavior and of basic strategies parents can use to reduce their children's negative behavior and guide their children's positive behavior.
Skills	Skills to help parents acquire knowledge about how physiology, stress, and family interactions influence the child's behavior, reflect on their attitudes (obedience, innate characteristics, respect for the child as a separate person needing nurturance and guidance), and develop skills of child guidance that are appropriate for their own child's temperament, development, and experience (observe child, interpret child's cues, set up environments and routines to reduce challenging behaviors, scaffold child's emotional regulation, state expectations positively)
Attitudes	Attitudes that support parents' respect for child autonomy (if culturally appropriate), value the role of parent in child guidance, and acknowledge parents' perspectives about obedience and punishment.

For full alignment see Appendix B.

The FLE Content Areas that are most applicable to this competency include:

Human growth and development	Understanding of the developmental changes (both typical and atypical) of individuals in families across the lifespan with an emphasis on knowledge of developmental domains
Parenting education and guidance	How parents teach, guide, and influence as the dynamic context of the parent–child relationship
Internal dynamics of families	Understanding of family strengths and weaknesses and how family members relate to each other
Interpersonal relationships	Understand the development and maintenance of interpersonal relationships

Note: Permission to reprint was granted from the National Council on Family Relations.

Knowledge

According to CUPID, home visitor should possess:

> Expanded knowledge of the role of family interaction patterns and adult mental health in child misbehavior and of basic strategies parents can use to reduce their children's negative behavior and guide their children's positive behavior.
>
> (CUPID, 2017)

Infant/Toddler Development Basics

Guiding infant/toddler behavior in ways that are appropriate for their age requires some basic knowledge of infant/toddler development. Infants and toddlers are changing at a rapid pace, and they are eager to use their newfound physical and cognitive abilities to explore, get messy, and test limits. Development is driven by autonomy, meaning an innate desire to be independent and do things for the self (Sroufe, 1979). Most parents would agree that they want their child to be self-sufficient, but the drive for autonomy also causes children to behave in ways that are less than pleasing to adults. Toddlers easily get upset when they cannot do something by themselves, and they have limited skills to manage these frustrations (a.k.a. self-regulation skills; Cole, Martin, & Dennis, 2004). This is a recipe for behaviors such as hitting, screaming, and tantrums.

It is important for parents and caregivers to realize that children are not going to behave the way adults want them to all of the time. In fact, adults who have unreasonable expectations about children's behavior often find themselves disappointed and stressed (Gartrell, 2004). The process of helping children understand how to use behaviors that are socially and culturally acceptable is socialization (Peterson & Rollins, 1987). Socialization takes time, and young children are going to make mistakes along the way. Dan Gartrell (2004) offers the wisdom that children's "misbehavior" is usually "mistaken behavior," and viewing it as such can alleviate the frustration parents often feel.

It is also crucial that adults recognize that all children are different. They will display different ranges of emotions, behaviors, and respond to guidance and discipline in various ways. Temperament is a set of inborn characteristics that remain stable across the lifespan – some infants are naturally more active, have more dramatic mood swings, or are less regular (e.g., eating, sleeping, bowel movements) and adaptable (Thomas & Chess, 1977). Parents are most successful in managing infant/toddler behavior when they recognize the unique aspects of their child's temperament and adapt their own behaviors to best meet the needs of their child.

Family Interaction Patterns

Family interaction patterns play a major role in shaping and guiding child behavior in three important ways: attachment, parenting styles, and issues in the family system.

Attachment. As was discussed in Chapter 6, as parents learn about and become "in tune" with their infants, they establish regular patterns of interaction that endure into childhood and beyond (Gross, 2019). These back-and-forth interactions form the basis of attachment, the special bond between parent and child (Bowlby, 1969/1982). Attachment relationships that are characterized by patterns of safety and security help children view themselves in a positive light and engage in prosocial behaviors with others (Sroufe, Carlson, & Shulman, 1993). In contrast, attachment relationships characterized by patterns of instability and inconsistency (i.e., insecure) often lead to behavior problems (van IJzendoorn, Schuengel, & Bakermans-Kranenburg, 1999). In extreme cases of trauma or maltreatment, disorganized attachment patterns can result in extreme maladaptive behaviors (Macfie, Cicchetti, & Toth, 2001).

Parenting styles. Parenting styles are patterns of parenting behaviors. Some families establish parenting styles that are a combination of sensitivity, warmth, and control. Diana Baumrind (1971) classified this as authoritative parenting. Parents who use authoritative parenting are responsive to their infant/toddlers' needs in a warm and positive manner, but also use high levels of control to monitor their children's actions and behaviors. In contrast, Baumrind's authoritarian parenting style is characterized by high levels of control and lower warmth and sensitivity. Parents who use this style are more rigid and controlling of their children's behavior and may use more punitive methods of discipline (Baumrind, 1971). Parents who are high on warmth and support, but exert little control in children's lives are classified as permissive. Finally, uninvolved parents are absent in both warmth and control. As discussed throughout the rest of this chapter, parenting styles are related

Guidance of Infant/Toddler Behaviors **217**

to children's behavior outcomes, but their exact impact on child behavior is often culturally dependent (Darling & Steinberg, 1993).

Issues in the family system. On the surface, some family issues may seem unrelated to infants and toddlers, but these issues can "trickle down" through the family system to eventually impact child behavior. To understand why, it is helpful to think of the family as made up of interconnecting parts—relationships and interactions between family members contribute to the system as a whole. Family systems theory specifically states that that interactions in one part of the system echo to all other parts of the system (Segrin & Flora, 2005). Thus, all interactions that occur within the family, even if they do not directly involve the child, can impact behavior. Infants and toddlers are particularly sensitive to issues occurring in the family system. Because their immature brains are still in the process of making new connections, they are more vulnerable to stress and trauma that interrupt these processes. For example, infants are more likely to have behavior and emotion regulation problems when they are exposed to intimate partner violence than older children (Carpenter & Stacks, 2009). Family issues also impact children's behavior because of the negative impact they have on parenting. For example, romantic relationship conflict worsens parents' mental health, which then reduces the ability to parent in a positive manner, which has a negative impact on child behavior (Krishnakumar & Buehler, 2000; Cummings & Davies, 2002). Stressful conditions, such as living in poverty, also affect child behavior via the family system: stress is taxing to parents' wellbeing, which impacts their parenting and ultimately children (Pachter, Auinger, Palmer, & Weitzman, 2006)

Adult Mental Health

Adult issues such as mood disorders, mental illness, or addiction can have a serious impact on infant/toddler behavior. As discussed above, child behavior develops within the contexts of the family, and parental mental health plays an important role in the family system. For example, mothers experiencing depressive symptoms are more likely to display increased negative parenting behaviors, particularly for mothers with young infants and mothers living in poverty (Lovejoy, Graczyk, O'Hare, & Neuman, 2000). Substance use can also have a harmful impact on parenting behaviors (Cohen, Hien, & Batchelder, 2008). Infants and toddlers growing up in homes in which parents have addiction issues are more likely to have greater internalizing (e.g., depression, anxiety) and externalizing (e.g., aggression) issues (Bagner, Pettit, Lewinsohn, & Seeley, 2010) than children whose parents do not struggle with addiction. These children are also at a higher risk for maltreatment (i.e., abuse or neglect) or other types of violence (Cohen et al., 2008; McKeganey, Barnard, & McIntosh, 2002).

Parental stress can impact infant/toddler behavior before birth. Evidence suggests that maternal stress during pregnancy can affect the developing fetus

218 *Guidance of Infant/Toddler Behaviors*

causing lower cognitive skills and increased fearfulness when they are toddlers (Bergman, Sarkar, O'Connor, Modi, & Glover, 2007). This occurs because the physiological experience of stress within the mother's body creates biological changes to the fetus's developing stress response system. Infants who are "hard-wired" for a stress response system on high alert are more reactive and may have more trouble modifying their own physiological arousal when emotions are running high (Davis, Glynn, Waffarn, & Sandman, 2011).

Reducing Negative Behaviors and Supporting Positive Behaviors

Behaviors in infancy. For infants, the best way to support positive behavior development is for parents to learn their baby's cues so they can meet their needs (hunger, comfort, etc.) in a sensitive and responsive manner. This helps build a secure relationship and instills a sense of trust in the parents, all of which lays the foundation for positive behaviors (Gross, 2019). Infants are going to cry and display a range of negative (or unhappy) behaviors, but parents can mitigate this by anticipating their babies' cues and be proactive in meeting their needs. Adults should keep the infant's immediate environment safe and only have things in their reach that are appropriate for them to play with. For example, infants who can sit up and reach/grasp for toys should only have access to toys around them that are safe for their age. Infants that can crawl or pull-to-stand need a larger safe area suited for their developmental needs. Keeping a safe, baby-friendly environment reduces the chance that the infant will get into something they are not supposed to. When that inevitably does occur, parents can use redirection to simply move the infant's attention to something more suitable (e.g., "Oops that glass cup is not a good toy for you. Look at this shiny rattle and the noise it makes!"). It is not appropriate to use physical punishment or yell at young infants for doing something "wrong," as they do not have the cognitive skills to fully understand the connection between their actions and a punitive response (e.g., Sobel & Kirkham, 2006).

Guiding behaviors. As infants turn to toddlers, specific behavior management strategies become more important. Guidance (as distinct from discipline and punishment) is the process of providing direction to children to help them use positive behaviors, and gently discourage or manage negative behaviors (Gartrell, 2004). Parents can provide better guidance when they understand the motives behind a specific behavior—is a toddler crying because they want attention? Are they hungry or tired? Or are they seeking affection? A parent may handle the situation differently depending on the answer. Guidance is never punitive—it is based on mutual respect between the adult and child (Essa, 2012).

There are many ways parents can use guidance to encourage positive behaviors. For one, they can model the behaviors they want to see from their toddler. For example, if a parent wants his toddler to share toys, he should model how to share when they play together. Or, if a parent wants her toddler to use a quiet voice in the grocery store, she should keep her voice calm and quiet also. When children act in positive ways, parents can increase the likelihood that children will repeat these behaviors with simple feedback such as, "Thank you for helping with …" or "I really like how you …." Positive feedback for positive behavior increases the likelihood that children will repeat the behavior. Parents can use also use simple strategies such as redirection (as described above), talking about and identifying feelings, or providing the child with choices whenever possible. Parents can also use natural consequences to help toddlers learn things on their own (within reason and safety). For example, rather than arguing about putting on his jacket, a parent can simply let their child step outside to see how cold it is for himself—which in all likelihood will result in him asking for his jacket.

Part of guidance is also taking steps to prevent misbehaviors in the first place. For example, moving all breakable items out of reach, watching for tired/hunger cues, and explaining behavior expectations ahead of time (e.g., "When we go in the grocery store you are going to sit in the cart and we are going to use quiet voices"). This helps toddlers understand what is expected of them, as they are still learning what is socially acceptable.

Discipline and punishment. Discipline is a specific reaction to a misbehavior (e.g., time out or other consequence). Toddlers need to understand cause-and-effect logic for discipline to be effective, so it is not developmentally appropriate to discipline young infants. For toddlers, discipline still needs to be within the realm of what is appropriate for their age. For example, time out should only be 1 minute per year of the child's age—the child needs time to calm down, but any longer and the child will not understand the consequence (Ryan, Sanders, Katsiyannis, & Yell, 2007). Other discipline methods include taking away materials (e.g., toys), privileges (e.g., screen time) or removing the child from the situation.

Punishment is distinct from discipline—it is an emotionally or physically painful consequence. This may include yelling, threatening, restraining, or spanking (hitting the child on the bottom without leaving a mark). Punishment for infants is never appropriate. For toddlers and preschoolers, there is general consensus among researchers that spanking does nothing to improve behavior and can even harm young children's development (Gershoff & Grogan-Kaylor, 2016; MacKenzie, Nicklas, Brooks-Gunn, & Waldfogel, 2015). Despite this, spanking is a common parenting practice for many U.S. parents with infants and toddlers (MacKenzie, Nicklas, Brooks-Gunn, & Waldfogel, 2011). A more nuanced look at this issue is discussed in the sections below.

FLE Content Area Knowledge and Knowledge of Guiding Infant/Toddler Behavior

Human growth and development: *Understanding of the developmental changes (both typical and atypical) of individuals in families across the lifespan with an emphasis on knowledge of developmental domains.*

220   *Guidance of Infant/Toddler Behaviors*

Knowledge in human growth and development helps home visitors conceptualize infant and toddler behavior as a combination of naturally unfolding development (e.g., nature and maturation) and experiences within the family (e.g., nurture). Families in EHS home visiting programs are more likely to be dealing with other stressors that strain the family system, just by way of living in poverty (Huston & Bentley, 2010). These issues may not involve the infant/toddler directly; instead, the stress trickles down the family system, affecting parental mental health, parenting practices, and ultimately infant/toddler behavior. Families living in economic disadvantage are at heightened risk for various issues such as parental depression/anxiety, family violence, food insecurity, and generalized feelings of stress (Evans & Kim, 2007). As home visitors work with families dealing with a variety of issues, the home visitor needs to keep in mind how these issues strain the family system and impact infants and toddlers indirectly. Home visitors should also recognize and capitalize on strengths within in the family system as protective factors for infant/toddler development. For example, low-income mothers often show more negative and punitive parenting behaviors, however, when these mothers are able to maintain higher levels of sensitivity, children's development is protected (Diener, Nievar, & Wright, 2003). Recognizing and capitalizing on support systems that help parents cultivate sensitive and responsive behaviors will in turn impact positive infant/toddler behavior. Moreover, the more supports and strengths families can draw from, the more children will thrive (Diener et al., 2003).

Knowledge of human growth and development can also guide home visitors in guidance and discipline techniques that are developmentally appropriate for the age of the infant or toddler. The developmental progression of young children's physical, cognitive, social, and emotional skills is directly linked to their behavior. For example, new motor skills such as crawling open new possibilities for the infant to explore their environment or seek out their caregiver, and new cognitive skills cause toddlers to insist that they do things by themselves. The more knowledge the home visitor has in the area of infant/toddler development, the better prepared they are to help parents guide misbehaviors and establish appropriate discipline strategies. For example, knowing that young infants learn through their senses helps parents understand why infants stick everything in their mouths. Or that toddlers have limited emotion regulation skills to calm themselves down in times of frustration, which is why they are prone to hitting, biting, and tantrums. Infants and toddlers learn about the world by actively exploring their environment, and are self-motivated, touch everything, push the boundaries, all with the goal of developing a mind of their own (Gross, 2019).

A developmental understanding of infant/toddler behavior also includes knowing how to tailor guidance and discipline strategies based on the unique characteristics of each child. For example, age of the child is critical: it is not appropriate to use discipline (especially punishment) with infants under 12 months, as these children do not have the cognitive understanding to connect

Table 10.1 Family Life Education Concepts and Resources that Align with Guidance of Infant/Toddler Behaviors

FLE Content Area: Human Growth and Development	Resources
Reciprocal relationship between individuals and families[1]; family interaction (patterns)[2]; mental health and disorders[2]; contexts of development[2]; parenting styles and children's behavior[2]	[1]Leventhal, J. (2015). Human growth and development across the lifespan. In M. J. Walcheski, & J. S. Reinke (Eds.), *Family life education: The practice of family science* (pp. 167–176). Minneapolis, MN: National Council on Family Relations. [2]Boyd, D., & Bee, H. (2015). Lifespan development (7th ed.). Upper Saddle River, NJ: Pearson.

their behavior to a consequence (Gross, 2019). Infants and toddlers also vary in temperament (e.g., activity level, adaptability, mood quality, and biological rhythmicity; Thomas & Chess, 1977). Children with an easy temperament are usually calm, adaptable, happy, and are more regular eaters/sleepers than children with a difficult temperament. These children tend to be more active, negative, fussy, and irregular eaters/sleepers. A difficult temperament is also related to a heightened stress-response system and greater reactivity to new stimuli (Buss, Davidson, Kalin, & Goldsmith, 2004; Kagan, 1994). As such, infant/toddlers with a difficult temperament may be more likely to act in ways that are unfavorable to parents, eliciting different types of parenting behaviors than young children who have an easier temperament (Roisman, Newman, Fraley, Haltigan, Groh, & Haydon, 2012). However, research suggests that when children with a difficult temperament experience high levels of maternal sensitivity across childhood, their behavior outcomes are similar (and sometimes better) than children with an easy temperament (Kennedy, 2013).

Parenting education and guidance: *An understanding of how parents teach, guide and influence children and adolescents as well as the changing nature, dynamics and needs of the parent/child relationship across the lifespan.*

Knowledge of parenting education and guidance can guide the home visitor in helping parents (and family members) understand their child's behavior and developing appropriate guidance and discipline strategies. Culture and intergenerational family experiences shape how parents approach these issues, making them tricky to navigate as professionals. In FLE, parenting education and guidance requires the professional to start where the parent is at (Jacobson, 2015). As such, it is important for the home visitor to start with how parents view their children's behavior and to develop a shared meaning about the goals they have for their child. They need to understand how parents view the purpose of guidance and discipline methods, and reasonings behind punishment decisions. Rather than

222 *Guidance of Infant/Toddler Behaviors*

flooding a family with information on the "right" way to use guidance and discipline, home visitors must gain insight to the family's values and past experiences to understand where they are coming from.

Nowhere is this more apparent than when it comes to the topic of appropriate discipline for infants and toddlers, specifically physical punishment. The Fragile Families and Child Wellbeing Study comprises nearly two thousand families who are demographically similar to the EHS population. Using data from this study, MacKenzie and colleagues (2011) found that about 15% of infants were spanked at 12 months, 40% by 18 months, and almost 50% at 20 months or older. African American children, particularly boys, were more likely to be spanked than children with white or Hispanic mothers. Young mothers, stressed mothers, and mothers who reported that their child has a difficult temperament were all more likely to use spanking, no matter their ethnicity (MacKenzie et al., 2011). A follow-up study found that after accounting for ethnicity and child sex, spanking in infancy/toddlerhood was associated with child aggression throughout early childhood and until age 9 (MacKenzie et al., 2015). Moreover, parents and children influenced each other in a bidirectional manner—spanking predicted later aggression, which in turn predicted more spanking. Most developmental scholars agree that spanking is an ineffective way to guide positive behaviors, and can be harmful for children's development (Berlin et al., 2009; Gershoff & Grogan-Kaylor, 2016).

Despite this, when working one-on-one with families, home visitors still need to meet families where they are and understand their views and goals regarding physical punishment. Parenting values and practices originate out of the cultural context within which the parent lives (Super & Harkness, 2002). For example, authoritarian discipline and physical punishment are more prevalent in African American families than white families, and some research suggests that it does not have the same effects on children. Slade and Wissow (2004) found that spanking across the first two years was associated with increased behavior problems in preschool for white children but not African American children. Studies with older children have found similar results (Deater-Deckard, Dodge, & Sorbring, 2005; Dodge, McLoyd, & Lansford, 2005). It is important to point out that multiple studies have found no difference by ethnicity (e.g., Berlin et al., 2009; MacKenzie et al., 2015). Additionally, an authoritative parenting style in which parents display high levels of engagement and warmth (while also maintaining high levels of control) is often held up as the "best" parenting style to support children's positive behaviors (Baumrind, 1971). In research with white, European, middle-class families, it is typically the case that authoritative parenting is associated with the best child behavior outcomes (Darling & Steinberg, 1993). However, research with African American families, and families living in poverty sometimes finds that children fare better in the context of a stricter, more authoritarian parenting style (Baumrind, 1972; Greening, Stoppelbein, & Luebbe, 2010). In Latino families, some research suggests that

Table 10.2 Family Life Education Concepts and Resources that Align with Guidance of Infant/Toddler Behaviors

FLE Content Area: Parenting Education and Guidance	Resources
Family conflict and guidance Educating parents with special circumstances (e.g., parenting in families with violence) and parenting in varying life circumstances[1,2]; parent–child interactions[1,2]; influences on parenting (e.g., social)[1]; prevent and respond to violence, abuse, and neglect[1]; sources of support for parenting[1]; importance of play and interaction for infants and toddlers[1]; developmentally and individually appropriate strategies[1]; mental health of parents (e.g., depression, substance abuse)[2]; family systems theory[2]; collaborative family atmosphere[2]; child maltreatment[2]; when to intervene[2]	[1]Jacobson, A. L. (2015). Parenting education and guidance. In M. J. Walcheski, & J. S. Reinke (Eds.), *Family life education: The practice of family science* (pp. 213–222). Minneapolis, MN: National Council on Family Relations. [2]Brooks, J. B. (2013). *The process of parenting* (9th ed.). New York: McGraw Hill.

the traditional parenting style framework does not capture Latino parenting, with Latino parents using a "protective" style based on lots of warmth, demandingness, but low autonomy-granting (Domènech Rodriguez, Donovick, & Crowley, 2009). Shared cultural norms and values regarding parenting may help explain these findings. For example, Darling and Steinberg (1993) emphasize that "parenting style" should be conceptualized as a context within which parenting behaviors occur. As such, parenting behaviors may have different impacts on child development depending on the parenting style context. An FLE perspective of parenting education and guidance must respect and seek to understand the "parenting context" their families are operating within, even if they diverge with the home visitor's personal views (Jacobson, 2015).

Internal dynamics of families: *Understanding of family strengths and weaknesses and how family members relate to each other.*

Knowledge of the internal workings of families prepares the home visitor to collaborate with parents (and other family members) to understand their child's behavior and develop guidance and discipline strategies. Knowledge of family systems theory is relevant here. Home visitors should conceptualize the family as a dynamic system of interconnected individuals and relationships (Segrin & Flora, 2005). From this perspective, both child behavior and guidance and discipline strategies employed, are both important components of the system.

224   *Guidance of Infant/Toddler Behaviors*

Rather than thinking of these issues in isolation, the home visitor should view them within the context of the overall family. For example, if a mother is struggling to manage her toddler's aggressive behavior, she may be feeling stressed and overwhelmed. These negative feelings can spillover to not only affect her toddler, but also her co-parenting relationship with her spouse, or interactions with her other children. As children get older, both mothers and fathers who have children with disruptive behavior issues report increased feelings of dissatisfaction as parents unless they are able to reframe these challenges in a positive light (Podolski, & Nigg, 2001).

As home visitors collaborate with families to develop appropriate guidance and discipline strategies, they also need to keep in mind how the internal workings of families affect parenting practices. For the EHS population, issues such as food insecurity, material deprivation, housing instability, and/or low wage jobs or unemployment are all taxing to the family system (Huston & Bentley, 2010). In EHS-HBO, it is key that home visitors consider these factors as they relate to parenting practices. Simply put, all of these issues strain the family system and make it more likely that parents will rely on harsh, punitive discipline techniques, be less responsive to their child's needs, and/or have less time to devote to cognitively stimulating activities (Evans, 2004). Strengths within each family can offset these issues, so that parents are better able to support their child's development. For low-income families, strengths such as communication skills, problem solving skills, family cohesion, and social support all create a context in which the family is better able so solve problems related to their children, meet their children's needs, and seek out the opportunities they need to succeed (Orthner, Jones-Sanpei, & Williamson, 2004).

Table 10.3 Family Life Education Concepts and Resources that Align with Guidance of Infant/Toddler Behaviors

FLE Content Area: Internal Dynamics of Families	Resources
Family conflict and guidance Family systems theory[1]; circumplex model of marital and family systems[1]; ABC-X model of family stress[1]; human ecology theory[1,2]; family development theory[1]; family dynamics[2]; communication[2]; parenting[2]; parenting styles[2]; stress, abuse, and family problems[2]; strengthening families[2]	[1]Reinke, J. S., & Walcheski, M. J. (2015). Internal dynamics of families. In M. J. Walcheski, & J. S. Reinke (Eds.), *Family life education: The practice of family science* (pp. 157–166). Minneapolis, MN: National Council on Family Relations. [2]Olson, D. H., DeFrain, J., & Skogrand, L. (2014). *Marriages and families: Intimacy, diversity, and strengths* (8th ed.). New York: McGraw Hill.

Interpersonal relationships: *An understanding of the development and maintenance of interpersonal relationships.*

Knowledge of interpersonal relationships also helps the EHS home visitor because it sheds light on important ways that the parent–child relationship (as well as surrounding interpersonal family relationships) affect infant/toddler behavior. Attachment relationships with parents (and other important caregivers) are the most critical interpersonal relationships that influence infant/toddler behavior and development (Bowlby, 1969/1982). They also reflect patterns of caregiving responses to young children's behaviors that were established during infancy and toddlerhood. For example, secure attachment relationships typically reflect a pattern of caregiving in which parents are responsive to infants' needs in a sensitive manner. Insecure attachment relationships typically reflect patterns of caregiving in which parents are inconsistent or are unresponsive when infants are in distress (Ainsworth, 1979). EHS home visitors can use this knowledge as a starting point for helping parents understand how relationships with their children set the foundation for behavior, and that toddler behavior issues can sometimes be resolved when these interpersonal issues are examined and addressed. For example, the Circle of Security attachment intervention framework starts with assessing attachment-caregiving practices, then building individual treatment goals to strengthen the adult-child relationship (Powell et al., 2014). One simple, but powerful strategy to enhance the parent–child relationship is to help parents reframe common misbehaviors as the child simply "seeking connection" (Powell et al., 2014). As adults, it is tempting to interpret young children's negative emotions as a personal attribute, or indication that the child is trying to annoy or frustrate parents on purpose (e.g., "My baby is screaming because she doesn't like me" or "My toddler won't pick up his toys because he wants to make me

Table 10.4 Family Life Education Concepts and Resources that Align with Guidance of Infant/Toddler Behaviors

FLE Content Area: Interpersonal Relationships	Resources
Family conflict and guidance Parents with infants and young children[1]; strengthening family relationships[2]; parenting in a positive way[2]	[1]Glotzer, R. (2015). Interpersonal relationships. In M. J. Walcheski, & J. S. Reinke (Eds.), *Family life education: The practice of family science* (pp. 189–202). Minneapolis, MN: National Council on Family Relations.
	[2]Hanna, S. L., Suggett, R., & Radtke, D. (2008). *Person to person: Positive relationships don't just happen* (5th ed.). Upper Saddle River, NJ: Pearson.

226 Guidance of Infant/Toddler Behaviors

mad"). Instead, these "misbehaviors" can be thought of as bid for connection from children (e.g., "My baby needs to feel close to me" or "My toddler needs my support").

Skills

The CUPID HV expanded competency for skills related to Knowledge of Infant/Toddler Development includes:

> Skills to help parents acquire knowledge about how physiology, stress, and family interactions influence the child's behavior, reflect on their attitudes (obedience, innate characteristics, respect for the child as a separate person needing nurturance and guidance), and develop skills of child guidance that are appropriate for their own child's temperament, development, and experience (observe child, interpret child's cues, set up environments and routines to reduce challenging behaviors, scaffold child's emotional regulation, state expectations positively).
>
> (CUPID, 2017)

Human growth and development

- Identify developmental stages and contexts

    o Recognizing infancy as an important time for social and emotional development.
    o Recognizing the role of family processes in the development of infant/ toddler behavior.

- Identify reciprocal influences on development

    o Recognizing the how child behavior is the results of interactions between parents and children.
    o Encourage parents to examine family-level issues when trying to understand their child's mis/behavior.
    o Encourage parents to consider their infant's temperament and how these inborn characteristics influence behavior.

- Recognize the impact of individual health and wellness on families

    o Recognize how adult mental health and other issues can have an impact on the entire family system and consequently infant/toddler behavior.
    o Facilitate parent knowledge about how individual health and wellness within the family system may be related to child behavior issues.
    o Help parents identify areas where individual health can be improved (and the resources necessary).

- Assist families with developmental transitions

Guidance of Infant/Toddler Behaviors 227

- o Support parents through the frustrations that come as their toddlers seek autonomy, test the limits, and learn to regulate their emotions.
- o Facilitate parent knowledge about the developmental changes that occur across 0–3, and what is expected and typical behavior.

- Guide practice using developmental theories

  - o Encourage parents to use guidance/discipline strategies that are appropriate for the cognitive maturity of the infant/toddler (Piaget's cognitive development theory).
  - o Encourage parents to use guidance/discipline strategies that promote a sense of safety and security (Erikson's psychosocial theory, attachment theory).
  - o Encourage parents to use guidance/discipline strategies that support children's developing autonomy (Erikson's psychosocial theory).

- Recognize socio-ecological influences on human development (e.g., trauma)

  - o Understanding how poverty affects infant/toddler development via the impact it has on the family system, particularly parenting practices.
  - o Recognize the cumulative nature of stress for infant/toddlers living in poverty.
  - o Recognize and help parents identify strengths within their family/community that will have a positive impact on their child's development/behavior.

Parenting education and guidance

- Promote healthy parenting from systems and lifespan perspectives

  - o Recognize that parenting is affected by (and affects) the family system.
  - o Recognize that parenting practices are passed down through generations.
  - o Help parents reflect on their own parenting practices and values and behaviors that have been passed down from previous generations.

- Promote healthy parenting from a child's and parent's developmental perspective

  - o Promote parenting practices that match the developmental characteristics of the infant/toddler.
  - o Help parents modify their behaviors and practices as their child's developmental needs change over the first three years.
  - o Have parents reflect on their goals for their child's behavior and match guidance and discipline techniques that help them meet these goals.

- Apply strategies based on child's age and stage and unique characteristics to support development

228 *Guidance of Infant/Toddler Behaviors*

- Help parents set realistic behavior expectations for their child at different ages.
- Help parents "tune in" to their infant's cues to lay the foundation for positive interactions.
- Help parents reframe misbehavior as "mistaken behavior" (Gartrell, 2004).
- Have parents analyze the motives behind children's challenging behaviors to better understand how to help them. For example, should a tantrum be ignored? Or is the tantrum a sign that the child needs connection?
- Set guidance and discipline goals with parents that are appropriate for their child's age, temperament, and other unique characteristics (e.g., special needs).
- Promote guidance methods as the first and most important steps they can take to support positive behaviors and reduce negative behaviors (e.g., modeling, positive feedback, redirection, talking, offering choices)
- Help parents arrange the home environment in ways that reduce the chance for misbehavior (e.g., moving breakable things out of reach, putting available toys on the floor, creating a space that is safe for infant exploration).
- Make a discipline plan with parents to handle specific negative behaviors. Guide parents to use non-punitive methods of discipline in developmentally appropriate ways (e.g., time out, removing materials/privileges, removal from the situation).

- Identify parenting styles and their related child outcomes

  - Through interactions and talking with parents, identify if parents use an authoritative, authoritarian, permissive or uninvolved style of parenting. Work with parents to understand what style of parenting feels normal for their family, and how they feel it supports their child's development and behavior.
  - Recognize that authoritative parenting is often the norm in families from white, European, and middle class backgrounds. For other families, a strict authoritarian style may be the norm.

- Evaluate various parenting strategies

  - Observe the effectiveness of guidance/discipline strategies and discuss these observations with parents. Find teachable moments to point out missed guidance opportunities or to offer suggestions and feedback.
  - Evaluate discipline strategies the family uses based on knowledge of child development and the cultural context of the family.
  - Pay special attention to punishment practices to determine if they are developmentally appropriate and ensure that practices are not emotionally or physically harmful to the child.

Guidance of Infant/Toddler Behaviors 229

- Recognize the impact of societal trends and cultural differences

  - Build a shared understanding with parents regarding their motives for using specific guidance/discipline strategies, and the goals they are trying to accomplish.
  - Build a shared understanding with parents about their motives for punishment, particularly physical punishment (e.g., spanking).
  - Work with families where they are in terms of how they approach guidance, discipline, and punishment. Recognize that not all families share the same parenting beliefs as the home visitor/program.

- Identify strategies to support children in various settings

  - Recognize when child misbehavior is severe and requires evaluation by a behavior analyst, developmental specialist, or other professional.

Internal dynamics of families

- Recognize and define healthy and unhealthy characteristics pertaining to family relationships and family development

  - Recognize aspects of the family system that promote positive child behaviors, including strengths that support parents in developing appropriate guidance/discipline techniques.
  - Recognize aspects of the family system that encourage negative child behaviors, including weaknesses that hinder parents in developing appropriate guidance/discipline techniques.

- Analyze family functioning using various theories

  - Conceptualize the family as a system of interconnecting relationships (family systems theory).
  - Recognize the attachment relationship between parents and infants/toddlers reflects different styles of how parents respond to and interact with their infants (attachment theory)
  - Conceptualize families living in poverty as nested within a series of ecological systems (e.g., local community, macro culture) that all impact on family functioning, which trickles down to child behavior (ecological systems theory).

- Assess family dynamics from a systems perspective

  - Conceptualize child behavior and parent practices as small pieces within a greater family system, which have an effect on (and are affected by) the entire system.
  - Observe child and parenting behaviors in relation to the functioning of the entire family system.

230 *Guidance of Infant/Toddler Behaviors*

- When parents are dealing with a misbehavior issue, redirect the parents' attention to aspects of the family system that may be contributing to the issue.

- Analyze family dynamics in response to stressors, stress, crises, and trauma

  - Support families in recognizing how stress, crises, and trauma affect infant/toddler behavior directly and indirectly through the effect it has on the parents themselves.
  - Support parents in finding resources for stress, crises, and trauma so they are better able to engage in parenting practices that meet their child's needs.
  - Facilitate and strengthen communication processes, conflict-management, and problem-solving skills.
  - Help parents (and other family members who are regularly involved in caregiving) identify sources of conflict related to managing infant/toddler behavior.
  - Work with parents (and other family members) to develop a plan to manage challenging behaviors with specific guidance/discipline strategies.

- Develop, recognize, and reinforce strategies that help families function effectively.

  - Work with families to foster cohesion (i.e., feelings of closeness) between family members as a way to support child behavior and development.
  - Identify and cultivate areas of social support (e.g., friends, family member, community) that support parental wellbeing.

Interpersonal relationships

- Recognize the impact of personality and communication styles

  - Recognize the parents' abilities to "tune in" to infant cues.
  - Recognize how the child's unique characteristics (temperament) elicit responses from parents.

- Recognize the developmental stages of relationships

  - Recognize that patterns of attachment are being established during infancy and toddlerhood, and that the quality of this relationship will have important implications for child behavior in the future.

- Analyze interpersonal relationships using various theoretical perspectives

  - Recognize that the parent–child relationship is built on the foundation of their attachment bond (Bowlby's attachment theory).

Guidance of Infant/Toddler Behaviors   231

- Recognize that toddlers' misbehavior can sometime be attributed to the quality of the parent–infant attachment relationship (Bowlby's attachment theory).

- Develop and implement relationship enhancement and enrichment strategies

  - Facilitate interactions between parents and infants that promote secure attachment. For example, help parents read and interpret their infant's cues, be responsive to their infant's needs, offer safety and security when the infant is distressed, support the infant's exploration of their environment.

- Develop and implement effective communication, problem solving, and anger and conflict management strategies

  - Help parents identify how their own communication and behavior towards their child sets the stage for developing a secure attachment relationship.
  - Model responsive language towards the child (e.g., "I see that you are upset, do you want a hug?").
  - Help parents identify when a "misbehavior" is actually the child seeking connection with the parent.
  - Help parents make connections between their own mental health and their child's behavior.

- Recognize the impact of violence and coercion in interpersonal relationships

  - Recognize that maltreatment (abuse and neglect) is a violation of the attachment relationship between parents and infants/toddlers and has serious consequences for later behavior issues.
  - Recognize the impact of extreme physical punishment on children's behavior.

- Recognize the influence of unhealthy coping strategies (e.g., substance abuse) on interpersonal relationships

  - Recognize the role of substance use (e.g., alcohol, drugs) on the parent's ability to interact with their infant/toddler in ways that will promote secure attachment.

Attitudes

The CUPID Expanded HV competency for attitudes related to Guiding Infant/Toddler Behaviors is as follows:

232 *Guidance of Infant/Toddler Behaviors*

> Attitudes that support parent respect for child autonomy (if culturally appropriate), value the role of parent in child guidance, and acknowledge parents' perspectives about obedience and punishment.
>
> (CUPID, 2017)

In building relationships with parents and families, NCFR's (2016) ethical principles state that the professional will "support and challenge parents to continue to grow and learn about parenting and their child's development," as well as "be proactive in stating child guidance principles and discipline guidelines and encourage non-violent child rearing." Moreover, according to Arcus and Thomas (1993) "family life education should be geared to the immediate needs of individuals and families and should be sensitive to the social and cultural changes that influence these needs" (p. 16). These principles of FLE reflect the attitude that both children and parents should be considered when EHS home visitors are working with families on guiding infant/toddler behavior. While it is important to foster parental respect for child autonomy, it is also necessary to assess the sociocultural beliefs of the parents regarding their child's behavior and parenting practices. Education through a strengths-based approach is a foundational principle of FLE (Darling et al., 2017), so adopting an attitude that gives space for parents' perspectives about infant/toddler behavior and appropriate discipline strategies as a starting point for setting goals, will lead to more productive collaboration with families. Collaborating with parents on how to manage toddler behavior and their beliefs about obedience and punishment can be challenging. Parents and families typically hold deeply rooted beliefs about infant/toddler behavior and it is easy for parents to feel offended if their beliefs are criticized or looked down upon by the home visitor. Family life educators hold the virtue of optimism (MCFR, 2009), which in this case helps the professional view the positive potential of parents for supporting their child's behavior. EHS home visitors can uphold this virtue by communicating respectfully and clearly with all family members (NCFR, 2016).

Box 10.1 CDA Home Visitor Competencies

The CDA Subject Areas and Competency Standards are national standards for Home Visitors. The subject area that is most relevant to this chapter includes **CDA Subject Area 8: Understanding principles of child development and learning.** Each competency standard comprises competency goals, functional areas, items, indicators, and examples. The competency goal that is most relevant to this chapter is "to support social and emotional development and provide positive guidance" (Council for Professional Recognition, 2017).

Guidance of Infant/Toddler Behaviors 233

Competency Goal	Functional Area	Example Items	Example Indicators
III. To support social and emotional development and provide positive guidance	**10 Guidance:** Home visitor helps parents provide a supportive environment, use effective strategies to promote their child's self-regulation, support acceptable behaviors, and effectively intervene for children with persistent challenging behaviors.	**Item 10.1:** Spaces and materials in the home are intentionally arranged according to children's developmental needs to promote positive interactions and limit disruptive behaviors.	Spaces and materials in the home anticipate children's behavioral and developmental needs
		Item 10.2: Helps parents learn and use positive guidance techniques.	Encourages parents to set realistic goals. Works with parents to help them understand the difference between punishment and discipline or guidance.
		Item 10.3: Helps parents to understand ways to gently guide children towards developing self-regulation and to establish methods for avoiding problems.	Helps parents develop their own skills to respect each child's dignity serving as a model of patience, understanding and acceptance. Discuss with parents ways that adults and children

(Continued)

234 Guidance of Infant/Toddler Behaviors

(Cont.)

Competency Goal	Functional Area	Example Items	Example Indicators
			learn self-regulation and ways to express discontent, anger, frustration, and anxiety.

Permission to reprint from the Council for Professional Recognition, 2019

Box 10.2 National Family Support Competency Framework for Family Support Professionals

The National Family Support Competency Framework for Family Support Professionals are competencies that include ten domains that are further clarified by dimensions (Institute for the Advancement of Family Support Professionals, 2018). There is one domain that is relevant to this chapter: (a) Parent–Child Interactions. Parent–Child Interactions includes three dimensions: influences on parenting, parent–child relationship, and developmentally appropriate guidance.

Domain 3	Dimension 13	Component b.	Levels of Competency
Parent–child interactions	Developmentally appropriate guidance	Positive guidance strategies	**1-Recognizing.** Understands positive guidance strategies including limit setting, providing choices, and natural and logical consequences
			3-Applying. Supports parents with information about positive guidance strategies and models the use of a variety of strategies
			5-Extending. Coaches parents to reflect on child's challenging behaviors and develop a list of positive guidance strategies to address these behaviors

Permission to reprint from the Institute for the Advancement of Family Support Professionals.

Summary

Working with parents to support infant/toddler behavior is a critical component of EHS-HBO programs. Home visitors have an ethical obligation to work with families in ways that will promote positive infant/toddler development. This is challenging work because parents' ideas and values about guidance, discipline, and punishment are rooted in sociocultural values. Knowledge in the FLE content areas human growth and development, parenting education and guidance, internal dynamics of families, and interpersonal relationships help establish the developmental foundations for understanding infant/toddler behavior and developmentally appropriate guidance and discipline strategies, how to work with parents effectively, particularly how to use attachment to build the foundations for healthy behaviors and navigate sensitive issues regarding physical punishment.

Key Concepts

- Attachment
- Authoritarian parenting
- Authoritative parenting
- Autonomy
- Developmentally appropriate
- Discipline
- Dyadic synchrony
- Guidance
- Parenting styles
- Punishment
- Redirection
- Socialization
- Temperament

Recommended Readings

Gartrell, D. (2004). *The power of guidance: Teaching social-emotional skills in early childhood classrooms.* Washington DC: National Association for the Education of Young Children.

MacKenzie, M. J., Nicklas, E., Brooks-Gunn, J., & Waldfogel, J. (2011). Who spanks infants and toddlers? Evidence from the fragile families and child well-being study. *Children and Youth Services Review, 33,* 1364–1373.

References

Arcus, M. E., & Thomas, J. (1993). The nature and practice of family life education. In M. E. Arcus, J. D. Schvaneveldt, & J. J. Moss (Eds.), *Handbook of family education: The practice of family life education* (pp. 1–32). Newbury Park, CA: Sage.

236 *Guidance of Infant/Toddler Behaviors*

Ainsworth, M. S. (1979). Infant–mother attachment. *American Psychologist, 34*(10), 932.

Bagner, D. M., Pettit, J. W., Lewinsohn, P. M., & Seeley, J. R. (2010). Effect of maternal depression on child behavior: A sensitive period?. *Journal of the American Academy of Child & Adolescent Psychiatry, 49*(7), 699–707.

Baumrind, D. (1971). Current patterns of parental authority. *Developmental Psychology, 4*, 1–103.

Baumrind, D. (1972). An exploratory study of socialization effects on black children: Some black–white comparisons. *Child Development, 43*, 261–267.

Bergman, K., Sarkar, P., O'Connor, T. G., Modi, N., & Glover, V. (2007). Maternal stress during pregnancy predicts cognitive ability and fearfulness in infancy. *Journal of the American Academy of Child & Adolescent Psychiatry, 46*(11), 1454–1463.

Berlin, L. J., Ispa, J. M., Fine, M. A., Malone, P. S., Brooks-Gunn, J., Brady-Smith, C., ... & Bai, Y. (2009). Correlates and consequences of spanking and verbal punishment for low-income White, African American, and Mexican American toddlers. *Child Development, 80*(5), 1403–1420.

Brooks, J. B. (2013). *The process of parenting* (9th ed.). New York: McGraw Hill.

Bowlby, J. (1969/1982). *Attachment and loss: Vol. 1. Attachment.* (2nd ed). New York: Basic Books.

Boyd, D., & Bee, H. (2015). *Lifespan development* (7th ed.). Upper Saddle River, NJ: Pearson.

Buss, K. A., Davidson, R. J., Kalin, N. H., & Goldsmith, H. H. (2004). Context-specific freezing and associated physiological reactivity as a dysregulated fear response. *Developmental Psychology, 40*, 583–594.

Carpenter, G. L., & Stacks, A. M. (2009). Developmental effects of exposure to intimate partner violence in early childhood: A review of the literature. *Children and Youth Services Review, 31*(8), 831–839.

Cohen, L. R., Hien, D. A., & Batchelder, S. (2008). The impact of cumulative maternal trauma and diagnosis on parenting behavior. *Child Maltreatment, 13*(1), 27–38.

Cole, P. M., Martin, S. E., & Dennis, T. A. (2004). Emotion regulation as a scientific construct: Methodological challenges and directions for child development research. *Child Development, 75*(2), 317–333.

Collaborative for Understanding the Pedagogy of Infant/toddler Development (CUPID). (2017). *Comprehensive competencies for educators of infants and toddlers in group care and home visiting settings.* Unpublished.

Council for Professional Recognition. (2017). *The Child Development Associate® National Credentialing Program and CDA® Competency Standards: Home visitor edition.* Washington DC: Council on Professional Recognition.

Cummings, E. M., & Davies, P. T. (2002). Effects of marital conflict on children: Recent advances and emerging themes in process-oriented research. *Journal of child psychology and psychiatry, 43*(1), 31–63.

Darling, C. A., Cassidy, D., & Rehm, M. (2017). Family life education: Translational family science in action. *Family Relations, 66*, 741–752. doi: 10.1111/fare.12286

Darling, N., & Steinberg, L. (1993) Parenting style as context: An integrative model. *Psychological Bulletin, 113*, 487–496.

Davis, E. P., Glynn, L. M., Waffarn, F., & Sandman, C. A. (2011). Prenatal maternal stress programs infant stress regulation. *Journal of Child Psychology and Psychiatry, 52*(2), 119–129.

Deater-Deckard, K., Dodge, K. A., & Sorbring, E. (2005). Cultural differences in the effects of physical punishment. In M. Rutter & M. Tienda (Eds.), *Ethnicity and causal mechanisms* (pp. 204–226). New York: Cambridge University Press.

Dodge, K. A., McLoyd, V. C., & Lansford, J. E. (2005). The cultural context of physically disciplining children. In V. C. McLoyd, N. E. Hill, & K. A. Dodge (Eds.), *African American family life: Ecological and cultural diversity* (pp. 245–263). New York: Guilford.

Diener, M. L., Nievar, M. A., & Wright, C. (2003). Attachment security among mothers and their young children living in poverty: Associations with maternal, child, and contextual characteristics. *Merrill-Palmer Quarterly (1982–),* 154–182.

Domènech Rodriguez, M. M., Donovick, M. R., & Crowley, S. L. (2009). Parenting styles in a cultural context: Observations of "protective parenting" in first-generation Latinos. *Family Process, 48,* 195–210.

Essa, E. L. (2012). *Introduction to early childhood education.* Belmont, CA: Wadsworth.

Evans, G. W. (2004). The environment of childhood poverty. *American Psychologist, 59* (2), 77–92.

Evans, G. W., & Kim, P. (2007). Childhood poverty and health: Cumulative risk exposure and stress dysregulation. *Psychological Science, 18,* 953–957.

Gershoff, E. T., & Grogan-Kaylor, A. (2016). Spanking and child outcomes: Old controversies and new meta-analyses. *Journal of Family Psychology, 30,* 453.

Glotzer, R. (2015). Interpersonal relationships. In M. J. Walcheski, & J. S. Reinke (Eds.), *Family life education: The practice of family science* (pp. 189–202). Minneapolis, MN: National Council on Family Relations.

Greening, L., Stoppelbein, L., & Luebbe, A. (2010). The moderating effects of parenting styles on African-American and Caucasian children's suicidal behaviors. *Journal of Youth and Adolescence, 39,* 357–369.

Gross, D. (2019). *Infancy: Development from birth to age 3* (3rd ed.). Lanham, MD: Roman & Littlefield.

Gartrell, D. (2004). *The power of guidance: Teaching social-emotional skills in early childhood classrooms.* Washington DC: National Association for the Education of Young Children.

Hanna, S. L., Suggett, R., & Radtke, D. (2008). *Person to person: Positive relationships don't just happen* (5th ed.). Upper Saddle River, NJ: Pearson.

Huston, A. C., & Bentley, A. C. (2010). Human development in societal context. *Annual Review of Psychology, 61,* 411–437.

Institute for the Advancement of Family Support Professionals. (2018). *National Family Support Competency Framework for Family Support Professionals.* Retrieved from: https://cppr-institute-prod.s3.amazonaws.com/modules/Approved%20National% 20Family%20Support%20Competency%20Framework_FINAL_7_18_2018.pdf

Jacobson, A. L. (2015). Parenting education and guidance. In M. J. Walcheski, & J. S. Reinke (Eds.), *Family life education: The practice of family science* (pp. 213–222). Minneapolis, MN: National Council on Family Relations.

Kagan, J. (1994). On the nature of emotion. In N. A. Fox (Ed.)., The development of emotion regulation: Biological and behavioral considerations. *Monographs of the Society for Research in Child Development, 59,* 7–24.

238 *Guidance of Infant/Toddler Behaviors*

Kennedy, E. (2013). Orchids and dandelions: How some children are more susceptible to environmental influences for better or worse and the implications for child development. *Clinical Child Psychology and Psychiatry, 18*(3), 319–321.

Krishnakumar, A., & Buehler, C. (2000). Interparental conflict and parenting behaviors: A metaanalytic review. *Family Relations, 49*, 25–44.

Leventhal, J. (2015). Human growth and development across the lifespan. In M. J. Walcheski, & J. S. Reinke (Eds.), *Family life education: The practice of family science* (pp. 167–176). Minneapolis, MN: National Council on Family Relations.

Lovejoy, M. C., Graczyk, P. A., O'Hare, E., & Neuman, G. (2000). Maternal depression and parenting behavior: A meta-analytic review. *Clinical Psychology Review, 20*, 561–592.

Macfie, J., Cicchetti, D., & Toth, S. L. (2001). The development of dissociation in maltreated preschool-aged children. *Development and Psychopathology, 13*, 233–254.

MacKenzie, M. J., Nicklas, E., Brooks-Gunn, J., & Waldfogel, J. (2011). Who spanks infants and toddlers? Evidence from the fragile families and child well-being study. *Children and Youth Services Review, 33*, 1364–1373.

MacKenzie, M. J., Nicklas, E., Brooks-Gunn, J., & Waldfogel, J. (2015). Spanking and children's externalizing behavior across the first decade of life: Evidence for transactional processes. *Journal of Youth and Adolescence, 44*, 658–669.

McKeganey, N., Barnard, M., & McIntosh, J. (2002). Paying the price for their parents' addiction: meeting the needs of the children of drug-using parents. *Drugs: Education, Prevention and Policy, 9*, 233–246.

Minnesota Council on Family Relations (MCFR). (2009). Ethical thinking and practice for parent and family life educators. In D. Bredehoft & M. Walcheski (Eds.), *Family life education: Integrating theory and practice* (pp. 233–239). Minneapolis, MN: National Council on Family Relations.

National Council on Family Relations (NCFR). (2016). *Family life educators code of ethics.* National Council on Family Relations. Retrieved from: https://www.ncfr.org/cfle-certification/cfle-code-ethics

Olson, D. H., DeFrain, J., & Skogrand, L. (2014). *Marriages and families: Intimacy, diversity, and strengths* (8th ed.). New York: McGraw Hill.

Orthner, D. K., Jones-Sanpei, H., & Williamson, S. (2004). The resilience and strengths of low-income families. *Family Relations, 53*, 159–167.

Pachter, L. M., Auinger, P., Palmer, R., & Weitzman, M. (2006). Do parenting and the home environment, maternal depression, neighborhood, and chronic poverty affect child behavioral problems differently in different racial-ethnic groups?. *Pediatrics, 117* (4), 1329–1338.

Peterson, G. W., & Rollins, B. C. (1987). Parent–child socialization. In G. W. Peterson & K. R. Bush (Eds.), *Handbook of marriage and the family* (pp. 471–507). Springer, Boston, MA.

Podolski, C. L., & Nigg, J. T. (2001). Parent stress and coping in relation to child ADHD severity and associated child disruptive behavior problems. *Journal of Clinical Child Psychology, 30*, 503–513.

Powell, B., Cooper, G., Hoffman, K., & Marvin, B. (2014). *The Circle of Security intervention.* New York: The Guilford Press.

Reinke, J. S., & Walcheski, M. J. (2015). Internal dynamics of families. In M. J. Walcheski, & J. S. Reinke (Eds.), *Family life education: The practice of family science* (pp. 157–166). Minneapolis, MN: National Council on Family Relations.

Roggman, L., Peterson, C., Cohen, R. C., Ispa, J., Decker, K. B., Hughes-Belding, K., Cook, G., & Vallotton, C. D. (2016). Preparing home visitors to partner with families of infants and toddlers. *Journal of Early Childhood Teacher Education, 37*, 301–313. http://dx.doi.org/10.1080/10901027.2017.1298369

Roisman, G. I., Newman, D. A., Fraley, R. C., Haltigan, J. D., Groh, A. M., & Haydon, K. C. (2012). Distinguishing differential susceptibility from diathesis–stress: Recommendations for evaluating interaction effects. *Development and Psychopathology, 24*, 389–409.

Ryan, J. B., Sanders, S., Katsiyannis, A., & Yell, M. L. (2007). Using time-out effectively in the classroom. *Teaching Exceptional Children, 39*, 60–67.

Segrin, C., & Flora, J. (2005). *Family communication.* Mahwah, NJ: Lawrence Erlbaum Associates.

Slade, E. P., & Wissow, L. S. (2004). Spanking in early childhood and later behavior problems: A prospective study of infants and young toddlers. *Pediatrics, 113*, 1321–1330.

Sobel, D. M., & Kirkham, N. Z. (2006). Blickets and babies: the development of causal reasoning in toddlers and infants. *Developmental Psychology, 42*, 1103–1115.

Sroufe, L. A. (1979). Socioemotional development. In J. Osofsky (Ed.), *Handbook of infant development* (pp. 462–516). New York: Wiley.

Sroufe, L. A., Carlson, E., Shulman, S. (1993). The development of individuals in relationships: From infancy through adolescence. In D. C. Funder, R. D. Prake, C. Tomlinson-Keasey, & K. Widaman (Eds.), *Studying lives through time: Approaches to personality and development* (pp. 315–342). Washington DC: American Psychological Association Press.

Super, C. M., & Harkness, S. (2002). Culture structures the environment for development. *Human Development, 45*, 270–274.

Thomas, A., & Chess, S. (1977). *Temperament and development.* New York: Brunner/ Mazel.

van IJzendoorn, M. H., Schuengel, C., & Bakermans-Kranenburg, M. J. (1999). Disorganized attachment in early childhood: Mata-analysis of precursors, concomitants, and sequelae. *Development and Psychopathology, 11*, 225–249.

11 Partnering with and Supporting Families

EHS-HBO is a "two-generation" program, meaning that supporting infant/toddler development is a primary goal of the program, in addition to partnering with and supporting parents (and other family members) as well (ACF, 2002). As set forth in the Head Start Act (ACF, 2007), EHS programs must "ensure that the level of services provided to families responds to their needs and circumstances" (Sec. 645A. [42 U.S.C. 9840A]). Many of the previous chapters have focused on the home visitor's knowledge and skills related to infant/toddler development and parenting. This chapter zooms out from the infant/toddler and instead focuses on how the home visitor partners with the family – specifically identifying family values, strengths, and circumstances. This chapter examines the CUPID Competency **Partnering with and Supporting Families** (CUPID, 2017; Roggman et al., 2016).

Competency	Establishing effective, regular, bi-directional communication with families to guide the use of practices that synthesize family and professional perspectives, and that work towards shared goals for the child.
Knowledge	Expanded knowledge of variability in family circumstances and values evident in family interactions, routines, organizations, possessions, and use of spaces
Skills	Skills for guiding parents to identify their own goals for children and use their family's resources to reach those goals, for collaborating with parents to establish common goals for home visits, and for adapting to individual communication styles and needs and to family culture and beliefs
Attitudes	Attitudes of willingness to defer to parents' strengths and preferences, and respect for parent as an expert on the child, the family as the child's primary environment, a wide range of family circumstances, and for the unique family resources for supporting child development

For the full alignment see Appendix B.

The FLE Content Areas that help expand this competency include:

Human sexuality	Understanding of the physiological, psychological, and social aspects of sexual development across the lifespan
Parenting education and guidance	How parents teach, guide, and influence as the dynamic context of the parent–child relationship
Family resource management	Understand the decisions individuals and families make about developing and allocating resources including time, money, material assets, energy, friends, neighbors, and space, to meet their goals
Professional ethics and practice	Understanding of the character and quality of human social conduct, and the ability to critically examine ethical questions and issues as they relate to professional practice
FLE methodology	Understand principles of FLE in tandem with planning and delivery of programs
Family law and public policy	Understand legal issues, policies, and laws influencing the wellbeing of families
Internal dynamics of families	Understanding of family strengths and weaknesses and how family members relate to each other

Note: Permission to reprint was granted from the National Council on Family Relations.

Knowledge

The CUPID expanded knowledge for partnering and supporting families is stated as:

> Expanded knowledge of variability in family circumstances and values evident in family interactions, routines, organizations, possessions, and use of spaces.
>
> (CUPID, 2017)

Family Partnerships Are Key

Family partnerships are key to supporting young children's outcomes. The degree to which families are involved in the home visiting program is the foundation of family partnerships. Korfmacher and colleagues (2008) define involvement as "the process of the parent connecting with and using the services of a program to the best of the parent's and the program's ability" (p. 173). Involvement includes aspects of program participation such as amount, frequency, and duration of home visits and time in the program. Involvement also includes emotional feedback. Parents have positive (or negative) emotional responses towards the

242   *Partnering with and Supporting Families*

program. The helping relationship is the emotional and goal-oriented partnership that develops between the home visitor and the family (Korfmacher et al., 2008). Home visitors must work to cultivate positive emotional responses and helping relationships while accounting for individual family circumstances and values.

Research on home visiting programs supports building relationships as critical to home visiting. A review of qualitative research on home visiting across a variety of programs determined that "building and preserving relationships with the [family] is the central focus of home visiting and provides a foundation for problem identification and problem solving" (McNaughton, 2000, p. 405). Relationships lay the foundation for all other work that goes into home visiting. Parents will be reluctant to open up about intimate aspects of family life without a quality relationship as the foundation. When families enter EHS-HBO, the home visitor is charged with establishing and maintaining these relationships. Home visitors in a variety of programs reported that it takes skill and experience to do this successfully (Heaman, Chalmers, Woodgate, & Brown, 2007). They have to learn to navigate sensitive issues around family needs, child assessment, and be open about the program's goals and expectations. Home visitors reported that the core areas of relationship-building with families include:

- Support: home visitors must provide support to the family
- Trust: home visitors and family members must learn to trust one another
- Partnership: home visitors must view their work as a collaborative effort with the family
- Boundaries: maintaining professional-client boundaries between the home visitor and family.

In EHS-HBO, family partnerships are seen as the foundation for home visiting success. For example, in EHS-HBO programs, quality engagement between families and home visitors has been associated with mothers' improved mental health at the end of the program (Raikes, Green, Atwater, Kisker, Constantine, & Chazan-Cohen, 2006). Additionally, fathers who interacted more with, were willing to learn from, and had an easy and pleasant relationship with their EHS home visitor were more engaged and involved in the program and with their infants (Roggman, Boyce, Cook, & Cook, 2002). Research with a national sample of EHS-HBO families from Roggman, Cook, Peterson, and Raikes (2008) suggests that home visiting programs can increase participation in the program by keeping families engaged with individualized home visits and being mindful of issues that may distract the family at home visits.

Since home visiting is a collaborative effort with families, parents and home visitors must establish shared goals for infants and toddlers in the program.

When the home visitor is able to facilitate interactions that involve both the parent and child, home visits are rated as higher in interaction quality and engagement (Peterson et al., 2018). Research with a national sample of EHS-HBO families has also found that the visit programs increase family participation in the program when they keep the visit focused on the child's individualized needs (Roggman et al., 2008). Child-focused home visits are also associated with children's increased cognitive and language skills at preschool-entry due to better home learning environments (Raikes et al., 2006). Home visitors need to understand the variety of family experiences in EHS-HBO as they work to establish these relationships and goals.

Variety of Family Experiences in Early Head Start

Many families enrolled in EHS-HBO have similar economic backgrounds, but family circumstances vary widely. EHS programs span urban and rural geographic areas across the U.S. Some EHS programs are operated by (or operate within) tribal communities. The eligibility requirements for families to participate in EHS-HBO are set forth by the Head Start Act (ACF, 2007). Families with children under three are eligible, but pregnant women may also enroll. Family income must fall below the federal poverty guidelines ($16,910/year for a parent and one child; U.S. Department of Health and Human Services, 2019), or the family must prove they are eligible for public assistance (e.g., TANF child-only payments). Some children in the program are homeless, or in foster care. Some children have documented disabilities.

The Early Head Start Family and Child Experiences Study (Baby FACES) is an ongoing descriptive study conducted by the Administration for Children and Families that examines the experiences of families in EHS programs nationwide. A 2015 report from the ACF provides a descriptive account of the various families in Early Head Start. Families report a variety of ethnicities, with 37% Hispanic, 37% white, 16% African American, 7% multi-racial non-Hispanic, 2% American Indian or Alaskan Native, and 1% other (ACF, 2015). In terms of family factors that confer risk, the Baby FACES study assessed if mothers were (1) single, (2) had their first baby as a teenager, (3) lacked a high school or equivalent GED, (4) received public assistance, and (5) unemployed or not in school. When toddlers were 24 months old, 58% of mothers reported less than three risk factors (low risk), and 17% reported four to five risk factors (high risk). Nearly a quarter of children in EHS had a documented special need (e.g., atypical hearing, speech, behavior, attention, or movement, or developmental delay). Many families in EHS lived in neighborhoods that scored high on negative neighborhood characteristics such deteriorating buildings, streets with potholes and litter, drug and alcohol paraphernalia, and fear of personal safety (ACF, 2015).

In sum, these demographic statistics point to the wide variety of family experiences in EHS programs. It is important for home visitors to recognize and understand the variability across families in their program so they can build partnerships that support their unique needs. The following sections explore how knowledge in many FLE content areas expands the home visitor's understanding of family circumstances and values in different aspects of family life.

A key component of FLE is "being with" families instead of "doing for" families (Petkus, 2015). Doing things for families implies that the home visitor is the "expert" coming to "fix" the family with their expert knowledge. In contrast, being with families implies that the home visitor works in a collaborative partnership by meeting families where they are.

FLE Content Area Knowledge and Knowledge of Partnering with and Supporting Families

Human sexuality. *Understanding of the physiological, psychological, and social aspects of sexual development across the lifespan.*

While much of this chapter is focused on partnering with and supporting families in terms of parent–child interactions and child outcomes, human sexuality is also relevant for families. Human sexuality is an important component to parents' health and wellbeing, but is also intertwined with family values, ethics, and religion. For FLE, content knowledge regarding human sexuality involves providing accurate information to families (regarding reproduction, contraception, sexual/gender identity, and other topics), understanding attitudes and values, assisting families in communication and decision-making regarding human sexuality topics, and helping families with responsible sexual behavior (Darling & Howard, 2015). Families in EHS-HBO are all either pregnant or have an infant or toddler – this means that most families in the program are in the child-bearing phase of life and are making decisions about family planning. Family planning involves all of the decisions families make regarding child-bearing and contraception. Families may turn to home visitors for accurate information or support regarding contraception options (e.g., condoms, birth control pills, intrauterine devices, etc.) and women's health care. Low-income families in EHS-HBO may be eligible for publicly-funded family planning services through Title X, Medicaid, or other programs. The Guttmacher Institute (2019) estimates that 20.2 million women (ages 13–44) needed publicly funded family planning services in 2014, and that every $1.00 in public funds invested in helping women avoid unintended pregnancies yields $7.09 in Medicaid expenditures. Home visitors have a responsibility to use an expanded knowledge of human sexuality to provide families with accurate information and resources regarding family planning services available to families in their programs, if they are seeking advice.

Home visitors will also encounter family members of various sexual orientations and gender identities. Sexual orientation is sexual and emotional attraction to others. Sexual minority young adults (e.g., lesbians, gays, bisexuals) are disproportionately more likely to experience depression, suicidality, and substance use (Watson, Wheldon, Wichstrøm, & Russell, 2015). Reviews of many scientific studies continue to find that child outcomes do not vary based on parents' sexual orientation, but LGB parents can face parenting challenges that stem from discrimination, such as less support from family and colleagues, or living in communities or states will less legal support (Goldberg, Gartrell, & Gates, 2014). Transgender people "are a diverse population of individuals who cross or transcend culturally defined categories of gender" (Bockting, Miner, Swinburne Romine, Hamilton, & Coleman, 2013, p. 943). An FLE perspective of human sexuality considers that health and wellbeing is comprise psychological, physiological, and cognitive wellbeing (Darling & Howard, 2015). Transgender people report high clinical levels of depression and anxiety, made worse by experiences of social oppression and discrimination (Bockting et al., 2013). As such, a strength-based approach to working with families requires that the home visitor respect the sexual and gender identities of individuals, including assisting families in seeking necessary resources and supports.

Working with families from a variety of backgrounds, with diverse experiences, means that families will have a range of values and attitudes about human sexuality. Family members and home visitors may not share the same ideas about contraception, decisions about child-bearing, what healthy sexual practices look like between romantic partners, or appropriate sexual/gender identities. An FLE approach to human sexuality "deals with examining issues honestly, and is not about telling others what to do" (Darling & Howard, 2015, p. 177). Home visitors must show respect for the values and preferences of individual family members. However, partnering with and supporting families also means that the home visitor has a responsibility to provide accurate and scientific information in this area.

Table 11.1 Family Life Education Concepts and Resources that Align with Partnering with and Supporting Families

FLE Content Area: Human Sexuality	Resources
Each families values, strengths, circumstances Make decisions based on laws and professional ethics[1]; balance accurate information with respect for values and preferences[1]; show respect for sexual diversity[1]; gender, sexuality, and sexual orientation[2]; ethics, religion, and sexuality[2]	[1]Darling, C. A., & Howard, S. (2015). Human sexuality across the lifespan. In M. J. Walcheski, & J. S. Reinke (Eds.), *Family life education: The practice of family science* (pp. 177–188). Minneapolis, MN: National Council on Family Relations. [2]Hyde, J. S., & Delamater, J. D. (2017). *Understanding human sexuality* (13th ed.). New York: McGraw Hill.

246 *Partnering with and Supporting Families*

Parenting education and guidance. *How parents teach, guide, and influence as the dynamic context of the parent–child relationship.*

Partnering with and supporting parents is a central component to the FLE content area of parenting education and guidance. An important aspect of this content area is understanding the beliefs and functions of families with background and characteristics that may differ from one's own (Jacobson, 2015), in this case the home visitor. The developmental niche (Super & Harkness, 2002) helps put parenting values and practices in context so home visitors can be better partners with families by understanding the values, practices, and motives of parents. The developmental niche comprises (1) the settings and environments children are exposed to, (2) the customs and values parents hold about child-rearing, and (3) the psychology and wellbeing of the parent (Super & Harkness, 2002). All of these things put together create a unique "niche" that is culturally-dependent and creates a context in which child development occurs. From this perspective home visitors partner with and support families by examining parenting while they consider questions such as:

- What opportunities do environments offer children for learning and practicing skills and competencies?
- What kind of competencies are valued in the community and why?
- At what ages are children expected to master particular skills, and what are the environmentally motived reason for doing so?
- What are the availability of parents, peers, siblings, and others to help children learn?

(Harkness, Super, Barry, Zeitlin, & Long, 2009, p. 133)

Table 11.2 Family Life Education Concepts and Resources that Align with Partnering with and Supporting Families

FLE Content Area: Parenting Education and Guidance	Resources
Each families' values, strengths, circumstances Parenting as a multi-generational and developmental process[1]; parenting as process[2]; understand beliefs and functions of families with backgrounds and characteristics different from own[1]; cultural influences on parenting[2]; role of routines[2]	[1] Jacobson, A. L. (2015). Parenting education and guidance. In M. J. Walcheski, & J. S. Reinke (Eds.), *Family life education: The practice of family science* (pp. 213–222). Minneapolis, MN: National Council on Family Relations. [2] Brooks, J. B. (2013). *The process of parenting* (9th ed.). New York: McGraw Hill.

Family resource management. *Understand the decisions individuals and families make about developing and allocating resources including time, money, material assets, energy, friends, neighbors, and space, to meet their goals.*

The interactions and routines that characterize daily family life are all informed by "planning, organizing, leading, and controlling the use of resources to accomplish their goals" (Moore & Asay, 2015, p. 205). According to Moore and Asay (2015), families strive to meet the individual needs of all family members, but also maintain the integrity of the whole family system. Families also have to find and make decisions about material resources (e.g., money, possessions) and human capital (e.g., earning potential, social support). Home visitors can use knowledge in this content area to answer this question: what values are evident in how families make decisions about family resource management?

Cultural factors play a major role in how families acquire and allocate resources (Moore & Asay, 2015). Depending on cultural background, families differ in how they balance the needs of the individual versus the needs of the group. These differences are seen in different cultural models, termed individualism and collectivism. Individualism can be defined as "a social pattern that consists of loosely linked individuals who view themselves as independent of collectives" (Triandis, 1995, p. 2). Families with an individualistic orientation tend to prioritize individual preferences, rights, and personal goals over the goals of the group. This cultural model tends to characterize families from Europe, North America, Australia and New Zealand (Brooks, 2013). Collectivism can be defined as "a social pattern consisting of closely linked individuals who see themselves as part of one or more collectives ... primarily motivated by the norms of, and duties imposed by, those collectives" (Triandis, 1995, p. 2). Families with a collectivist orientation tend to prioritize the needs of the group over the needs of the individual and emphasize family connectedness. This cultural model is characteristic of families of Asian, African, or South American descent (Brooks, 2013). These cultural models are not mutually exclusive, but they do help define how families make decisions regarding family resource management. A family with an individualistic orientation may be more willing to put money, time, and emotional resources towards something that will fulfill the personal happiness of one family member, at the expense of the group. For example, a mother may end her romantic relationship with her child's father for the sake of her personal happiness, or parents may be very focused on promoting their toddler's independence. In contrast, a family with a collectivist orientation may be more apt to utilize family resources in ways that favor the entire system, at the expense of the personal happiness of individual family members. For example, a mother may feel morally obligated to provide care for extended family members, or be more apt to emphasize their child's connections and relationships with others. A home visitor's role is to be mindful of families' cultural values as they guide the decision-making process of acquiring and utilizing family resources, as these models are the foundation for what families' value and the decisions they make.

248 *Partnering with and Supporting Families*

Table 11.3 Family Life Education Concepts and Resources that Align with Partnering
with and Supporting Families

FLE Content Area: Family Resource Management	Resources
Each families' values, strengths, circumstances[1] Cultural influences[1]; environmental influences and circumstances[1,2]; develop personal resources[1]; clarify values as basis for choice[1,2]; resources to meet basic family needs[1]; decision making-process[1,2]	[1]Moore, T. J., & Asay, S. M. (2015). Family resource management. In M. J. Walcheski, & J. S. Reinke (Eds.), *Family life education: The practice of family science* (pp. 205–212). Minneapolis, MN: National Council on Family Relations. [2]Moore, T. J., & Asay, S. M. (2018). *Family resource management* (3rd ed.). Thousand Oaks, CA: Sage.

Professional ethics and practice. *Understanding of the character and quality of human social conduct, and the ability to critically examine ethical questions and issues as they relate to professional practice.*

According to Palm (2015), ethics play a critical role in all FLE work because work with families is inherently intimate; home visitors are privy to many aspects of families' lives, and can cause real harm if situations are not handled in an ethical manner. The Minnesota Council on Family Relations (MCFR) outlines three approaches to ethics for FLE professionals (MCFR, 2009): (1) a relational ethics approach to working with families in which caring and relationships between the home visitor and family provide the context for making ethical decisions; (2) a principles approach to ethics that clarifies specific organized principles to guide ethical interactions with families; and (3) virtue ethics which are "dispositions to do the right thing for the right reasons" such as being caring, using practical wisdom or prudence, and being hopeful or optimistic with families (MCFR, 2009, p. 4). Put together, these ethical approaches provide a framework for partnering with and supporting families in ways that nurture and support the caring relationship between the home visitor and family, with principles in place to guide ethical decision making.

Home visitors very often find themselves in situations in which they hold conflicting values with the family on any number of issues – child discipline practices, developmentally appropriate child behaviors, family planning, use of community resources, etc. As discussed throughout this chapter, home visitors must prioritize families' values, but also have a duty to provide accurate information as professionals. MCFR's (2009, pp. 6–7) ethical principles for working with parents and families include:

- Respecting cultural beliefs, backgrounds, and differences and engage in practice that is sensitive to the diversity of child-rearing values and goals.

Partnering with and Supporting Families 249

Table 11.4 Family Life Education Concepts and Resources that Align with Partnering with and Supporting Families

FLE Content Area: Professional Ethics and Practice	Resources
Each families' values, strengths, circumstances Ethical principles as one type of value[1]; ethical values as a guide to conduct[1]	[1]Palm, G. F. (2015). Professional ethics and practice. In M. J. Walcheski, & J. S. Reinke (Eds.), *Family life education: The practice of family science* (pp. 235–241). Minneapolis, MN: National Council on Family Relations.

- Supporting and challenging parents to continue to grow and learn about parenting and their child's development.
- Communicating openly and truthfully about the nature and extent of services provided.
- Supporting diverse family values by acknowledging and examining alternative parenting practices that support healthy family relationships.

As discussed in Chapter 5, home visitors must engage in their own self-reflection on their values and attitudes regarding family life and working with families who differ from their own. Truly partnering *with* families (as opposed to doing things *for* families) requires this self-reflection and integration of professional ethics.

FLE methodology. *Understand principles of FLE in tandem with planning and delivery of programs.*

FLE methodology applied in a home visiting setting starts with a needs assessment of the family, developing goals and objectives for the family's time in the program, implementation of the program, and continual evaluation (Covey, 2015). Per the Head Start Performance Standards (ACF, 2016), individual EHS-HBO programs are in charge of setting up the assessment-evaluation cycle and make decisions on which tools they use to accomplish this (see Chapter 9). Given this, home visitors working in EHS-HBO programs must work within the structural boundaries of their given program as they partner with and support families.

Home visitors can facilitate partnerships with families by integrating elements of FLE methodology related to effective instruction and engagement. First, the home visitor can foster more meaningful instruction when they ask parents to "activate" what they already know (Merrill, 2001). As an example, say a home visitor wants to teach a parent information about toddler self-regulation to help the parent better understand why his toddler gets so frustrated and has outbursts. The home visitor might start with asking the parent to think of a time when they were frustrated but no one understood why. Or ask the

250 *Partnering with and Supporting Families*

parent to think of a time they tried to help their toddler's outburst but were not successful. The home visitor can also foster more meaningful instruction by demonstrating new information or skills to the parent (Merrill, 2001). Continuing the example above, rather than simply giving the parent information about toddler self-regulation, they can demonstrate the knowledge to the parent. Duncan and Goddard (2011) suggest that home visitors ask parents "what they would normally say under such circumstances" (p. 89) to activate an automatic response. The home visitor can then lead the parent through a series of questions to analyze the effectiveness of this response, demonstrating to the parent why a new strategy might be more effective.

Additionally, as described in the sections above, families in EHS-HBO have a wide range of experiences, cultural backgrounds, and needs. FLE methodology also provides guidance for the home visitor to reach audiences with diverse needs (Covey, 2015). It is necessary to sensitize, or "tune in," to the varying backgrounds, experiences, and needs of each family (Duncan & Goddard, 2011). Families also hold a variety of values that will impact how they interact with a program, such as:

- The value placed on individual accomplishment versus family or social group wellbeing.
- Communication preferences such as comfort level for self-disclosure, or how direct comments/questions are interpreted.
- Action oriented in creating and setting program goals versus being more reflective.
- Value placed on honoring history and ancestors.
- The value placed on household functioning in isolation versus reliance on extended family and friends.

(Duncan & Goddard, 2011)

Table 11.5 Family Life Education Concepts and Resources that Align with Partnering with and Supporting Families

FLE Content Area: FLE Methodology	Resources
Each families' values, strengths, circumstances Meeting needs of diverse audiences[1,2,3]; sensitivity and respect for diversity[1]; values[2,3]; characteristics and needs of various groups[2]	[1]Covey, M. (2015). Family life education methodology. In M. J. Walcheski, & J. S. Reinke (Eds.), *Family life education: The practice of family science* (pp. 243–251). Minneapolis, MN: National Council on Family Relations.
	[2]Darling, C. A., & Cassidy, D. (2014). *Family life education: Working with families across the*

(*Continued*)

Partnering with and Supporting Families 251

Table 11.5 (Cont.)

FLE Content Area: FLE Methodology	Resources
	lifespan (3rd ed.). Long Grove, IL: Waveland.
	[3]Duncan, S. F., & Goddard, H. W. (2017). *Family life education: Principles and practices for effective outreach* (3rd ed.). Thousand Oaks, CA: Sage.

Family law and public policy. *Understand legal issues, policies, and laws influencing the wellbeing of families.*

Partnering with and supporting families also involves knowledge related to family law and public policy. Families do not exist in isolation. Ecological systems theory states that families are nested not only within communities, but within an even larger macrosystem (Bronfenbrenner & Morris, 2006). The macrosystem is comprised of the policies and laws that govern individuals' lives and choices. "Even though families are inherently private, they are inevitably affected by public policy" (Bogenschneider, 2015, p. 223). For example, for low-income families, a range of child health care needs are supported by policies related to Medicaid and the Children's Health Insurance Program (CHIP). Both provide publicly funded options for children to receive basic health services (well-baby visits, vaccines) as well as services related to disabilities (e.g., rehabilitation therapy [speech, occupational, or physical], genetic testing, adaptive technology [wheelchairs, prosthetics, orthotics, etc.]). Families can also receive food or housing assistance from the Supplemental Nutrition Assistance Program (SNAP) and the Special Supplemental Nutrition Program for Women, Infants, and Children (WIC), and Temporary Assistance for Needy Families (TANF). Daily family life in EHS-HBO is greatly affected by changes in laws and polices related to these programs, particularly with shifts in the political climate of the macrosystem.

Families also interact with the legal system for marriage, divorce, and child custody issues. Laws and policies related to child protection also play a major role protecting children within families. As mandated reporters, home visitors also have a legal obligation to the children in the program to report any instances of suspected maltreatment. An estimated 192,660 infants and toddlers experience maltreatment each year, and infants under the age of 12 months are the most likely to die as the result of maltreatment (U.S. Department of Health & Human Services, 2018). Maltreatment is defined as abuse (physical, emotional, sexual) or neglect, with rates of neglect much higher for infants than abuse (U.S. Department of Health & Human Services, 2018). Child Protection Services (CPS) received

252 *Partnering with and Supporting Families*

Table 11.6 Family Life Education Concepts and Resources that Align with Partnering with and Supporting Families

FLE Content Area: Family Law and Public Policy	Resources
Each families' values, strengths, circumstances Evaluate and comprehend laws relating to marriage, divorce, family support, child custody, child protection and rights, and family planning[1]; support family functioning[1]; collaboration[2]	[1]Bogenschneider, K. (2015). Family law and public policy. In M. J. Walcheski, & J. S. Reinke (Eds.), *Family life education: The practice of family science* (pp. 223–234). Minneapolis, MN: National Council on Family Relations. [2]Bogenschneider, K. (2014). *Family policy matters: How policymaking affects families and what professionals can do* (3rd ed.). New York: Routledge.

approximately 4.1 million reports in 2016 (U.S. Department of Health & Human Services, 2018). The vast majority of reports are determined to be unsubstantiated, meaning that no evidence of maltreatment was found. For families with substantiated cases of maltreatment, families have interactions with CPS that range from no services, to in-home services, to removal of the child to foster care (Berger & Font, 2015). In the case of removal from the home, families do not typically lose access to their EHS-HBO services.

Partnering with and supporting families also means that the home visitor is current on macrosystem-level initiatives that affect EHS families. One example is the Strengthening Families Initiative by The Center for the Study of Social Policy (CSSP), which is a macrosystem-level initiative to support vulnerable families (CCSP, 2015). The four main ideas include (1) focusing on protective factors (e.g., social connections, knowledge of parenting and child development, support in times of need, social and emotional competence of children), (2) enhancing interactions with parents by building supportive relationships, (3) aligning with the science on child development by using research-based evidence to improve practices with families, (4) making small but significant changes in many settings by applying the ideas to the wide variability of family circumstances. Initiatives that put forth macro-level perspectives of strengthening vulnerable families provide programs and professionals with a framework for structuring services and interactions with families in ways that optimize family and child wellbeing.

Internal dynamics of families. *Understanding of family strengths and weaknesses and how family members relate to each other.*

An understanding of the internal dynamics of families, particularly how families respond to stress and crisis, can help EHS-HBO home visitors and families partner to develop effective solutions. All families experience stress, which is defined as tension that taxes a family's capabilities (Lamana, Reidmann, & Stewart, 2012). Stress originates from negative events, but also seemingly positive events (e.g., moving, having a baby). A family moves to a state of crisis if the stressful event paralyzes the family system – the family has to find new patterns of action immediately. It is a time of instability and marks a turning point for the family with possible outcomes in either positive or negative directions (Lamana et al., 2012). The double ABC-X model of stress helps explains how crisis affects the internal workings of the family system (McCubbin & Patterson, 1983). The first part of the model (Aa) states the stressor event itself (A), and the current demands, hardships, and pileups (a) the family is already dealing with. The family's ability to cope and manage the crisis with their current resources is factored in (B), as well as how the family interprets the event (C). Aa, B, and C work together to produce the crisis experience for the family (X) (McCubbin & Patterson, 1983). For example, say a mother and her infant are about to be evicted from their current home (A – the event). This mother has already lost her housing once before, because she struggles to find affordable rent given her low wage employment (a – demands, hardships, and pileups). The mother has family close by to take her in if necessary, and the support of her EHS-HBO home visitor to help her find new housing (B – current resources). Because of this, the mother is upset that she is losing her current housing, but is hopeful that things will work out (C – interpretation of the event). As a result (X) this crisis is manageable. One can imagine alternative scenarios for the (B) and (C) components of the model, which lead to worse outcomes for the family. EHS-HBO home visitors need to be aware of how stress and crisis affect the internal workings of families in various ways – this will allow them to be better partners to work together to find solutions when issues arise. It also speaks to how diverse family experiences play a role in affecting how families react to and interpret stressful events in their lives.

Table 11.7 Family Life Education Concepts and Resources that Align with Partnering with and Supporting Families

FLE Content Area: Internal Dynamics of Families	Resources
Each families' values, strengths, circumstances ABC-X model of family stress[1]; human ecology theory[1]; cultural diversity[2]; family	[1]Wadsworth, S. M. M., Roy, K. M., & Watkins, N. (2015). Families and individuals in societal contexts. In M. J. Walcheski & J. S. Reinke (Eds.), *Family life education: The*

(*Continued*)

254 *Partnering with and Supporting Families*

Table 11.7 (Cont.)

FLE Content Area: Internal Dynamics of Families	Resources
strengths and challenges[2]; family dynamics[2]; communication[2]; power in the family[2]; managing economic resources[2]; parenthood[2]; stress, abuse, family problems[2]	*practice of family science* (pp. 147–155). Minneapolis, MN: National Council on Family Relations [2]Olson, D. H., DeFrain, J., & Skogrand, L. (2014). *Marriages and families: Intimacy, diversity, and strengths* (8th ed.). New York: McGraw Hill.

Skills

According to CUPID, home visitors should possess the following skills for partnering with and supporting families:

> Skills for guiding parents to identify their own goals for children and use their family's resources to reach those goals, for collaborating with parents to establish common goals for home visits, and for adapting to individual communication styles and needs and to family culture and beliefs.

> (CUPID, 2017)

Human Sexuality

- Recognize the biological and psychological aspects of human sexuality

  - Recognize individual family members' needs regarding family planning and use of contraceptives.
  - Recognize and understand various sexual orientations (e.g., heterosexual, gay, lesbian, bisexual).
  - Recognize and understand various gender identities, including transgender people.

- Address human sexuality from positions respectful of values

  - Respect family values regarding family planning and contraception, but provide accurate information regarding contraception access and resources for women's health care when requested.
  - Recognize that individual family members may have differing values regarding a range of human sexuality topics than the home visitor. Meet families where they are and provide accurate information when necessary.

Parenting Education and Guidance

- Promote healthy parenting from systems and lifespan perspectives and a child's and parent's developmental perspective

  - Take time to learn about the "developmental niche" (Super & Harkness, 2002) of each family. What settings and environments are children in? What are the customs and values parents hold? What is the parent's understanding of parenting practices and motivation for implementation?
  - Promote parenting strategies that make sense to parents in terms of their developmental niche.

- Apply strategies based on child's age and stage and unique characteristics to support development

  - Using knowledge of human development, help tailor parenting strategies to meet children's unique characteristics (e.g., age, sex, temperament, etc.), while considering how these parenting strategies are shaped by the developmental niche.

- Recognize various parenting roles and their impact on families

  - Observe how parents structure family routines, interactions, and physical spaces. For example, in terms of infant sleeping practices, what is the routine for putting baby to sleep? How does the parent interact with the baby (swaddling, rocking, singing, etc.)? Where does the infant sleep (crib, bed, etc.)? What is the parent's role in developing these interactions, and how does it impact the family?

- Identify strategies to support children in various settings

  - Use the concept of the developmental niche to customize how the home visitor goes about partnering with and supporting each family.
  - Understand that the developmental niche may include multiple settings depending on where the child spends their time each day (e.g., childcare, grandparent's house, public park).

Family Resource Management

- Recognize the multiplicity of resources families need, acquire, and manage (e.g., personal, familial, professional, community, environmental)

  - Recognize that family resources include material and economic resources such as money, material possessions, access to institutions (e.g., health care, education).
  - Recognize that family resources also include individual human resources such as the earning potential, emotional energy, and social support.

256   *Partnering with and Supporting Families*

- Inform individuals and families of consumer rights, responsibilities, and choices of action/advocacy

  - Talk with parents and family members about decisions related to acquiring and allocating family resources. What are their expectations for balancing individual needs versus the needs of the family system? How do they make decisions about allocating resources?

- Recognize and facilitate the reciprocal relationship between individual/family/community choices and resources

  - Help families identify material and human resources necessary to achieve the family's ideal balance between individual and group needs.
  - Have knowledge of community resources and provide referrals that help families achieve these goals.

- Apply and facilitate effective decision-making processes (e.g., assessment of individual and family needs, identification and evaluation of options and resources, implementation of decision, evaluation of outcomes)

  - Work with families to assess current family resources and how they are allocated. Identify and evaluate the resources families need, or areas where allocation needs to be improved. Create an action plan and evaluate progress.

- Understand the impact of values and goals in the decision-making process

  - Understand the impact of different cultural models (individualism and collectivism) on values and decision-making regarding the acquiring and allocation of family resources.

- Apply organizational and time management strategies; use basic financial management tools and principles

  - Assist families with allocating resources appropriately by discussing prioritization, delegation of family tasks, creating daily schedules, mock budgets, etc.

Professional Ethics and Practice

- Demonstrate professional attitudes, values, behaviors, and responsibilities to clients, colleagues, and the broader community, that are reflective of ethical standards and practice: (1) Understand the domains and scope of practice for family life educators and the role of collaboration; (2) Establish and maintain appropriate personal and professional boundaries; (3) Create a personal ethics plan to support/reflect the standards of the profession; (4) Maintain current knowledge and skills in the field

Part of establishing and maintaining personal and professional boundaries is reflecting on and recognizing when one's personal values are creeping into home visiting practices.

Instead, create a personal ethics plan that balances respecting diverse family values and practices, but also provide accurate information that supports family wellbeing. This leaves the home visitor's personal values out of the equation.

Maintain current knowledge in relevant fields (e.g., child development, guidance and discipline, family planning, and other issues relevant to EHS-HBO families) to provide accurate, up-to-date scientific information.

- Identify and apply appropriate strategies to deal with conflicting values

    - Engage in reflective practices (see Chapter 5).
    - Support parents where they are, but challenge them to grow and learn (MCFR, 2009).
    - Be open and truthful when providing information to the family (MCFR, 2009).

- Demonstrate respect for diverse cultural values

    - Start by understanding families where they are. No matter if this issue is child discipline practices, developmentally appropriate child behaviors, family planning, or use of community resources, work to understand how the family's cultural beliefs and background influence their thinking.
    - Acknowledge diverse family practices and encourage practices that support family wellbeing (MCFR, 2009).

FLE Methodology

- Employ strategies to meet the needs of different audiences and implement adult education principles into work with individuals, parents, and families, and demonstrate group process and facilitation skills

    - Use demonstrations to help parents learn. For example, model the behavior or words you want the parent to use. Or, ask parents to start with what they would normally do – then ask questions that help them break down their current response and demonstrates to them that there may be a better solution.
    - Have parents "activate" what they already know about a topic. Pose hypotheticals or ask parents to reflect on their own lived experiences.
    - For child-related issues, have parents "activate" what they know by reflecting on how they think their child perceived a situation, or have the parent think of a time in which they did not handle a situation successfully.

258 *Partnering with and Supporting Families*

- Create learning environments that support individual differences and develop culturally competent materials and experiences

  - Observe family values related to individualism/collectivism, communication preferences, action/reflective orientation, honoring the past, and household functioning.
  - Use these observations to develop culturally sensitive goals and strategies.

- Demonstrate sensitivity to diversity

  - Become sensitized to the individual cultures, backgrounds, experiences and needs of each family.
  - Tailor interactions with each family to honor their values.

Family Law and Public Policy

- Identify current laws, policies, and initiatives that influence professional conduct and services and that affect families

  - Identify laws, policies, and initiatives that affect family wellbeing for a variety of family issues – food insecurity, housing, healthcare access.
  - Identify laws, policies, and initiatives that affect child wellbeing through child protective services.

- Inform families, communities, and policy makers about public policies, initiatives, and legislation that affect families at local, state, and national levels

  - Be able to inform families about the process of referral and access to state and local food, housing, and healthcare programs.
  - Be familiar with the CPS process to support families who are reported for child maltreatment.

Internal Dynamics of Families

- Recognize and define healthy and unhealthy characteristics pertaining to family relationships and family development

  - Recognize and define the terms stress and crisis.

- Analyze family dynamics in response to stress, crises, and trauma

  - Use the double ABC-X model to breakdown how a stressor or crisis is affecting the family system. Identify the stressful event (A), the family's current demands and hardships (a), the family's current resources (B), and the family's interpretation of the event (C) that interact to produce the crisis (X).

Partnering with and Supporting Families 259

- Develop, recognize, and reinforce strategies that help families function effectively
  - Using the ABC-X model as a guide, help families recognize and address current hardships and pileups as well as identify and strengthen resources to mitigate the effects of a future crisis.
  - For families experiencing a crisis, recognize that how the family interprets the event will shape their experience of the event. For example, one family may interpret a divorce as a happy event, whereas another family interprets it as catastrophic.

Attitudes

The attitudes developed by CUPID that home visitors should adopt to effectively partner with, and support families are:

> Attitudes of willingness to defer to parents' strengths and preferences, and respect for parent as an expert on the child, the family as the child's primary environment, a wide range of family circumstances, and for the unique family resources for supporting child development.
>
> (CUPID, 2017)

These attitudes place parents and family at the center of improving child wellbeing and emphasize respect for a range of family circumstances. Many FLE values and ethical principles compliment these attitudes. The CFLE code of ethics devotes an entire section of ethical principles for working with parents in this manner (NCFR, n.d.). Specifically, respecting "cultural backgrounds, beliefs, and differences" and accepting "parents and other family members for who they are." The code also emphasizes that "parents have the primary responsibility as educators, nurturers and limit-setters for their children" (NCFR, n.d.). Working with diverse groups of families, who all have unique cultural backgrounds, needs, and life experiences is no easy feat, especially when trying to partner with and support each family member effectively. Home visitors will no doubt find themselves in ethical dilemmas in which the values of the family and home visitor collide. As a starting point to address these issues, MCFR's (2009) guidelines suggest: (1) starting with understanding the complexities of the family system, (2) developing respect for the family's cultural beliefs and background, (3) placing parents and family members at the center of problem solving and decision-making, and (4) ensuring that the program nurtures all family members. Keeping these guidelines in mind will ensure that home visitors maintain an attitude that places parents and family members at the center of developing and supporting the child's outcomes, while also cultivating positive relationships between the home visitor and caregivers.

260 *Partnering with and Supporting Families*

Box 11.1 CDA Home Visitor Competencies

The CDA Subject Areas and Competency Standards are national standards for Home Visitors. The subject area that is most relevant to this chapter includes **CDA Subject Area 4: Understanding family systems and development.** The competency goal that is most relevant to this chapter is "To establish positive and productive partnerships with families" and "To ensure a well-run, coherent and purposeful program responsive to the needs of the families in his or her caseload" (Council for Professional Recognition, 2017).

Competency Goal	Functional Area	Example Items	Example Indicators
IV. To establish positive and productive partnerships with families	**11 Families:** Home visitor establishes a positive, responsive, and cooperative relationships with each family, engages in two-way communication with families, encourages the parents to take leadership in personal and family education, and supports the relationship of the families with their children.	**Item 11.1:** Parents/families are appreciated and they are the center of the program **Item 11.2:** Help parents recognize that they are the center of the program. Item 11.3: Uses information about families' cultures, religions, and childrearing practices in program experiences.	Home toys, materials, and equipment reflect respect for family's culture, religion, and child rearing practices Implements a family centered-responsive home visitor practice. Helps family members to identify and value their family's beliefs, culture and values.

Permission to reprint from the Council on Professional Recognition, 2019

Box 11.2 National Family Support Competency Framework for Family Support Professionals

The National Family Support Competency Framework for Family Support Professionals are competencies that include ten domains that are further clarified by dimensions (Institute for the Advancement of Family Support Professionals, 2018). There is one domain that is relevant to this chapter: (a) Relationship-Based Family Partnerships, which includes three dimensions: respect and responsiveness, positive communication, and collaboration

Domain 7	Dimension 27	Component a.	Levels of Competency
Relationship-based family partnerships	**Collaboration**	Role of the family support professional	**1-Recognizing.** Understands the role of the Family Support Professional
			3-Applying. Supports parents by collaborating to develop mutual roles and expectations
			5-Extending. Coaches parents to engage in parent leadership in decision making and planning

Permission to reprint from the Institute for the Advancement of Family Support Professionals.

Summary

Developing effective partnerships with families is essential for home visiting to support child and family wellbeing. To do this, home visitors must have knowledge in the variety of family values and circumstances of the families in their program (CUPID, 2017; Roggman et al., 2016). Knowledge in the FLE content area human sexuality, parenting education and guidance, family resource management, professional ethics and practice, FLE methodology, family law and public policy, and internal dynamics of families all help expand and clarify how home visitors can create effective partnerships with families.

Key Concepts

- ABC-X model
- Child protective services
- Collectivism
- Developmental niche
- Family planning
- Gender identity
- Helping relationship
- Individualism

262 *Partnering with and Supporting Families*

- Involvement
- Macrosystem
- Maltreatment
- Sexual orientation
- Three approaches to ethics

Recommended Readings

Boss, P., Bryant, C. M., & Mancini, J. A. (2016). *Family stress management: A contextual approach*. Sage Publications.

Michalopoulos, C., Faucetta, K., Hill, C. J., Portilla, L. B., Lee, H., Duggan, A., ... & Nerenberg, L. (2019). *Impacts on family outcomes of evidence-based early childhood home visiting: Results from the Mother and Infant Home Visiting Program evaluation*. Mathematica Policy Research.

References

Administration for Children and Families (ACF). (2002). *Making a difference in the lives of infants and toddlers and their families: The impacts of Early Head Start: Vol. 1. Final technical report*. Washington, DC: U.S. Department of Health and Human Services.

Administration for Children and Families (ACF). (2007). *Head Start Act*. U.S. Department of Health and Human Services.

Administration for Children and Families (ACF). (2015). *The Faces of Early Head Start: A National Picture of Early Head Start Programs and the Children and Families They Serve*. OPRE Report #2015-29, Washington, DC: Office of Planning, Research, and Evaluation, Administration for Children and Families, U.S. Department of Health and Human Services.

Administration for Children and Families (ACF). (2016). *Head Start Performance Standards 45 CFR Chapter XIII September 2016*. U.S. Department of Health and Human Services.

Collaborative for Understanding the Pedagogy of Infant/toddler Development (CUPID) (2017). *Comprehensive competencies for educators of infants and toddlers in group care and home visiting settings*. Unpublished.

Berger, L. M., & Font, S. A. (2015). The role of the family and family-centered programs and policies. *The Future of Children*, 155–176.

Bockting, W. O., Miner, M. H., Swinburne Romine, R. E., Hamilton, A., & Coleman, E. (2013). Stigma, mental health, and resilience in an online sample of the US transgender population. *American Journal of Public Health*, *103*, 943–951.

Bogenschneider, K. (2014). *Family policy matters: How policymaking affects families and what professionals can do* (3rd ed.). New York: Routledge.

Bogenschneider, K. (2015). Family law and public policy. In M. Walcheski & J. Reinke (Eds.) *Family life education: The practice of family science* (pp. 223–225). Minneapolis, MN: National Council on Family Relations.

Bronfenbrenner, U., & Morris, P. A. (2006). The bioecological model of human development. In R. M. Learner & W. Damon (Eds.) *Handbook of child psychology* (pp. 793–828). Hoboken, NJ: John Wiley & Sons Inc.

Brooks, J. (2013). *The process of parenting* (9th ed.). New York, NY: McGraw Hill.

Center for the Study of Social Policy (CSSP). (2015). *Strengthening families*. Retrieved from: https://cssp.org/resource/strengtheningfamilies101/

Council for Professional Recognition. (2017). *The Child Development Associate® National Credentialing Program and CDA® Competency Standards: Home visitor edition*. Washington DC: Council on Professional Recognition.

Covey, M. (2015). Family life education methodology. In M. Walcheski & J. Reinke (Eds.) *Family life education: The practice of family science* (pp. 243–251). Minneapolis, MN: National Council on Family Relations.

Darling, C. A., & Cassidy, D. (2014). *Family life education: Working with families across the lifespan* (3rd.). Long Grove, IL: Waveland.

Darling, C. A., & Howard, S. (2015). Human sexuality across the lifespan. In M. Walcheski & J. Reinke (Eds.) *Family life education: The practice of family science* (pp. 177–179). Minneapolis, MN: National Council on Family Relations.

Duncan, S. F., & Goddard, H. W. (2011). *Family life education: Principles and practices for effective outreach*. Thousand Oaks, CA: Sage Publications.

Duncan, S. F., & Goddard, H. W. (2017). *Family life education: Principles and practices for effective outreach* (3rd ed.). Thousand Oaks, CA: Sage.

Goldberg, A. E., Gartrell, N. K., & Gates, G. J. (2014). *Research report on LGB-parent families*. UCLA School of Law: The Williams Institute.

Guttmacher Institute. (2019). *Publicly funded family planning*. Retrieved from https://www.guttmacher.org/united-states/contraception/publicly-funded-family-planning

Harkness, S., Super, C. M., Barry, O., Zeitlin, M., Long, J., & Sow, S. (2009). Assessing the environment of children's learning: The developmental niche in Africa. *Multicultural Psychoeducational Assessment*, 133–155.

Heaman, M., Chalmers, K., Woodgate, R., & Brown, J. (2007). Relationship work in an early childhood home visiting program. *Journal of Pediatric Nursing, 22*(4), 319–330.

Hyde, J. S., & Delamater, J. D. (2017). *Understanding human sexuality* (13th ed.). New York: McGraw Hill.

Institute for the Advancement of Family Support Professionals. (2018). *National family support competency framework for family support professionals*. Retrieved from: https://cppr-institute-prod.s3.amazonaws.com/modules/Approved%20National%20Family%20Support%20Competency%20Framework_FINAL_7_18_2018.pdf

Jacobson, A. L. (2015). Parenting education and guidance. In M. J. Walcheski, & J. S. Reinke (Eds.), *Family life education: The practice of family science* (pp. 213–222). Minneapolis, MN: National Council on Family Relations.

Korfmacher, J., Green, B., Staerkel, F., Peterson, C., Cook, G., Roggman, L., Faldowski, R. A., & Schiffman, R. (2008). Parent involvement in early childhood home visiting. *Child & Youth Care Forum, 37*, 171–196.

Lamana, M. A., Reidmann, A., & Stewart, S. (2012). *Marriages, families and relationships* (12th ed.). Stamford, CT: Cengage Learning.

McCubbin, H. I., & Patterson, J. M. (1983). The family stress process: The double ABCX model of adjustment and adaptation. *Marriage & Family Review, 6*, 7–37.

McNaughton, D. B. (2000). A synthesis of qualitative home visiting research. *Public Health Nursing, 17*, 405–414.

264 Partnering with and Supporting Families

Merrill, M. D. (2001). First principles of instruction. *Journal of Structural Learning and Intelligence Systems, 14,* 456–466.

Minnesota Council on Family Relations (MCFR). (2009). *Ethical thinking and practice for parent and family life educators.* St. Paul, MN: Minnesota Council on Family Relations.

Moore, T. J., & Asay, S. M. (2015). Family resource management. In M. J. Walcheski, & J. S. Reinke (Eds.), *Family life education: The practice of family science* (pp. 205–212). Minneapolis, MN: National Council on Family Relations.

Moore, T. J., & Asay, S. M. (2018). *Family resource management* (3rd ed.). Thousand Oaks, CA: Sage.

National Council on Family Relations (NCFR). (n.d.). *Family life educators code of ethics.* Retrieved https://www.ncfr.org/sites/default/files/cfle_code_of_ethics_2.pdf

Olson, D. H., DeFrain, J., & Skogrand, L. (2014). *Marriages and families: Intimacy, diversity, and strengths* (8th ed.). New York: McGraw Hill.

Palm, G. (2015). Professional ethics and practice. In M. J. Walcheski, & J. S. Reinke (Eds.), *Family life education: The practice of family science* (pp. 235–237). Minneapolis, MN: National Council on Family Relations.

Peterson, C. A., Hughes-Belding, K., Rowe, N., Fan, L., Walter, M., Dooley, L., Wang, W., & Steffensmeier, C. (2018). Triadic Interactions in MIECHV: Relations to Home Visit Quality. *Maternal and Child Health Journal,* 1–10.

Petkus, J. (2015). A first-hand account of implementing a Family Life Education model: Intentionality in Head Start home visiting. In M. J. Walcheski, & J. S. Reinke (Eds.), *Family life education: The practice of family science* (pp. 325–331). Minneapolis, MN: National Council on Family Relations.

Raikes, H., Green, B. L., Atwater, J., Kisker, E., Constantine, J., & Chazan-Cohen, R. (2006). Involvement in Early Head Start home visiting services: Demographic predictors and relations to child and parent outcomes. *Early Childhood Research Quarterly, 21*(1), 2–24.

Roggman, L. A., Boyce, L. K., Cook, G. A., & Cook, J. (2002). Getting dads involved: Predictors of father involvement in Early Head Start and with their children. *Infant Mental Health Journal, 23*(1-2), 62–78.

Roggman, L. A., Cook, G. A., Peterson, C. A., & Raikes, H. H. (2008). Who drops out of early head start home visiting programs? *Early Education and Development, 19*(4), 574–599.

Roggman, L., Peterson, C., Cohen, R. C., Ispa, J., Decker, K. B., Hughes-Belding, K., Cook, G., & Vallotton, C. D. (2016). Preparing home visitors to partner with families of infants and toddlers. *Journal of Early Childhood Teacher Education, 37,* 301–313. http://dx.doi.org/10.1080/10901027.2017.1298369

Super, C. M., & Harkness, S. (2002). Culture structures the environment for development. *Human Development, 45,* 270–274.

Triandis, H. C. (1995). *Individualism and collectivism.* New York, NY: Routledge.

U.S. Department of Health & Human Services. (2018). *Child maltreatment 2016.* Retrieved from https://www.acf.hhs.gov/cb/research-data-technology/statistics-research/child-maltreatment

U.S. Department of Health and Human Services. (2019). *U.S. federal poverty guidelines used to determine financial eligibility for certain federal programs.* Retrieved from https://aspe.hhs.gov/poverty-guidelines

Wadsworth, S. M. M., Roy, K. M., & Watkins, N. (2015). Families and individuals in societal contexts. In M. J. Walcheski & J. S. Reinke (Eds.), *Family life education: The practice of family science* (pp. 147–155). Minneapolis, MN: National Council on Family Relations

Watson, R. J., Wheldon, C. W., Wichstrøm, L., & Russell, S. T. (2015). Cross-national investigation of health indicators among sexual minorities in Norway and the United States. *Social Sciences, 4,* 1006–1019.

12 Diversity and Inclusion with an Emphasis on Supporting Families of Infants/Toddlers with Special Needs

Diversity refers to many aspects of family life – for example, culture, language, family history, and disability. These aspects of family life are important to understand because they guide the goals parents have for their children, family values and attitudes, as well as caregiving practices. Families in EHS-HBO come from a variety of cultural backgrounds and histories. Additionally, EHS-HBO is dedicated to serving infants/toddlers with developmental delays and disabilities and their families as a part of the diverse population receiving services. This chapter will explore the CUPID competency **Diversity and Inclusion with an Emphasis on Supporting Families of Infants/Toddlers with Special Needs** (CUPID, 2017; Roggman et al., 2016).

Competency	Using strength-based, family-centered, and collaborative practices to support infants and toddlers with special needs, guided by requirements of IDEA Part C, including implementing screening and referrals, and working with other professionals to identify and implement the best supports for children
Knowledge	Expanded knowledge of how culture and prior family experiences affect home life in family interactions, routines, and other activities; expanded knowledge of child and parent rights
Skills	Individualize to each family's culture and home language to help parents reflect on how their culture, values, and family history influence their parenting and decisions about their child, and to guide parent to use the family's traditions as opportunities to support child development. Skills to help parents understand policies and child and parent rights, available services, information about common disabilities, and strategies to adapt to natural environments
Attitudes	Attitudes of respect for differing perspectives, values, and beliefs about home life. Attitudes that support family centered practice in the natural environment

For full alignment see Appendix B.

The FLE Content Areas that help expand this competency include:

Parenting education and guidance	How parents teach, guide, and influence as the dynamic context of the parent–child relationship
Family resource management	Understand the decisions individuals and families make about developing and allocating resources including time, money, material assets, energy, friends, neighbors, and space, to meet their goals
Families and individuals in societal contexts	Understanding families in regard to other institutions
FLE methodology	Understand principles of FLE in tandem with planning and delivery of programs
Family law and public policy	Understand legal issues, policies, and laws influencing the wellbeing of families
Internal dynamics of families	Understanding of family strengths and weaknesses and how family members relate to each other

Note: Permission to reprint was granted from the National Council on Family Relations.

Knowledge

According to CUPID's home visitor competencies, expanded knowledge home visitors should possess related to diversity and inclusion includes:

> Expanded knowledge of how culture and prior family experiences affect home life in family interactions, routines, and other activities; Expanded knowledge of child and parent rights.

> (CUPID, 2017)

Culture and Family Experiences

Culture encompasses,

> how particular groups of people live. It is the way we eat, sleep, talk, play, care for the sick, relate to one another, think about work, arrange our kitchens, and remember our dead. It includes the language we speak, the religion or spirituality we practice (or do not), and the clothing, housing, food, and rituals/holidays with which we feel most comfortable.

> (Derman-Sparks & Edwards, 2010, p. 55)

In other words, culture shapes every aspect of family life. Every decision parents make about caring for their infants (from sleeping arrangements,

268 Diversity and Inclusion

feeding practices, discipline methods, expressions of emotion, conversations practices, among endless others) is shaped by culture. The developmental niche is the culturally-constructed context for child development (Super & Harkness, 2002). In other words, cultural values inform parenting in terms of the settings parents and children interact within, as well as the activities that take place on a daily basis (Bornstein & Cheah, 2006). The routines, activities, and interactions that occur within a family are going to be shaped by this developmental niche. It is also going to shape what parents think is important for their infants and toddlers in terms of caregiving practices, developmental skills they want to promote, and family values they want to impart to the next generation.

According to García Coll and colleagues (1996), families of color also have to deal with the fallout of discrimination and oppression. Here we use the term families of color to refer to "a socially created category referring collectively to the groups that have historically been and currently are targets of racism" (Derman-Sparks & Edwards, 2010, p. xiii). The experiences of racism for families of color play a role in how they navigate social institutions such as school, health care, and influence residential and economic segregation, all of which impact family life and child wellbeing (García Coll et al., 1996). Families can also experience marginalization based on other aspects of their identities such as language, religion, economic status, disability, sexual orientation, and/or gender identity.

Additionally, many children in EHS-HBO are dual language learners (DLLs), According to the Office of Head Start,

> dual language learner means a child who is acquiring two or more languages at the same time, or a child who is learning a second language while continuing to develop their first language. The term "dual language learner" may encompass or overlap substantially with other terms frequently used, such as bilingual, English language learner (ELL), Limited English Proficient (LEP), English learner, and children who speak a Language Other Than English (LOTE).
>
> (ACF, 2016, p. 109)

Families in EHS-HBO have infants and toddlers who are at the beginning stages of language development. Infants coo and babble and start to say one-word utterances around 12 months – but they are also taking in all of the language sounds in their home (whether it be one language, two, or more; Gross, 2019). It is critical that the family's home language is supported. Research suggests that DLLs do better academically when they have strong language and literacy support in their native language, in addition to English (Espinosa, 2013). Home language support is an essential part of EHS-HBO (ACF, 2018a). The Head Start Performance Standards stipulate that bilingualism be recognized as a strength for the child, that native language development is supported, and that interactions with parents be conducted in the home language whenever possible (ACF, 2016).

Infant/Toddler Special Needs

A developmental delay is defined as the percentage gap between an infant/toddler's chronological age and their developmental age (as determined by appropriate assessment instruments) (Pellegrino, 2013). For example, if a 24-month-old's communication skills are evaluated at an 18-month developmental age, then the toddler presents a 25% delay in typical communication skills (developmental age divided by chronological age, then subtracted from one). In contrast, a disability can be defined as a reduction "in the ability to perform some action, engage in some activity, or participate in some real-life situation or setting" (Pellegrino, 2013). It's important to note that a delay is determined with the expectation that with additional supports and services, an infant/toddler will close the gap of the delay and will get back on the typical developmental track (Pellegrino, 2013). In contrast, a diagnosed disability is expected to affect a person's skill and ability level to some extent for the rest of their life (Pellegrino, 2013). The most commonly diagnosed disabilities in infants/toddlers are: autism spectrum disorder, cerebral palsy, genetic syndromes (e.g., Down syndrome, fragile x syndrome), ADHD, intellectual disability, hearing loss, vision impairment, and learning disabilities (e.g., dyslexia, dysgraphia, dyscalculia) (Boyle et al., 2011).

The Individuals with Disabilities Education Act (IDEA) is a federal law that was initially authorized by Congress in 1975 (under the name Education for All Handicapped Children Act) to enforce that a free appropriate public education (FAPE) be provided to all individuals with an identified disability aged three to 21 (Part B of the current law; IDEA, 2004). Early Intervention guidelines were added to the law through a revision made in 1986, which mandated that states expand disability services to individuals aged birth to three (Part C of the current law; IDEA, 2004). IDEA is frequently changing and updating, with the most recent reauthorization in 2004 and most recent revision in 2015. This chapter will explore what this law means for families, and what role home visitors play in explaining and upholding these rights.

Supporting the rights as outlined in IDEA, EHS-HBO reserves at least 10% of their enrollment for infants and toddlers with identified developmental delays or disabilities (ACF, 2016). EHS-HBO typically surpasses this number due to supporting inclusion for infants/toddlers with delays and disabilities, and having a higher rate of identifying these needs in infants/toddlers already enrolled in the program (Children with Disabilities in EHS). In the most recent EHS statistics report from 2015–2016, 12.5% (23,907) of the total number of infants and toddlers enrolled in an EHS program (147,519) had identified needs that qualified for services under Part C of IDEA (ACF, 2018b). Home visitors are required to monitor a child's on-going developmental progress, regardless of there being concerns or not (ACF, 2018b). Through screening and assessment, home visitors can determine if there are concerns

270 *Diversity and Inclusion*

for an infant/toddler's development that would be cause for a referral to Part C services. When needs have been identified, home visitors should adjust their curriculum accordingly to meet children where they are in terms of developmental skills (ACF, 2018b). For infants and toddlers, Part C services under IDEA typically determine eligibility for services based on a developmental delay in cognitive, communication, physical, self-help, or social-emotional skills (IDEA, 2004). This is due to a developmental delay being the first concern that typically presents in an infant/toddler with a disability. IDEA identifies an additional 13 categories of diagnosed disabilities that are recognized: autism; deaf-blindness; deafness; visual impairment (including blindness); emotional disturbance; hearing impairment; intellectual disability; multiple disabilities; orthopedic impairment; other health impairment; specific learning disability; speech or language impairment; traumatic brain injury (IDEA, 2004). These 13 categories are used nationally to determine eligibility for Part B services for individuals aged three to twenty-one.

Disability and Child/Parent Rights

IDEA outlines the rights for infants and toddlers under the age of three and their families in Part C of the current law. Part C outlines the federal requirements for identifying delays and disabilities and the services that should follow through a program called Early Intervention Services (EI) (IDEA, 2004). Under IDEA, general EI services are outlined, but each state in the United States has the right to tailor some parts of the program according to the state's own preferences. EI services generally have a screening process to identify infants/toddlers who should be formally assessed, a formal assessment process to determine eligibility, a process to write the Individualized Family Service Plan (IFSP), and requirements for meeting service obligations (IDEA, 2004). Other national requirements include using a family-centered approach where parents ultimately make all decisions for their infant/toddler, and providing services in a natural environment (e.g., home, childcare classroom, grandparent's house, public park, etc.) (IDEA, 2004). States can individualize their program by choosing the screening and assessment tools used, determining what level of delay or disabilities qualify for eligibility, how to write the IFSP, and how services are delivered (IDEA, 2004).

EHS-HBO home visiting is an essential introduction to the world of inclusion and the least restrictive environment. Home visiting can assist families in finding their new "normal" after their infant/toddler is identified as having a developmental delay or disability. EHS-HBO honors the idea of inclusion for infants/toddlers with disabilities by teaching caregivers how to include the infant/toddler in the family's typical daily activities and routines, by inviting the family to participate in community activities alongside typically developing children, and by sometimes enrolling the child into the EHS preschool program for additional support (ACF, 2016). To be fully included, an infant/toddler should be placed in the least restrictive environment possible, meaning modifications should be made in the home and community environments so the infant/toddler can always participate alongside typically developing peers as often as possible and only removed from the inclusive setting if their impairment requires specialized instruction or therapy that cannot be given in the current setting (IDEA, 2004). Home visiting combines these two terms to help families adapt their interactions and their home and community environments to allow their infant/toddler to fully participate in daily activities and routines. Home visitors have an important role in educating families about delays or disabilities that may affect their infant/toddler, providing strategies that use an infant/toddler's known strengths to help develop areas of need, and identifying and referring to appropriate resources.

FLE Content Area Knowledge and Knowledge of Diversity and Inclusion

Parenting education and guidance. *How parents teach, guide, and influence as the dynamic context of the parent–child relationship.*

Content knowledge of parenting education and guidance includes adapting home visiting practices so they are culturally sensitive to all families. In terms of parenting practices, home visitors should seek to understand the beliefs and functions of parenting decisions, values, and behaviors, rather than making assumptions about why parents do what they do (Jacobson, 2015). Home visiting programs likely reflect the values of the dominant culture. The dominant culture is not the majority, but rather the culture of "the people who hold the social, political, and economic power" (Derman-Sparks & Edwards, 2010, p. 57), which in the U.S. tends to be white, English-speaking, middle-class, and Christian. Families experience cultural discontinuity when parenting practices and beliefs at home are viewed as "wrong" by a program (Derman-Sparks & Edwards, 2010). This can cause discomfort or shame among family members, which is the opposite of a FLE strengths-based approach. This is illustrated in even simple infant decisions such as putting a baby to sleep (Burnham, 2013). Many babies in the U.S. sleep in cribs, or another apparatus, separately from parents. Many parents in the U.S. also advocate strict sleep/feeding schedules to help "train" the infant to sleep through the night. This is not the norm for all cultures – African American, Japanese, Chinese, and many European families all report higher rates of bed-sharing with their infants than white parents from the U.S. (Burnham, 2013). Beliefs about soothing infants back to sleep at night is also culturally bound (Burnham, 2013). Rather than labeling parents as "wrong" for the decisions they make about sleep practices, the home visitor should understand their

272 Diversity and Inclusion

beliefs and functions of their behaviors. Home visitors should also be aware that many of the practices that are held up as developmentally appropriate, tend to emphasize individualistic cultural models of self-sufficiency, independence, and individual rights (Derman-Sparks & Edwards, 2010). Families with a collectivist cultural model may be more focused on parenting behaviors that reinforce interdependence and group wellbeing.

A culturally sensitive parent educator also recognizes the importance of the family's native home language environment in promoting healthy parenting practices and infant/toddler development. Children and families fare better when the native language is embraced and respected (Espinosa, 2013). Home visits should be conducted in parents' native language if possible, and bilingual language development for infants/toddlers should be encouraged. Infants/ toddlers learning more than one language have their own developmental timeline for language acquisition. For example, DLL children have two (or more) vocabularies to learn, which creates a different developmental trajectory for early language and literacy as compared to young children learning one language (i.e., monolingual) (Hammer et al., 2014). This needs to be accounted for in parenting education. Culturally sensitive parent education also recognizes the unique needs of families with an infant/toddler with special needs, which may need to be tailored to include specialized education on the child's disability or delay, how parents need to adapt their interactions and home environments to allow their child to participate fully in daily activities and routines, or teaching parents how to advocate for their child's needs.

Table 12.1 Family Life Education Concepts and Resources that Align with Diversity and Inclusion

FLE Content Area: Parenting Education and Guidance	Resources
Cultural influences on parenting and family life Seek to understand beliefs and functions underlying differences rather than making assumptions[1]; develop cultural competence[1]; include extended family members when appropriate[1]; understand parenting as a multigenerational development process[1]; recognize influences on parenting (e.g., cultural)[1]; Identify sources to support parenting of varied parenting situations[1]; culture[2]; strong families[2]; learning disabilities[2]; support groups[2]	[1]Jacobson, A. L. (2015). Parenting education and guidance. In M. J. Walcheski, & J. S. Reinke (Eds.), *Family life education: The practice of family science* (pp. 213–222). Minneapolis, MN: National Council on Family Relations. [2]Brooks, J. B. (2013). The process of parenting (9th ed.). New York: McGraw Hill.

Family resource management. *Understand the decisions individuals and families make about developing and allocating resources including time, money, material assets, energy, friends, neighbors, and space, to meet their goals.*

In FLE, culture and environment play a major role in family resource management (Moore & Asay, 2015). Because family life is rooted in culture, and culture is part of a broader network of values, attitudes, and behaviors, the decisions families make about utilizing resources and assets is also culturally-dependent (Moore & Asay, 2015). Families may have different values about how they maintain their home, the materials they choose to put in their home, patterns of consumption, and more (Goldsmith, 2013). Individualistic versus collectivist cultural models also dictate how families manage resources. A parent with a more collectivist orientation may be more inclined to dedicate materials and energy to activities that benefit the group than a parent more focused on individual success. Resource management is also driven by environmental influences such as access to resources – either geographically or economically (Moore & Asay, 2015). Resources that are limited typically incur more costs to a family than resources that are abundant (Moore & Asay, 2015). For example, if a family has to travel great distances to take their infant to see a developmental specialist, that incurs more costs in terms of time, resources, money, and energy. Families living in poverty often lack the resources they need to meet the family's needs effectively. Poverty obviously comes with a lack of economic resources and material assets, but the stress also drains energy and time (e.g., working multiple jobs and night shifts). Home visitors can work with families to connect them to community resources and help families structure time, assets, and energy in ways that maximize family wellbeing. They can also help cultivate resources such as friends, neighbors, and support, that bring the family strength.

Parents of infants/toddlers with delays and disabilities may have many doctor, specialist, and therapy appointments to manage, while trying to maintain "normal" life tasks (e.g., job, grocery shopping, siblings' needs, etc.). Parents will determine the priorities of these tasks based on their culture, as discussed above, but having an infant/toddler with a disability can also influence a family's decision-making dynamic. A once individualist family may become more collectivist to support one another in the task of raising an infant or toddler with a delay or disability. In contrast, a once collectivist parent may become more individualist with their focus shifting only to their infant/toddler with a delay or disability, minimizing other family members or tasks. Home visitors can assist families in making decisions to allocate resources in the most effective way possible.

There are many national resources for families with an infant/toddler with a delay or disability to support family life, assist with access to services, and include the family in the community (DHHS, 2019). The Early Childhood Technical Assistance Center (ECTA) is a national resource in place to assist

274   *Diversity and Inclusion*

Table 12.2 Family Life Education Concepts and Resources that Align with Diversity and Inclusion

FLE Content Area: Family Resource Management	Resources
Cultural influences on parenting and family life Understand that one cultural influence is one's own family experience[1]; practice resource consumption and conservation in family life[17]; decision-making process[1]; understanding family diversity[2]; parents and parenting[2]; culture (communication, family dynamics, family management, family needs, human rights, rituals of, etc.)[2]; policy-specific definitions (legal system, life insurance, taxes, FMLA, gray areas, etc.)[2]; families within cultural contexts[2]	[1]Moore, T. J., & Asay, S. M. (2015). Family resource management. In M. J. Walcheski, & J. S. Reinke (Eds.), *Family life education: The practice of family science* (pp. 205–212). Minneapolis, MN: National Council on Family Relations. [2]Moore, T. J., & Asay, S. M. (2018). *Family resource management* (3rd ed.). Thousand Oaks, CA: Sage.

families in understanding their rights under IDEA and refer families to resources in relation to their legal rights. There are many organizations that provide respite care, given to a caretaker of an individual with a disability so the caretaker can have a break or complete other tasks (e.g., personal doctor's appointment, grocery shopping, going to a movie), such as the ARCH National Respite Network and Resource Center. There are also many resources for including infants/toddler with a delay or disability and their family in the community, such as Kids Together, Inc., through advocacy and coordination of community events.

Families and individuals in societal contexts. *Understanding families in regard to other institutions*

When considering variation in family cultures, home language, and abilities, knowledge of families and individuals in societal contexts helps root the home visitor's understanding of these issues within the contexts that shape daily family life. From ecological and lifespan perspectives, the shared family histories of groups are passed down from generation to generation. It is important that the home visitors are able to understand the families they work with in terms of this shared family history. For example, African American families share a history around slavery (Cohen, 2018). This includes shared trauma of forced family separations, extreme physical and mental abuse, and the resulting discrimination and marginalization that continues to this day (Williams et al., 2017). For many Mexican American families, a shared family history revolves around immigration. Many Mexican families were not immigrants to the U.S. – they became citizens when U.S./Mexico boundaries changed as a result of the Mexican-American War in 1848 (Cohen, 2018). As immigration policies in the U.S. continue to change, many Latino families are connected by a shared history with the immigration system in some way. These shared contexts shape family values and practices that are passed down from generation to generation. In addition to shaping family values and practices, they also impact how families approach interactions with institutions such as health care and education. Home visitors need to be aware of families' shared histories. For example, low income African American families may be weary of seeking services from social services and mental health institutions because of structural biases and racism that exist in these systems, as they are often unprepared to deal with the race-related stress and the psychological trauma many people of color face (Franklin, Franklin, & Kelly, 2006). As another example, undocumented immigrant parents may be reluctant to engage with certain community resources if they fear their immigrant status will be an issue. Many undocumented parents are raising children who are U.S. citizens, which brings a unique set of challenges to parenting (Yoshikawa, 2011). For DLLs, language experiences at home also affect the family's abilities to engage with institutions. Depending on the parent's own language abilities (e.g., child is a DLL but parent is monolingual Spanish-speaker), communication with institutions that do not support their native language is challenging.

For families with infants/toddlers with special needs, understanding families in regard to other institutions is critical, because historically children with disabilities have been excluded from important institutions such as education. Prior to the initial enactment of IDEA in 1975 (under the name Education for All Handicapped Children Act), children with disabilities did not have access to a free appropriate public education (FAPE; IDEA, 2004). Guidelines to include infants and toddlers were not added to IDEA until 1986 (IDEA, 2004). Due to institutions having a large influence on society's views and attitudes, society is still adjusting to being inclusive of people with special needs. Access to FAPE is mandated by law, but full inclusion is not (IDEA, 2004). Inclusion is "the right of every infant and young child and his or her family, regardless of ability, to participate in a broad range of activities and contexts as full members of families, communities, and society" (DEC/NAEYC, 2009, p. 2). DEC/NAEYC (2009) list three factors of inclusion: (1) access to a variety of settings/environments, activities, and learning opportunities, (2) participation through individualized accommodations and support, and (3) support at a systems-level through adult education on effective practices and collaboration of stakeholders. As stated, inclusion is not mandated by IDEA; however, it is widely followed by special education providers in school settings. For example, in a preschool classroom, inclusion may look like providing a specialized support chair and specialized

276 *Diversity and Inclusion*

crayons for an infant/toddler with cerebral palsy so he/she can join peers in coloring at a small table during a group activity. When a child with a delay or disability enters preschool or elementary school, inclusion should be supported by their Individual Education Plan/Program (IEP; IDEA, 2004). Inclusion applies not only to a school setting, but society overall in family settings (e.g., the family's home), community settings (e.g., the park, grocery store, or sporting event), and professional settings (e.g., a person's workplace). As mentioned previously, a home visitor can assist a family in creating an inclusive home environment as the first step towards an inclusive lifestyle for their infant/toddler. If a parent learns how to create an inclusive environment at home, it will be easier for the parent to support an inclusive environment for their child in the community.

Another factor that can help shift society's attitudes towards inclusion of individuals with disabilities is people first language. Clarke, Embury, Knight, & Christensen, (2017) define people first language as "the way we speak, write, and portray people with disabilities that eliminates disparagement or pity" (p. 74). Instead of saying "the autistic toddler," we should be saying "the toddler with autism." This separates the person from their disability, as they truly are a person who happens to also have a disability. Using people first language provides an opportunity for society to then focus on other aspects of the person, such as their personality, intelligence, or physical traits.

Table 12.3 Family Life Education Concepts and Resources that Align with Diversity and Inclusion

FLE Content Area: Families and Individuals in Societal Contexts	Resources
Cultural influences on parenting and family life Family interactions and social systems[1]; ecological perspective[1]; lifespan perspective[1]; culture, cultural groups, and cultural norms[2]; changing social environments and positive responses[2]; cultural diversity and family strengths and challenges[2]; family coping strategies[2]; domestic violence[2]; child abuse and neglect[2]; sibling and child-to-parent abuse[2]; alcohol problems[2]	[1]Wadsworth, S. M. M., Roy, K. M., & Watkins, N. (2015). Families and individuals in societal contexts. In M. J. Walcheski & J. S. Reinke (Eds.), *Family life education: The practice of family science* (pp. 147–155). Minneapolis, MN: National Council on Family Relations [2]Olson, D. H., DeFrain, J., & Skogrand, L. (2014). *Marriages and families: Intimacy, diversity, and strengths* (8th ed.). New York: McGraw Hill.

Table 12.4 Family Life Education Concepts and Resources that Align with Diversity and Inclusion

FLE Content Area: FLE Methodology	Resources
Cultural influences on parenting and family life Understanding and respect for all forms of diversity[1]; cultural competence[2,3]; diversity of family experience (abuse, mental illness, conflict, poverty, stress, social support, family size, etc.)[3]; cultural deficit or compensatory model[2]; cultural response sets[2]; culture[2]; social exchange theory[2]; family systems theory[2]; family as an ecosystem[2]; family developmental theory[2]; family stress theory[2]	[1]Covey, M. (2015). Family life education methodology. In M. J. Walcheski, & J. S. Reinke (Eds.), *Family life education: The practice of family science* (pp. 243–251). Minneapolis, MN: National Council on Family Relations. [2]Darling, C. A., & Cassidy, D. (2014). *Family life education: Working with families across the lifespan* (3rd ed.). Long Grove, IL: Waveland. [3]Duncan, S. F., & Goddard, H. W. (2017). *Family life education: Principles and practices for effective outreach* (3rd ed.). Thousand Oaks, CA: Sage.

FLE methodology. *Understand principles of FLE in tandem with planning and delivery of programs*

Part of FLE methodology is understanding and respecting all forms of diversity, recognizing that cultural competence is a critical component of program development and delivery (Covey, 2015). The first step is appreciating that the term diversity actually encompasses many social identities. Social identities denote "membership in groups that are defined by society, are shared with many other people, and have societal advantages and disadvantages attached to them" (Derman-Sparks & Edwards, 2010, p. xiii). These include language, religion, economic status, disability, sexual orientation, gender identity, age, and more. Home visitors should conduct a self-assessment of their own social identity categories and reflect on which aspects of their identity have provided them with social advantages (or disadvantages). This is the first step in developing an understanding of the experiences of families whose social identities may differ from one's own. FLE recognizes that diverse family experiences contribute to a variety of family values and attitudes, such as how the individual is perceived in comparison to the group, communication styles, orientations towards time and action, work ethic, and family structure (Darling & Cassidy, 2014).

Family law and public policy. *Understand legal issues, policies, and laws influencing the wellbeing of families*

According to Bogenschneider (2015), a FLE perspective of family law and policy can be understood as "family policy is what is enacted, and family law is how what

278   *Diversity and Inclusion*

is enacted is interpreted and applied" (p. 224). Furthermore, a family impact lens is a way of examining the indirect impact of policy on family life (Bogenschneider, 2015). For example, housing and health care policies do not explicitly discuss family life, but how those policies are enacted have an impact on many facets of family wellbeing. For families with an infant/toddler with a disability or delay, family life is greatly affected by law and policy. Each state has its own procedural safeguards in place for families, but there are general rights provided to all families through IDEA. El services are governed by the Health Insurance Portability and Accountability Act (HIPAA) and the Family Educational Rights and Privacy Act (FERPA), so parents have the right to complete confidentiality of their infant/toddler's medical and education records (IDEA, 2004). A release of information/records must be signed by a parent to allow any additional participants in their infant/toddler's El services (IDEA, 2004). Parents have the right to consent for all offered services, meaning that providers' roles are to present all appropriate options and recommendations to a family, but ultimately parents make all decisions for their infant/toddler's services (IDEA, 2004). To be fully prepared for all decision-making, parents have the right to review any part of their infant/toddler's records at any time (IDEA, 2004). In accordance with this, parents have the right to prior written notice of all major juncture meetings (e.g., assessments, creation of or changes to the IFSP, changes in or refusal of services (by parent or program), etc.) to ensure the parents have adequate time to review records, invite advocates, or consider decisions before meeting with providers (IDEA, 2004). IDEA requires the prior written notice must be in a parent's native language. States may have additional procedural safeguards per their individual program policies, but the above is the minimum that the federal government requires.

Parents may face challenges to maintaining their legal rights. A qualitative study by Shannon (2004) found that many parents feel they are not always fully informed on service or program options available, so they cannot make fully informed decisions. The study also found that programs sometimes make decisions based on the possibility of insurance reimbursement, rather than making family-centered decisions (Shannon, 2004). With the variability of El programs in different states, a family may also encounter providers who are not fully trained or informed on procedural safeguards, so mistakes may occur. Additionally, many states have limited access to necessary services due to shortages of specialists and therapists needed to provide the services. This can lead to extended waits for infants and toddlers who need specialized testing, diagnoses, or therapies to support their growth and development. Due to the need for specialized services, families must also wait for approval by insurance companies to move forward with services. Many challenges can arise for parents of infants and toddlers with special needs, so a home visitor should not only be an advocate for families but also teach parents how to be an advocate for their child.

Diversity and Inclusion   279

Table 12.5 Family Life Education Concepts and Resources that Align with Diversity and Inclusion

FLE Content Area: Family Law and Public Policy	Resources
Cultural influences on parenting and family life Distinguish family policy and family law that are germane to families[1]; use a family impact lens[1,2]; understand legal protection of and for family members[1]; understand laws relating to child protection and rights[1]; individual rights[2]; disabilities, legislation and processes[2]; how society shapes families[2]; getting families involved in policy[2]	[1]Bogenschneider, K. (2015). Family law and public policy. In M. J. Walcheski, & J. S. Reinke (Eds.), *Family life education: The practice of family science* (pp. 223–234). Minneapolis, MN: National Council on Family Relations. [2]Bogenschneider, K. (2014). *Family policy matters: How policymaking affects families and what professionals can do* (3rd ed.). New York: Routledge.

If a parent feels that any of their procedural safeguards have been violated, they have the right to file a complaint (IDEA, 2004). Each state has the right to develop their own process for complaints, but there is a typical route that is followed. Initially, parents should report any concerns to their service coordinator. If the issue cannot be resolved or the parent does not feel comfortable discussing the matter with their service coordinator, the parent should report the concern to their EI program through the provider's supervisor or the program director. Again, if the concern cannot be resolved or the parent does not feel comfortable addressing it with the program, the parent can file a formal written complaint to the Part C office in their state (IDEA, 2004). The Part C office will investigate all sides of the claim to reach a formal decision about whether a parent's rights were violated. If a parent's rights were violated, the Part C office will work with the program and family to ensure that the violation is corrected appropriately. IDEA also outlines that the Part C office can offer mediation as a resolution to issues; mediation can be used along with or instead of filing a formal written complaint. Mediation allows a family and their EI program to meet with a neutral party to discuss solutions to any concerns. Parents also have the right to request a due process hearing with a neutral hearing officer (IDEA, 2004). Typically, families are encouraged to address concerns in one of the above routes prior to filing a due process request, however they can go straight to a due process hearing if they feel. After a decision has been made by a hearing officer, families and programs have the right to appeal a decision through a neutral review officer (IDEA, 2004). Once the final decision has been made by a review officer, parents or the EI program can take the decision into the court system if they feel unsatisfied (IDEA, 2004).

Internal dynamics of families. *Understanding of family strengths and weaknesses and how family members relate to each other*

Content knowledge on the internal dynamics of families highlights the "inner workings" of families (Reinke & Walcheski, 2015). Diversity in family culture, ethnicity, language, ability, and other social identities, is a critical part of these inner workings. According to García Coll and colleagues' (1996) integrative model, families of color (and other marginalized groups) face added stressors of racism, oppression, discrimination, and segregation – all of which have implications for family processes and child development. While these factors can have a negative impact on family life, the model also accounts for strengths that families develop in response to these pressures. Families develop an adaptive culture that includes their traditions and cultural legacies, as well as family histories that been shaped by social and political forces (García Coll et al., 1996). Home visitors should work with families to learn about and appreciate their unique experiences so they can understand how the inner workings of each family are shaped by cultural experiences. If a family is experiencing a crisis, the home visitor can also use this knowledge to inform the ABC-X model (McCubbin & Patterson, 1983). The crises families face (A), their resources to deal with the crisis (B), and their interpretation of the event (C) will all be shaped and informed by adaptive culture.

Families with infants and toddlers with delays and disabilities face many unique stressors and challenges that shape family life (Smith, Oliver, & Innocenti, 2001). Time management of additional appointments with doctors, specialists, and therapists in addition to trying to lead a typical family life place a burden onto families who are seeking support for their child (Smith et al., 2001). With all these additional services come extra costs for families, not only additional medical costs but also additional transportation and childcare expenses along with a possible reduction in income due to time off work. Managing collaboration between various providers can be difficult as services may be provided by various agencies who are not connected. The burden falls onto the family to relay information and make informed decisions based on various opinions and recommendations. Families may also experience various degrees of grief as they come to terms with the diagnosis of a delay or disability; family stress can rise when family members experience various levels of grief at different times (Blaska, 1998). Stress and conflict may also form when parents are trying to balance the needs of an infant/toddler with disabilities with the needs of their other children or family members (Blaska, 1998). It can be easy to become consumed with the needs of a child with a delay or disability, but regular routines and activities also need to continue for the family. Home visitors should be sensitive to the extra stress placed on a family with an infant/toddler with special needs by assessing the overall family's needs and referring to appropriate resources.

Diversity and Inclusion 281

Table 12.6 Family Life Education Concepts and Resources that Align with Diversity and Inclusion

FLE Content Area: Internal Dynamics of Families	Resources
Cultural influences on parenting and family life Understand rights and responsibilities of family members[1]; understand influences on family interaction patters (e.g., cultural)[1]; family systems theory[1]; circumplex model of marital and family systems[1]; ABC-X model of family stress[1]; human ecology theory[1]; family development theory[1]; culture, cultural groups, and cultural norms[2]; changing social environments and positive responses[2]; cultural diversity and family strengths and challenges[2]; family coping strategies[2]; domestic violence[2]; child abuse and neglect[2]; sibling and child-to-parent abuse[2]; alcohol problems[2]	[1]Reinke, J. S., & Walcheski, M. J. (2015). Internal dynamics of families. In M. J. Walcheski, & J. S. Reinke (Eds.), *Family life education: The practice of family science* (pp. 157–166). Minneapolis, MN: National Council on Family Relations. [2]Olson, D. H., DeFrain, J., & Skogrand, L. (2014). *Marriages and families: Intimacy, diversity, and strengths* (8th ed.). New York: McGraw Hill.

Skills

The skills home visitors should have related to diversity and inclusion include:

Individualize to each family's culture and home language to help parents reflect on how their culture, values, and family history influence their parenting and decisions about their child, and to guide parent to use the family's traditions as opportunities to support child development. Skills to help parents understand policies and child and parent rights, available services, information about common disabilities, and strategies to adapt to natural environments.

(CUPID, 2017)

Parenting Education and Guidance

Adapting to Family Cultures and Home Language

* Promote healthy parenting from a child's and parent's developmental perspective

282 *Diversity and Inclusion*

- o Promote developmentally appropriate parenting practices that support healthy child development and healthy parent–child interactions.
- o Promote the family's native home language as important for development.
- o For infants/toddlers learning English in addition to another language, promote bilingual language development.

- Apply strategies based on child's age and stage and unique characteristics to support development

  - o For infants/toddlers with special needs, promote parent–child interactions and home environments that allow the child to participate fully in daily routines and activities.

- Evaluate various parenting strategies

  - o Work with parents to understand their beliefs about parenting behaviors.
  - o Understand the functions of parenting values, behaviors, and strategies.
  - o For infants/toddlers with special needs, evaluate if parent–child interactions and the home environment allow the child to participate fully in daily life.

- Recognize various parenting roles and their impact on families

  - o Recognize that parents may be trying to balance the cultural practices of their family with messages from the dominant culture about the "right" parenting practices.
  - o Recognize that parents who have an infant/toddler with a disability or delay must balance the special needs of their child with a dominant culture that is not always inclusive of people with special needs.

- Recognize the impact of societal trends and cultural differences

  - o Recognize how the family's parenting practices are viewed in terms of the dominant culture.
  - o Recognize and validate if the family experiences cultural discontinuity.
  - o Recognize if parenting practices from an individualistic cultural model are at odds with a family's collectivist cultural model (or vice versa).

- Identify strategies to support children in various settings

  - o Support parents in supporting their DLL children and bilingual language development during infancy and toddlerhood so they are more successful upon preschool entry.
  - o Teach parents how to advocate for the rights and needs of their child's disability or delay.

Diversity and Inclusion   283

Family Resource Management

Adapting to Family Cultures and Home Language

- Recognize and facilitate the reciprocal relationship between individual/family/community choices and resources

  - Help families determine resources available in their communities.
  - Help families access needed resources in the communities.
  - Recognize how accessing resources in the community affects the family's own resources (e.g., time for transportation, money, energy, etc.). Help families manage these barriers if possible.

- Understand the impact of values and goals in the decision-making process

  - Understand that individualism and collectivism cultural models impact how families decide to utilize resources.
  - Understand that families have different values and goals when it comes to maintain their home, accessing and utilizing materials and assets for their home and children, how money is allocated, energy is expended, and more.
  - Understand that for many families in EHS-HBO, the experiences of living in poverty may shape how they make decisions about allocating limited economic and material resources.
  - Recognize if limited family resources (or misappropriate resource management) is negatively affecting the family system (e.g., parent feels there is too little time to spend with infant; parent feels that all their energy is drained by work; parent has limited access to medical care for their child).
  - Recognize family resources that are strengths to the family system (e.g., time spent with family, friends, neighbors; resources in the community, puzzles and books to help children learn).

Disabilities

- Inform individuals and families of consumer rights, responsibilities, and choices of action/advocacy

  - Refer families to national or state level resources that support individuals with disabilities and their families.

- Recognize the multiplicity of resources families need, acquire, and manage (e.g., personal, familial, professional, community, environmental)

  - Evaluate a family's strengths and areas of needs in all facets of family life.
  - Refer caregivers to respite care as needed to ensure typical family routines are still occurring.

284   *Diversity and Inclusion*

- Apply and facilitate effective decision-making processes (e.g., assessment of individual and family needs, identification and evaluation of options and resources, implementation of decisions, evaluation of outcomes)

  o Assess the family system to determine if resources are being allocated effectively.
  o Guide the family in managing their resources most effectively.
  o Consider how individualistic vs collectivist attitudes influence this decision making.

Families and Individuals in Societal Contexts

Adapting to Family Cultures and Home Language

- Identify the influence of local and global systems on individuals and families

  o Recognize how shared family histories affect the decisions parents make for their families and children.
  o Understand that laws and policies have an influence on the way society views and includes individuals with disabilities and their families.

- Identify contemporary and historical factors that influence individuals and families

  o Learn the family histories of the population(s) home visitors will be working with.
  o Understand the importance of inclusion as a major milestone for the educational rights of children with special needs.

- Identify social and cultural influences on family composition and family life

  o Identify how shared family histories affect family life, specifically historical oppression, racism, immigration status.
  o Identify how historical cultural experiences affect how families interact with institutions (e.g., health care, education, etc.).
  o Identify how different language abilities (e.g., monolingual, bilingual, DLL children) affect how families approach and interact with institutions.
  o Recognize that differing cultures may have unique interpretations and reactions to delays and disabilities.
  o Understand that society is still adjusting to the inclusion model.

- Recognize reciprocal interactions between individuals, families, and systems

  o Recognize barriers within institutions and communities that impact families of diverse cultures, languages, and abilities.
  o Use people first language when speaking to and about individuals with disabilities.

- Assess the impact of demographics (e.g., race, ethnicity) on families

  - Assess the impact of shared family histories on families.
  - Assess the impact of marginalization and discrimination on families.
  - Assess the impact of disability on families.
  - Recognize that all families are unique and general difference among groups may not reflect each family's experience.

FLE Methodology

Adapting to family cultures and home language

- Employ strategies to meet the needs of different audiences

  - Recognize each family's social identities, including the social advantages and disadvantages associated with each.
  - Talk with families about their experiences related to their social identities.

- Employ techniques to help the learner do hands-on learning

  - Use materials already available in the family's home to promote parent–child interactions and child development.

- Create learning environments that support individual differences

  - Ground all parenting education and coaching in the family's cultural context.
  - Implement home visiting practices in the family's native language whenever possible.

- Demonstrate sensitivity to diversity and develop culturally competent materials and experiences

  - In terms of diverse cultures/ethnicities, this may include

    - Reviewing materials for bias.
    - Ensuring that the needs of families of color are visible to the program.
    - Listening and understanding the motives and behaviors behind parenting values, beliefs, and practices.
    - Connecting families with services and community resources that support cultural traditions.

  - For families with DLLs this may include (adapted from Howard et al., 2007)

    - Bilingual office staff.
    - Staff training in cross-cultural awareness.

286   *Diversity and Inclusion*

- □ Communication with parents in native language.
- □ Identify and utilize community language resources.

- o For families with infants/toddlers with special needs this may include

  - □ Use of people first language.
  - □ Following a model of inclusion.
  - □ Educating families and staff about parent procedural safeguards under IDEA.
  - □ Recognizing the unique stressors parents of infants/toddlers with a delay or disability face.

- o Home visitors can analyze and reflect on their own social identities, particularly the aspects of their identities that have provided them with social advantages.

- Identify sources of evidence-based information and implement evidence-based programs

  - o Ensure that all program curricula, assessments, and materials are validated for use with the populations of families in the EHS-HBO program.

- Implement adult education principles into work

  - o Recognize that adult learning styles will vary according to cultural differences, such as how the individual is perceived in comparison to the group, communication styles, orientations towards time and action, work ethic, and family structure (Darling & Cassidy, 2014).

Family Law and Public Policy

Disabilities

- Understand policy processes

  - o Understand the Individuals with Disabilities Education Act (IDEA), specifically PART C that mandates services for infants and toddlers age birth to three and their families.
  - o Understand parent and children's legal rights under IDEA, specifically PART C rights that mandate procedural safeguards for infants and toddlers age birth to three and their families.

- Identify current laws, policies, and initiatives that influence professional conduct and services and that affect families

  - o Use a family impact lens to identify ways in which family policies and laws affect day-to-day family life.

Diversity and Inclusion   287

- o Use a model of inclusion in family, community, and professional settings.
- o Use people first language when speaking (or writing) to or about an individual with a disability.

- • Distinguish between advocacy and others (e.g., lobbying)

  - o Understand who can be a stakeholder.

- • Analyze policy resources for evidence of bias (e.g., unintended, inherent, political, self-interest)

  - o Understand the reasoning for an individual or organization to support or oppose a policy or law.

- • Inform families, communities, and policy makers about public policies, initiatives, and legislation that affect families at local, state, and national levels

  - o Educate families on their legal rights through Part C of IDEA.
  - o Be an advocate for family's rights at local, state, and national levels.

Internal Dynamics of Families

Adapting to Family Cultures and Home Language

- • Recognize and define healthy and unhealthy characteristics pertaining to family relationships and family development

  - o Recognize that the inner workings of family life are shaped by diverse family experiences.
  - o Recognize that some families may experience racism, oppression, discrimination, and segregation, and this impacts family life and child development.
  - o Recognize that families with infants/toddlers with disabilities must learn to manage new routines, procedures, and/or emotions after a diagnosis.
  - o For families with DLLs, recognize the importance of native language development in promoting healthy family relationships and connections with culture.

- • Analyze family functioning using various theories

  - o Use ecological systems theory to understand how families are nestled within multiple layers of context, and how their family culture relates to their microsystems (family, school, friends), exosystems (community, neighborhoods), and macrosystem (social and political climate).
  - o Analyze family stress and crisis with the ABC-X model (McCubbin & Patterson, 1983), but recognize the ways in which culture and

288 *Diversity and Inclusion*

diverse family experiences inform crises families face (A), their resources to deal with the crisis (B), and their interpretation of the event (C).

- Assess family dynamics from a systems perspective

  - Assess how families' adaptive cultures are sources of strength for the family system.
  - Assess how families with infants/toddlers with disabilities manage the special needs and services for their child, and how this affects the family system.

- Facilitate and strengthen communication processes, conflict-management, and problem-solving skills and develop, recognize, and reinforce strategies that help families function effectively

  - Talk with families about their lived experiences.
  - Help families identify strengths within their adaptive culture to capitalize on in times of stress/crisis.
  - Be available for families to grieve the diagnosis of a delay or disability.
  - Help families establish new routines that help their infant/toddler with a disability be a full participant in family life.
  - The home visitor should help families come to terms with the changes their family will need to make to accommodate a child with disability/delay.
  - The home visitor can provide support and resources related to stress management due to a diagnosis of disability/delay, time and financial burdens, "grieving" process of a diagnosis.

Attitudes

CUPID's attitudes for home visitors to support diversity and inclusion are stated as:

> Attitudes of respect for differing perspectives, values, and beliefs about home life; attitudes that support family centered practice in the natural environment.
>
> (CUPID, 2017)

Values reflected here are respect for the home lives of all families. This has critical implications for developing relationships with parents and children – if parents (and children) feel cultural discontinuity between their home life and the EHS-HBO program, home visitors will be unable to work with families effectively. A guiding CFLE principle is, "I will respect cultural beliefs, backgrounds and differences and engage in practice that is sensitive to the diversity of child-rearing values and goals" (NCFR, n.d.). The core value of a strengths-based perspective for all FLE is also central to these attitudes. A strengths-based view of family life is valuing the role all

Diversity and Inclusion 289

individuals play in their own growth – this means that prevention and education efforts are true partnerships with families rather than an exercise in "instilling knowledge" (Darling, Cassidy, & Rehm, 2017). Centering home visiting practices in a deep respect for families' cultures and lived experiences is an important part of this perspective.

Moreover, for families with infants/toddlers with special needs, people-first language is also a major component of respecting the diversity of family life. People-first language places the infant/toddler before the disability. This respects the fact that the disability does not define the infant/toddler and can even impact how people with disabilities are perceived by society (e.g., Feldman et al., 2002). Another form of respect for families with infants/toddler with disabilities is recognizing when they themselves need professional guidance. All infants/toddlers present disabilities and delays in different ways, so home visitors should reach out and seek advice when they have questions. This is in line with professional standards for CFLEs such as, "I will define our role as parent and family life educators and practice within our level of competence" (NCFR, n.d.).

Box 12.1 CDA Home Visitor Competencies

The CDA Subject Areas and Competency Standards are national standards for Home Visitors. The subject areas that are most relevant to this chapter include **CDA Subject Area 7: Working across the child welfare continuum** and **CDA Subject Area 8: Understanding principles of child development and learning.** Each competency standard is comprised of competency goals, functional areas, items, indicators, and examples. The competency goals that are most relevant to this chapter are "To support social and emotional development and provide positive guidance," and "To establish positive and productive partnerships with families" (Council for Professional Recognition, 2017).

Competency Goal	Functional Area	Example Items	Example Indicators
III. To support social and emotional development and provide positive guidance.	**9 Social:** Candidate helps parents to ensure that each child functions effectively in the family, learns to express feelings,	Item 9.2: A non biased-environment is provided.	Diverse activities, materials, curricula and/or events reflect an understanding of others' cultures and

(Continued)

290   *Diversity and Inclusion*

(Cont.)

Competency Goal	Functional Area	Example Items	Example Indicators
	acquires social skills, and makes friends, and helps parents promote mutual respect among children and adults in their lives.		the value of non-bias and anti-bias.
IV. To establish positive and productive partnerships with families	**11 Families:** Home visitor establishes a positive, responsive, and cooperative relationships with each family, engages in two-way communication with families, encourages the parents to take leadership in personal and family education, and supports the relationship of the families with their children.	Item 11.3: Uses information about families' cultures, religions, and childrearing practices in program experiences.	Helps family members to identify and value their family's beliefs, culture and values.
V. To ensure a well-run, coherent and purposeful program responsive to the needs of the families in his or her caseload.	**12 Program Management:** Home visitor is a manager who uses and facilitates all available resources (in the community and elsewhere) to meet the needs and interests of the families. The home visitor is	Item 12.3: Candidate knows the social service, health, and educational resources of the community and uses them when appropriate.	Refers families to relevant agencies when parents need social services or when they suspect children may have developmental challenges. Refers families to relevant agencies when parents suspect children

(Continued)

(Cont.)

Competency Goal	Functional Area	Example Items	Example Indicators
	a competent organizer, planner, record keeper, communicator, and cooperative team player.		may have developmental delays.

Permission to reprint from the Council for Professional Recognition, 2019

Box 12.2 National Family Support Competency Framework for Family Support Professionals

The National Family Support Competency Framework for Family Support Professionals are competencies that include ten domains that are further clarified by dimensions (Institute for the Advancement of Family Support Professionals, 2018). There is one domain that is relevant to this chapter: (a) Cultural and Linguistic Responsiveness. This includes three dimensions: cultural competency, cultural humility, and linguistic responsiveness.

Domain 8	Dimension 28	Component b.	Levels of Competency
Cultural and Linguistic Responsiveness	**Cultural competence**	Knowledge of culture	**1-Recognizing.** Understands the process of acculturation
			3-Applying. Supports parents by utilizing active listening in order to recognize and acknowledge the family's definition of its culture/cultural affiliation and values
			5-Extending. Coaches parents by actively seeking new knowledge regarding diversity in cultural beliefs and practices in order to provide effective family support services to individual families

Permission to reprint from the Institute for the Advancement of Family Support Professionals.

Summary

Diversity is a wide-ranging topic and includes a variety of family experiences and social identities related to culture, ethnicity, language, and ability. All of which inform parenting values, beliefs, and practices. The home visitor's expanded content knowledge of parenting education and guidance, family resource management, families and individuals in societal contexts, FLE methodology, family law and public policy, and internal dynamics of families prepares the home visitor to work with families in a culturally competent manner.

Key Concepts

- Adaptive culture
- Cultural discontinuity
- Culture
- Developmental delay
- Developmental niche
- Disability
- Dominant culture
- Dual language learners
- Early intervention services
- Families of color
- Family impact lens
- Individuals with Disabilities Education Act (IDEA)
- Least restrictive environment
- People-first language
- Social identities

Recommended Reading

Individuals with Disabilities Education Act. Resources for Educators and Service Providers. Retrieved from https://sites.ed.gov/idea/educators-service-providers/

Child Trends. (2014). *Dual language learners: Indicators of child and youth wellbeing.* Retrieved from https://www.childtrends.org/wp-content/uploads/2014/11/127_Dual_Language_Learners.pdf

Derman-Sparks, L., & Edwards, J. O. (2010). *Anti-bias education for young children and ourselves.* Washington, DC: National Association for the Education of Young Children.

Yoshikawa, H. (2011). *Immigrants raising citizens. Undocumented parents and their children.* New York, NY: Russell Sage Foundation.

References

Administration for Children and Families (ACF). (2016). *Head Start Performance Standards 45 CFR Chapter XIII September 2016*. U.S. Department of Health and Human Services.

Administration for Children and Families (ACF). (2018a). *Home Language Support*. U.S. Department of Health and Human Services. Retrieved from https://eclkc.ohs.acf.hhs.gov/culture-language/article/home-language-support.

Administration for Children and Families (ACF). (2018b). *Special Needs Infographic*. U.S. Department of Health and Human Services. Retrieved from https://eclkc.ohs.acf.hhs.gov/sites/default/files/pdf/special-needs-infographic-text-only.pdf

Blaska, J. K., (1998). Cyclical grieving: Reoccurring emotions experienced by parents who have children with disabilities. Retrieved from: https://files.eric.ed.gov/fulltext/ED419349.pdf

Bogenschneider, K. (2014). *Family policy matters: How policymaking affects families and what professionals can do* (3rd ed.). New York: Routledge.

Bogenschneider, K. (2015). Family law and public policy. In M. Walcheski & J. Reinke (Eds.), *Family life education: The practice of family science* (pp. 223–225). Minneapolis, MN: National Council on Family Relations.

Bornstein, M. H. & Cheah, C.S.L. (2006). The place of "culture and parenting" in the ecological contextual perspective on developmental science. In K.H. Rubin & O. Boon Chung (Eds.), *Parental beliefs, parenting, and child development in cross-cultural perspective* (pp. 3–33). London, UK: Psychology Press.

Boyle, Coleen A., Boulet, S., Schieve, L. A., Cohen, R. A., Blumberg, S. J., Yeargin-Allsopp, M., Visser, S. and Kogan, M. D. (2011). Trends in the prevalence of developmental disabilities in US children, 1997–2008. *Pediatrics, 127(6)*, 1034–1042.

Brooks, J. B. (2013). *The process of parenting* (9th ed.). New York: McGraw Hill.

Burnham, M. M. (2013). Co-sleeping and self-soothing during infancy. In A. R. Wolfson, H. Montgomery-Downs (Eds.), *The Oxford handbook of infant, child, and adolescent sleep and behavior* (pp. 127–139). New York: Oxford University Press.

Clarke, L. S., Embury, D. C., Knight, C., & Christensen, J. (2017). People-first language, equity, and inclusion: How do we say it, and why does it matter? *Learning Disabilities: A Multidisciplinary Journal, 22(1)*, 74–79.

Cohen, P. (2018). *The family: Diversity, inequality, and social change.* New York, NY: W.W. Norton & Company.

Collaborative for Understanding the Pedagogy of Infant/toddler Development (CUPID). (2017). *Comprehensive competencies for educators of infants and toddlers in group care and home visiting settings*. Unpublished.

Council for Professional Recognition. (2017). *The Child Development Associate® National Credentialing Program and CDA® Competency Standards: Home visitor edition*. Washington DC: Council on Professional Recognition.

Covey, M. (2015). Family life education methodology. In M. Walcheski & J. Reinke (Eds.), *Family life education: The practice of family science* (pp. 243–251). Minneapolis, MN: National Council on Family Relations.

Darling, C. A., & Cassidy, D. (2014). *Family life education: Working with families across the lifespan* (3rd ed.). Long Grove, IL: Waveland.

294 Diversity and Inclusion

Darling, C. A., Cassidy, D., & Rehm, M. (2017). Family life education: Translational family science in action. *Family Relations, 66,* 741–752. doi: 10.1111/fare.12286

DEC/NAEYC. (2009). *Early childhood inclusion: A joint position statement of the Division for Early Childhood (DEC) and the National Association for the Education of Young Children (NAEYC).* Chapel Hill: The University of North Carolina, FPG Child Development Institute.

Department of Health and Human Services (DHHS). (2019). *National resources. State of Nevada.* Retrieved from http://dhhs.nv.gov/Programs/IDEA/ProjectASSIST/National-Resources/.

Derman-Sparks, L., & Edwards, J. O. (2010). *Anti-bias education for young children and ourselves.* Washington, DC: National Association for the Education of Young Children.

Duncan, S. F., & Goddard, H. W. (2017). *Family life education: Principles and practices for effective outreach* (3rd ed.). Thousand Oaks, CA: Sage.

Espinosa, L. (2013). *Early education for dual language learners: Promoting school readiness and early school success.* Washington, DC: Migration Policy Institute.

Feldman, D., Gordon, P. A., White, M. J., & Weber, C. (2002). The effects of people-first language and demographic variables on beliefs, attitudes and behavioral intentions toward people with disabilities. *Journal of Applied Rehabilitation Counseling, 33,* 18–49.

Franklin, A. J., Franklin, N. B., & Kelly, S. (2006). Racism and invisibility: Race-related stress, emotional abuse, and psychological trauma for people of color. In L. V. Blitz & M. P. Greene (Eds.), *Racism and racial identity: Reflections on urban practice in mental health and social services* (pp. 9–30). New York, NY: Routledge Press.

García Coll, C. G., Crnic, K., Lamberty, G., Wasik, B. H., Jenkins, R., García, H. V., & McAdoo, H. P. (1996). An integrative model for the study of developmental competencies in minority children. *Child Development, 67,* 1891–1914.

Gross, D. (2019). *Infancy: Development from birth to age 3* (3rd ed.). Lanham, MD: Roman & Littlefield.

Goldsmith, E. B. (2013). *Resource management for individuals and families.* Upper Saddle River, NJ: Pearson Education, Inc.

Hammer, C. S., Hoff, E., Uchikoshi, Y., Gillanders, C., Castro, D. C., & Sandilos, L. E. (2014). The language and literacy development of young dual language learners: A critical review. *Early Childhood Research Quarterly, 29(4),* 715–733.

Howard, E. R., Sugarman, J., Christian, D., Lindholm-Leary, K. J., & Rogers, D. (2007). *Guiding principles for dual language education* (2nd ed.). Washington, DC: Center for Applied Linguistics.

Jacobson, A. L. (2015). Parenting education and guidance. In M. Walcheski & J. Reinke (Eds.) *Family life education: The practice of family science* (pp. 243–251). Minneapolis, MN: National Council on Family Relations.

Individuals with Disabilities Education Act (IDEA), 20 U.S.C. §§ 1400–1444 (2004).

Institute for the Advancement of Family Support Professionals. (2018). *National Family Support Competency Framework for Family Support Professionals.* Retrieved from: https://cppr-institute-prod.s3.amazonaws.com/modules/Approved%20National%20Family%20Support%20Competency%20Framework_FINAL_7_18_2018.pdf

McCubbin, H. I., & Patterson, J. M. (1983). The family stress process: The double ABCX model of adjustment and adaptation. *Marriage & Family Review, 6,* 7–37.

Moore, T. J., & Asay, S. M. (2015). Family resource management. In M. J. Walcheski, & J. S. Reinke (Eds.), *Family life education: The practice of family science* (pp. 205–212). Minneapolis, MN: National Council on Family Relations.

Moore, T. J., & Asay, S. M. (2018). *Family resource management* (3rd ed.). Thousand Oaks, CA: Sage.

NCFR. (n.d.). *Family life educators code of ethics.* Retrieved https://www.ncfr.org/sites/default/files/cfle_code_of_ethics_2.pdf

Olson, D. H., DeFrain, J., & Skogrand, L. (2014). Marriages and families: Intimacy, diversity, and strengths (8th ed.). New York: McGraw Hill.

Pellegrino, L. (2013). Patterns in development and disability. In Batshaw, M. L., Roizen N. J., Lotrecchiano, G. R. (Eds.), *Children with disabilities* (pp. 231–242). Chelsea, MI: Sheridan Books, Inc.

Reinke, J. S., & Walcheski, M. J. (2015). Internal dynamics of families. In M. J. Walcheski, & J. S. Reinke (Eds.), *Family life education: The practice of family science* (pp. 157–166). Minneapolis, MN: National Council on Family Relations.

Roggman, L., Peterson, C., Cohen, R. C., Ispa, J., Decker, K. B., Hughes-Belding, K., Cook, G., & Vallotton, C. D. (2016). Preparing home visitors to partner with families of infants and toddlers. *Journal of Early Childhood Teacher Education, 37,* 301–313. http://dx.doi.org/10.1080/10901027.2017.1298369

Shannon, P. (2004). Barriers to family-centered services for infants and toddlers with developmental delays. *Social Work, 49,* 301–308.

Smith, T. B., Oliver, M. N. I., & Innocenti, M. S. (2001). Parenting stress in families of children with disabilities. *American Journal of Orthopsychiatry, 71(2),* 257–261.

Super, C. M., & Harkness, S. (2002). Culture structures the environment for development. *Human Development, 45,* 270–274.

Wadsworth, S. M. M., Roy, K. M., & Watkins, N. (2015). Families and individuals in societal contexts. In M. J. Walcheski & J. S. Reinke (Eds.), *Family life education: The practice of family science* (pp. 147–155). Minneapolis, MN: National Council on Family Relations

Williams, B. K., Sawyer, S. C., & Wahlstrom, C. M. (2017). *Marriage, Families, & Intimate Relationships* (4th ed). New York, NY: Pearson.

Yoshikawa, H. (2011). *Immigrants raising citizens. Undocumented parents and their children.* New York, NY: Russell Sage Foundation.

13 Professionalism

It is important to understand that EHS-HBO is an evidence-based model but there are other models (e.g., Parents as Teachers). There are variations across home visiting models and goals, which are evident in theories of change and logic models that undergird programs. There are many facets of professional development to promote quality practice of home visitors and to advance the professionalism of the home visiting workforce. The Collaborative for Understanding the Pedagogy of Infant/Toddler Development (CUPID) drafted a set of competencies for the Infant/Toddler Workforce that includes **Professionalism**. This competency encompasses engaging in the broader profession and learning and applying evidence-based practices in one's work (CUPID, 2017; Roggman et al., 2016).

See full alignment in Appendix B.

Competency	Engaging in the broader profession by articulating the importance of work with young children and families, and by seeking out and applying evidence-based practices and standards for one's work.
Knowledge	Expanded knowledge includes understanding the underlying logic model and evidence base behind and surrounding home visiting programs (Roggman et al., 2016) as well as other topics, such as policies and professional development (Roggman et al., 2018). Also, knowledge of this competency includes understanding variations in home visiting programs (Roggman et al., 2016).
Skills	Skills for advocating for families and seeking opportunities to develop and increase competencies from a wide range of topics and across disciplines that are germane to home visiting (Roggman et al., 2016; Roggman et al., 2018).
Attitudes	Attitudes include commitment to learning about children and families, parenting, adult development and learning, and community resources (Roggman et al., 2018).

FLE Content Areas that are most germane to this expanded competency for home visitors include:

FLE methodology	Understanding of FLE principles in tandem with planning and delivery of programs
Professional ethics and practice	Understanding the character and quality of human social conduct and critically examine ethical questions and issues as they relate to professional practice
Human growth and development across the lifespan	Understanding of the developmental changes (both typical and atypical) of individuals in families across the lifespan with an emphasis on knowledge of developmental domains
Family law and public policy	Understand legal issues, policies, and laws influencing the wellbeing of families

Note: Permission to reprint was granted from the National Council on Family Relations.

Knowledge

The detailed description of the knowledge that home visitors should possess regarding professionalism includes:

> CUPIDs Home Visitor Expansion of Competency: Detailed knowledge of home visiting evidence; logic models behind home visiting programs; variations in program models; adult development.
>
> (CUPID, 2017)

According to CUPID, knowledge of policies and professional development are also crucial to this expanded competency (Roggman et al., 2018).

Basics and Background

Home visiting evidence. We are in an era of evidence-based programming. Evidence-based programs and practice are different; the former is a multi-dimensional intervention and the latter is a core component of a larger intervention (Mattox & Kilburn, 2012). There are three types of program evidence that are important in order for a home visiting program to earn an evidence-based program status, these include: (a) cost-benefit analysis, (b) process or implementation evaluation, and (c) impact or outcome evaluation (Cannon, 2018). A pilot study that explores a home visiting model by including a process or implementation evaluation is helpful before conducting a randomized control trial with impact or outcome evaluations.

EHS-HBO is an evidence-based program (HomVEE, 2016a) and is a well-known and comprehensive home visiting program. Evidence-based home visiting models should be followed with fidelity, including structural components, such as dosage, and other aspects, such as family and home visitor interaction (Daro, 2010).

We know that there are home visiting skills supported by research, including: (a) establishing positive relationships with the parent, child, and other family members, (b) responding to each family's unique strengths, (c) promoting developmentally supportive parent–child interactions, and (d) establishing a collaborative and professional partnership with the parent (Marshall & Virmani, 2017). A home visit that includes time spent in triadic interaction (parent, child, and home visitor) that focuses on coaching parent–child interaction is an important part of home visiting quality (Peterson et al., 2018).

There are several observational measures of research-based home visiting quality. For example, the Home Visitor Rating Scales—Adapted and Extended to Excellence (HOVRS-A+) is used to collect data on effective home visiting practices. HOVRS is a quantifiable rating system that includes seven scales of a home visit: (1) Home Visitor Responsiveness to Family; (2) Home Visitor–Family Relationship; (3) Home Visitor Facilitation of Parent–Child Interaction; (4) Home Visitor Non-Intrusiveness/Collaboration with Family; (5) Parent–Child Interaction During Home Visit; (6) Parent Engagement During Home Visit; and (7) Child Engagement During Home Visit (Roggman et al., 2012). Observational measures that explore developmental parenting include: Parent Interactions with Children: Checklist of Observations Linked to Outcomes (PICCOLO; Roggman, Cook, Innocenti, Norman, & Christiansen, 2013) or Home Observation Measurement of the Environment (HOME; Caldwell & Bradley, 2003). To determine how home visits support child development, measures such as the Ages and Stages Questionnaire (ASQ: Squires, Potter, & Bricker, 1999) or the Brigance Infant and Toddler Screen (see Glascoe, 2002) may be used. The aforementioned tools are neither an exhaustive list nor an endorsement of any tool. Home visitors can think about how child development assessments and screenings link to the Head Start Early Learning Outcomes Framework (Head Start Early Childhood Learning & Knowledge Center, 2018).

Logic Models

Logic models are graphical depictions that include text to communicate what happens in the program and how it leads to results (McCawley, 2001). Darling and Cassidy (2014) explain that logic models represent key components of the program, such as inputs (e.g., resources), activities (e.g., techniques), outputs (e.g., number of participants served), and outcomes (e.g., benefits or changes to participants as a result of activities). Parents as Teachers provides a logic model and suggests that model enhancements might be needed to address families' needs and strengths (Parents as Teachers National Center, 2018). In the PAT logic model, examples of inputs include "Implementing agency leadership and support" and "The Foundational Curricula, Model Implementation and Supervisor's Handbook" (Parents as Teachers National Center, 2018). Samples of activities include: "Reflective supervision and professional development" and "Child screening" (Parents as Teachers National Center, 2018). Also in the PAT logic model, examples of outputs include "Staff receive regular reflective supervision and participate in professional development" and "Children receive regular developmental screening and a health review, including hearing and vision" (Parents as Teachers National Center, 2018). Finally, examples of outcomes include "Increased healthy pregnancies and improved birth outcomes" and "Improved child health and development" (Parents as Teachers National Center, 2018).

Maternal Infant and Early Childhood Home Visiting (MIECHV) programs also have logic models. For an example, please see Connecticut's MIECHV Program logic model (http://www.ct.gov/oec/lib/oec/familysupport/miechv/application/2016/attachment_1_-_logic_model.pdf)

Variations in Program Models

While there are several topics that are common across models, such as serving families in poverty, there are differences, such as how home visitors serve families that substantially differ across models (Wasik & Bryant, 2001). The processes and content of program models need more attention and are often considered a black box (Hebbeler & Gerlach-Downie, 2002; Korfmacher et al., 2008). EHS-HBO is funded by the federal government and serves pregnant women and families with children younger than the age of three. "Early Head Start uses a comprehensive, two-generation approach to enhance child development and support family self-sufficiency and well-being" (Roggman, Cook, Peterson, & Raikes, 2008, p. 576). EHS-HBO programs that use curriculum, such as Parents as Teachers (PAT), are expected to focus on parental efficacy, knowledge of child development, and using everyday learning opportunities in the home (Hebbeler & Gerlach-Downie, 2002). This may not be enough, however, to accomplish the EHS mission of working with the whole family and family strengths and needs beyond the parent–child interaction (Walsh, Mortensen, Edwards, & Cassidy, in press).

For a full list of home visiting models and evidence of the model's effectiveness, please visit the Home Visiting Evidence of Effectiveness (HomVEE). One example of a national model is the Home Instruction for Parents of Preschool Youngsters (HIPPY), which focuses on child development and school readiness (HomVEE, 2013). Another example of a national model is Healthy Families America (HFA), which aims to reduce child maltreatment and promote parent–child interactions, children's social-emotional health, and children's school readiness (HomVEE, 2017). Finally, another example is Nurse Family

300   *Professionalism*

Partnership (NFP), which is for first-time mothers and children from low-income families and promotes prenatal health, child health, and families' self-sufficiency (HomVEE, 2016b).

Policies

As of August 1, 2018, all home visitors in home-based EHS programs must have a minimum of a home-based CDA credential or comparable credential course-work and demonstrate competency in home visiting (Marshall & Virmani, 2017). See Chapter 2 of this textbook for more information on the current state of EHS-HBO. The Head Start Performance Standards include staff qualifications and requirements and are an authoritative source on all necessary information about the formal structure and governance of the home visiting agency. For instance, an agency must have a policy council and a policy committee, and this can be the same body depending on the operational responsibilities of the agency (Administration for Children and Families, 2016).

It will be important to read the agency's policies and to think about their role in the successful delivery of the home visiting program. Home visiting agencies will typically provide training on their model and policies over several days and then offer additional training on a variety of topics, such as child development, reflective practice, and trauma-exposure (Schultz, Jones, Pinder, Wiprovnick, Groth, Shanty, & Duggan, 2018). As outlined by the Administration for Children and Families, "a program must provide ongoing training and professional development to support staff in fulfilling their roles and responsibilities" (2016, p. 54). Thus, actively pursuing and reflecting upon professionalization opportunities is important for all home visitors.

Professional Development

Professional development can include a variety of strategies, such as coaching and mentoring, reflective supervision, and technical training and support. Child abuse and neglect, family engagement, family services, and knowledge of the content in Head Start Early Learning Outcomes Framework: Ages Birth and Five are important topics included in training (Administration for Children and Families, 2016).

Program procedures, such as confidentiality, are also important to professionalism and consider confidentiality as synonymous with privacy and as extremely important to quality services of home visiting, particularly given the personal nature of home visiting. In general, home visitors should not state the names of the families outside of reflective supervision and in discussion with other professionals at the site, and these discussions should always be done in private (Wasik & Bryant, 2001). Codes of ethics and standards of the field emphasize confidentiality and provide guidance on working with families. There are a variety of ethical codes and standards available, including those offered by the: (a) National Association of Social Workers, (b) PAT, (c) National Association for the Education of Young Children, and (d) National Council on Family Relations. In addition, each site or agency should have guidelines and procedures for working with families that endorse the process of ethical decision making.

Professional organizations and conferences are important for professional development. The Ounce for Prevention (https://www.theounce.org/) and the Home Visiting Applied Research Collaborative or HARC (https://www.hvresearch.org/) offer meetings and conferences to help home visitors learn about cutting-edge research and practice in the field. The National Research Conference on Early Childhood (NRCEC) presented by the Administration for Children and Families is also an important conference for the home visiting field. The National Council on Family Relations has a home visiting focus group for NCFR members. Parents as Teachers has an annual conference that offers a variety of workshop tracks, such as serving all families. Webinars, journals, and online courses are also helpful for promoting professional growth.

Respecting the other professionals you work with is as important as respecting the families and young children in your care. Christie (2018) asserts that caring is the process of welcoming another's strengths and needs while putting aside your own choices, preferences, and ideas. Relationships are important and take time to build; keep in mind that your relationships with families are not friendships. The family's relationship with the home visitor is important to successful home visiting (Brookes, Summers, Thornburg, Ispa, & Lane, 2006; Korfmacher, Green, Spellman, & Thornburg, 2007). The home visitor and family relationship is an unrequited relationship in which the home visitor focuses on the family and engages in minimal self-disclosure. The idea of being with families (rather than doing for) draws attention to the importance of boundaries in home visiting (Petkus, 2015).

Talking about caring, collaborative relationships, boundaries, and other topics of this nature can help home visitors be realistic in their expectations and prevent burnout. The average salary for an Early Head Start home visitor is approximately $31,740 annually (PayScale, 2018). While determining if you have any additional skills (e.g., being bilingual) or credentials that might increase pay, one strength of the home visiting workforce is that 90% of children from Spanish-speaking homes have a home visitor who speaks Spanish (Marshall & Virmani, 2017). It is important to keep in mind that the aforementioned home visitor salary is, unfortunately, consistent with the low pay that currently characterizes the early childhood field. It is important to recognize that burnout can result from low pay and that support from a supervisor, tending to personal needs (e.g., adequate sleep, exercise, family or social time), and promoting one's skill set are all important to preventing burnout.

In addition to preventing burnout, it is helpful for home visitors to know about secondary traumatic stress (STS) and it tends to come from the home visitor's relationship with a family that has experienced trauma (Gurwitch & Williams, 2017). A home visitor experiencing STS might have symptoms, such as emotional exhaustion, lack of interest in the job, and others (Gurwitch & Williams, 2017). One warning sign of this is that the home visitor has diminished self-care (Gurwitch & Williams, 2017). The subscale of secondary trauma on the Professional Quality of Life Scale (ProQOL) is recommended as a starting place (see ProQOL.org) to promote discussions with supervisors and other home visiting professionals.

Adult Development

Home visitors will need opportunities to be introduced to new content and its importance, to practice skills through techniques such as role playing, and to reflect and receive feedback (Schultz et al., 2018). Theories of adult learning will help professionals understand why people respond differently to learning experiences (see Kolb, 1984; Mezirow, 2000). The home visiting field needs more work to explore how home visitors' knowledge and skills actually transfer to their work with families (Schultz et al., 2018). Home visitors should be aware of the adult learning principles and the transfer of skills to understand their own work with families but also to understand their families. In other words, being familiar with andragogy is essential. Home visitors bring their own experiences related to their age and stage of development, values, beliefs, and other unique characteristics to home visits. Parents, whether in adolescence, emerging adulthood, adulthood, or late adulthood, also bring their unique experiences and characteristics to visits.

Parents' engagement in the home visit will depend upon several of their own characteristics, such as their psychological functioning (e.g., parents with better mental health are more likely to engage in a collaborative relationship), their motivation for program services, and demographic features of the parent (e.g., parents who work more will have less time to engage), to name a few (Korfmacher et al., 2008).

EHS HV focuses on the whole family and this means that home visitors need to be cognizant that what the parents or other adults bring to the visit is important, as is understanding adult development in order to develop and maintain a trusting relationship with the whole family. Understanding the concepts, theories, and research that are hallmarks of each age and stage of development is paramount to understanding how families think, feel, and physically change across the lifespan.

FLE Content Area Knowledge and Knowledge of Professionalism

Four FLE content areas and the most relevant guideline(s) within these content areas were selected through the process described in Appendix B as aligning with CUPID's HV expanded competency. The FLE content areas include: (1) FLE methodology, (2) Professional ethics and practice, (3) Human growth and development, and (4) Family law and public policy.

Next, we consider the topics from CUPID's HV expanded competency on professionalism as aligning with content guidelines within these FLE content areas. We commence with a brief explanation of the gist of each FLE content area and then discuss the most relevant knowledge in this content area to the professionalism HV expanded competency by CUPID that was fully described at the start of this chapter. The readings featured in the tables in this section are either included in the "Resource List for the Certified Family Life Educator (CFLE Exam)" see NCFR (2015) or are chapters in Walcheski and Reinke's (2015) "Family Life Education: The Practice of Family Science."

FLE methodology. *Understanding of FLE principles in tandem with planning and delivery of programs.*

Training in FLE methodology prepares the home visitor with knowledge in program planning, implementation, and evaluation. For example, family life educators have experience with a variety of evaluation types, including formative evaluations, as well as experiences with using a logic model to understand the outcomes of a program (Darling & Cassidy, 2014). This prepares home visitors to understand an if-then method of looking at a program and to comply with program standards for delivery and evaluation efforts. FLEs have been trained to consider evidence-based programs as the gold standard. HomVEE is an example of a resource for evidence-based programs (Darling & Cassidy, 2014). Knowledge of a program's theory of change and how to promote program fidelity are crucial to evidence-based home visiting programs' implementation (Asmussen, 2011). Professionals may try to understand the active ingredients or what elements of the model result in favorable outcomes (HARC, 2018). Proactive (i.e., intentional and planned) and reactive (i.e., handling challenges as they surface) adaptations to evidence-based programs are possible (see Ballard, Tyndall, Baugh, Bergeson, & Littlewood, 2016).

A foundation in research and theory helps FLEs to appreciate the intentional nature of research and to demarcate objectivity from subjectivity (Darling, Cassidy, & Rehm, 2017). Theories relevant to adult learning and development are also key (Darling et al., 2017). For example, Erikson's psychosocial stages of development is an example of a theory of adult development, particularly the stages of intimacy versus isolation, generativity versus stagnation, and identity versus despair (Erikson, 1998). It is important to understand the developmental stages of families as they pertain to individual and family needs (Darling & Cassidy, 2014). Also keep in mind that adult learners bring their own characteristics and experiences with them and tend to be responsible for their own lives and can demonstrate self-direction, which sets the stage for the professional to use the facilitator role with this group (Darling & Cassidy, 2014).

304   *Professionalism*

Table 13.1 Family Life Education Concepts and Resources that Align with
Professionalism

FLE Content Area: Family Life Education Methodology	Resources
Home Visiting Evidence Evidence-based[1]; evidence-based programs[2,3]; parent education via home visiting[2]; home visiting programs[3] **Models** Logic models[1,2,3]; program models[1] **Adult Development** Andragogy[1]; adult development[2]; adult learners[3]	[1]Covey, M. (2015). Family life education methodology. In M. J. Walcheski, & J. S. Reinke (Eds.), *Family life education: The practice of family science* (pp. 243–251). Minneapolis, MN: National Council on Family Relations. [2]Darling, C. A., & Cassidy, D. (2014). *Family life education: Working with families across the lifespan* (3rd ed.). Long Grove, IL: Waveland. [3]Duncan, S. F., & Goddard, H. W. (2017). *Family life education: Principles and practices for effective outreach* (3rd ed.). Thousand Oaks, CA: Sage.

Facilitators help adults gain access to the knowledge and skills that they possess within themselves (Duncan & Goddard, 2017).

Professional ethics and practice. *Understand the character and quality of human social conduct, and the ability to critically examine ethical questions and issues as they relate to professional practice.*

An important topic of to home visitors' professional development is ethics. In particular, new professionals must consider whether a situation represents a true ethical dilemma or is an issue that could be resolved with more developed knowledge and skills (MNCFR, 2009, 2016; NCFR, 2018). The Family Life Educators Code of Ethics and a five-step ethical decision-making process may promote thoughtful professionals Please see the Winter 2018 (Vol.31.1) *CFLE Network* for the entire list of ethical principles used in the case study process.

The ethical decision-making process includes five steps to help explore solutions and actions in response to an ethical dilemma. The first step is to identify all the important and potential relationships in the case (MNCFR, 2009, 2016; NCFR, 2018). It will be important to consider any site policies that may also influence the decision-making process. Consideration of these factors may help the professional identify possible solutions (the fourth step) and select an action or actions (the fifth step) that may be implemented after consulting with the appropriate people, such as a director or parents (MNCFR, 2009, 2016).

Reflective supervision can be considered ongoing professional development for home visitors (Watson, Bailey, & Storm, 2016) particularly when it is part

Table 13.2 Family Life Education Concepts and Resources that Align with Professionalism

FLE Content Area: Professional Ethics and Practice	Resources
Home visiting evidence Ethical decision-making[1,2]	[1]Palm, G. F. (2018). Professional ethics and practice in family life education. In *Tools for ethical thinking and practice in family life education* (4th ed., pp. 1–10). Minneapolis, MN: National Council on Family Relations.
	[2]National Council on Family Relations. (2018). *Tools for ethical thinking and practice in family life education* (4th ed.). Minneapolis, MN: National Council on Family Relations.

of a larger system of support. The reflective supervision relationship should be an opportunity to discuss the decision-making process and share information without judgment from the supervisor. In other words, the content of the discussion should not be tied to the home visitor's evaluation. Reflective practice through the form of self-assessment and examining strengths and challenges may also support professional development (Parlakian, 2001). Reflection may promote sensitive and supportive interactions with families and, in turn, support the intended outcomes and goals of the home visiting program.

The Family Life Educators Code of Ethics (see NCFR, 2016) is an important guide to sign and to utilize. In other words, all CFLEs must read and sign this document but, perhaps more importantly, professionals should work to internalize the principles within the code of ethics. These principles, such as "I will be aware of the impact/power we have on parents and family relations" (see NCFR, 2016), should undergird an ethical decision making process.

Human growth and development across the lifespan. *Understand the development changes (both typical and atypical of individuals in families across the lifespan with an emphasis on knowledge of developmental domains).*

Young adulthood (approximately ages 20–40) and middle adulthood (approximately ages 40–60) are typically times of taking on new roles, such as entering the workforce, having a long-term romantic partnership or getting married, and potentially becoming a parent (Walsh, DeFlorio, Burnham, & Weiser, 2017). For most, physical changes occur and one's lifestyle may slow down or accelerate the aging process (Walsh et al., 2017). Smoking, alcohol use, and a poor diet increase the rate of the aging process, whereas exercise, a healthy diet, and abstaining from drugs and alcohol may slow down the aging process (Walsh et al., 2017). Regarding an aspect of social and emotional development, identity continues to develop in adulthood and an individual's disposition may be a better predictor of

306 *Professionalism*

Table 13.3 Family Life Education Concepts and Resources that Align with Professionalism

FLE Content Area: Human Growth and Development	Resources
Adult development Development across the lifespan including early adulthood, middle adulthood, late adulthood[1,2]	[1]Leventhal, J. (2015). Human growth and development across the lifespan. In M. J. Walcheski, & J. S. Reinke (Eds.), *Family life education: The practice of family science* (pp. 167–176). Minneapolis, MN: National Council on Family Relations. [2]Boyd, D., & Bee, H. (2015). *Lifespan development* (7th ed.). Upper Saddle River, NJ: Pearson.

an emotional crisis than would their chronological age (Walsh et al., 2017). In terms of cognitive development, most adults tend to possess sufficient memory skills (Walsh et al., 2017) but abstract, hypothetical thought has wide variation with some adults not demonstrating this advanced cognition.

There are several theories about adult development; some were mentioned in the family life education methodology section in this chapter. Other theories, such as Piaget's theory of the stages of cognitive development, might help to understand the possibilities and limitations of concrete operational thought and formal operational thought. Not all adults reach the formal operational stage (Sutherland, 1982). Kohlberg (1969) extended Piaget's work by discussing moral development. Perry (1970) discussed cognitive development beyond formal thought.

Family law and public policy. *Understand legal issues, policies, and laws influencing the wellbeing of families.*

Knowledge of policies, such as those in the Head Start Performance Standards (Administration for Children and Families, 2016) and local, agency-specific policies is important. At times, national and local policies may overlap. Policy is a course of action or plan and is implemented through a law, rule, or similar regulations (Bogenschneider, 2015). It is important for family professionals to be familiar with family policy, such as parental leave (Bogenschneider, 2014). It is also important to know the facts of the field in order to advocate for families and for services. For example, children enrolled in Early Head Start services have better outcomes (e.g., language, social-emotional) when home visiting is combined with center-based services compared to center-only services (Love et al., 2005, as cited in Bogenschneider, 2014).

Home visiting is the best story to tell of how an idea is transformed into law (Bogenschneider, 2014). Although home visiting was commenced over a hundred

Table 13.4 Family Life Education Concepts and Resources that Align with Professionalism

FLE Content Area: Family Law and Public Policy	Resources
Home visiting evidence Evidence-based home visiting[2]; home visiting legislation[2] **Models** Programs (e.g., prevention)[2]; develop, implement, and evaluation policy[1]	[1]Bogenschneider, K. (2015). Family law and public policy. In M. J. Walcheski, & J. S. Reinke (Eds.), *Family life education: The practice of family science* (pp. 223–234). Minneapolis, MN: National Council on Family Relations. [2]Bogenschneider, K. (2014). *Family policy matters: How policymaking affects families and what professionals can do* (3rd ed.). New York: Routledge.

years ago, it did not undergo serious evaluation (i.e., randomized control trials) until the 1960s (Bogenschneider, 2014). The Obama administration noticed the positive outcomes of home visiting programs and their support by various advocacy groups on children and parenting, such as on maternal health and child development (Bogenschneider, 2014). Between 2010 and 2014, this story had a positive ending with $1.5 billion made available to states for maternal, infant, and early childhood home visiting programs with most funding allocated to evidence-based programs (Bogenschneider, 2014).

Skills

To advance FLE practice within EHS-HBO, the CUPID HV expanded competency for Skills related to Professionalism include:

> Skills to advocate for families and seek opportunities to develop home visiting competencies from a wide range of training and education topics, across multiple disciplines, that are relevant to the unique challenges of home visiting.
>
> (CUPID, 2017)

FLE Methodology

- Employ strategies to meet the needs of different audiences; Employ techniques to help the learner do hands-on learning
  - Use evidence-based practices and modify only when needed, such as in the case of a family in crisis.
  - Follow the foundational curricula (e.g., for home visitors in PAT programs) to achieve fidelity and positive short-term and intermediate outcomes.

308 *Professionalism*

- Create learning environments that support individual differences

  - Connect individuals and families to community resources when more support is needed beyond the home visit.
  - Deliver models as they are intended to be delivered and make intentional adaptations in consideration of culture and context as they fit the local audience.

- Demonstrate group process and facilitation skills

  - Respect and promote adult development by serving as a facilitator (cf., expert).
  - Promote individualized learning that is self-directed.
  - Maintain boundaries between FLE and other domains of practice (e.g., family therapy).

- Develop culturally competent materials and experiences

  - Identify cultural factors that are important to each family and to the program and create materials that support these.
  - Utilize proactive and reactive adaptations to evidence-based programs to ensure culturally appropriate experiences.

- Identify sources of evidence-based information and implement evidence-based programs

  - Participate in professional development opportunities that present the latest research and evidence-based information in home visiting.
  - Demonstrate knowledge of Early Head Start Home Visiting as an evidence-based program by reviewing information in HomVEE.
  - Demonstrate knowledge of evidence-based curriculum, such as PAT, by reviewing information in HomVEE.

- Design educational experiences from start to finish (needs assessment to outcome measures)

  - Explain evidence-based programs and curriculums and how to achieve fidelity.
  - Design proactive adaptations to evidence-based programs and curriculums.
  - Describe the logic model and/or theory of change that guides the program.

- Promote and market educational programs

  - Build trust with families to promote their program attendance.
  - Effectively promote and market socialization events at the agency and in the community by using a variety of recruitment techniques.

- Implement adult education principles in work with individuals, parents, and families

  - Identify issues that adults face and identify strategies and content that can be useful.

Professional Ethics and Practice

- Demonstrate professional attitudes, values, behaviors, and responsibilities to clients, colleagues, and the broader community that are reflective of ethical standards and practice: (1) Understand the domains and scope of practice for family life educators and the role of collaboration; (2) Establish and maintain appropriate personal and professional boundaries; (3) Create a personal ethics plan to support/reflect the standards of the profession; (4) Maintain current knowledge and skills in the field

  - Explain the code of ethics and five step decision-making process to colleagues.
  - Maintain confidentiality of families.
  - Identify and describe empirical information from prevention science that underscores ethical interactions and apply this to home visits.
  - Engage in personal reflection and reflection during supervision that involves a personal ethics plan.
  - Demonstrate understanding and practice within the domain of FLE (cf., family therapy and family case management); discuss boundaries with families and supervisor.

- Identify and apply appropriate strategies to deal with conflicting values

  - Practice viewing conflicting values as differences rather than deficits.
  - Apply the five step decision-making process to demonstrate a thoughtful proposal of solutions and actions to ethical dilemmas.

- Demonstrate respect for diverse cultural values

  - Engage in an ongoing discussion with families about their culturally preferred practices.
  - Regarding refugee and other families, ask families good questions about what life was like in a different country to promote acculturation.
  - Participate in personal reflection and reflective supervision about how cultural factors can be considered in practice.

Human Growth and Development Across the Lifespan

- Guide practice using developmental theories

310 *Professionalism*

- Consider adult development theories (e.g., Erikson, Piaget, Kohlberg, Perry) and theories of adult learning (e.g., Kolb, Mezirow) as points of entry to understanding aspects of families and how practices might be received by them.

- Recognize socio-ecological influences on human development (e.g., trauma)

  - Identify influences that affect your wellbeing and influences that affect families' wellbeing.

Family Law and Public Policy

- Understand policy processes

  - Identify and describe policy and procedures that are relevant to home visiting and to families served.

- Identify current laws, policies, and initiatives that influence professional conduct and services and affect families

  - Identify laws, policies, and initiatives that are supportive of families and opportunities to advocate for change.

- Distinguish between advocacy and others (e.g., lobbying); Inform families, communities, and policy makers about public policies, initiatives, and legislation that affect families at local, state, and national levels

  - Participate in work that promotes advocating for policy change and describe how it is different from other types of work.

Box 13.1 CDA Home Visitor Competencies

The CDA Competency Standards are national standards for home visitors. The subject area that is most relevant to this chapter includes **CDA Subject Area 6: Maintaining a commitment to professionalism**. Each standard is comprised of competency goals, functional areas, items, indicators, and examples. The competency goal that is most relevant to this chapter is "To maintain a commitment to professionalism" (Council for Professional Recognition, 2016, p. 99).

Competency Goal	Functional Area	Example Item	Example Indicators
III. To maintain a commitment	13 Professionalism:	Item 13.3: Identifies and	Is a member of a professional

(Continued)

(Cont.)

Competency Goal	Functional Area	Example Item	Example Indicators
to professionalism	Home visitor makes decisions based on knowledge of research-based early childhood practices and adult learning, promotes high quality childcare services, and takes advantages of opportunities to improve knowledge and competence, both for personal and professional growth and for the benefit of children and families.	recognizes areas of own professional growth and gains the needed skills to provide high quality home visits.	organization and attends meetings, learning sessions and conferences Finds ways to meet his or her own needs and maintain energy and enthusiasm

Permission to reprint from the Council for Professional Recognition

Box 13.2 National Family Support Competency Framework for Family Support Professionals

The National Family Support Competency Framework for Family Support Professionals are competencies that include ten domains that are further clarified by dimensions (Institute for the Advancement of Family Support Professionals, 2018). The domain that is most germane to this chapter is Professional Practice, which includes five dimensions: ethical and legal practice, reflective practice, professional development, professional boundaries, and quality improvement.

Domain 10	Dimension 36	Component a.	Levels of Competency
Professional Practice	**Professional Development**	**Continuous Learning**	**1-Recognizing.** Understands and identifies specific areas for

(Continued)

312 *Professionalism*

(Cont.)

Domain 10	Dimension 36	Component a.	Levels of Competency
			additional growth and development
			3-Applying. Supports parents through building professional skills by seeking out training, feedback, or other opportunities for ongoing learning development
			5-Extending. Coaches parents to become continuous learners by developing personal growth goals and timelines, and accountability checks

Permission to reprint from the Institute for the Advancement of Family Support Professionals

Attitudes

CUPIDs Home Visitor Expansion of Competency: Attitudes that reflect a commitment to learn not only about children but also about families, parenting, and adult development, and a commitment to advocate for families (see Roggman et al., 2016; CUPID, 2017).

Principles of FLE that align with CUPIDs attitude. Societal issues, such as parenting, within the context of the family are important to FLE (Darling, Cassidy, & Rehm, 2017). A foundation in research and theory, which includes adult learning and development, is a foundational principle of family life education (Darling et al., 2017). Family life educators take a strengths-based approach, another foundational principle, to understand families' felt needs (Darling et al., 2017).

Virtues of FLE are also relevant to this discussion. For example, one virtue is prudence/practical wisdom or recognizing conflicting needs through reflection and professional discussions (Palm, 2018). This suggests that professionals should carefully consider the needs of children as well as other members of the family and propose solutions that carefully consider any tensions or conflicting needs. Several ethical principles are germane to this attitude (see MNCFR, 2016).

There were four FLE content areas addressed in this chapter:

- FLE methodology,
- Professional ethics and practice,
- Human growth and development across the lifespan, and
- Family law and public policy.

Family life educators practicing within EHS HV should adopt and internalize the principles, virtues, and relational ethics that are inherent within these content areas. FLE principles, virtues, relationship ethics, and the understanding and practice of content areas work to align with CUPID's emphasis on a commitment to learn about the entire family, and associate topics, issues, and strengths within the family context.

Summary

CUPID's home visitor expanded competency of professionalism arises from CUPIDs Infant/Toddler Workforce competency of professionalism. Topics within the expanded competency of professionalism include: home visiting evidence, logic models, variations in program models, policies, professional development, and adult development. The knowledge, skills, and attitudes within this competency align with four FLE content areas: FLE Methodology, Professional Ethics and Practice, Human Growth and Development Across the Lifespan, and Family Law and Public Policy.

Key Concepts

- Andragogy
- Burnout
- Code of ethics
- Confidentiality
- Ethical decision-making process
- Evidence-based practice
- Evidence-based program
- Fidelity
- Logic models
- Professional development
- Professional organizations
- Secondary traumatic stress

Recommended Readings

Alitz, P. J., Geary, S., Birriel, P. C., Sayi, T., Ramakrishnan, R., Balogun, O., Salloum, A., & Marshall, J. T. (2018). Work-related stressors among Maternal, Infant, and Early Childhood Home Visiting (MIECHV) home visitors: A qualitative study. *Maternal and Child Health Journal, 22*, 62–69. doi: 10.1007/s10995-018-2536-8

Jones Harden, B., Denmark, N., & Saul, D. (2010). Understanding the needs of staff in Head Start programs: The characteristics, perceptions, and experiences of home visitors. *Children and Youth Services Review, 32,* 371–379. doi: 10.1016/j.childyouth.2009.10.008

West, A. L, Berlin, L. J., & Jones Harden, B. (2018). Occupational stress and well-being among Early Head Start home visitors: A mixed methods study. *Early Childhood Research Quarterly, 44,* 288–303. doi: 10.1016/j.ecresq.2017.11.003

References

Administration for Children and Families (2016). *Head Start Program Performance Standards.* Retrieved from: https://eclkc.ohs.acf.hhs.gov/policy/45-cfr-chap-xiii

Asmussen, K. (2011). *The evidence-based parenting practitioner's handbook.* Abingdon, UK: Routledge.

Ballard, S. M., Tyndall, L. E., Baugh, E., Bergeson, C. B., & Littlewood, K. (2016). Framework for best practices in family life education: A case example. *Family Relations, 65,* 393–406. doi: 10.1111/fare.12200

Bogenschneider, K. (2014). *Family policy matters: How policymaking affects families and what professionals can do* (3rd ed.). New York: Routledge.

Bogenschneider, K. (2015). Family law and public policy. In M. J. Walcheski, & J. S. Reinke (Eds.), *Family life education: The practice of family science* (pp. 223–234). Minneapolis, MN: National Council on Family Relations.

Boyd, D., & Bee, H. (2015). *Lifespan development* (7th ed.). Upper Saddle River, NJ: Pearson.

Brookes, S. J., Summers, J. A., Thornburg, K. R., Ispa, J. M., & Lane, V. J. (2006). Building successful home visitor–mother relationships and reaching program goals in two Early Head Start programs: A qualitative look at contributing factors. *Early Childhood Research Quarterly, 21,* 25–45. doi: 10.1016/j.ecresq.2006.01.005

Caldwell, B. M., & Bradley, R. H. (2003). *Home observation for measurement of the environment: Administration manual.* Tempe, AZ: Family & Human Dynamics Research Institute, Arizona University.

Cannon, J. (2018). Planning ahead or an impact evaluation. Presentation at the Ounce for Prevention, Washington, D. C.

Christie, T. (2018). Respect: The heart of serving infants and toddlers. *Young Children, 73,* 10–15.

Collaborative for Understanding the Pedagogy of Infant/toddler Development (CUPID). (2017). *Comprehensive competencies for educators of infants and toddlers in group care and home visiting settings.* Unpublished.

Council for Professional Recognition. (2016). *The Child Development Associate® National Credentialing Program and CDA® competency standards: Home visitor edition.* Washington, DC: Council for Professional Recognition.

Covey, M. (2015). Family life education methodology. In M. J. Walcheski, & J. S. Reinke (Eds.), *Family life education: The practice of family science* (pp. 243–251). Minneapolis, MN: National Council on Family Relations.

Darling, C. A., & Cassidy, D. (2014). *Family life education: Working with families across the lifespan* (3rd ed.). Long Grove, IL: Waveland.

Darling, C. A., Cassidy, D., & Rehm, M. (2017). Family life education: Translational family science in action. *Family Relations, 66*, 741–752. doi: 10.1111/fare.12286

Daro, D. (2010). Replicating evidence-based home visiting models: A framework for assessing fidelity. Retrieved from http://citeseerx.ist.psu.edu/viewdoc/download?doi=10.1.1.296.529&rep=rep1&type=pdf

Duncan, S. F., & Goddard, H. W. (2017). *Family life education: Principles and practices for effective outreach* (3rd ed.). Thousand Oaks, CA: Sage.

Erikson, E. H. (1998). *The life cycle completed.* New York, NY: Norton.

Glascoe, F. P. (2002). The Brigance Infant and Toddler Screen: Standardization and validation. *Developmental and Behavioral Pediatrics, 23*, 145–150. doi: 0196-206X/00/2303-0145

Gurwitch, R., & Williams, J. (2017). Understanding how family stress and trauma impacts home visitors. Webinar from the National Center on Early Childhood Development, Teaching and Learning.

HARC (2018). Introduction to precision home visiting. Retrieved from https://www.hvresearch.org/introduction-to-precision-home-visiting/

Head Start Early Childhood Learning & Knowledge Center. (2018). Head Start Early Learning Outcomes Framework. Retrieved from https://eclkc.ohs.acf.hhs.gov/school-readiness/article/head-start-early-learning-outcomes-framework

Hebbeler, K. M., & Gerlach-Downie, S. G. (2002). Inside the black box of home visiting: A qualitative analysis of why intended outcomes were not achieved. *Early Childhood Research Quarterly, 17*, 28–51. doi: 10.1016/S0885-2006(02)00128-X

HomVEE. (2013). Home Instruction for Parents of Preschool Youngsters (HIPPY). Retrieved from https://homvee.acf.hhs.gov/Model/1/Home-Instruction-for-Parents-of-Preschool-Youngsters–HIPPY–sup—sup-/13/1

HomVEE. (2016a). Early Head Start-Home Visiting (EHS-HV). Retrieved from https://homvee.acf.hhs.gov/Model/1/Early-Head-Start-Home-Visiting–EHS-HV-/8/1

HomVEE. (2016b). Nurse Family Partnership (NFP). Retrieved from https://homvee.acf.hhs.gov/Model/1/Nurse-Family-Partnership–NFP–sup—sup-/14/1

HomVEE. (2017). Healthy Families America (HFA). Retrieved from https://homvee.acf.hhs.gov/Model/1/Healthy-Families-America–HFA–sup—sup-/10/1

Institute for the Advancement of Family Support Professionals. (2018). *National Family Support Competency Framework for Family Support Professionals.* Retrieved from: https://cppr-institute-prod.s3.amazonaws.com/modules/Approved%20National%20Family%20Support%20Competency%20Framework_FINAL_7_18_2018.pdf

Kolb, D. (1984). *Experiential learning: Experience as the source of learning and development.* Upper Saddle River, NJ: Prentice-Hall.

Kohlberg, L. (1969). *Stages in the development of moral thought and action.* New York: Hold, Reinhart and Winston.

Korfmacher, J., Green, B., Spellmann, M., & Thornburg, K. R. (2007). The helping relationship and program participation in early childhood home visiting. *Infant Mental Health Journal, 28*, 459–480. doi: 10.1002/imhj.20148

Korfmacher, J., Green, B., Staerkel, F., Peterson, C., Cook, G., Roggman, L., Faldowski, R. A., & Schiffman, R. (2008). Parent involvement in early childhood home visiting. *Child & Youth Care Forum, 37*, 171–196. doi: 10.1007/s10566-008-9057-3

316 Professionalism

Leventhal, J. (2015). Human growth and development across the lifespan. In M. J. Walcheski, & J. S. Reinke (Eds.), *Family life education: The practice of family science* (pp. 167–176). Minneapolis, MN: National Council on Family Relations.

Marshall, E., & Virmani, E. A. (2017). Professional development for home visitors. National Center on Early Childhood Development, Teaching and Learning. Retrieved https://eclkc.ohs.acf.hhs.gov/video/professional-development-home-visitors

Mattox, T., & Kilburn, M. R. (2012). Understanding evidence-based information for the early childhood field. *Zero to Three, 32*, 4–10.

McCawley, P. F. (2001). The logic model for program planning and evaluation. University of Idaho. Retrieved from https://www.cals.uidaho.edu/edcomm/pdf/CIS/CIS1097.pdf

Mezirow, J. (2000). *Fostering critical reflection in adulthood: A guide to transformative and emancipatory learning.* San Francisco, CA: Jossey-Bass.

Minnesota Council on Family Relations (MNCFR). (2009). Ethical thinking and practice for parent and family life educators. In D. Bredehoft & M. Walcheski (Eds.), *Family life education: Integrating theory and practice* (pp. 233–239). Minneapolis, MN: National Council on Family Relations.

Minnesota Council on Family Relations (MNCFR). (2016). *Ethical thinking and practice for parent and family life education.* Minneapolis, MN: Ethics Committee, Parent and Family Education Section. Retrieved from https://mn.ncfr.org/resources/

National Council on Family Relations (NCFR). (2015). *Resource list for the Certified Family Life Educator (CFLE) Exam.* Retrieved from https://www.ncfr.org/sites/default/files/2017-01/2015_cfle_exam_resources.pdf

National Council on Family Relations (NCFR). (2016). Family Life Educators Code of Ethics. Retrieved from https://www.ncfr.org/sites/default/files/cfle_code_of_ethics_2.pdf

National Council on Family Relations (NCFR). (2018). *Tools for ethical thinking and practice in family life education* (4th ed.). Minneapolis, MN: National Council on Family Relations.

Palm, G. F. (2018). Professional ethics and practice in family life education. In *Tools for ethical thinking and practice in family life education* (4th ed., pp. 1–10). Minneapolis, MN: National Council on Family Relations.

Parents as Teachers National Center. (2018). Logic model. Retrieved from https://parentsasteachers.org/logic-model/

Parlakian, R. (2001). *Look, listen, and learn: Reflective supervision and relationship-based work.* Washington, DC: Zero to Three.

PayScale. (2018). Early Head Start Home Visitor salary. Retrieved from https://www.payscale.com/research/US/Job=Early_Head_Start_Home_Visitor/Hourly_Rate

Perry, W. G. (1970). *Forms of intellectual and ethical development in the college years.* New York: Rinehart and Winston.

Peterson, C. A., Hughes-Belding, K., Rowe, N., Fan, L., Walter, M., Dooley, L., Wang, W., & Steffensmeier, C. (2018). Triadic interactions in MIECHV: Relations to home visiting quality. *Maternal and Child Health Journal, 22*, 3–12. doi: 10.1007/s10995-018-2534-x

Petkus, J. (2015). A first-hand account of implementing a Family Life Education model: Intentionality in Head Start home visiting. In M. J. Walcheski, & J. S. Reinke (Eds.), *Family life education: The practice of family science* (pp. 325–331). Minneapolis, MN: National Council on Family Relations.

Roggman, L. A., Cook, G. A., Peterson, C. A., & Raikes, H. H. (2008). Who drops out of Early Head Start home visiting programs? *Early Education and Development, 19,* 574–599. doi: 10.1080/10409280701681870

Roggman, L. A., Cook, G. A., Innocenti, M. S., Norman, V. J. & Christiansen, K. (2013). *Parenting Interactions with Children: Checklist of Observations Linked to Outcomes (PIC-COLO) User Guide.* Baltimore: Brooks.

Roggman, L. A., Cook, G. A., Innocenti, M. S., Jump Norman, V. K., Christiansen, K., Boyce, L. K., ... Hallgren, K. (2012). Home Visit Rating Scales—Adapted & Extended to Excellence: (HOVRS-A+). Unpublished measure.

Roggman, L. A., Peterson, C. A., Chazan-Cohen, R., Ispa, J., Decker, K. B., Hughes-Belding, K., Cook, G. A., & Vallotton, C. D. (2016). Preparing home visitors to partner with families of infants and toddlers, *Journal of Early Childhood Teacher Education, 37,* 301–313.

Roggman, L., Peterson, C., Ispa, J., Cohen, R. C., Cook, G., Hughes-Belding, K., Valloton, C., Decker, K., & CUPID. (2018). *CUPID: A scholarship of teaching and learning effort to improve teaching and enhance practice for those serving infants, toddlers, and their families.* Washington, DC: The National Research Conference on Early Childhood.

Schultz, D., Jones, S. S., Pinder, W. M., Wiprovnick, A. E., Groth, E. C., Shanty, L. M., & Duggan, A. (2018). Effective home visiting training: Key principles and findings to guide training developers and evaluators. *Maternal and Child Health Journal, 22,* 1563–1567. doi: 10.1007/s10995-018-2554-6

Squires, J., Potter, L., & Bricker, D. (1999). *The ASQ user's guide* (2nd ed.). Baltimore, MD: Brookes.

Sutherland, P. (1982). An expansion of Peel's describer-explainer stage theory. *Educational Review, 34,* 69–76.

Walcheski, M. J., & Reinke, J. S. (2015). *Family life education: The practice of family science.* Minneapolis, MN: National Council on Family Relations.

Walsh, B. A., DeFlorio, L., Burnham, M. M., & Weiser, D. A. (2017). *Introduction to human development and family studies.* New York: Taylor & Francis.

Walsh, B. A., Mortensen, J. A., Edwards, A. L., & Cassidy, D. (in press). The practice of family life education within Early Head Start home visiting. *Family Relations.*

Watson, C. L., Bailey, A. E., & Storm, K. J. (2016). Building capacity in reflective practice: A tiered model of statewide supports for local home-visiting programs. *Infant Mental Health Journal, 37,* 640–652. doi: 10.1002/imhj.21609

Wasik, B. H., & Bryant, D. M. (2001). *Home visiting: Procedures for helping families* (2nd ed.). Thousand Oaks, CA: Sage.

14 Supporting Competencies in Adults

In EHS-HBO, while many program goals are focused on infant/toddler development, many of the actual home visiting interactions are between the home visitor and parent (or other adult family members). A national survey of families in EHS-HBO found that when children were 24 months old, home visitors spent about half of the time on child-focused activities. The rest of the time was focused on 14% parent–family activities, 15% parent–child activities, and 17% staff–family relationship building activities (ACF, 2015). This included adult-focused activities such as providing education/information, setting goals, observing/assessing, problem solving, emotional support, feedback on parent–child interactions, and crisis management (ACF, 2015). These data illustrate that much of the home visitor's job is spent working with adults. As such, home visitors must have expanded knowledge in how to support adult learning and behavior, particularly in ways that will help parents support young children's development (Roggman et al., 2016). The CUPID competency for **Supporting Competencies in Adults** includes (CUPID, 2017; Roggman et al., 2016):

Competency	Supporting adult learners (e.g., parents, colleagues) to develop the competencies and sense of efficacy to support children's development and learning
Knowledge	Knowledge of adult/adolescent development, learning, behavior change, parenting, and mental health
Skills	Skills for: collaborating with and coaching parents to engage in interactions that support positive infant/toddler development; helping parents reflect on their lives; supporting parenting efficacy; guiding parent problem solving to increase the quality of the home environment; and for mentoring adult achievement of self-sufficiency goals
Attitudes	Attitudes reflecting compassion and understanding for the challenges of adult life, the difficulty of parenting when experiencing depression or anxiety, and the influence from a parent's earlier life experiences

For full alignment see Appendix B.

The FLE Content Areas that help expand this competency include:

Human growth and development	Understanding the developmental changes (both typical and atypical) of individuals in families across the lifespan with an emphasis on knowledge of developmental domains
Parenting education and guidance	How parents teach, guide, and influence as the dynamic context of the parent–child relationship
Families and individuals in societal contexts	Understanding families in regards to other institutions
FLE methodology	Understand principles of FLE in tandem with planning and delivery of programs

Note: Permission to reprint was granted from the National Council on Family Relations.

Knowledge

CUPID's expanded home visitor knowledge for supporting adult competencies is:

> Knowledge of adult/adolescent development, learning, behavior change, parenting, and mental health.
>
> (CUPID, 2017)

Adolescence and Early Adulthood

In a recent national survey of EHS families, mothers were an average of 20 years old when they had their first child (ACF, 2015). This statistical average means that parents in EHS-HBO range from adolescents to young adults, meaning that home visitors will work with parents who are at different development stages themselves.

The developmental period of adolescence begins with the onset of puberty (usually around age 12, with girls typically a little earlier), in which the gonads (ovaries and testes) mature and begin producing hormones (estrogen and testosterone) that cause male and female adult sex characteristics to develop (Kuther, 2017). Adolescence is often portrayed as a chaotic and stressful time in life. In the early 1900s, G. Stanley Hall famously coined the phrase "storm and stress" to describe the supposedly tumultuous developmental period that carried children from childhood to adulthood (Arnett, 1999). Society and the media often characterize teens as hormonal, moody, and angry. However, research suggests a much more positive view of adolescent development. Kuther (2017) summarizes that many teens report feeling close and happy

320   *Supporting Competencies in Adults*

with their parents, and that there is little relation to hormonal swings and moody behaviors—moodiness instead is often a product of social and psychological stressors (e.g., peers, school). Even though adolescents are increasingly capable of thinking and reasoning like adults, they are still undergoing considerable brain development in areas related to problem-solving, impulse control, risk assessment, and formal reasoning (Kuther, 2017).

Early adulthood spans the ages of about 18 to 40, and is a developmental period characterized by fewer physical changes, but more mature cognitive processes (Kuther, 2017). Young adulthood is also marked by important social changes such moving away and establishing oneself away from the family of origin (i.e., the household in which one was raised; Williams et al., 2017). As they begin to pair with romantic partners and have children of their own, young adults begin to establish their family of procreation (Williams et al., 2017). Most women have their first child in their mid-20s, with lower-income women and women without a college education typically having children earlier than women with more education and wealth (Penman-Aguilar, Carter, Snead, & Kourtis, 2013).

EHS-HBO programs serve many teen parents. Since the 1990s, the U.S. has experienced a steady downward trend in teen pregnancies and teen births. The teen birth rate, which is defined as the number of births per 1,000 females (ages 15 to 19) decreased from 61.8 to 24.2 across 1990–2014 (Patton & Livingston, 2016). Teen pregnancy and birth rates remain higher for African American and Hispanic teens (Patton & Livingston, 2016), as well as teens from low-income families (Martin, Hamilton, Osterman, Driscoll, & Drake, 2018). In a sample of 1,700 white, African American and Latina EHS mothers, one-third had their child before age 19 (Berlin, Brady-Smith, & Brooks-Gunn, 2002). When these mothers were video-taped playing with their child at 24 months old, they were observed to use less supportive parenting behaviors, and were more intrusive, detached, and hostile than older mothers (Berlin et al., 2002). As such, EHS-HBO is an important point of intervention for these young families.

Learning and Behavior Change Related to Parenting

If home visitors want parents to become better supports for their young children's development, they must have an understanding of how young adults learn and create changes in their behavior, particularly when it comes to parenting. Learning is a life-long process, and the way humans process new information changes throughout the lifespan. The manner in which adolescents and adults learn has a direct impact on how home visitors should approach the home visiting process. Adolescence and early adulthood are distinct stages marked by unique characteristics and cognitive processes, which in turn affects parental development (Steinberg, 2017; Jacobson, 2015). Parenting is a life-long process that changes as parents and children develop together. Parents in

EHS-HBO are either pregnant or have an infant or toddler, meaning that they at the beginning of their parenting journey.

The goals of EHS-HBO are to foster healthy change in parenting and family interactions in ways that improve child wellbeing. EHS-HBO strives to collaborate with parents to coach them in supporting their child's development and developing their own self-efficacy. Self-efficacy is a term derived from Albert Bandura's social learning theory, and is the belief about one's capabilities to achieve a certain level of performance that exerts influence over their own life (Bandura, 1994). The way parents perceive their own self-efficacy will dictate their motivation, behaviors, and feelings about parenting and family life. For example, a parent with low self-efficacy about managing their toddler's tantrums may feel stressed, defeated, and have little motivation to do anything about it because they feel that there is no point – they are not going to have any effect, so why bother? Parents who feel efficacious in their abilities to parent are less stressed, and report a higher level of satisfaction in their life (Çattık & Aksoy, 2018). Home visitors should not only coach parents on making changes in parenting interactions and the home environment, but should also teach parents how to access information and resources in the community to build their self-efficacy and confidence in self-sufficiency. Home visitors should not only focus on providing information to parents, but also teach parents how to make their own informed decisions based on available information and resources. This will truly build a parent's efficacy in their own skills and decisions. The features of the adolescent and young adult developmental time periods, including unique cognitive processes, learning behaviors, and strategies to support and coach are elaborated in the following sections.

Parental Mental Health

If home visitors are going to expect adults to learn, change, and become more sensitive, responsive, and self-sufficient parents as a result of the EHS-HBO program, they must recognize the role adult mental health plays in being able to do these things effectively. Parental mental health is an important mediator of all family processes. This is depicted in the family stress model (Conger et al., 2002). For families in poverty, low incomes and resulting hardships contribute to increased feelings of economic pressure (i.e., feeling that one's family does not have enough to make ends meet), which in turn contributes to worse mental health, such as increased depressive symptoms. These symptoms translate to relationship conflict and less nurturing parenting, ultimately impacting child development (Conger et al., 2002).

Depression is a major risk factor for poor parent–child relationships during infancy and toddlerhood. According to the American Psychiatric Association (APA, 2013), depression is pervasive and interferes with everyday life. Symptoms may include (but are not limited to) feeling sad, anxious, tired, guilty,

322 *Supporting Competencies in Adults*

worthless, helpless, sleeping issues (too much or too little), and physical symptoms such as aches, pains, headaches, stomach problems, or thoughts about suicide or self-harm (APA, 2013). Postpartum depression specifically occurs in women during the postpartum period (the first year after having a baby), and is experienced by about 13% of mothers (Beck, 2001). There are many risk factors for postpartum depression including, a history of depression, prenatal anxiety, an unplanned/unwanted pregnancy, life stress, a lack of social support, and socioeconomic status (Beck, 2001).

Depression is the most toxic to parent–child relationships and child development when it occurs early in the child's life (Goodman et al., 2011). It is a major risk factor for developing insecure or disorganized attachment (Goodman & Brand, 2009), which has lifelong negative consequences for children (van Ijzendoorn et al., 1999). Persistent maternal depressive symptoms over an infant's first year have been associated with hyperactivity, physical aggression, and separation anxiety at age three (Kingston et al., 2018). Living in the context of poverty also exacerbates the negative associations between parental depression and young children's behavior problems (Goodman et al., 2011). Depression can also negatively impact a person's ability to learn and recall new information, making it difficult for parents with depression to learn new information and adjust their parenting behaviors (Kizilbash, Vanderploeg, & Curtiss, 2002). Individual EHS-HBO programs may screen for postpartum depression, and depressive symptoms in parents (see Chapter 9). Home visitors are not trained to diagnose or manage depression, so it is the responsibility of the program to have a plan to refer parents for mental health services as necessary. However, the home visitor should still understand how parental mental health affects their work with parents, as is elaborated in the next sections.

FLE Content Knowledge and Knowledge of Supporting Competencies in Adults

Human growth and development. *Understanding the developmental changes (both typical and atypical) of individuals in families across the lifespan with an emphasis on knowledge of developmental domains.*

Content knowledge of human growth and development across the lifespan prepares the home visitor to understand adolescence and early adulthood as unique developmental stages. Understanding the unique characteristics of each stage helps explain why people think and behave the way they do at different ages. Some EHS-HBO parents are teenagers who are at a different developmental stage than older parents. Adolescent thinking is more mature than childhood, but it is not without limitations. While children's thinking is tied to concrete experiences, adolescents are able to engage in more formal types of reasoning (Kuhn, 2008). Formal reasoning involves being able to think at an abstract level, pose hypotheticals, and draw inferences using deductive logic

(Kuther, 2017). According to Steinberg (2017), adolescents are able to weigh possibilities and generate systematic solutions to problems. They are able to use metacognition (thinking about thinking) as well. Despite this, they are prone to egocentrism (i.e., a heightened sense of importance), which limits their thinking in a few ways (Steinberg, 2017). Egocentrism may cause teens to erroneously believe that everyone is focused on their behavior, or that they have an "imaginary audience." This may cause adolescent parents to feel more scrutiny about becoming parents or their parenting skills. They are also prone to maintaining a personal fable, again erroneously thinking that their life experiences are unique. This can become hazardous when adolescents refuse to believe that they will not fall victim to the consequences of risky behaviors (e.g., reckless driving, unprotected sex). This can make it difficult for home visitors to instill changes in adolescent parent behaviors. For home visitors working with young parents, it is important to be aware of how adolescents process information and risk.

Some researchers have documented "emerging adulthood" as an extended transition between adolescence and early adulthood, about the ages of 18 to 25 (Arnett, 2000). This period is characterized as a time of "change and exploration" in terms of identity, relationships, education, and career possibilities (Arnett, 2000). Some researchers argue however that emerging adulthood is entirely dependent on the social context, meaning that only adolescents who have the luxury of changing and exploring options experience this "stage" (Steinberg, 2017). For some in EHS-HBO, young parenthood and economic disadvantage may leave little freedom for these pursuits. Traditionally, early adulthood is marked as ages 18 to 40, but is not as clear-cut of a developmental period as other points in the lifespan (e.g., infancy vs. early childhood), and the changes that take place over adulthood are largely idiosyncratic, meaning based on individual experiences due to differences in environment and opportunity (Hoyer & Rybash, 1994). In contrast to teens, young adults are able to engage in postformal reasoning, meaning that they are better able to combine abstract thought with practical considerations (Sinnott, 1998). According to Kuther (2017), "young adults who demonstrate postformal thinking recognize that most problems have multiple causes and solutions, that some solutions are better choices than others, and that all problems involve uncertainty" (p. 376). As young adults gain more experience with others (and more education), they process information in increasingly complex ways (Kuther, 2017). Young adults may focus on facts that they perceive as "right" or "wrong" no matter the person or setting, but some young adults are more flexible in their thinking, recognizing that knowledge is often subjective to the person and context. The most advanced post-formal thought involves taking in contradictory perspectives and evaluating evidence accordingly (Yan & Arlin, 1995). Due to young adults having more complex reasoning skills, it may be easier for home visitors to mentor young adult parents into making informed lasting changing in their parenting.

324 *Supporting Competencies in Adults*

Some researchers argue that parenthood can be thought of as a developmental stage of adulthood in itself because parenthood is:

(1) a major life stage with powerful potential for parents' reorganization of self (e.g., mastery of intrapsychic conflicts, increased self-esteem) and of environment (e.g., heightened focus on family relationships, decreased focus on other relationships); (2) a life stage of some duration with at least a clear beginning, middle, and end (paralleling the child's development).

(Demick, 2002, p. 391)

The transition to parenthood (i.e., conception through the first few years of parenthood) kicks off this stage (e.g., Demick, 2002). No matter when it occurs in an individual's lifespan, it represents a period of destabilization for the individual in which they have to adopt the parenting role as part of their sense of self and reorganize their social contexts to adjust to a new baby. This is challenging for all parents, but can be especially difficult for young parents. From a life course perspective, adolescent parenthood is "off time" with social norms for having a baby, which has consequences for how teen parents may see themselves (Neugarten & Neugarten, 1996). In terms of mental health, some people are biologically predisposed to developing depressive symptoms (Abkevich et al., 2003), but the social adjustment to new parenthood can be a catalyst for symptoms, particularly for adolescent mothers (Birkeland, Thompson, & Phares, 2005). Depressive symptoms can be fueled by unique social

Table 14.1 Family Life Education Concepts and Resources that Align with Supporting Competencies in Adults

FLE Content Area: Human Growth and Development	*Resources*
Adult/adolescent development Ages and stages including adulthood (early to late) and adolescence[1,2] **Learning** Learning and learning theories[2] **Behavior change** Behavior and parental behaviors[2] **Parenting** Parental behaviors, parental responsiveness, and parenting styles[2] **Mental health** Mental health and mental disorders[2]	[1]Leventhal, J. (2015). Human growth and development across the lifespan. In M. J. Walcheski, & J. S. Reinke (Eds.), *Family life education: The practice of family science* (pp. 167–176). Minneapolis, MN: National Council on Family Relations. [2]Boyd, D., & Bee, H. (2015). *Lifespan development* (7th ed.). Upper Saddle River, NJ: Pearson.

issues that go along with teen parenting, such as social isolation from peers and school, low feelings of self-efficacy (i.e., believing in one's ability to succeed), and worries about how pregnancy will change their bodies (Birkeland et al., 2005). African American and Latina adolescent mothers are at greater risk for depression and resulting consequences such dropping out of school (Barnet et al., 1996; Birkeland et al., 2005; Leadbeater, 1999).

Parenting education and guidance. *How parents teach, guide, and influence as the dynamic context of the parent–child relationship.*

Knowledge of the FLE content area parenting education and guidance can prepare home visitors for coaching and collaborating with parents to support child development. The manner in which EHS-HBO home visitors actually go about this will be at least partially guided by the research-based curriculum individual programs implement at home visits. For example, Parents as Teachers (PAT) is used by many EHS-HBO programs around the country. The curriculum provides expert knowledge to parents about parenting practices and child development, including how development changes over the first three years of life. The logic is that improved knowledge helps parents feel more competent in their one-on-one interactions with their child and setting up the environment in ways that support healthy development (Parents as Teachers National Center, 2019). As such, coaching and support is focused on increasing parent knowledge, attitudes, and behaviors (Wagner et al., 2002). The Home Visit Rating Scales (HOVRS-A+; Roggman et al., 2010), is an assessment of home visitor–parent relationships, including how the home visitor facilitates parent–child interactions. According to the measure, high quality coaching of parent–child interactions has three elements: (1) encouraging parental leadership during parent–child interactions, (2) responding to both parents and children when coaching, and (3) using toys and supplies that are already available in the home as materials to facilitate parent–child interactions (Roggman et al., 2010). In FLE, collaboration with parents is essential, and as such home visitors must situate parents as the leaders during parent–child interactions instead of stepping in as the "expert" to "fix" what's wrong (Darling & Cassidy, 2014). Utilizing materials already available in the home further exemplifies the principle of "being with" families instead of doing things for them (Petkus, 2015). Parents will get more from coaching sessions if they can implement the strategies with materials they already have, versus specialized materials that the home visitor supplies. Parents will get more out of coaching and home visitor interaction if home visitors are able to implement curriculum accurately, and are able to foster healthy relationships with families.

In FLE, knowledge of parenting education and guidance also involves coaching and collaborating with parents to support their own self-efficacy (Jacobson, 2015). In terms of parenting and family life, parents should feel that they have the abilities necessary to make meaningful contributions to their child's development and supporting their family as needed. Researchers argue parental self-efficacy is a mediational pathway between parent–child characteristics and parental behaviors (Teti, O'Connell, & Reiner, 1996). That is, individual characteristics of parents (e.g., personality, mental health) and children (e.g., temperament) affect sensitive parent–child interactions, but mostly indirectly via the effect the have on parental self-efficacy. This makes self-efficacy and important point of intervention for changing family behaviors.

According to Bandura (1994), the four main sources of self-efficacy include mastery experiences, beliefs, social models, and negative stress reduction. First, mastery experiences come from experiencing successes through sustained efforts. For parents, this may include small victories such as learning to soothe their crying infant or larger hurdles like finding employment. Second, beliefs in one's self-efficacy can be facilitated when others tell them that they have what it takes; for this to work, however, home visitors must be realistic in parents' capabilities, or parents will only be disappointed when results do not match expectations. Here the home visitor's personal relationship with the family is critical—when home visitors know their parents well and have a close and warm relationship with them, they will be better equipped to provide appropriate support that boosts self-efficacy. A related concept here is scaffolding. Coined by theorist Lev Vygotsky, scaffolding is when a "more knowledgeable other" helps someone accomplish something that is just beyond their current skill level—this is where the most learning occurs (Brooks, 2013). Home visitors must work in collaboration with parents, but they can scaffold parent–child interactions to help parents see their achievements and build motivation to continue until mastery is achieved. Third, social models provide individuals with a reference for success. Parents watch those around them succeed (or fail) and internalize it as part of their own self-efficacy. Home visitors are important social models for developmentally appropriate parent–child interactions. Attending parent groups as part of the EHS-HBO program also provides parents with social models of other parents who are share similar struggles and parenting issues. Even providing information about child development plays an important role in self-efficacy. For example, when parents have high knowledge of child development, combined with high self-efficacy, they are more likely to provide highly sensitive care to their infants (Hess, Teti, & Hussey-Gardner, 2004). Finally, negative emotions and stress get in the way of self-efficacy, making it challenging to interpret anything one is doing in a positive light (Bandura, 1994). Feelings of depression create a giant cloud, obscuring parents' perceptions of their abilities and accomplishments (Leahy-Warren, McCarthy, & Corcoran, 2012). This is particularly concerning for adolescent parents, or mothers with postpartum depression. It is essential for home visitors to identify family stress and mental health concerns, and refer families to appropriate community resources and supports.

Table 14.2 Family Life Education Concepts and Resources that Align with Supporting Competencies in Adults

FLE Content Area: Parenting Education and Guidance	Resources
Adult/adolescent development Adolescents and adults within the context of family[1]; adolescence and adulthood[2] **Learning** Teaching and learning of life skills[1]; learning theories and learning to parent[2] **Behavior change** Modifying behavior[2] **Parenting** Parent education and parenting[1,2]; parenting in various circumstances[2] **Mental health** Mental disorders[2]	[1]Jacobson, A. L. (2015). Parenting education and guidance. In M. J. Walcheski, & J. S. Reinke (Eds.), *Family life education: The practice of family science* (pp. 213–222). Minneapolis, MN: National Council on Family Relations. [2]Brooks, J. B. (2013). *The process of parenting* (9th ed.). New York: McGraw Hill.

Families and individuals in societal contexts. *Understanding families in regards to other institutions.*

In terms of supporting competencies in adults, content knowledge in families and individuals in societal contexts bring in to focus how the context of living in poverty exacerbates many of the issues discussed in this chapter. As discussed earlier, the family stress model lays out the pathways by which poverty, and the associated stressors and hardship that go along with it, affect parent and child wellbeing (Conger et al., 2002). A major pathway is the negative effect economic hardship has on parental mental health (Conger et al., 2002). Research has also shown that the effects of living in poverty on young children's cognitive development is exacerbated by maternal depression (Petterson & Albers, 2001). The youngest parents in EHS-HBO are also dealing with the fact that society views their entry in to parenthood as "off time" in the life course, plus additional stress and negative emotions that goes along with adolescent parenthood (Hans & Thullen, 2009). Huang and colleagues (2014) found that adolescent mothers' stress (and lack of social support) was associated with increased feelings of depression, which in turn affected children's wellbeing at 12 months. Home visitors are not trained to diagnose and treat mental health issues, but this research underscores the importance of screening for depression as a regular home visiting practice. Parental mental health is the foundation for supporting competencies in adults—parents and home visitors working together in the program will only go so far if parental mental health is not addressed. This is all the more challenging for

328   Supporting Competencies in Adults

low-income parents because of barriers to healthcare institutions (Santiago, Kaltman, & Miranda, 2013). These include logistical barriers (e.g., cost, lack of insurance, public transportation issues, lack of childcare, and shift work schedules), individual perception barriers (e.g., stigma for families of color or immigration status, family/community disapproval of mental health services), and systems-level barriers (e.g., lack of services in native language or by people of color, inadequate training and screening across the mental health fields). EHS-HBO home visitors may be able to do little to address systems-level barriers, but they can work with families to overcome logistical and individual perception barriers to mental health care.

Cultivating self-efficacy and self-sufficiency in parents is also influenced by the context of poverty. For parents, these traits are assets, meaning that having high feelings of self-efficacy helps parents act in ways that are beneficial to their child's development. Raikes and Thompson (2005) examined self-efficacy as a "psychological resource" for Early Head Start mothers to protect them from feelings of parenting stress. For these mothers, the mere fact of living in poverty was not associated with parenting stress. Instead, ecological risk factors that stemmed from living in poverty (no high school diploma, health problems, recently divorced, homeless or incarcerated, child has a health or developmental concern, alcohol or drug abuse, domestic violence) were stronger predictors of stress (Raikes & Thompson, 2005). Plus, family income was only associated with parenting stress when mothers also had low feelings of self-efficacy (Raikes & Thompson, 2005). Ways of promoting self-efficacy were discussed earlier, but it's important to mention here that feelings of self-efficacy are partially informed by the messages parents receive from others about their competence (Bandura, 1994). Parents living in poverty, including adolescent parents and families of color, may have to manage stigmatization and prejudices from society. Deidra Kelly (1996, p. 445) identified a "cycle of stigma" in society for young parents, especially those in poverty, which negatively influences policies and programs that should be supporting parents in need. There are many programs designed to assist families in poverty, but many parents report feeling degraded with little sympathy given to complex situations in order to receive the assistance (Reutter et al., 2009). Reutter et al. (2009, p. 302) interviewed a mother living in poverty who reported "It makes me feel like I'm not worth anything. I feel like I can't provide for myself or my daughter," when she attempts to apply for additional assistance. Home visitors must reflect on their own attitudes and biases in order to build an encouraging relationship with parents where efficacy can grow. For home visitors working with adolescent parents, their own mothers may also be heavily involved in helping them adjust to parenthood (Hans & Thullen, 2009), which adds another dimension of complexity in managing expectations from others. It is important for home visitors to recognize that parents in EHS-HBO may also be managing these types of perceptions and feelings from other, which can affect how they perceive themselves as capable parents.

Supporting Competencies in Adults 329

Table 14.3 Family Life Education Concepts and Resources that Align with Supporting Competencies in Adults

FLE Content Area: Families and Individuals in Societal Contexts	Resources
Adult/adolescent development Life course perspective[1]; adolescence and adulthood[2] **Learning** Lifelong learning and the education system[1]; learners and learning theories[2] **Behavior change** Behaviorists[2]; change (e.g., resistance to, stress, flexibility)[2] **Parenting** Ecological perspective[1]; parenthood and parent education[2] **Mental health** Well-functioning families[2]; wellness[2]; stress and family problems[2]	[1]Wadsworth, S. M. M., Roy, K. M., & Watkins, N. (2015). Families and individuals in societal contexts. In M. J. Walcheski & J. S. Reinke (Eds.), *Family life education: The practice of family science* (pp. 147–155). Minneapolis, MN: National Council on Family Relations [2]Olson, D. H., DeFrain, J., & Skogrand, L. (2014). *Marriages and families: Intimacy, diversity, and strengths* (8th ed.). New York: McGraw Hill.

FLE methodology. *Understand principles of FLE in tandem with planning and delivery of programs.*

Content knowledge in FLE methodology emphasizes the importance of adult learning styles when planning programs for parents, as well as methods for tailoring program implementation for specialized populations (Covey, 2015), such as adolescent parents or mothers with postpartum depression.

Trivette, Dunst, Hamby, and O'Herin (2009) state that adult learning describes involves a process of planning, application, and understanding that can be applied to working with adults in home visiting:

- Planning
  - Introduce: engage the learner in a preview of the material, knowledge or practice that is the focus of instruction or training.
  - Illustrate: Demonstrate or illustrate the use or applicability of the material, knowledge or practice for the learner.

- Application
  - Practice: Engage the learner in the use of the material, knowledge or practice.

330 *Supporting Competencies in Adults*

- ○ Evaluate: Engage the learner in a process of evaluating the consequence or outcome of the application of the material, knowledge or practice.
- Deep understanding
  - ○ Reflection: Engage the learner in self-assessment of his or her acquisition of knowledge and skills as a basis for identifying "next steps" in the learning process.
  - ○ Mastery: Engage the learner in a process of assessing his or her experience in the context of some conceptual or practical model or framework, or some external set of standards or criteria. (Trivette et al., 2009, p. 3)

In a home visiting context, it is important for home visitors to understand that learning is a process – parents are not going to magically take in and perfectly apply all of the information that the home visitor brings. It takes planning, practice, and evaluation to move to a real state of understanding.

Given FLE methodology, home visiting implementation should be altered when working with specialized populations. For home visitors working with adolescent parents, grandmother involvement is likely, and requires special considerations for program implementation. First, home visitors may need to spend program time directly addressing the parent–grandparent relationship, or grandparent wellbeing (Hans & Thullen, 2009). This may dictate program activities and how the home visitor goes about observing and understanding the family's daily life. Second, grandparents serve as major sources of parenting expertise for teen parents, thus the home visitor must be aware that advice on best practices for supporting infant/toddler development may stand in contrast to advice from grandparents (Hans & Thullen, 2009). For home visitors working with depressed parents, particularly mothers with postpartum depression, they must be aware that these parents are likely experiencing impairments that affect their learning such as, negative emotionality, cognitive biases (leading to negative self-perceptions), and trouble reading emotional cues in others (O'Hara & McCabe, 2013). Research suggests that other underlying issues related to depression include parents' own poor emotion regulation, low motivation, and rumination of negative thoughts (Psychogiou & Parry, 2014). Because of this, depressed parents may be less likely to take their infant to well-baby checks, get immunizations, put their baby in safe sleeping positions, and they are more likely to develop negative patterns of interaction with their infants/toddlers (O'Hara & McCabe, 2013). Management of depressive symptoms must be overseen by a mental health professional, but the home visitors should be aware of these challenges to help tailor program implementation for the unique challenges these parents may face.

Table 14.4 Family Life Education Concepts and Resources that Align with Supporting Competencies in Adults

FLE Content Area: FLE Methodology	Resources
Adult/adolescent development Age-appropriate techniques[1]; adulthood and adolescence[2,3]	[1]Covey, M. (2015). Family life education methodology. In M. J. Walcheski, & J. S. Reinke (Eds.), *Family life education: The practice of family science* (pp. 243–251). Minneapolis, MN: National Council on Family Relations.
Learning Learning styles[1,2]; transformative learning theory[1]; active engagement[1,3]; learning by doing[2]; learning theories[2]; lifelong learning[2]	[2]Darling, C. A., & Cassidy, D. (2014). *Family life education: Working with families across the lifespan* (3rd ed.). Long Grove, IL: Waveland.
Behavior change Behaviorism[2]; behavioral change and theories[3]; behavior modification models[3]; behaviorist educational philosophy[3]	[3]Duncan, S. F., & Goddard, H. W. (2017). *Family life education: Principles and practices for effective outreach* (3rd ed.). Thousand Oaks, CA: Sage.
Parenting Parenting education and parenting[2,3]	
Mental health Mental health issues and personal wellbeing[3]	

Transformative learning theory is the continual appraisal of new information in light of previous knowledge or experiences (Taylor, 2017). Adults all use frames of reference to situate new information but can revise the meaning they hold for knowledge (i.e., transform) through reflection and renewed appraisal of information. Parents are going to approach parenting and family issues from their current frames of reference, and home visitors are working with them to reflect on new information. With continued practice, evaluation, and evidence of progress, home visitors can help parents develop mastery of best practices in supporting their infant/toddler's development and self-efficacy in their own skills.

Skills

Skills for home visitors related to supporting competencies in adults include:

> Collaborating with and coaching parents to engage in interactions that support positive infant/toddler development; helping parents reflect on their lives; supporting parenting efficacy; guiding parent problem solving to increase the quality of the home environment; and for mentoring adult achievement of self-sufficiency goals.
>
> (CUPID, 2017)

332 *Supporting Competencies in Adults*

Human Growth and Development

- Identify developmental stages and contexts

  - Identify adolescence (approximately 12 to 18) as a unique developmental stage characterized by puberty and formal reasoning (with egocentric limitations).
  - Identify early adulthood (approximately 18 to 40) as a unique developmental stage characterized by increasingly complex postformal thinking and important social changes such as moving from the family of origin to a family of procreation.

- Identify reciprocal influences on development

  - Recognize that the cognitive processes of adolescents/young adults are shaped by their developmental capabilities as well as their social experiences with others/education.
  - Recognize that mental health issues are a combination of biological predisposition and social factors (such as the transition to parenthood).

- Recognize the impact of individual health and wellness on families

  - Recognize the negative effect parental depressive symptoms, particularly postpartum depression has on parent–child relationships and infant development.
  - Recognize that parental depression has the most negative impact on child development when it occurs during infancy/toddlerhood.
  - Recognize that depression rates are highest for young African American and Latina mothers

- Assist families with developmental transitions

  - Assist parents in understanding child development and healthy parenting practices in ways that match with their own developmental level.
  - Screen parents, particularly mothers, for mental health concerns.
  - Connect families with appropriate services and referrals for any mental health concerns.

- Guide practice using developmental theories

  - Consider the developmental level of the parent (adolescent versus early adult) and use knowledge of cognitive development to guide practices.
  - For young parents, recognize how limitations to adolescent thinking (e.g., egocentrism, invisible audience, personal fable) impact the information and advice presented to them during the home visit.
  - For young parents, be mindful of adjusting discussions if they are not capable yet of relativistic thinking or reflective judgement.

Supporting Competencies in Adults 333

- Recognize socio-ecological influences on human development (e.g., trauma)

  - Using the family stress model (Conger et al., 2002), recognize how the stress associated with living in poverty affects relationships and wellbeing, which impacts parenting and ultimately infant/toddler development.

Coaching and Collaborating with Parents to Support Child Development

- Promote healthy parenting from systems and lifespan perspectives

  - Promote parental leadership during parent–child interactions.
  - Coach parents using toys and materials available in their home.
  - Collaborate with parents so they are at the center of parent–child interactions
  - Model developmentally appropriate parent–child interactions with the child.

- Promoting healthy parenting from a child's and parent's developmental perspective

  - Scaffold parents' knowledge of child development.
  - Address the needs of parents at the transition to parenthood, for example, sleep, self-care, infant feeding, childbirth recovery, adjustment to family life, etc.
  - Support parental self-efficacy.

    - Help parents achieve small and large parenting victories.
    - Model developmentally appropriate interactions with infants and toddlers.
    - Encourage parents to attend EHS parent groups to connect with other parents.
    - Provide encouragement and scaffolding to parents.
    - Screen and refer parents with depressive symptoms to appropriate mental health services.

- Apply strategies based on child's age and stage and unique characteristics to support development

  - Scaffold parents' knowledge of child development as infants grow from newborns to toddlers.
  - Model developmentally appropriate parenting behaviors.

- Identify parenting styles and their related child outcomes & Evaluate various parenting strategies

  - Observe parents in actions and watch for opportunities to scaffold the parent to victory, model developmentally appropriate behaviors, or provide encouragement.

334   *Supporting Competencies in Adults*

- ○ Analyze how parental mental health affects self-efficacy and subsequent parenting strategies.

- Recognize various parenting roles and their impact on families

  - ○ Recognize parents' role as the expert on their child.
  - ○ Recognize the role of parents' mental health in self-efficacy.

- Recognize the impact of societal trends and cultural differences

  - ○ Respect individual preferences regarding coaching and scaffolding.
  - ○ Respect individual preferences on discussing mental health issues or seeking mental health services.

- Identify strategies to support children in various settings

  - ○ Coach parents in identifying their child's needs and seeking out appropriate referrals (e.g., health care services, screenings for developmental delays, nutrition services, clothing, child care, etc.)

Coaching/Collaborating/Mentoring Parents to Support Parent Efficacy and Self-Sufficiency

- All of the above
- Analyze various parenting programs, models, and principles

  - ○ Ensure that home visit interactions include

    - □ Placing parents at the center and as leaders in parent–child interactions.
    - □ Using materials and toys available in the home.
    - □ Modeling developmentally appropriate parenting behaviors.
    - □ Scaffolding child development knowledge, parent–child interactions, and other relevant family needs.
    - □ Supporting parents in small and large victories with their children.
    - □ Providing positive encouragement.
    - □ Recognizing the role of mental health, specifically depression, in self-efficacy.

- Recognize parenting issues within family structures

  - ○ Grandparents may play a large role in a young parent's life, and thus influence the family system, especially when it comes to accepting new information regarding infant/toddler rearing and development.

- Recognize various pathways to parenting and their associated issues

  - ○ Recognize that parents may face different issues depending on when where they are in their own development—e.g., adolescent parent versus a parent in early adulthood.

Supporting Competencies in Adults

Families and Individuals in Societal Contexts

Coaching and Collaborating with Parents to Support Child Development

- Identify the influence of local and global systems on individuals and families
  - Identify the needs that families have from living in poverty and identify corresponding supports in the community.
  - Identify mental health services in the community that are available to low-income families.
  - Identify logistical barriers parents have to accessing mental health services (e.g., child care, transportation, work schedule, etc.).
- Identify factors that influence individuals and families from contemporary and historical perspectives
  - Validate parents (particularly adolescent parents or parents of color) who feel stigmatized by society.
- Identify social and cultural influences on family composition and family life
  - Identify individual perception barriers parents have to accessing mental health services (stigma due to immigration status, families of color, etc.).
  - Coach parents on accessing information and resources available in their community to build self-efficacy and self-sufficiency.
  - Coach parents on how to make their own informed decisions based on available information and resources.
- Recognize reciprocal interactions between individuals, families, and systems
  - Recognize that society's expectations of parents contributes to their feelings of self-efficacy.
  - Recognize that there may be structural barriers that prevent parents from seeking mental health services (e.g., lack of training or access of mental health services, lack of services in native language)
- Assess the impact of demographics (e.g., class) on families
  - Identify how living in poverty affects individuals and families.
  - Conduct needs assessments to assess material hardship for each family.
  - Assess family income, but also other family risk factors such as no high school diploma, health problems, recently divorced, homeless or incarcerated, child has a health or developmental concern, alcohol or drug abuse, or domestic violence.

336 *Supporting Competencies in Adults*

Coaching/Collaborating/Mentoring Parents to Support Parent Efficacy and Self-Sufficiency

• All of the above

FLE Methodology

Coaching and Collaborating with Parents to Support Child Development

• Employ strategies to meet the needs of different audiences

   ○ Introduce material (e.g., child development knowledge, parenting techniques, etc.) in a variety of ways with discussion, relaxation exercises, writing, etc. (Trivette et al., 2009).
   ○ Illustrate the applicability of new material in a variety of ways with discussion, role playing, etc. (Trivette et al., 2009).
   ○ Include grandparents as important members in the home visit if appropriate.

• Employ techniques to help the learner do hands-on learning

   ○ Have parents practice using new material. For example, role play new guidance/discipline techniques with the home visitor, model the home visitor's actions, talk about their understanding of a child development concept, etc.
   ○ Evaluate parents' use of new material.
   ○ Have parents engage in self-assessment of their use of new material.
   ○ Have parents engage in a cycle of practice and evaluation until they develop mastery with the material.

• Create learning environments that support individual differences

   ○ Recognize individual differences in adolescent/adult learning.
   ○ For adolescent parents, create learning environments that include grandparents.
   ○ Be mindful of the role that parental mental health, particularly depression, plays in adult learning.

• Develop culturally competent materials and experiences

   ○ Be sure that materials and experiences respect the frames of reference parents are entering the home visiting program with.
   ○ Be mindful that developmentally appropriate parenting skills may contradict advice from grandparents.

• Identify sources of evidence-based information and implement evidence-based programs

- Ensure that program curriculum is flexible to implement with parents that may have specialized needs such as adolescent parents or depressed parents.

- Design educational experiences from start to finish

  - Design educational experiences from start to finish with planning (introduce, illustrate), application (practice, evaluate), and understanding (reflection, mastery) (Trivette et al., 2009).

Coaching/Collaborating/Mentoring Parents to Support Parent Efficacy and Self-Sufficiency

- All of the above
- Demonstrate group process and facilitation skills
- Demonstrate sensitivity to diversity and community needs, concerns, and interests

  - Home visitors can support families of diverse backgrounds by advocating for programs that provide mental health services in various native languages or by people of color.

Attitudes

The attitudes that help home visitors support adult competencies include:

> Attitudes reflecting compassion and understanding for the challenges of adult life, the difficulty of parenting when experiencing depression or anxiety, and the influence from a parent's earlier life experiences.
>
> (CUPID, 2017)

These attitudes reflect a strengths-based approach to working with adults, recognizing that the wellbeing of children hinges on the wellbeing of the adults in their families. One of code of ethics for CFLEs is "I will provide a program environment that is safe and nurturing to all family members" (NCFR, n.d.). This includes parents and other important adults in the family (e.g., grandparents). Parental mental health has been a big focus of this chapter, but it is important to recognize that adults vary in their willingness to seek services or treatment when there are problems. The CFLE code of ethics also stipulates "I will support family members as they make decisions about the use of resources to best meet family needs" (NCFR, n.d.). There are many reasons why adults may not feel comfortable seeking mental health support, but home visitors can support families of diverse backgrounds by advocating for programs that provide mental health services in various native languages or by people of color. As the CUPID (2017) attitudes reflect, adult life is complicated and

338   *Supporting Competencies in Adults*

helping parents support their own wellbeing can be difficult. Despite these challenges, the primary goal of FLE is to support the wellbeing of the entire family system, with parents' mental health and self-efficacy the foundation for family wellbeing.

Box 14.1 CDA Home Visitor Competencies

The CDA Subject Areas and Competency Standards are national standards for Home Visitors. The subject area that is most relevant to this chapter includes **CDA Subject Area 4: Understanding family systems and development.** Each competency comprises competency goals, functional areas, items, indicators, and examples. The competency goals that are most relevant to this chapter are "To establish positive and productive partnerships with families" and "To maintain a commitment to professionalism" (Council for Professional Recognition, 2016).

Competency Goal	Functional Area	Example Items	Example Indicators
IV. To establish positive and productive partnerships with families	**11 Families:** Home visitor establishes a positive, responsive, and cooperative relationships with each family, engages in two-way communication with families, encourages the parents to take leadership in personal and family education, and supports the relationship of the families with their children.	**Item 11.2:** Help parents recognize that they are the center of the program. Item 11.4: Uses a variety of techniques, including information dissemination, referral, and brokering to help families meet their young children's needs.	Builds the parents' self-esteem and efficacy by identifying and praising effective parenting behavior and efforts towards personal development. Encourages parents in specific activities that foster learning in the home and community.
VI: To maintain a commitment to professionalism	**13 Professionalism:** Home visitor makes decisions based on knowledge of	**Item 13.1:** Works with parents and other professionals as an advocate for	Advocates for the needs of children and families Works with parents and other

(Continued)

Supporting Competencies in Adults   339

(Cont.)

Competency Goal	Functional Area	Example Items	Example Indicators
	research-based early childhood practices and adult learning, promotes high quality child care services, and takes advantages of opportunities to improve knowledge and competence, both for personal and professional growth and for the benefit of children and families.	children and families.	professionals to develop effective strategies to communicate to decision makers the need for quality services.

Permission to reprint from the Council for Professional Recognition, 2019

Box 14.2 National Family Support Competency Framework for Family Support Professionals

The National Family Support Competency Framework for Family Support Professionals are competencies that include ten domains that are further clarified by dimensions (Institute for the Advancement of Family Support Professionals, 2018). There is one domain that is relevant to this chapter: (a) Community Resources and Support. This includes three dimensions: building community relationships, service system coordination and referral, and advocacy.

Domain 6	Dimension 24	Component a.	Levels of Competency
Community resources and support	**Advocacy**	Empowering families	**1-Recognizing.** Understands situations in which a family might seek legal assistance to assert a right or entitlement

(Continued)

340 *Supporting Competencies in Adults*

(Cont.)

Domain 6	Dimension 24	Component a.	Levels of Competency
			3-Applying. Supports parents in becoming advocates for themselves and their children
			5-Extending. Coaches parents in evaluating the results of advocacy, celebrating small wins, adjusting strategies if necessary, and encouraging persistence

Permission to reprint from the Institute for the Advancement of Family Support Professionals.

Summary

Supporting competencies in adults is critical for home visitors to meet EHS-HBO program goals for young children's development, healthy parent–child relationships, and overall family wellbeing. Adolescence and early adulthood are important developmental time periods, and mental health issues, particularly depression, play a major role in how parents' approach learning in the home visiting program. The FLE content areas human growth and development, parenting education and guidance, families and individuals in societal contexts, and FLE methodology give home visitors greater content knowledge on adolescent and young adult development, coaching parents' self-efficacy, understanding the unique contexts of families in poverty, and tailoring home visiting practices for adult learning, including unique populations.

Key Concepts

- Adolescence
- Adult learning
- Depression
- Early adulthood
- Family of origin
- Family of procreation
- Family stress model
- Formal reasoning
- Home Visit Rating Scales
- Postformal reasoning

- Postpartum depression
- Scaffolding
- Self-efficacy
- Teen birth rate
- Transformative learning theory
- Transition to parenthood

Recommended Readings

National Institute of Mental Health. (n.d.). *Depression in Women.* U.S. Department of Health and Human Services. Retrieved from https://www.cdc.gov/tobacco/campaign/tips/diseases/depression-anxiety.html

Taylor, K., & Marienau, C. (2016). *Facilitating learning with the adult brain in mind: A conceptual and practical guide.* San Francisco, CA: John Wiley & Sons.

References

Abkevich, V., Camp, N., Hensel, C. H., Neff, C. D., Russell, D. L., Hughes, D. C., et al. (2003). Predisposition locus for major depression at chromosome 12q22–12q23.2. *American Journal of Human Genetics, 73,* 1271–1281.

Administration for Children and Families (ACF). (2015). *The faces of Early Head Start: A national picture of Early Head Start programs and the children and families they serve.* OPRE Report #2015-29, Washington, DC: Office of Planning, Research, and Evaluation, Administration for Children and Families, U.S. Department of Health and Human Services.

American Psychological Association (APA). (2013). *Diagnostic and statistical manual of mental disorders* (5th ed.). Arlington, VA: American Psychiatric Publishing.

Arnett, J. J. (1999). Adolescent storm and stress, reconsidered. *American Psychologist, 54* (5), 317.

Arnett, J. J. (2000). Emerging adulthood: A theory of development from the late teens through the twenties. *American Psychologist, 55*(5), 469.

Bandura, A. (1994). Self-efficacy. In V. S. Ramachaudran (Ed.), *Encyclopedia of human behavior* (vol. 4, pp. 71–81). New York: Academic Press. (Reprinted in H. Friedman [Ed.], *Encyclopedia of mental health.* San Diego: Academic Press, 1998).

Barnet, B., Joffe, A., Duggan, A. K., Wilson, M. D., & Repke, J. T. (1996). Depressive symptoms, stress, and social support in pregnant and postpartum adolescents. *Archives of Pediatrics and Adolescent Medicine, 150*(1), 64.

Beck, C. T. (2001). Predictors of postpartum depression: An update. *Nursing Research, 50*(5), 275–285.

Berlin, L. J., Brady-Smith, C., & Brooks-Gunn, J. (2002). Links between childbearing age and observed maternal behaviors with 14-month-olds in the Early Head Start Research and Evaluation Project. *Infant Mental Health Journal, 23*(1–2), 104–129.

Birkeland, R., Thompson, J. K., & Phares, V. (2005). Adolescent motherhood and postpartum depression. *Journal of Clinical Child and Adolescent Psychology, 34*(2), 292–300.

342 Supporting Competencies in Adults

Boyd, D., & Bee, H. (2015). *Lifespan development* (7th ed.). Upper Saddle River, NJ: Pearson.

Brooks, J. B. (2013). *The process of parenting* (9th ed.). New York: McGraw Hill.

Çattık, M., & Aksoy, V. (2018). An examination of the relations among social support, self- efficacy, and life satisfaction in parents of children with developmental disabilities. *Education & Science, 43(195)*, 65–77.

Collaborative for Understanding the Pedagogy of Infant/toddler Development (CUPID). (2017). *Comprehensive competencies for educators of infants and toddlers in group care and home visiting settings.* Unpublished.

Conger, R. D., Wallace, L. E., Sun, Y., Simons, R. L., McLoyd, V. C., & Brody, G. H. (2002). Economic pressure in African American families: A replication and extension of the family stress model. *Developmental psychology, 38*(2), 179–193.

Council for Professional Recognition. (2016). The Child Development Associate National Credentialing Program and CDA Competency Standards, Home Visitor Edition. Washington DC: Council for Professional Recognition.

Covey, M. (2015). Family life education methodology. In M. Walcheski & J. Reinke (Eds.) *Family life education: The practice of family science* (pp. 243–251). Minneapolis, MN: National Council on Family Relations.

Darling, C. A., & Cassidy, D. (2014). *Family life education: Working with families across the lifespan.* Long Grove, IL: Waveland Press.

Demick, J. (2002). Stages of parental development. In M. Bornstein (Ed.) *Handbook of Parenting: Vol. 3. Being and Becoming a Parent* (pp. 389–413). Mahwah, NJ: Lawrence Erlbaum Associates.

Duncan, S. F., & Goddard, H. W. (2017). *Family life education: Principles and practices for effective outreach* (3rd ed.). Thousand Oaks, CA: Sage.

Goodman, S. H., & Brand, S. R. (2009). Infants of depressed mothers. In *Handbook of infant mental health* (pp. 153–170). New York: Guilford Publications.

Goodman, S. H., Rouse, M. H., Connell, A. M., Broth, M. R., Hall, C. M., & Heyward, D. (2011). Maternal depression and child psychopathology: a meta-analytic review. *Clinical Child and Family Psychology Review, 14*(1), 1–27.

Hans, S. L., & Thullen, M. J. (2009). The relational context of adolescent motherhood. In C. H. Zeanah (Ed.), *Handbook of infant mental health* (pp. 214–229). New York, NY: The Guildford Press.

Hess, C. R., Teti, D. M., & Hussey-Gardner, B. (2004). Self-efficacy and parenting of high-risk infants: The moderating role of parent knowledge of infant development. *Journal of Applied Developmental Psychology, 25*, 423–437.

Hoyer, W. J., & Rybash, J. M. (1994). Characterizing adult cognitive development. *Journal of Adult Development, 1*(1), 7–12.

Huang, C. Y., Costeines, J., Kaufman, J. S., & Ayala, C. (2014). Parenting stress, social support, and depression for ethnic minority adolescent mothers: Impact on child development. *Journal of Child and Family Studies, 23*, 255–262.

Institute for the Advancement of Family Support Professionals. (2018). *National Family Support Competency Framework for Family Support Professionals.* Retrieved from: https://cppr-institute-prod.s3.amazonaws.com/modules/Approved%20National%20Family%20Support%20Competency%20Framework_FINAL_7_18_2018.pdf.

Jacobson, A. L. (2015). Parenting education and guidance. In M. Walcheski & J. Reinke (Eds.) *Family life education: The practice of family science* (pp. 243–251). Minneapolis, MN: National Council on Family Relations.

Kelly, D. M. (1996). Stigma stories: Four discourses about teen mothers, welfare, and poverty. *Youth & Society, 27*(4), 421–449.

Kingston, D., Kehler, H., Austin, M. P., Mughal, M. K., Wajid, A., Vermeyden, L., ... & Giallo, R. (2018). Trajectories of maternal depressive symptoms during pregnancy and the first 12 months postpartum and child externalizing and internalizing behavior at three years. *PloS one, 13*(4).

Kizilbash, A.H., Vanderploeg, R. D., & Curtiss, G. (2002). The effects of depression and anxiety on memory performance. *Archives of Clinical Neuropsychology, 17*(1), 57–67.

Kuhn, D. (2008). Formal operations from a twenty-first century perspective. *Human development, 51*(1), 48–55.

Kuther, T. L. (2017). *Lifespan development: Lives in context*. Thousand Oaks, CA: Sage Publications.

Leadbeater, B. J. (1999). School outcomes for minority-group adolescent mothers at 28–36 months postpartum: A longitudinal follow-up. *Cognitive and Moral Development, Academic Achievement in Adolescence, 2*(4), 237.

Leahy-Warren, P., McCarthy, G., & Corcoran, P. (2012). First-time mothers: social support, maternal parental self-efficacy and postnatal depression. *Journal of Clinical Nursing, 21*(3-4), 388–397.

Leventhal, J. (2015). Human growth and development across the lifespan. In M. J. Walcheski, & J. S. Reinke (Eds.), *Family life education: The practice of family science* (pp. 167–176). Minneapolis, MN: National Council on Family Relations.

Martin, J.A., Hamilton, B.E., Osterman, M.J.K., Driscoll, A.K., & Drake, P. (2018). Births: Final data for 2017. *National Vital Statistics Reports, 67*(8). 1–50.

Neugarten, B. L., & Neugarten, D. A. (1996). The changing meanings of age. In *The meanings of age: Selected papers of Bernice L. Neugarten* (pp. 72–78) Chicago, IL: University of Chicago Press.

O'Hara, M. W., & McCabe, J. E. (2013). Postpartum depression: current status and future directions. *Annual Review of Clinical Psychology, 9*, 379–407.

Olson, D. H., DeFrain, J., & Skogrand, L. (2014). *Marriages and families: Intimacy, diversity, and strengths* (8th ed.). New York: McGraw Hill.

Parents as Teachers National Center. (2019). *Evidence-based model*. Retrieved from https://parentsasteachers.org/evidence-based-model.

Patton, E., & Livingston, G. (2016). *Why is the teen birth rate falling?* Pew Research Center. Retrieved from http://www.pewresearch.org/fact-tank/2016/04/29/why-is-the-teen-birth-rate-falling/

Penman-Aguilar, A., Carter, M., Snead, M.C., & Kourtis, A.P. (2013). Socioeconomic disadvantage as a social determinant of teen childbearing in the US. *Public Health Reports, 128*, 5–22.

Petkus, J. (2015). A first-hand account of implementing a Family Life Education model: Intentionality in Head Start home visiting. In M. J. Walcheski, & J. S. Reinke (Eds.), *Family life education: The practice of family science* (pp. 325–331). Minneapolis, MN: National Council on Family Relations.

Petterson, S. M., & Albers, A. B. (2001). Effects of poverty and maternal depression on early child development. *Child Development, 72*(6), 1794–1813.

Psychogiou, L., & Parry, E. (2014). Why do depressed individuals have difficulties in their parenting role? *Psychological Medicine, 44*(7), 1345–1347.

NCFR. (n.d.). *Family life educators code of ethics.* Retrieved https://www.ncfr.org/sites/default/files/cfle_code_of_ethics_2.pdf

Raikes, H. A., & Thompson, R. A. (2005). Efficacy and social support as predictors of parenting stress among families in poverty. *Infant Mental Health Journal, 26,* 177–190.

Roggman, L. A., Cook, G. A., Innocenti, M. S., Jump Norman, V. K., Christiansen, K., Boyce, L. K., Aikens, N., Boller, K., Paulsell, D., & Hallgren, K. (2010). Home Visit Rating Scales—Adapted and Extended (HOVRS-A+) version 2. Adapted from Roggman, L. A., et al. (2008). Home Visit Rating Scales. In L. Roggman, L. Boyce, and M. Innocenti, *Developmental Parenting* (pp. 209–217). Baltimore: Paul H. Brookes Publishing.

Roggman, L., Peterson, C., Cohen, R. C., Ispa, J., Decker, K. B., Hughes-Belding, K., Cook, G., & Vallotton, C. D. (2016). Preparing home visitors to partner with families of infants and toddlers. *Journal of Early Childhood Teacher Education, 37,* 301–313. http://dx.doi.org/10.1080/10901027.2017.1298369

Reutter, L. I., Stewart, M. J., Veenstra, G., Love, R., Raphael, D., & Makwarimba, E. (2009). "Who do they think we are, anyway?": Perceptions of and responses to poverty stigma. *Qualitative Health Research, 19*(3), 297–311.

Santiago, C. D., Kaltman, S., & Miranda, J. (2013). Poverty and mental health: How do low-income adults and children fare in psychotherapy?. *Journal of Clinical Psychology, 69*(2), 115–126.

Sinnott, J. (1998). *The development of logic in adulthood: Postformal thought and its applications.* Springer Science & Business Media.

Steinberg, L. (2017). *Adolescence, Eleventh Edition.* New York, NY: McGraw Hill Education.

Taylor, E. W. (2017). Transformative learning theory. In A. Laros, T. Fuhr, & E. W. Taylor (Eds.), *Transformative Learning Meets Bildung* (pp. 17–29). Rotterdam, Netherlands: Sense Publishers.

Teti, D. M., O'Connell, M. A., & Reiner, C. D. (1996). Parenting sensitivity, parental depression and child health: The mediational role of parental self-efficacy. *Early Development and Parenting: An International Journal of Research and Practice, 5,* 237–250.

Trivette, C. M., Dunst, C. J., Hamby, D. W., & O'Herin, C. E. (2009). Characteristics and consequences of adult learning methods and strategies. *Winterberry Research Syntheses, 2*(2), 1–33.

Van Ijzendoorn, M. H., Schuengel, C., & Bakermans–Kranenburg, M. J. (1999). Disorganized attachment in early childhood: Meta-analysis of precursors, concomitants, and sequelae. *Development and Psychopathology, 11*(2), 225–250.

Wadsworth, S. M. M., Roy, K. M., & Watkins, N. (2015). Families and individuals in societal contexts. In M. J. Walcheski & J. S. Reinke (Eds.), *Family life education: The practice of family science* (pp. 147–155). Minneapolis, MN: National Council on Family Relations.

Wagner, M., Spiker, D., & Linn, M. I. (2002). The effectiveness of the Parents as Teachers program with low-income parents and children. *Topics in Early Childhood Special Education, 22*(2), 67–81.

Williams, B. K., Sawyer, S. C., & Wahlstrom, C. M. (2017). *Marriage, Families, & Intimate Relationships* (4th ed). New York, NY: Pearson.

Yan, B., & Arlin, P. K. (1995). Nonabsolute/relativistic thinking: A common factor underlying models of postformal reasoning? *Journal of Adult Development, 2*(4), 223–240.

15 Promises and Challenges for the Interface of Home Visiting and Family Life Education

Home visiting is uniquely supportive of family life (Wasik & Bryant, 2001). FLE and EHS home-based programs both emphasize family self-sufficiency and wellbeing and share important overlaps that position families' individual needs at the forefront of programming (Petkus, 2015; Walsh, 2017, 2019). This chapter provides ways to expand linkages between FLE/CFLE to EHS home-based services.

As the home visiting field grapples with the tensions and unknowns of universal home visiting and precision home visiting, it is apparent that new ways of thinking are the future. Universal home visiting approaches serve all families regardless of criteria, such as income, age, risk, or others (Stetler et al., 2018). Precision prevention focuses on the appropriate intervention for the appropriate population by making programs more efficient and effective and thus promoting participant engagement and retention (Home Visiting Applied Research Collaborative, 2018; Supplee, Parekh, & Johnson, 2018). The calls have been made to provide home visiting services to all in a manner that allows individualized services to co-exist with program models. This is complex work and it demands a home visiting workforce that has credentials, such as CFLE, and training on an FLE approach. We need to prepare now and expand the current linkages between FLE/CFLE and home visiting.

It is a crucial time for FLE to be deliberate about practice, research, and other efforts that keep the future of home visiting in mind. The opportunities and challenges in the home visiting field fuel FLE to gain momentum and inspire CFLEs to have an important role now and in the future of home visiting.

Family Life Education

FLE focuses on the whole family and shares that focus with EHS home-based services (Walsh, 2019). In general, professionals need to continue with efforts that endorse the value of families and home visiting in programs, practices, and policies (Bogenschneider, 2014).

More specifically, the promise is that home visitor preparation can be subsumed within the existing CFLE framework. The training needed for home visitors exists within the established framework of FLE. CFLEs providing home visiting services live out the principles of FLE in their work with families (Guardado, 2019). As demonstrated in this book, Petkus (2015) guided a philosophical shift from a toy-centered and child-centered approach to an FLE approach in an EHS-HBO. In order to guide this paradigm shift, Petkus applied the domains of family practice model (see Myers-Walls, Ballard, Darling, & Myers-Bowman, 2011) to home visiting and tasked home visitors with staying in the domain of FLE. As demonstrated in Chapter 4, focus groups at the aforementioned program confirmed that many principles of FLE were endorsed at the site. The focus group clarified that while the parent–child relationship is important, the parent–child–home visitor triad is essential to progress and to building upon the strengths of individual families as well as supporting the professionalism of the home visitor.

Parents as Teachers

Of the approximately 1,300 Parents as Teachers (PAT) affiliates in the United States, approximately 180 programs offer EHS service. PAT emphasizes three areas that should be the focus of every home visit: (1) parent–child interaction, (2) development-centered parenting, and (3) family wellbeing (HomVEE, 2017). There is a dearth of research on PAT but there is some support that the curriculum promotes positive child and parent outcomes (Lahti, Goodman, & LeCroy, 2019). PAT programs produce better child academic outcomes and positive parenting behavior more so than the control (i.e., non-PAT) and thus findings support home visiting services (Lahti et al., 2019).

Training in the PAT model might not be enough to arm home visitors with the knowledge base and skills to effectively address family needs and strengths beyond parent–child interactions (Walsh, Mortensen, Edwards, & Cassidy, in press). FLE and EHS-HBO may widen the scope of PAT models by emphasizing the whole family (Walsh et al., in press). Because FLE and EHS-HBO are a natural fit, FLE modules and enhancements to EHS-HBO using PAT as the curriculum may strengthen model fidelity rather than raise concerns about modules and enhancements jeopardizing it.

348 *Promises and Challenges*

Appendix C provides a starting point to considering linkages between FLE and PAT. FLE can potentially be a viable proactive adaptation to PAT (Walsh, 2019).

Principles of FLE as a Metaframework

As discussed in Chapter 3, FLE includes foundational principles of education, prevention, and strengths-based approaches, and a strong understanding of theory and research (see Darling, Cassidy, & Rehm, 2017). Home visiting and family life education both value these principles. A foundation in FLE also necessarily includes operational components of culture, contexts, content, and practice (see Darling et al., 2017). All of the aforementioned principles of FLE are a metaframework that is not model specific, which means FLE principles are applicable to all home visiting models. Researchers and practitioners interested in pursuing FLE as a metframework for home visiting might learn lessons from Facilitating Attuned Interactions (FAN) as a guide for conceptualization (Gilkerson, 2015).

The next step is to develop a measure of fidelity for home visitor implementation of the principles. The seven principles could be the core components of the measure. It will then be necessary to think about what items will be important indicators of the core components. The process of creating the items might be guided by thinking about how the home visitor may demonstrate these principles. Once the items are finalized, anchors will need to be created for the scale. Devellis (2012) provides helpful information about developing a scale. Using the scale with video-recorded observations of home visits may help refine the scale. Initial reliability of the scale in terms of response consistency would need to be examined via Cronbach's alpha. It will also be important to solicit qualitative feedback from those completing the measure. This will most likely help to address clarity, understanding, and any missing information regarding the instrument. Test–retest reliability should be completed using tests of differences (t-tests) and correlations. The factor structure of the measure should be examined using CFA, testing the degree to which the obtained data fits the theoretical structure. Discriminant and convergent validity should be established by testing linear relationships (correlations, regressions) between the newly developed tool and Roggman et al.'s (2019) HOVRS-3 (convergent validity). A measure will need to be determined for discriminant validity. It is then important to establish normative data and then validate the scale for a variety of participants.

Pre-Service Training in Higher Education and Competencies

Future research may survey administrators of family science (or similar nomenclature) programs with an emphasis on NCFR-approved CFLE programs to determine the extent to which courses prepare students for a career as a home visitor (Walsh et al., in press). Participants in Walsh et al.'s study had copious suggestions about how academic programs in higher education might prepare future home visitors.

Researchers should explore perspectives via focus groups of what faculty at institutions of higher education, students, and stakeholders think about components of home visiting training these contexts. Focus group questions should address current coursework, expansion of coursework, interdisciplinary models, classroom collaboration with professionals, home visiting experiences, home visiting practicum/internship/field experience efforts, and home visiting labs (Roggman et al., 2016). The analysis should consider distinctions between CFLE approved programs and CFLE non-approved programs. It will be helpful to have ideas emerge from the focus groups and to pilot-test ideas before further developing and finalizing recommendations for IHEs through the Delphi Method.

Pre-service home visitor training and the competencies to guide it warrant more attention. Chapters 5 to 14 have aligned the ten FLE content areas with the Collaborative for Understanding the Pedagogy of Infant/Toddler Development's expanded core competencies for pre-service home visitors (CUPID 2017; Roggman et al., 2016). See Appendix B for the entire competency alignment.

In-Service Training

Chapter 16 includes four online modules about FLE for EHS in-service home visitors. Walsh et al. (in press) asserted that NCFR could develop online modules that target Darling et al.'s foundational and operational principles of FLE.

Similarly, Walsh, Cassidy, and Hoover (2019) invited NCFR members to complete a survey on the potential use of online modules to promote the ten FLE content areas. Many participants (69%) supported this potential endeavor and resource. Online module about the content areas may provide in-service home visitors with content area knowledge as well as help home visiting professionals, students, and others prepare to take the CFLE exam (Walsh, 2019).

There are opportunities for CFLEs to complete online home visiting training in order to acquire or to renew the CFLE credential through continuing education credit. For example, the Ounce of Prevention Fund's (the Ounce) online training program for home visitors and supervisors, Achieve OnDemand, is applicable across home visiting models, and includes both self-paced online courses and support (Walsh, 2019).

Coaching

There is consensus in the home visiting field that coaching is important to home visitors' development and growth, but little is known about coaching home visiting professionals (Walsh, Innocenti, & the Community of Practice for Professional Development, Ounce of Prevention Fund, in review). Coaching is individual

350 *Promises and Challenges*

professional development for home visitors through engagement in a process of promoting individual goal setting through training and support (Walsh et al., in review).

Allen's (2016) family life coaching, or a technique used by Certified Family Life Educators (CFLEs), may inform home visitors as coachees receiving coaching. Because the scholarship on coaching home visitors is emergent, it is important to consider the existing literature in multiple fields with an emphasis on the possibilities for home visiting (Walsh et al., in review). There are common themes of coaching professionals from other fields. For example, there are several extant literature reviews, content analyses, and think pieces on coaching professionals in the early childhood field (e.g., Artman-Meeker, Fettig, Barton, Penney, & Zeng, 2015; Elek & Page, 2018; Gupta & Daniels, 2012; Isner et al., 2011; Rush, Shelden, & Hanft, 2003; Schachter, 2015). An empirical foundation for coaching home visitors is needed.

Being a Professional to a Profession

Home visiting typically refers to service delivery and is a unique method to strengthen parents and children (Manz & Bracaliello, 2016). Service delivery is typically thought of as a function of family needs and family receptivity to home visiting services (Smith, 2005). The role "home visitor" is not an occupation recognized in the *Occupational Outlook Handbook* (U.S. Bureau of Labor Statistics, 2018), CareerOneStop (U.S. Department of Labor, 2019), nor O*Net OnLine (U.S. Department of Labor, 2018). Closely related job titles to home visitor, such as family support worker are identified for social and human service assistants. Similarly, family life educator is not explicitly identified. It is imperative that continued effort and thought is given to recognize family life educators as qualified service providers at the state level. Furthermore, although it may not be surprising that family life educators and home visitors often have difficulty identifying their professional roles, continued efforts are needed to help the professions and beyond create clear identities for these professionals.

CFLE Recognition in EHS

Providing family services is complex and warrants credentials, training, and supports for home visitors (Wasik & Bryant, 2001). It is imperative that NCFR seeks inclusion of CFLE by the Office of Head Start for fulfillment of requirements under Section 1302.91 of the Head Start Program Performance Standards, Staff Qualifications and Competencies. As scholarship and practice that expands the linkages between CFLE and EHS-HBO continue to grow, it will be imperative to work with the National Head Start Association. Other suggestions include working with the Head Start Early Childhood Learning and Knowledge Center and the Ounce (see Walsh, 2019). Synergy and overlap between CFLE/FLE and EHS should be explored (see Walsh et al., in press).

Summary

Calls for universal home visiting and precision home visiting have been made by leaders in the home visiting field. This is complex work and it demands a home visiting workforce that has credentials, such as CFLE and training within an FLE approach. Researchers and practitioners should continue to create linkages between CFLE/FLE to EHS-HBO. Further developing the principles of FLE as a metatheory for home visiting as well as developing a measure of fidelity for home visitor implementation of the FLE principles will strengthen linkages. This may lead to discussions about further possibilities. For example, could FLE become an evidence-based home visiting service delivery model? Are FLE researchers and practitioners prepared to substantially increase the empirical foundation of FLE research as well as research on FLE within the context of EHS-HBO? Similarly, are we prepared to conduct rigorous evaluations that are necessary for FLE to gain evidence-based status in HomVEE? Would efforts be better spent creating modules (or enhancements) to the PAT curriculum in EHS-HBO? Finally, we believe that getting CFLE approves by the Office of Head Starts for fulfillment of staff requirements in the Head Start Performance Standards is a necessary next step to advancing the discussion and the interface of FLE within EHS home visiting.

Key Concepts

- Competencies
- Metaframework
- Parents as Teachers
- Precision home visiting
- Service delivery
- Universal home visiting

Recommended Reading

McCurdy, K., & Daro, D. (2001). Parent involvement in family support programs: An integrated theory. *Family Relations, 50,* 113–121. doi: 10.1111/j.1741-3729.2001.00113.x

References

Allen, K. (2016). *Theory, research, and practical guidelines for family life coaching.* Switzerland: Springer.

Artman-Meeker, K., Fettig, A., Barton, E. E., Penney, A., & Zeng, S. (2015). Applying an evidence-based framework to the early childhood coaching literature. *Topics in Early Childhood Special Education, 35,* 183–196. doi: 10.1177/0271121415595550

Bogenschneider, K. (2014). *Family policy matters: How policymaking affects families and what professionals can do* (3rd ed.). New York: Taylor & Francis.

352 Promises and Challenges

Collaborative for Understanding the Pedagogy of Infant/toddler Development (CUPID). (2017). *Comprehensive competencies for educators of infants and toddlers in group care and home visiting settings.* Unpublished.

Darling, C. A., Cassidy, D., & Rehm, M. (2017). Family life education: Translational family science in action. *Family Relations, 66,* 741–752. doi: 10.1111/fare.12286

DeVellis, R. F. (2012). *Scale development: Theory and application* (3rd ed.). Thousand Oaks, CA: Sage.

Elek, C., & Page, J. (2018). Critical features of effective coaching for early childhood educators: A review of empirical research literature. *Professional Development in Education, 45,* 567–585. doi: 10.1080/19415257.2018.1452781

Gilkerson, L. (2015). Facilitating attuned interactions: Using the FAN approach to family engagement. *Zero to Three, 35,* 46–48.

Guardado, M. D. (2019). Family life education within an Early Head Start home-based program. *CFLE Network, 32,* 22–23.

Gupta, S. S., & Daniels, J. (2012). Coaching and professional development in early childhood classrooms: Current practices and recommendations for the future. *NHSA Dialog, 15,* 206–220. doi: 10.1080/15240754.2012.665509

Home Visiting Applied Research Collaborative (HARC). (2018). Introduction to precision home visiting. Retrieved from https://www.hvresearch.org/precision-home-visiting/introduction-to-precision-home-visiting/

Home Visiting Evidence of Effectiveness (HomVee). (2017). Parents as Teachers—Model overview. Retrieved from https://homvee.acf.hhs.gov/Model/1/Parents-as-Teachers–PAT–Model-Overview/16/2

Isner, T., Tout, K., Zaslow, M., Soli, M., Quinn, K., Rothenberg, L., & Burkhauser, M. (2011). Coaching in early care and education programs and Quality Rating and Improvement Systems (QRIS): Identifying promising features. *Child Trends.* Retrieved from https://www.childtrends.org/wp-content/uploads/2014/09/2011-47CoachingEarlyCareEducation.pdf

Lahti, M., Evans, C. B. R., Goodman, G., & LeCroy, C. W. (2019). Parents as Teachers (PAT) home visiting intervention: A path to improved academic outcomes, school behavior, and parenting skills. *Children and Youth Services Review, 99,* 451–460. doi: 10.1016/j.childyouth.2019.01.022

Manz, P. H., & Bracaliello, C. B. (2016). Expanding home visiting outcomes: Collaborative measurement of parental play beliefs and examination of their association with parents' involvement in toddler's learning. *Early Childhood Research Quarterly, 36,* 157–167. doi: 10.1016/j.ecresq.2015.12.015

Myers-Walls, J., Ballard, S., Darling, C., & Myers-Bowman, K. (2011). Reconceptualizing the domains and boundaries of family life education. *Family Relations, 60,* 357–372. doi: 10.1111/j.1741-3729.2011.00659.x

Petkus, J. (2015). A first-hand account of implementing a Family Life Education model: Intentionality in Head Start home visiting. In M. J. Walcheski, & J. S. Reinke (Eds.), *Family life education: The practice of family science* (pp. 325–331). Minneapolis, MN: National Council on Family Relations.

Roggman, L. A., Cook, G. A., Innocenti, M. S., Jump Norman, V. K., Boyce, L. K., Olson, T. L. … Peterson, C. A. (2019). The Home Visit Rating Scales: Revised, restructured, and revalidated. *Infant Mental Health Journal, 40,* 315–330. doi: 10.1002/imhj.21781

Roggman, L. A., Peterson, C. A., Chazan-Cohen, R., Ispa, J., Decker, K., Hughes-Belding, K., Cook, G. A., & Vallotton, C. D. (2016). Preparing home visitors to partner with families of infants and toddlers. *Journal of Early Childhood Teacher Education, 37,* 301–313. doi: 10.1080/10901027.2016.1241965

Rush, D. D., Shelden, M. L., & Hanft, B. E. (2003). Coaching families and colleagues: A process for collaboration in natural settings. *Infants and Young Children, 16,* 33–47.

Schachter, R. E. (2015). An analytic study of the professional development research in early childhood education. *Early Education and Development, 26,* 1057–1085. doi: 10.1080/10409289.2015.1009335

Smith, B. D. (2005). Parental employment and home visiting program service delivery. *Journal of Family Strengths, 8,* 1–17.

Stetler, K., Silva, C., Manning, S. E., Harvey, E. M., Posner, E., Walmer, B., … Kotelchuck, M. (2018). Lessons learned: Implementation of pilot universal postpartum nurse home visitation program, Massachusetts 2013–2016. *Maternal and Child Health Journal, 22,* 11–16. doi: 10.10007/s10995-017-2385-x

Supplee, L. H., Parekh, J., & Jonhson, M. (2018). Principles of prevention science for improving recruitment and retention of participants. *Prevention Science, 19,* 689–694. doi: 10.1007/s11121-018-0884-7

U.S. Bureau of Labor Statistics. (2018). *Occupational outlook handbook.* Retrieved from https://www.bls.gov/ooh/

U.S. Department of Labor. (2018). O*Net Online. Retrieved from https://www.onetonline.org/

U.S. Department of Labor. (2019). CareerOneStop. Retrieved from https://www.careeronestop.org/

Walsh, B. A. (2017). Setting the stage for families in poverty as catalysts: A family life education approach to Early Head Start Home Visiting. *Family Focus, 73,* 8–10.

Walsh, B. A. (2019). The interface of FLE and Early Head Start home-based services: Past, present, and future. *CFLE Network, 32,* 11–13.

Walsh, B. A., Cassidy, D., & Hoover, M. (2019). *Exploring online modules to promote content and practice in FLE content areas.* Presentation at the National Council on Family Relations annual conference in Fort Worth, TX.

Walsh, B. A., Innocenti, M., & Community of Practice for Professional Development, Ounce of Prevention Fund (in review). Coaching home visitors: A thematic review with an emphasis on cross-field perspectives emphasizing research needs.

Walsh, B. A., Mortensen, J. A., Edwards, A. L., Cassidy, D. (in press). The practice of family life education within Early Head Start home visiting. *Family Relations.*

Wasik, B. H., & Bryant, D. M. (2001). *Home visiting: Procedures for helping families* (2nd ed.). Thousand Oaks, CA: Sage.

16 Training to Promote a Family Life Education Approach to Early Head Start Home Visiting

Scant attention has been paid to the professional development of home visitors in the early childhood context (Jones Harden, Denmark, & Saul, 2010) and we know little about the quality of the professional development (Schultz, Jones, Pinder, Wiprovnick, Groth, Shanty, & Duggan, 2018). Home visitors are integral to EHS-HBO and should have an array of professional development and training experiences available to them (US Department of Health and Human Services, Administration for Children and Families, Administration on Children, Youth, and Families, Head Start Bureau, n.d.). Early Head Start home visitors have diverse educational backgrounds, characteristics, and professional experiences (Wasik & Roberts, 1994; Sama-Miller, Akers, Mraz-Esposito, Zukiewicz, Avellar, Paulsell, & Del Grosso, 2018) and thus training and professional development that fits their diverse needs, strengths, and backgrounds is needed (Gill, Greenberg, Moon, & Margraf, 2007; West, Berlin, & Jones Harden, 2018). There are few formal educational experiences available that are specifically tailored to home visitors, meaning that much of their training is from outside of higher education (Wasik & Bryant, 2001). To our knowledge, there is no widely available training focused on a family life education (FLE) approach to home visiting. This study explored Early Head Start home visiting professionals' experiences with FLE professional development. Because there are empirical linkages among home visiting staff qualifications, program goals, family characteristics, and child and family outcomes (Jones Harden et al., 2010; Schachner, Gaylor, Chen, Hudson, & Garcia, 2017), it is intuitive that training for home visitors should acknowledge these factors. We also believe that there is a wide array of topics that home visitors can benefit from, such as knowledge and guidance on FLE, and that online modules with coaching as an additional support is a viable mode for this training.

There is a paucity of literature on training experiences of home visitors, particularly training that emphasizes forming respectful and healthy relationships with families (Azzi-Lessing, 2011). Early Head Start home visitors should receive, at minimum, training that focuses on program goals, philosophies, and implementation (Administration for Children and Families, 2016). There are also guidelines about ongoing training beyond the orientation or minimum that focuses on topics such as family engagement, in a manner that builds home visitors' knowledge and competencies (Administration for Children and Families, 2016).

Training is available to home visitors in a variety of modes (e.g., video) and on a variety of topics. For example, there are videos designed for home visitors on family support, child abuse and neglect prevention, and many other topics. In a review of audio-visual training materials for home visitors, Wasik, Thompson, Shaeffer, and Herrmann (1996) provided reviews of 58 home visiting training videos with an emphasis on the content (e.g., family diversity), presentation (e.g., clear and orderly presentation), and production (e.g., high-quality vignettes). To our knowledge, the researchers did not capture home visitors' experiences and perspectives about any of the training.

Mental health, substance abuse, and domestic violence have also been the focus of training for home visitors in urban contexts, and their experiences with the training have been captured. Tandon, Mercer, Saylor, and Duggan (2008) conducted focus groups with paraprofessional home visitors to understand their perspectives about the adequacy of the training and their preparation outside of the training to work with families with risk factors. One theme demonstrated that home visitors were provided with enough knowledge on the topics but desired more information on strategies as well as guidance on how to work with families in the areas of mental health, substance abuse, and domestic violence. Although Tandon et al.'s (2008) work may or may not generalize to professional home visitors, it sheds light on the need for multi-faceted training that targets knowledge and skills. In particular, the findings suggest that training should be accompanied by coaching or similar interventions to provide guidance and feedback, and to discuss skills germane to the training.

In addition to considering coaching, Oborn and Johnson (2015) applied technology strategies in the form of electronic performance feedback to promote home visitor training. Retrospectively, the researchers acknowledged that the coaching was often one-way with the coach providing electronic feedback via email. They suggested that coaching be broadened to include bi-directional communication that emphasizes self-reflection. Our current study included one-on-one coaching sessions delivered face-to-face with the purpose of promoting home visitor reflection.

Providing the actual content of home visitor training in online modules is not a new idea. For example, in 2012, Nebraska provided free online training to home visitors working with parents (Zero to Three, 2016). The training program, which includes seven modules, was in response to home visitors stating that in-person training was difficult to add to their existing schedules (Zero to Three, 2016). The Substance Abuse and Mental Health Services Administration (SAMHSA), coupled with Head Start, offered online training on a variety of topics, such as maternal depression, motivational interviewing, and mental health consultation. Another online visiting training, called Achieve OnDemand, is offered by The Ounce of Prevention Fund (Ounce) and covers topics such as the basics of home visiting, trauma and mental health, domestic violence, and safety planning (Ounce of Prevention Fund, 2018). There is a fee for enrolling in the courses and there are interactive components, such as discussion boards to promote interaction with other users (Ounce of Prevention Fund, 2018). The Institute for the Advancement of Family Support Professionals has a variety of online modules for home visitors and supervisors. These are a few examples of existing online training for home visitors.

Little is known about using online modules coupled with face-to-face coaching to promote content knowledge and skills on the topic of FLE. Knowing how to work with families from a variety of backgrounds should be a high-priority focus of home visitor training (Azzi-Lessing, 2011). Along this vein, collaborating and working effectively with all families is the heart of FLE (Darling & Cassidy, 2014) and tenets of our FLE training are described next.

Family Life Education Training and Current Study

To our knowledge, in addition to our present study, there was one other instance of professional development on FLE provided to Early Head Start home visitors. One Early Head Start/Head Start home visiting site transitioned from an approach that favored modeling, therapy, and intervention as well as bringing toys into the home to a family life education approach (Petkus, 2015). Petkus noted that their professional development to prompt their transition to a FLE approach included hosting Drs. Lori Roggman and Mark Innocenti to discuss home visiting and to provide training on the HOVRS (Petkus, 2015). This training also included a presentation from Dr. McWilliam and others (Petkus, personal communication). Petkus also conducted several presentations with discussions at the site about what FLE looks like in philosophy and in practice (Petkus, personal communication). Data were not collected on either the training or the transition to an FLE approach at this site.

Home visiting sites and systems should consider that professional development is important to maintaining a competent home visiting workforce (Schreiber, 2010) and that evidence-informed practice and explorations are therefore needed to develop an understanding of FLE with regard to home visiting. FLE has a strong foundation for home visitors, such as the domains of family practice (Myers-Walls et al., 2011), principles of FLE (Arcus & Thomas, 1993), ethics and virtues of FLE (Palm, 2018), case study process (MNCFR, 2016), FLE content areas (NCFR, 2015; Walcheski & Reinke, 2015), best practices in FLE (Ballard & Taylor, 2012), and professional support via the CFLE, conferences, and ongoing communication (Darling et al., 2017). In the present work, we used the following to create four online modules:

- family life education keystones, theories, and best practices
- adult learning theories
- Petkus' approach to EHS home visiting (HV) via FLE
- tenets and evidence included in HomVEE about EHS

- evidence from our qualitative study at one EHS-HBO declaring use of FLE as their approach (see Chapter 4)
- robust home visiting findings
- our own professional experiences.

Additionally, it was also essential to consider guiding principles of the Head Start Early Learning Outcomes Framework: Ages Birth to Five (U.S. Department of Health & Human Services, 2017) as well as the nine principles of Early Head Start Home Visiting (Home Visiting Evidence of Effectiveness, 2016). We created professional development modules in FLE in the context of EHS-HBO and explored participants' perspectives using a researcher-created measure developed for this study.

The present chapter is the first step in exploring quantitative and qualitative results in regard to training home visitors in a FLE approach to their work. For those desiring to implement a FLE approach to EHS HV, using the professional development modules featured in this chapter at local EHS agencies might be the best place to start. Additionally, the professional development modules or iterations of them could be used in institutions of higher education in courses that prepare home visitors or family service workers.

Method

Research Design

This study explored home visiting professionals' experiences with professional development modules, which aimed to promote knowledge of FLE. The main research questions of the present chapter were: (1) Were there differences in reported professional development module quality by condition (comparison, professional development, professional development plus coaching)? (2) What factors of the professional development modules were helpful and unhelpful to participants? (3) Were there differences in scores in FLE content assessments by condition (comparison, professional development, professional development plus coaching)? (4) What responses were elicited by the FLE content? These questions were addressed by using a mixed-methods approach. The first and the third questions were addressed by quantitative methods. The second and the fourth questions were addressed by qualitative methods.

Measure

We designed four versions of a survey to explore what participants thought about the professional development modules and a variety of topics germane to FLE and an FLE approach within EHS home-based practices. There were four survey distribution points, approximately ten days apart. The surveys

Training to Promote a FLE Approach

were administered via PsychData from August 2017 to September 2017. Question logic was used based on condition in PsychData, which means that the total number of questions answered by each participant varied.

Sensitizing concepts informed the development of our survey questions. Sensitizing concepts or "starting points" (Charmaz, 2003, p. 259) included: principles of FLE (Arcus & Thomas, 1993), best practices in FLE (Ballard & Taylor, 2012), domains of family practice (Myers-Walls et al., 2011) and concepts related an FLE approach to EHS home visiting (Petkus, 2015; Walsh, 2017).

Professional Development Modules

The research team created four videos over a period of five months. The focus of the videos was informed by the sensitizing concepts. See Table 16.1 for the topic of the video as well as a link to each video.

Each video was accompanied by an information sheet (see Chapter 16 Appendices A, B, C, and D) and a discussion board via Padlet© to allow participants the opportunity to ask questions, share insights, or make comments about the content of each video. The lengths of the videos were, respectively: 11:02, 25:37, 25:21, and 12:17.

To ensure the quality of the videos, three raters independently scored the technical qualities of the modules. They used a rubric with a four-point rating scale ranging from insufficient (1) to distinguished (4) to evaluate each video on five domains. The videos mostly received distinguished and proficient ratings with a few of its qualities receiving emergent ratings. Ratings of insufficient were not received. See Table 16.2 for inter-rater reliability.

Context and Participants

A focus group with one site was conducted approximately one year prior to this study. Coding and analysis of this focus group's data revealed that the site

Table 16.1 Video Web Links

Title of Video	Video Web Link
Overview of FLE	https://youtu.be/gXMOach0RGI
Home Visiting: A FLE Approach	https://youtu.be/UBuXd2E6GoY
A FLE Perspective: Empowering Families	https://youtu.be/UMKySyhfFYw
Making It Your Own	https://youtu.be/hVZAtAmpDKI

Training to Promote a FLE Approach   359

Table 16.2 Inter-Rater Reliability of Videos

Scale		% Agreement	Fleiss' Kappa
All		81.7	.673
Video			
	1	66.7	.013
	2	73.3	.444
	3	100.0	1.000
	4	86.7	.779
Domain			
	Audio	66.7	.314
	WLC	100.0	1.000
	VDR	83.3	.833
	VDCT	58.3	.268
	Lighting	100.0	1.000

WLC: Written Language Conventions; VDR-Visual Definition Resolution; VDCT Visual Definition Camera Technique

had a need and an interest in learning about FLE, and that online methods would fit in their day-to-day routines. A discussion with the supervisor at the other home visiting site revealed that training, particularly via online modules, would be welcome.

Both home visiting sites were Parents as Teachers affiliate sites at the time of the study. One site serves families in rural areas and the other site is an EHS-HBO in an urban setting. Only one site was an Early Head Start site, but both had the broad goals of promoting child and family development. Supervision practices at both sites continued in a business as usual fashion throughout the study and after it.

This study included a purposive sample. Twenty study participants were evenly divided among three groups; Group 1 received professional development in FLE through professional development modules; Group 2 received the professional development modules and supplementary coaching; and Group 3, the comparison group, received neither videos nor coaching. The rationale for coaching is that professionals' engagement in coaching helps participants explore the materials and increase the likelihood of changing thinking and practice (Rush, Shelden, & Hanft, 2003). Participants ranged in age from 60 years to 18 years ($M = 31.20$, $SD = 13.33$). Participants' range of experience working at Early Head Start ranged from 18 years to 0 years ($M = 3.47$, $SD = 5.59$).

360 *Training to Promote a FLE Approach*

Participants' years of experiences working with children and families ranged from 30 years to 0 years ($M = 10.21$, $SD = 9.02$). Details of the sample ($N = 20$) are outlined in Table 16.2.

Procedures

After obtaining Institutional Review Board (IRB) approval from one university, we recruited participants. Six participants were recruited from one EHS-HBO and were assigned to the condition of professional development modules plus coaching. Four participants were from a different home visiting site and were assigned to the condition of professional development modules. The comparison group included ten participants, all of whom were recruited from one family science class at one university.

Each week for four weeks, the intervention conditions received professional development modules, which included one video link (see Table 16.1), an information sheet (see Chapter 16 Appendices A–D), a discussion board link, and a survey. The professional development plus coaching condition also received a link to an online booking tool, youncanbookme©, to sign up for one professional coaching session per week. Each week, the comparison group received a survey. After the study ended, the comparison group received an email with all of professional development module materials.

Quantitative Analyses

Non-parametric analyses and cross tabulations with Pearson's chi square were conducted to examine differences across groups.

Qualitative Analyses

Participants' open-ended responses were divided into two datasets. Most responses to open-ended questions included three sentences, although responses ranged from a few words to multiple paragraphs. The first dataset focused on perspectives about the professional development modules and the second dataset focused on their perspectives of family life education content knowledge in the context of home visiting. For each dataset, we followed the same analyses.

Memos were used prior to coding to help establish rigor (Saldaña, 2016). Two researchers independently coded the data. One researcher is the first author of this work. A third researcher independently coded the data as well to ensure validity.

The researchers read the responses to the survey questions multiple times. Each researcher independently coded their thoughts about analysis and coding (Saldaña, 2016). The open-ended survey data was analyzed in several phases:

Table 16.3 Sample Characteristics

	n	%			n	%
Gender Identity			Are you a Certified Life Educator (CFLE)?			
Male	1	5.0		No	18	94.7
Female	19	95.0		Yes	1	5.3
Ethnicity			Do you have a professional license?			
Caucasian	15	75.0		No	16	84.2
African American	2	10.0		Yes	3	15.8
Native American/American Indian	1	5.0				
Other (please specify)	2	10.0	What is your position at Early Head Start?			
				Home Visitor	7	36.8
Highest Level of Education				Supervisor	2	10.5

(*Continued*)

Table 16.3 (Cont.)

			How familiar are you with family life education?			
High school	7	35.0				
Associate's degree	3	15.0				
Bachelor's degree	8	40.0	How familiar are you with family life education?			
Master's degree	1	5.0		Unfamiliar	2	10.5
Other (please specify)	1	5.0		Neutral	10	52.6
				Familiar	6	31.6
Degree in Family Science?				Very familiar	1	5.3
Yes	5	25.0				
No	15	75.0				

initial, focused, subthemes, and major themes (see Saldaña, 2011). MAXQDA Analytics Pro 12 was the Computer Assisted Qualitative Data Analysis Software (CAQDAS) used for this study. MAXQDA was used for all coding phases to analyze all data line-by-line. Additionally, we used MAXQDA to calculate inter-rater reliability (see Tables 16.4 and 16.6).

Table 16.4 Coding Analysis

Themes			
Focused codes	*Cohen's Kappa*	*Percentage Agreement*	*Exemplary Quote*
Experiences with Professional Development Modules on FLE and EHS HV			
Positive experiences	.84	88.00	"I enjoyed that the information was clear and not drawn out. It got right to the point and the length of the video was an element I could commit to as a professional."
Negative experiences	.94	95.24	"The video is very difficult to see it is at an hard angle to see what presenter is pointing at."
Attitudes about FLE			
Clarity about FLE/CFLE gained	.62	71.43	"I'm reminded with every video just how crucial my role as a home visitor is. A difference can be made that has generation effects. Empowering families with confidence and self-worth to face challenges and even advocate for their children."
Resistance to FLE/CFLE	.83	87.5	"The only issue I could see happening is if we decide to move to becoming FLEs it is a lot of time and effort that would have to put in outside work hours to become a CFLE."
Knowledge about FLE in context of EHS HV			
FLE hallmarks and principles	.71	78.57	"FLE is being therapeutic without being therapy."

(*Continued*)

364 Training to Promote a FLE Approach

Table 16.4 (Cont.)

Themes

Focused codes	Cohen's Kappa	Percentage Agreement	Exemplary Quote
Alignment of FLE and EHS HV	.73	80.00	"The examples that were given to put the FLE approach into the visits, for example joining in what the family already doing when you arrived, having the parent/family drive the visit and bring ideas, and I really liked the idea of redirecting the child back to the parent if the child and parent becomes disengaged."
None	1.00	100.00	
Overall	.83	84.52	

Results and Discussion

Research Question #1

The first research question asked: were there differences in reported professional development module quality by condition (comparison, professional development, professional development plus coaching)? Due to limitations in sample size, differences in groups were tested using a variety of non-parametric analyses to assess for within subjects and between subjects differences. Results did not yield any significant differences for either within or between subject effects, all $p > .05$, indicating that reported scores on video perceptions could not be discriminated by time or group. Examination of the trends suggests that regardless of time or group, participants reported favorable responses to videos, evidenced by scores all trending towards a positive direction. This may suggest that the videos are strong enough to stand on their own without coaching. From a cost perspective, these results might support that there is not an additive benefit to providing coaching with the professional development modules. The coaching was well received as demonstrated by pre- and post-evaluations (see Walsh & Steffen, 2018); nonetheless, the results suggest that there were similar gains and experiences from both professional development groups. It may mean that the videos accompanied by assessments are the necessary elements that are needed to achieve good outcomes. It is plausible that coaching has other benefits that were not captured in this study. The one minor exception to this was attitudes towards participating in online discussions, which was consistently the lowest scoring (while still in the positive direction) across times and groups. See Figure 16.1.

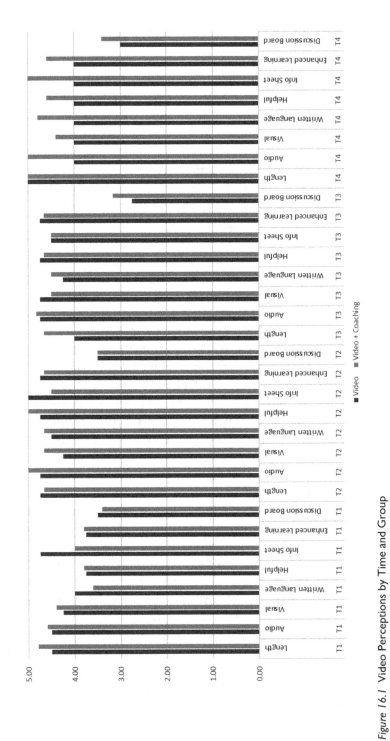

Figure 16.1 Video Perceptions by Time and Group

Research Question #2

The second research question asked: what factors of the professional development modules were helpful and unhelpful to participants? See Table 16.4 for the coding analysis.

The theme Experiences with Professional Development Modules on FLE and EHS HV captured both positive and negative experiences with the FLE modules. Participants were prompted to discuss what features of the modules seemed helpful as well as the problems and barriers within the modules. From coding and analysis it became evident that participants had a variety of experiences with the four modules. Participants reported that there were good technical qualities of the modules, professional and engaging videos, appropriate length, and that most features were helpful. On the other hand, an equal number of negative experiences were reported with poor technical qualities and inappropriate length of the videos cited. It is possible that videos around 10 to 15 minutes in length might be important to consider compared to videos that are 25 minutes in length. Participants appreciated that the first, second, and fourth videos showed the speaker but they appreciated that the third video had greater technical qualities. In the future, it might be worthwhile to use video software, such as Camtasia©, that allows the presenter to appear in a box throughout the presentation.

The theme Attitudes about FLE captured participants' expressions of their feelings and perspectives about FLE. Home visitors stated that they gained knowledge about FLE and CFLE throughout the intervention. They also expressed that they now have a foundation in FLE and through learning this material they felt valued as professionals. Other participants' statements demonstrated resistance to FLE and becoming a CFLE. Similar to another study (see Walsh, Mortensen, Edwards, & Cassidy, in press), participants expressed that a culture change would be needed for their home visiting site to adopt FLE. Participants stated that the CFLE requirements would require much time and effort and require work outside of their regular work hours. Several participants questioned FLE as a field, suggesting that it is in the nascent stages compared to other areas of study and that FLE might be too optimistic for the families served. While much FLE literature focuses on primary and secondary prevention (e.g., Myers-Walls et al., 2011), it is often appropriate to use FLE as tertiary prevention to help people handle complicated and chronic problems (Darling & Cassidy, 2014; Darling, Cassidy, Rehm, 2017), which may be more characteristic of the Early Head Start population.

The theme Knowledge about FLE in Context of EHS HV captured participants' expressions on a variety of FLE hallmarks such as family empowerment, strengths-based work, domains of family practice, ten FLE content areas, and family theories. The fourth video underscored alignment of EHS and FLE principles, and participants discussed examples stated in the video that demonstrated alignment of these two approaches. Participants also reiterated parts of the shared alignment, such as the parent as the child's first teacher (Darling & Cassidy, 2014; Jacobson, 2015).

Research Question #3

The third research question explored: were there differences in scores, if any, in FLE content assessments by condition (comparison, professional development, professional development plus coaching)? Responses to FLE content areas by group were analyzed using Crosstabulations with Pearson's chi square. Results found no significant differences across groups, indicating similar proportions of responses across groups. It should be noted that participants across groups had large proportions of selecting the "right" answer, which may suggest that item content was not difficult and that more rigorous items are needed. In the future, a delayed post-test will help to determine decay or maintenance of content knowledge. The comparison group included college students enrolled in a HDFS program, which may suggest that they had similar motivation to the intervention groups about a FLE approach to EHS HV and to respond correctly. See Table 16.5 for FLE content knowledge by group.

Table 16.5 FLE Content Knowledge by Group

	Comparison		Video		Video + Coaching	
	n	%	*n*	%	*n*	%
FLE, family therapy, and family case management all share the goal of: Strong healthy families	9	100	3	100	5	100
FLE generally is an educational rather than therapeutic approach True	8	88.9	3	100	5	100
False	1	11.1	0	0.0	0	0.0
Words that describe the work of FLE are?						
Preventive, educational, and collaborative	7	70.0	4	100	4	80.0
Therapy and case management	3	30.0	0	0.0	1	20.0

(*Continued*)

368   *Training to Promote a FLE Approach*

Table 16.5 (Cont.)

	Comparison		Video		Video + Coaching	
	n	%	n	%	n	%
Which of the following is a green flag of an effective visit?						
Parent and child interact during most of the visit	7	70.0	4	100	4	80.0
Therapy and case management	3	30.0	0	0.0	1	20.0
FLE has commonalities with family therapy and social work but it is a distinct area						
True	10	100	4	100	4	80.0
False	0	0.0	0	0	1	20.0
Within a FLE approach, the main focus is on the home visitor and child interaction						
True	2	25.0	0	0.0	0	0.0
False	6	75.0	4	100	6	100

The open-ended responses demonstrated differences in understanding with some responses identifying hallmarks of FLE and other responses demonstrating application of concepts of FLE to home visiting.

Research Question #4

The fourth research questions explored: what were the responses to family life education content? See Table 16.6 for coding analysis.

The theme Hallmarks of FLE Germane to Home Visiting captured keystones of FLE, such as principles of FLE (Arcus & Thomas, 1993), domains of family practice (Myers-Walls et al., 2011), best practices in FLE (Ballard & Taylor, 2012), and Petkus's (2015) FLE model of home visiting. The codes reflected that home visitors genuinely experienced identifying and understanding concepts of FLE in their responses.

Home visitors demonstrated awareness of FLE in their current thinking and practice. The theme Sense of Doing FLE in Current HV Work captured their views on an FLE approach or components of it in their current work. One focused code captured that home visitors were mindful of the unique nature of each family and the need to individualize services. Other home visitors

Table 16.6 Coding Analysis

Themes			
Focused Codes	*Cohen's Kappa*	*Percentage Agreement*	*Exemplary Quote*
Hallmarks of FLE germane to home visiting			
Principles of FLE	.56	66.67	"I remind myself before every visit to approach with respect and compassion."
Best practices in FLE and domains of family practice model	.88	91.36	"Cultivate strengths within the family and focus on individual and family strengths"
FLE model in HV	.60	70.00	"joint problem solving, involving everyone in the home during the visit"
Sense of doing FLE in current HV work			
Individualize HV services to meet needs of families	.78	83.33	"So 'being with' will look different for each family."
Applying hallmarks of FLE to home visits	.84	87.80	"Currently, I feel that I use FLE principles every visit, with success that is dependent on where the parent is. I know that as home visitors we work to see things from a strengths based perspective and celebrate the everyday successes with our families."
Challenges of FLE in HV			
Home visitors practice in all domains of family practice	.81	85.71	"I see that home visitors practice elements of all three models of family practice. There is always case management when it comes to the needs of the families, while in the home personal stories come up in which therapy applies."
CFLE needs more recognition	1.00	100.00	"Soon policy makers will appreciate family life education and federal agencies will require home visitors to be certified through an approved university."

(Continued)

Table 16.6 (Cont.)

Themes

Focused Codes	Cohen's Kappa	Percentage Agreement	Exemplary Quote
Obtaining CFLE is challenging	1.00	100.00	"In all honesty, the CFLE may be too much time in school for some of us to complete. With a full time job and families it can be overwhelming."
Paradigm shifts require care and caution	.67	75.00	"I think the home visitor would have to be willing to shift to FLE and make the changes that each home visitor is comfortable with."
Alignment between FLE and HV			
HV and FLE are similar	.91	93.33	"FLE and HV sound very similar."
FLE and PAT align	1.00	100.00	"FLE is the approach our Parents As Teachers curriculum uses in order to help demonstrate evidence based information."
FLE and EHS HV align	1.00	100.00	"From what it seems, the EHS home visiting expectation already meets the majority of FLE characteristics."
FLE professional development as a catalyst			
Readiness to incorporate FLE into practice	.60	70.00	"All of the core ideas of family life education I would like to work into my current practices because I feel like the families I am with will have better visits as well as better outcomes if the core ideas of family life education are used in home visiting."
Reaffirmed value as a HV	1.00	100.00	"It is a good reminder that what home visitors do is important."
Other	.85	88.89	"To have presentations be large"
Overall	.87	87.30	

asserted that they already use components of FLE in their work. For instance, one participant identified a component, such as taking a strengths-based approach in thinking and in practice, and stated that this is done and speculated that much depends on the family's state and characteristics.

Although home visitors identified and expressed knowledge of FLE gleaned from the modules, and some stated that they do FLE in their current home visiting work, the theme Challenges of FLE captured barriers or problems thought to be currently associated with FLE in the context of home visiting. One home visitor stated that home visitors currently operate in the three domains of family practice (see Myers-Walls et al., 2011). While operation in three domains is sometimes needed in home visiting, the primary focus should be the home visitor as a family life educator rather than as a family therapist who is tasked with fixing the family (Petkus, 2015). When the home visitor operates primarily as a FLE, this may promote the professionalization of home visitors and mitigate burnout (Petkus, 2015). Some home visitors highlighted that the CFLE needs more recognition, as well as challenges to obtaining the CFLE credential. This finding is consistent with previous research on a FLE approach to EHS home visiting (see Chapter 4). Home visitors also highlighted that changing thinking and practice requires care and caution. We agree, particularly given that a paradigm shift to FLE from a child-centered and toy-based approach that previously tasked home visitors with fixing families resulted in 100% turnover (Petkus, 2015). The video links featured earlier in this chapter along with this book should form a foundation for site discussions about a FLE foundation for home visiting. It is important to maintain a competent home visiting workforce and Schreiber (2010) raises questions about training systems, resources to support home visitors and supervisors, and incentives for professional development.

The theme Alignment between FLE and HV included alignment of HV and FLE in general. In this focused code, participants expressed that the goals of HV align with FLE and that the roles of a family life educator and home visitor are similar. Other participants expressed that Parents As Teachers (PAT) and FLE align. One participant expressed that she thought that FLE is the approach that PAT already employs. The third focused code in the theme captured participants' statements that EHS HV and FLE align. This is not surprising given that the fourth module (video and information sheet) underscored the nine dimensions of EHS HV (Home Visiting Evidence of Effectiveness, 2016) alignment with keystones of FLE (see Walsh, 2017).

The final theme, FLE Professional Development as a Catalyst, captured participants' desires to incorporate FLE into their practice. One participant called the FLE training an "aha moment" that helped her to see how all of her other training and the approaches of her site converge. Participants also expressed that the FLE training reaffirmed her value as a home visitor and that she felt ready to serve families after experiencing the FLE training.

Additional Limitations and Directions for Future Research

This is the first study on home visitors' experiences and perspectives on FLE professional development. This study has a small sample and limited statistical power. Home visitors were from one region of one southwestern U.S. state. Participants from a different regional area may have demonstrated different ways of thinking about FLE. We did not measure social desirability and thus we do not know if participants responded candidly or in ways they thought would be pleasing to the researchers.

Future studies should examine home visitors practice through observation and video prior to, during, and after the training. This should be in the context of knowing family characteristics and program goals. Home visiting measures from the existing literature will help to capture the quality of the visits. All in all, this may shed light on practice change in the context of FLE training.

One site of home visitors in the present study participated in a focus group and expressed an interest in FLE training in a way that worked with their schedules, such as online. It would be interesting to compare the findings of online modules and face-to-face formats. Future students should also consider their attitudes about their home visiting practice before, during, and after the training. This may help to make the training more meaningful, particularly if their attitudes can be discussed in coaching in light of recommended attitudes (e.g., accepting families as they are) for home visitors (Roggman et al., 2016).

Supervision is important to home visitors and an outlet for promoting professional growth and to help home visitors serve families (Wasik & Bryant, 2001). As linkages between FLE and EHS-HBO develop, it will be helpful to determine the most appropriate content and training processes for experienced service providers.

Summary

EHS home visitors have varying professional backgrounds and levels of training (Sama-Miller et al., 2016). There are empirical linkages among home visitor qualifications, program goals, and child and family outcomes (Jones Harden et al., 2010). This study is an important part of the line of research that has the larger question: is FLE, or components of it, a viable option for promoting home visiting effectiveness? Petkus (2015) provides a first-hand account of implementing a FLE model with EHS home visiting. Unfortunately, no data were collected. FLE has a strong foundation for home visitors, such as the domains of family practice (Myers-Walls et al., 2011), principles of FLE (Arcus & Thomas, 1993), ethical principles and virtues of FLE (e.g., Palm, 2018), case study process (MNCFR, 2016), FLE content areas (NCFR, 2015; Walcheski & Reinke, 2015), best practices in FLE (Ballard & Taylor, 2012), and professional support via the CFLE, conferences, and ongoing communication (Darling et al., 2017). The authors created four professional development modules (videos, information sheets, and discussion boards) that provided information about FLE, alignment with EHS (see Walsh, 2017), and Petkus's (2015) model as well as extensions of it (see Chapter 4). Three raters thought that most dimensions of the videos were proficient to distinguished (compared to emergent and insufficient), and the raters had the most agreement on the lighting, written language conventions, and visual definition of the videos. We aimed to explore home visiting professionals' experiences with FLE professional development.

Due to limitations in sample size, differences in groups were tested using a variety of non-parametric analyses to assess for within-subjects and between-subjects differences. Results did not yield any significant differences ($p > .05$), indicating that reported scores could not be discriminated by time or group. Nonetheless, examination of the trends suggests that regardless of time or group, participants reported favorable response to videos, evidenced by scores all trending toward a positive direction. Responses to FLE content questions by group were analyzed using crosstabulations with Pearson's chi square. There were no significant differences across groups, indicating similar proportions of responses across groups. Participants across groups had large proportions of selecting the correct answer, which suggests that item content needs further consideration in future interventions.

The present qualitative findings support that participants had positive experiences with the videos and were receptive to FLE in the context of home visiting. Participants shared their knowledge of principles of FLE (Arcus & Thomas, 1993), domains of family practice (Myers-Walls et al., 2011), best practices in FLE (Ballard & Taylor, 2012), and Petkus's (2015) FLE model of home visiting. Participants noted similarities between home visiting and FLE as well as specific similarities between EHS HV and FLE. Although not directly addressed in the modules, participants also noted similarities between PAT and FLE, which perhaps suggests an appetite for delineating how FLE compares to and enhances existing home visiting curriculums is an important step for future research. It is certainly notable that participants also had a sense of doing FLE in their current work; nonetheless, similar to other work (see Walsh et al., in press) professionals questioned the legitimacy of the CFLE credential and noted challenges to obtaining it, particularly given its lack of recognition by EHS at the time of this study. Finally, participants indicated a readiness to incorporate FLE and felt valued as a professional, both suggesting that the modules underscored in this chapter fit home visitor needs and interests.

Key Concepts

- Evidence-informed
- Family life coaching

374 *Training to Promote a FLE Approach*

- Framework for best practices in FLE
- Non-parametric analyses
- Online modules
- Principles of FLE
- Professional development
- Sensitizing concepts

Recommended Readings

Small, S., & Huser, M. (2015). Principles for improving family programs: An evidence-informed approach. In M. J. Walcheski & J. S. Reinke (Eds.), *Family life education: The practice of family science* (pp. 255–265). Minneapolis, MN: National Council on Family Relations.

Roberts, A. R., & Yeager, K. R. (2004). *Evidence-based practice manual: Research and outcome measures in health and human services.* New York: Oxford University Press.

References

Administration for Children and Families (2016). *Head Start Program Performance Standards.* Retrieved from: https://eclkc.ohs.acf.hhs.gov/policy/45-cfr-chap-xiii

Allen, W. D., & Blaisure, K. R. (2015). Family life education and the practice of cross-cultural competence. In M. J. Walcheski, & J. S. Reinke (Eds.), *Family life education: The practice of family science* (pp. 27–37). Minneapolis, MN: National Council on Family Relations.

Arcus, M. E., & Thomas, J. (1993). The nature and practice of family life education. In M. E. Arcus, J.D. Schvaneveldt, & J. J. Moss (Eds.), *Handbook of family life education: The practice of family life education* (pp. 1–32). Newbury Park, CA: Sage.

Office of Planning Research and Evaluation, Administration for Children and Families, U.S. Department of Health and Human Services.

Azzi-Lessing, L. (2011). Home visitation programs: Critical issues and future directions. *Early Childhood Research Quarterly, 26,* 387–398. doi: 10.1016/j.ecresq.2011.03.005

Ballard, S. M., & Taylor, A. C. (2012). Best practices in family life education. In S. M. Ballard & A. C. Taylor (Eds.). *Family life education with diverse populations* (pp. 1–18). Thousand Oaks, CA: Sage.

Charmaz, K. (2003). Grounded theory: Objectivist and constructivist methods. In N. K. Denzin & Y. S. Lincoln (Eds.), *Strategies for qualitative inquiry* (2nd ed., pp. 249–291). Thousand Oaks: CA: Sage.

Darling, C. A., & Cassidy, D. (2014). *Family life education: Working with families across the lifespan* (3rd ed.). Long Grove, IL: Waveland.

Darling, C. A., Cassidy, D., & Rehm, M. (2017). Family life education: Translational family science in action. *Family Relations, 66,* 741–752. doi: 10.1111/fare.12286

Duncan, S. F., & Goddard, H. W. (2017). *Family life education: Principles and practices for effective outreach*(3rd ed.). Thousand Oaks, CA: Sage.

Gill, S., Greenberg, M. T., Moon, C., & Margraf, P. (2007). Home visitor competence, burnout, support, and client engagement. *Journal of Human Behavior in the Social Environment, 15,* 23–44. doi: 10.1300/J137v15n01_02

Home Visiting Evidence of Effectiveness (HomVEE). (2016). *Early Head Start—Home Visiting: Program model overview*. Retrieved from https://homvee.acf.hhs.gov/Model/1/Early-Head-Start-%20Home-Visiting-%28EHS-HV%29/8/2

Jacobson, A. L. (2015). Parenting education and guidance. In M. J. Walcheski & J. S. Reinke (Eds.), *Family life education: The practice of family science* (pp. 213–222). Minneapolis, MN: National Council on Family Relations.

Jones Harden, B., Denmark, N., & Saul, D. (2010). Understanding the needs of staff in Head Start programs: The characteristics, perceptions, and experiences of home visitors. *Children and Youth Services Review, 32*, 371–379.

Leventhal, J. (2015). Human growth and development across the lifespan. In M. J. Walcheski, & J. S. Reinke (Eds.), *Family life education: The practice of family science* (pp. 167–176). Minneapolis, MN: National Council on Family Relations.

Minnesota Council on Family Relations. (MNCFR). (2016). *Ethical thinking and practice for parent and family life education*. Minneapolis, MN: Ethics Committee, Parent and Family Education Section. Retrieved from https://mn.ncfr.org/resources/

Myers-Walls, J. A., Ballard, S. M., Darling, C. A., & Myers-Bowman, K. S. (2011). Reconceptualizing the domain and boundaries of family life education. *Family Relations, 60*, 357–372. doi: 10.1111/j.1741-3729.2011.00659.x

National Council on Family Relations. (NCFR). (2015). Family life education content areas: Content and practice guidelines. Retrieved from https://www.ncfr.org/sites/default/files/fle_content_and_practice_guidelines_2015_0.pdf

Oborn, K. M. K., & Johnson, L. D. (2015). Coaching via electronic performance feedback to support home visitors' use of caregiver coaching strategies. *Topics in Early Childhood Special Education, 35*, 157–169. doi: 10.1177/0271121415592411

Ounce of Prevention Fund. (2018). Achieve OnDemand: Online home visiting training you can depend on. Retrieved from https://www.theounce.org/achieveondemand/

Palm, G. (2018). Professional ethics and practice in family life education. In *Tools for ethical thinking and practice in family life education* (4th ed., pp. 1–10). Minneapolis, MN: National Council on Family Relations.

Petkus, J. (2015). A first-hand account of implementing a family life education model: Intentionality in Head Start home visiting. In M. J. Walcheski, & J. S. Reinke (Eds.), *Family life education: The practice of family science* (pp. 325–331). Minneapolis, MN: National Council on Family Relations.

Roggman, L. A., Peterson, C. A., Chazan-Cohen, R., Ispa, J., Decker, K., Hughes-Belding, K., Cook, G. A., & Vallotton, C. D. (2016). Preparing home visitors to partner with families of infants and toddlers. *Journal of Early Childhood Teacher Education, 37*, 301–313. doi: 10.1080/10901027.2016.1241965

Rush, D. D., Shelden, M. L., & Hanft, B. E. (2003). Coaching families and colleagues: A process for collaboration in natural settings. *Infants & Young Children, 16*, 33–47. doi: 10.1097/00001163-200301000-00005

Saldaña, J. (2011). *Fundamentals of qualitative research: Understanding qualitative research*. New York: Oxford.

Saldaña, J. (2016). *The coding manual for qualitative researchers* (3rd ed.). Thousand Oaks, CA: Sage.

Sama-Miller, E., Akers, L., Mraz-Esposito, A., Zukiewicz, M., Avellar, S., Paulsell, D., & Del Grosso, P. (2018). *Home visiting evidence of effectiveness review: Executive summary*.

Office of Planning, Research and Evaluation, Administration for Children and Families, US Department of Health and Human Services. Washington, DC. Retrieved from https://homvee.acf.hhs.gov/Publications/9/Publications/55/

Schachner, A., Gaylor, E., Chen, W. B., Hudson, L., & Garcia, D. (2017). RISE home visiting evaluation: Final evaluation report. Retrieved from https://del.wa.gov/sites/default/files/public/RISE_Final_Eval_Report_FINAL_2017_send.pdf

Schreiber, L. (2010). Key components of a successful early childhood home visitation system: A self-assessment tool for states. Retrieved from https://www.zerotothree.org/resources/174-key-components-of-a-successful-early-childhood-home-visitation-system

Schultz, D., Jones, S. S., Pinder, W. M., Wiprovnick, A. E., Groth, E. C., Shanty, L. M., & Duggan, A. (2018). Effective home visiting training: Key principles and findings to guide training developers and evaluators. *Maternal and Child Health Journal, 22*, 1563–1567. doi: 10.1007/s10995-018-2554-6

Tandon, S. D., Mercer, C. D., Saylor, E. L., & Duggan, A. K. (2008). Paraprofessional home visitors' perspectives on addressing poor mental health, substance abuse, and domestic violence: A qualitative study. *Early Childhood Research Quarterly, 23*, 419–428. doi: 10.1016/j.ecresq.2008.02.002

U.S. Department of Health and Human Services, Administration for Children and Families, Administration on Children, Youth, and Families, Head Start Bureau (n. d.). Program administrator's checklist: For the Head Start home-based program option. Retrieved from https://eclkc.ohs.acf.hhs.gov/program-planning/article/program-administrators-checklist-head-start-home-based-program-option

U.S. Department of Health & Human Services (2017). Interactive Head Start Early Learning Outcomes Framework: Ages birth to five. Retrieved from https://eclkc.ohs.acf.hhs.gov/interactive-head-start-early-learning-outcomes-framework-ages-birth-five

Walsh, B. A. (2017). Setting the stage for families in poverty as catalysts: A family life education approach to Early Head Start Home Visiting. *National Council on Family Relations Family Focus, 73*, 8–10.

Walsh, B. A., Mortensen, J. A., Edwards, A. L., Cassidy, D. (in press). The practice of family life education within Early Head Start home visiting. *Family Relations*.

Walsh, B.A., & Steffen, R. (November, 2018). *Evaluating FLE use of family life coaching technique with EHS home visitors*. Presentation at the National Council on Family Relations annual conference, San Diego, CA.

Walcheski, M. J., & Reinke, J. S. (2015). *Family life education: The practice of family science*. Minneapolis, MN: National Council on Family Relations.

Wasik, B. H., & Bryant, D. M. (2001). *Home visiting: Procedures for helping families* (2nd ed.). Thousand Oaks, CA: Sage.

Wasik, B. H., Thompson, E. A., Shaeffer, L., & Herrmann, S. (1996). *A guide to audio visual training materials for home visitors*. Chapel Hill: The Center for Home Visiting, University of North Carolina at Chapel Hill.

Wasik, B. H., & Roberts, R. N. (1994). Survey of home visiting programs for abused and neglected children and their families. *Child Abuse & Neglect, 18*, 271–283.

West, A. L, Berlin, L. J., & Jones Harden, B. (2018). Occupational stress and well-being among Early Head Start home visitors: A mixed methods study. *Early Childhood Research Quarterly, 44*, 288–303. doi: 10.1016/j.ecresq.2017.11.003

Zero to Three. (2016). Nebraska online home visiting training modules. Retrieved from https://www.zerotothree.org/resources/872-nebraska-online-home-visiting-training-modules

An Overview of Family Life Education (FLE)
Please view the video at: https://youtu.be/gXMOachORGI

Key Terms of Family Life Education

- Empowerment
- Strengths
- Education and Skill-Building
- Prevention
- Collaboration
- Doing for versus Being With
- Evidence Based and Evidence Informed
- Multidisciplinary
- Relationship Based
- Family Systems
- Attachment

Domains of Family Practice Model

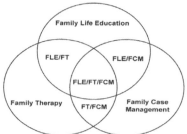

FLE:
- FLE methodology
- Normal, healthy functioning
- Broad, inclusive knowledge base
- Education/prevention focus

MFT:
- Therapeutic intervention
- Assessment and diagnosis
- Psychotherapy

FCM:
- Coordination of services
- Family advocacy
- Focus on meeting family needs

FLE/MFT:
- Interpersonal relationship skills
- Healthy sexual functioning
- Life course perspective

FLE/FCM:
- Family resource management
- Family policy

MFT/FCM:
- Focus of family problems
- Intervention techniques
- Treatment goals/methods
- Management of client records
- Closure of cases

FLE/FT/FCM:
- Family Systems Theory
- Sensitivity to diversity
- Research-based practice
- Ecological context
- Values and ethics

Myers-Walls et al. (2011)

Content Areas of FLE

- Families and individuals in society
- Internal dynamics of families
- Human growth and development
- Human sexuality
- Interpersonal relationships
- Parent education and guidance
- Family resource management
- Family law and public policy
- Professional ethics and practice
- Family life education methods

Certified Family Life Educator

- Values prevention, education, and collaboration and other key terms of FLE
- Has the goal of healthy and strong families
- Similar but unique from FT and FCM
- Skills and competencies in content areas of FLE
- Adheres to the National Council on Family Relations (NCFRs) code of ethics https://www.ncfr.org/sites/default/files/cfle_code_of_ethics_2.pdf
- Completed national exam OR completed coursework in the 10 content areas from an NCFR approved program

For more info about becoming a CFLE, please visit the NCFR website: https://www.ncfr.org/cfle-certification

Dr. Walsh, bridgetw@unr.edu

Home Visiting: A FLE Approach

Please view the video at: https://youtu.be/UBuXd2E6GoY

Strong, Healthy Families

- Family life education, family therapy, and family case management all share of the same goal of strong, healthy families
- The domains of family practice model acknowledges that there are similarities and differences in the work of these three professions

Myers-Walls, Ballard, Darling, and Myers-Bowman (2011)

Prevention, Education, Coach

- FLE and coach
- Joint problem solving
- Collaborative planning approach
- Parent demonstration of learned skills; Encourage through narration of parent-child interaction
- Family systems theory, siblings
- Adverting later problems, through empowering self-sustainability
- Encourage long-term self-confidence and skill building in parents
- Discourage reliance on service provider
- Guide parents to understanding child health, safety, nutritional needs and avenues to promote these
- Parent education through focus on attachment; parental understanding of child development; parental responsiveness to child

Why Does this Sound Like Signs of an Effective Visit?

- ☐ Parent and child interact during most of the visit
- ☐ Child turns to the parent when HV arrives
- ☐ HV narrates positive parent-child interactions
- ☐ Other family members, if available, are involved in the visit

Could you elaborate on ways you see EHS HV and FLE interact?

Dr. Walsh, bridgetw@unr.edu

A Family Life Education Perspective of Empowering Families with Young Children

Please view the video at: https://www.youtube.com/watch?v=UMKySyhfFYw

The FLE philosophy
- Family-strengths perspective
- Families as systems rooted in ecological contexts
- Prevention focus

Why is family empowerment important for families with young children?
- Family wellbeing is community wellbeing. Everyone benefits
- Transition to parenthood is an important time for the family system – and stressful!

What is family empowerment?
- Knowledge, skills, resources to make decisions that contribute to healthy family functioning
- Strengths-based
- Comes from within the family system

"Cultivating" family empowerment
- Cultivated from within the family system
- Families do the work, professions scaffold
- Nurture strengths when times are good.
- Draw on strengths in times of stress

Family processes that give families strength.

Shared belief systems ➤ Family organization ➤ Patterns of communication

- Building nurturing relationships
- Establishing routines
- Maintaining expectations
- Adaptability to challenges
- Community connections

Think about your own practices:
- Do you cultivate these strengths with the families you work with?
- Do you focus on family strengths?
- How would cultivating these strengths benefit?

The role of the professional.

- "Doing for" vs. "Being with"
- Focus on relationships
- Validate challenges
- Start with family's priorities and interests

"The professional task shifts from the expert holder of knowledge to facilitating **democracy and shared action**"
(Roehlkepartain & Syvertsen, 2014, p. 18)

Think **about your own practices.**

Strength-based or Deficit-based?

Approach with respect and compassion?

All families have the capacity to grown and flourish?

Focus on family interactions that cultivate empowerment?

Check in with yourself as a professional

"By concentrating on only a family's problems and family's failings, we ignore the fact that it **takes a positive approach in life to succeed.** The family strengths perspective is a **world-view or orientation** toward life and families that is **positive and optimistic**"
(DeFrain & Asay, 2007, p. 3)

Making It Your Own!

Please view the video at: https://youtu.be/hVZAtAmpDKI

Alignment of Principles

EHS-HBO Principles (HomVEE, 2016)	FLE Principles (included in Walsh, 2017)
"High quality services	Qualified professionals are crucial to high quality FLE (Arcus, Schvaneveldt, & Moss, 1993)
Activities that promote healthy development and identify atypical development at the earliest stages possible	Typical and atypical development (Leventhal, 2015)
Positive relationships and continuity, with an emphasis on the role of the parent as the child's first, and most important, relationship	Importance of parenting and parent education (Darling & Cassidy, 2014; Jacobson, 2015)
Activities that offer parents a meaningful and strategic role in the program's vision, services, and governance	Shared educational goals and practices (Arcus et al., 1993; Duncan & Goddard, 2017); parents as members of community and world (Doherty, Erickson, & Cutting, 2015)
Inclusion strategies that respect the unique developmental trajectories of young children in the context of a typical setting, including children with disabilities	Supporting families with children with medical or other special needs (Jacobson, 2015)
Cultural competence that acknowledges the profound role that culture plays in early development	Cross-cultural competence (Ballard & Taylor, 2012; Allen & Blaisure, 2015) and respecting different values (Arcus et al., 1993)
Comprehensiveness, flexibility, and responsiveness of services that allow children and families to move across various program options over time as their life situation demands	Based on needs of individuals and families (Arcus et al., 1993); Offered in many different settings (Arcus et al., 1993)
Transition planning	Developmental transitions through ages and stages (Leventhal, 2015) and other life transitions (Arcus et al., 1993; Duncan & Goddard, 2017)
Collaboration with community partnerships that allow programs to expand their services"	Collaboration for strong, healthy families (Myers-Walls et al., 2011)

Principles and Practices

Cultural Competence, Flexibility, and Responsiveness ⟶ Present and future needs; families strengths; shared goal setting

Relationships that Put Families First and High Quality Services ⟶ Triad (HV, Parents, Child) Observing, narrating, modeling, coaching, collaborating

Meaningful Family Life ⟶ Families systems theory suggests that families members interact in an interdependent manner and that change in one or some members may be enhanced or sabotaged; Involve or engage multiple family members

Dr. Walsh, bridgetw@unr.edu

Appendix A

Introduction to Early Head Start Home Visiting

One Program's Description

Tracy Casbarro, Milagro Guardado, Shauna Herrick, Christina Martin, Maria Reyes-Vargas, Jamie Gehrman-Selby, and Karyn Sholund

University of Nevada, Reno, Early Head Start-Home-Based Option

> It is not your job to save everyone. Some people are not even ready to be helped. Focus on being of service to those who are and be wise and humble enough to know when the best service you can offer is to guide them toward help in another direction.
>
> (Anna Taylor)

Background

An Early Head Start-Home-Based Option (EHS-HBO) philosophy is designed to provide a formal structure for parents and other primary caregivers to use their strengths to provide a nurturing, educational environment for their children. Through a collaborative approach, parents and home visitors are encouraged to work together to create an enjoyable, yet structured plan to facilitate and promote healthy and safe child development. Throughout this chapter, the word *parent* will be used to refer to individuals essential to a child, this may include parents, and other primary caregivers. Respect is valued as an expectation to be modeled within the parent, child, and home visitor triad. Families are provided the opportunity to have a voice in policy council and/or governing body for the program.

As a federally funded program, families living at or below the current federal poverty guidelines are deemed eligible for services. For the year 2019, a family of three living within the continental United States must have earned less than $21,330 (Office of the Assistant Secretary for Planning and Evaluation, 2019). There are exceptional factors that make a family categorically eligible, i.e. homelessness, foster care, disability (SSI), and Temporary Assistance for Needy Families (TANF). Throughout the years, home visitors have experienced working with a range of diverse families. Home visiting services provides the flexibility to meet every family's unique context and structure. The program model and curriculum are adaptable for pregnant women, teen parents, single-parent homes, two parent households, foster families, families with disabilities, and justice system involved families.

The greatest benefit observed comes from the parent–child interactions promoted during each home visit. Access to resources (such as childcare) and connections to community resources is something often requested by parents. Families in an EHS-HBO program are provided opportunities to socialize in small and large group settings. An advantage of socialization opportunities is the strengthening of school-readiness skills in children, as well as parent-to-parent interactions that happen. Formal and informal opportunities are organized to provide such experiences for the families, opportunities such as playgroups, community events, and resource fairs. Program flexibility is practiced by meeting parents in their home environment or otherwise requested location.

Long-term outcomes (e.g., school readiness) are discussed with families at various intervals during their home visiting experience. Goals that revolve around school readiness, access to health care, and family self-sufficiency are discussed with each participant and reviewed according to their unique abilities. The EHS-HBO program model provides tools to be used within visits and promote parental observation that bring awareness of child development. Additionally, assessments in development, nutrition and health screenings are completed and discussed with the families to monitor healthy child development and growth. Oftentimes, when conducting screenings and assessments, home visitors find themselves having conversations with families regarding child development, child behaviors and physical abilities the children have experienced.

Individualizing the curriculum to meet the families wants and needs, makes a difference when aiming for effective home visiting. Every home visit is individualized to meet each family at their level of understanding and capacity. Meeting families where they are at often includes the home visitor asking powerful questions to the parents and at the core of this is a sense of attunement to the family. Trusting relationships are the basis between home visitors and parents to promote the discovery of that family's strengths and needs. Getting to know the family and the relationship that evolves from those interactions provides the tools and knowledge to individualize visits. Relationships thrive when mutual respect, responsiveness and follow-through of each party is established. Some of the factors that contribute to establishing quality working relationships are validated through consistency and communication.

Relationships allow for clear communication to be shared and to shape the visits. We strive to allow families to feel confident and honest during visits to encourage families to provide valid answers during assessments. This information can be seen through results found in child development screenings, observations, health assessments, curriculum, the Parent Gauge Needs assessment and parent input. The information gathered by these assessments identifies strengths and needs of each child and family and the creation of the follow-up visits comes into design.

384   *Appendix A*

A variety of developmental screenings are available for programs to use within their agency. One such screening is the Ages and Stages Questionnaire (ASQ). The ASQ is a set of questions designed to be completed by parents at any point for a child between ages 1 month to 5½ years. The questions are organized into five areas covering developmental domains (communication, gross motor, fine motor, problem solving, and personal social). Parental answers will range depending if the child performs the skill, *sometimes*, or *not yet* (Squires, Twombly, Bricker, & Potter, 2009). For example, when a child scores in the area of concern in a certain domain of the ASQ, the family and home visitor will be alerted to plan activities to strengthen that specific area of development. A common scenario is, an eight-month-old child scores in the grey area of the gross motor development section of the ASQ. A highlighted milestone at that age is the ability for infant to sit upright on the floor using their hands to lean on for support or perhaps sitting up straight without leaning on their hands. With this milestone noted as needing work, the home visitor might mention activities that will strengthen the skill. Families also have the opportunity to suggest what activities work best within their home. Reflecting on the scenario while being in the home allows families and home visitors to brainstorm about what is available to use as props, tools, and activities that will help strengthen the skill the family is focusing on.

Home visiting as a profession, is a career that has a comprehensive approach. There are skills and requirements that vary from being mandatory by agency and voluntary based on a professional desire to expand knowledge. In one EHS-HBO program based in Northern Nevada, Washoe County licensing requires that all staff must complete the following training: Child Abuse and Neglect Prevention, Signs and Symptoms of Illness including Blood-borne Pathogens, CPR and First Aid training, SIDS Training, Child Development/Positive Guidance, Obesity Prevention and Nutrition, Shaken Baby, Medication Administration, and Emergency Disaster Preparedness. Continued early childhood education (ECE) hours are required per year licensing year and must be approved by the early childhood professional development system. The additional 24 hours of training each year can be scheduled to meet home visitors' professional needs. Topics of interest for additional training apart from the 24 hours required for ECE compliance might include information for situations home visitors are often placed in. In this particular EHS-HBO program, home visitors have attended training discussing breast-feeding, brain development, trauma, domestic violence, mental health, discipline and guidance, and child development among others.

Head Start Early Learning Outcomes Framework (Administration for Children and Families [ACF], 2015) was written to establish practices and policies to help prepare young children for success in school. It is based on current research of what young children should know before they enter school and to help adults better understand what they can do to support children in

Appendix A 385

achieving those outcomes. It is organized into five domains: approaches to learning; social and emotional development; language and literacy; cognition and perceptual, motor and physical development. The Framework uses developmental progressions to describe the skills, behaviors and concepts that children will demonstrate as they progress towards a given goal within an age period. The Learning Outcomes can be used to help guide curriculum and engage families in their children's learning. During the first five years of development, children grow and learn at an incredible rate. They are learning to talk, walk, explore, develop friendships, etc. Since children can have very different experiences, their learning and development can also be very different. These differences can have lasting impact on later school success. The guiding principles for the Framework are as follows (Administration for Children and Families [ACF], 2015, p. 3):

1. Each child is unique and can succeed—with appropriate support, all children can be successful learners and achieve the skills, behaviors, and knowledge described in the Framework;
2. Learning occurs within the context of relationships—responsive and supportive interactions with adults are essential to children's learning;
3. Families are children's first teacher and most important caregivers, teachers, and advocates—families have unique knowledge, skills and backgrounds that contribute to their child's school readiness;
4. Children learn best when they are emotionally and physically safe and secure—when children receive nurturing, responsive and consistent care, they are able to engage fully in learning experiences;
5. Areas of development are integrated, and children learn many concepts and skills at the same time;
6. Teaching must be intentional and focused on how children learn and grow—children are eager to learn so by providing developmentally appropriate opportunities for exploration and play can build on their intrinsic strengths to learn;
7. Every child has diverse strengths rooted in their family's culture, background, language and beliefs—effective teaching practices and learning experiences build on the unique backgrounds and prior experiences of each child.

Home visitors can help give parents the support and resources to support their child's development and learning success. Home visitors can use the guiding principles when designing their home-based curriculum to support the learning outcomes and children's future school success. The Framework can be used discuss skills that children are developing and to identify strategies that support and reinforce children's learning and development. Home visitors can partner with parents and families, providing individualized learning

386 *Appendix A*

opportunities that promote strong child outcomes (Administration for Children and Families [ACF], 2015).

The Head Start Program Performance Standards (HSPPS) provide guidance on how to implement the performance standards required for all Head Start and Early Head Start grantees (Administration for Children and Families [ACF], 2016). It covers the areas of program governance, program operations, financial and administrative requirements and federal administrative procedures. The home-based option for Early Head Start must deliver the same full range of comprehensive services as a center-based option except for the areas specifically addressed under the home-based option. The EHS-HBO delivers the services with the child's parents, primarily in the home and through group socializations (§302.22, ACF, 2016). Home visitors may only carry a caseload of 10–12 families. Home visitors are to offer one home visit per week that lasts for 90 minutes. The program must offer 46 home visits and 22 socializations over the course of the program year. They must use a home visiting curriculum that is research based, can demonstrate fidelity, and is aligned with the Head Start Early Learning Outcomes Framework.

Home Visits and More

A day in the life of an Early Head Start home visitor is never the same from day-to-day. There are many different layers when it comes to being a home visitor. For home visiting, flexibility is the key word. The following sections will provide examples of home visitor perspectives from home visitors at an EHS-HBO program. When we come in to the office, we connect with co-workers and discuss the day's plan. A designated work space is needed for home visitors to email, plan, and organize a visit. Planning a visit can look differently per home visitor and unique family. Reflecting on the last visit is a great way to beginning the planning session. We ask ourselves, "what concerns, or questions did the family have? What strengths did they demonstrate?". The PAT curriculum is used to prepare each visit (see Parents as Teachers National Center, 2015). When a family is new or shared little input in planning for the next visit, foundational visits from PAT are used to guide the next visit.

PAT supports the use of materials that are often times found in a home. However, the gathering of supplies that might be needed, but the family lacks, is a duty a home visitor must do to prepare for the parent–child activity. Getting to know the family is an essential process that influences the preparation of a visit. Many families in an EHS-HBO program are living below the poverty line. Limited access to resources can have an impact in implementing the visit. For example, knowing that the family doesn't have the adequate kitchen utensils helps a home visitor come prepared with the supplies needed to create Play-Doh with the family.

The first visit has the potential of being the most nerve-wracking visit. Personal safety must be considered for every visit; however, extreme measures should be taken on *every* first visit. Planning a new route, parking in a strange place upon arrival, locating the home/apartment and walking into the home of strangers is not for the faint of heart. Home visitors are encouraged to be highly aware of their surroundings. Distraction from a cell phone is discouraged when walking to and from a vehicle. Staying alert within the home is a priority. On the first visit especially, personal items such as car keys and cell phone are recommended to remain on the home visitor's body (pockets) for quick access in case of emergency departure.

Building a connection with the family begins from the moment the home visitor contacts the family. From that point on, building a trusting relationship is essential to the support a home visitor can provide; relationship building is a constant work in work progress. We learn bits and pieces about the family at every single visit. While some parents tend to enjoy sharing facts about their family and experiences, there are others who are more reserved and share bits of knowledge as the weeks/months progress and the professional relationship builds.

What might a visit look like? Home visitors sit on the floor during parent–child interaction; this helps model for the family that being on the child's level facilitates interactions with their child. The home visitor encourages the family to participate in the parent–child activity. However, the home visitor may have to adapt the plan if the family member is unable to get on the floor. During the visits we also cover developmental centered parenting skills that provide a universal look at parenting challenges regardless of age, culture, race, or gender. Families often share goals and struggles in terms of their overall family's health and wellbeing.

Parent–child interaction opportunities are a great time for parents and home visitors to discuss the child's skills and parenting behaviors that the parents may use during that time. When siblings or other children are present, discussions of social skills such as sharing toys or aggressive behaviors might be observed. As a visit is wrapping up, the following steps enhance parent investment that leads to the success of the next visit—**review** with the family on how they felt the activity went, **plan** for the next visit and **schedule** the next visit time.

Once back at the office, paperwork and data entry are next on the to-do list. The visit plans will be scanned in and attached in the necessary locations of the data system (e.g., Child Plus). In this particular EHS-HBO program, there are child development observations that will need to be documented in the ongoing developmental assessment data system (e.g., Teaching Strategies Gold).

Sometimes visits can leave home visitors in a high emotional state. Just as they can cause excitement from hearing about a family's triumphs, visits can also leave you feeling stressed, hurt, worried, or overwhelmed from the challenges and troubles families share. Sharing these thoughts and feelings with a trusted supervisor is one strategy used by home visitors to reduce the secondary trauma that can occur from those emotionally difficult visits. Reflective supervision allows a supervisor to provide mentoring and coaching to support the home visitor. It's a time where a home visitor finds a listening ear and a time to brainstorm for ideas and resources. Research has shown when the supervisor is more engaged with reflective supervision, impact is shown to have increase in positive behaviors, performance and career satisfaction (Gallen, Ash, Smith, Franco & Willford, 2016).

We are a highly educated group of professionals but most home visiting programs have minimum educational requirements. This may include a high school diploma with experience, CDA certificate, or an associate's degree in an early childhood field. Other preferred education might include bachelor's degrees with early childhood experience or a license in a particular field such as social work or nursing. Many home visiting programs will require that the home visitor meet state or county child care licensing requirements with background clearances (arrest and child abuse), specific training such as first aid, CPR, and mandated reporting, and registration in certain childcare or home visiting professional organizations. Some programs may require that a home visitor be certified in a certain curriculum or areas of specialty (i.e. lactation education, birth educator, infant mental health etc.). Many programs require that home visitors take annual continuing education credits in their field to help support on going learning and staying up to date with the latest research to share with families. Home visitors should have a strong knowledge in parenting education, child development, and typical compared to atypical development. Other professional characteristics that home visitors should have are flexibility, tolerance, strengths-based perspective, caring, warmth, outgoing, listening, empathy and strong professional boundaries and ethics.

Working with PAT

The EHS and PAT models support each other in providing opportunities to strengthen and encourage the development of protective factors that help a family's outcomes. The EHS model and PAT models have similar missions; they both assist families in having healthy prenatal results and they both support the development of infants and toddlers in different areas of development (cognitive, social–emotional, motor, language) for later success in school, all while supporting the parents along the way. The Early Head Start mission is "to support healthy prenatal outcomes and enhance intellectual, social, and emotional development of infants and toddlers to promote later success in school." Parents as Teachers supports optimal early development, learning and health of children by supporting and engaging their parents and caregivers (https://parentsasteachers.org).

The goal of the Parents as Teachers curriculum is to provide parents with child development knowledge and parenting support provide early detection of developmental delays, and health issues, prevent child abuse and neglect and increase children's school readiness. It is a comprehensive professional curriculum that is evidence based and has been shown to be effective. The program is designed to empower parents as their child's first teacher.

The PAT model includes consistent visits in the family's home or anywhere that is convenient for them to meet; visits range from once a week to once a month. In contrast, our Early Head Start program requires weekly, 90-minute visits. EHS-HBO services are available to pregnant woman and visits are 60 minutes long until their baby is born. Children are part of the EHS-HBO program until their third birthday. In addition, EHS center-based families have the opportunity for parent meetings four times a year, using the PAT six-week curriculum series, "What you Do Matters." PAT provides structured home visit plans that cover, but are not limited to, the topics of child development, family well-being, parent–child interactions, prenatal and/or parenting behaviors, and development-centered parenting at every visit.

When planning for the first eight visits, the home visitor pulls information from each section and brings information to families after using an already completed PAT foundational visit form or creating a personal visit planning guide. These foundational visits are a requirement for all new families and after the arrival of a newborn into the family. After the foundation visits are completed, families and home visitors have full range to design the visits with topics of that family's highest need and/or interest. Within the personal planning guide there is an opening section, parent child interaction, developmental-centered parenting, family wellbeing and closing section.

There are areas designed within the curriculum for parent educators to read, expand, and refresh on their knowledge in specific areas prior to home visits. Within the curriculum, there are links that connect home visitors to outside resources and further information to expand working knowledge in specific areas.

The parent–child interaction activity sheets are broken down into age specific activities and developmental domains. Each activity provides a list of items required for the activity—found in the section "What do we have?" The "How do we do it?" section provides a step-by-step list of how to complete each activity. "What's in it for us?" discusses what learning domains are being exercised, what is taking place during the activity and additional observations the caregiver can add. Caregivers keep the activity sheets and may recreate the activity at a later date with their child(ren).

Why Our Early Head Start Program Selected PAT

According to Sherry Waugh (2019), Director of the Child and Family Research Center at the University of Nevada, Reno, as a university affiliated program, UNR Early Head Start is committed to utilizing evidence-based program models that are supported by well-designed research. When it came time to select a curriculum for our home-based program, the Parents as Teachers program clearly emerged as a national leader in parent education. By providing materials that support and engage parents as well as ongoing professional development for home visitors, PAT continues to be our chosen curricular model.

Box A.1 One Parent's Experience at UNR's Early Head Start (EHS) Home Visit Program

My name is Marlen Yanes, mother of three children. Their ages are two, five, and seven years old. I have been in the program since June 2017, and I was referred to EHS by the Nevada Early Intervention Service (NEIS). I never had a doubt to sign up to EHS program because I heard great things about the program. Since the first time my home visitor came to my house, I sensed that I was going to learn much fun and interesting information to help my daughter to grow with her learning and development. I was not wrong; certainly it is amazing how little by little I have been learning important parenting strategies that I apply every day with my three children. It is very impressive how I spend time playing with my children now. Before my home visitor came to my house, I did not comprehend the importance of reading books to my children. Now I have reading routines with them. During the home visits, my husband sometimes joins us in the activities. He recognizes that our home visitor provides us with great support for parenting, and our two-year-old daughter has had a great improvement on every area. For example, in language my daughter is verbally expressing herself very well. She also has learned many songs and does really well in problem solving. My home visitor reminds me to follow up with physical checks, dental care, and to practice good eating habits and manners with my children. Every day my daughter talks about our home visitor; she remembers what we worked on during past home visits and tells her dad when he comes back from work. When I tell her that it is "home visit day", she waits for our home visitor to come while watching out by the window. My older children love her and they cannot wait to be off from school to play with us during the home visit. I cannot lie, even I feel happy when my home visitor comes. I never miss my visits; I like this time so much because we talk about many important topics including nutrition, family wellbeing, school involvement, and health.

I am very thankful for my EHS-HBO program; we work together to create positive educational and wellbeing outcomes for our children. I notice that parenting is not an easy responsibility. In my house we are very happy and feel fortunate to be in this program. I have attended the play groups that the program provides. It is amazing how they provide transportation for us to make it to these play groups. During these play groups, my daughter is learning to play and share the materials with other children in the program. I truly appreciate the EHS-HBO program for their amazing work. I thank my home visitor for her creativity, respect, patience, and her passion for working with families and their children. She helps me be a strong parent.

Funding Source

The Patient Protection and Affordable Care Act greatly expanded the availability of home visiting in the United States to create the Maternal and Infant Early Childhood Home Visiting Program (Michalopoulos, Lee, Duggan, Lundquist, Tso, Crowne, Burrell, Somer, Filene, & Knox, 2015). Maternal and Infant Early Childhood Home Visiting (MIECHV) is a funding source that provides either additional funding support to programs or MIECHV can act as a stand-alone funding for programs. MIECHV was designed to improve outcome for families in at risk communities that include property, crime, domestic violence, adverse birth outcomes such as premature birth and infant mortality, high school dropouts, substance abuse, unemployment, and child maltreatment (Michalopoulos et al., 2015). Originally MIECHV funding was created to fill funding gaps to programs, however after initial reviews the funding was given to programs as a stand-alone funding source.

MIECHV funding requires programs to collect and report data. The data collected by the programs will be used to focus on specific benchmarks for the following program year. This data is then reported to the Health Resources and Services Administration (HRSA) for approval for the program year benchmarks. Examples of data collected to create benchmarks may include but are not limited to literacy, breastfeeding, school readiness, domestic violence, and mental health. The data is collected by specific questionnaires that are approved by HRSA. The home visitor will collect the information by both conducting interviews and requests of the parent to complete questionnaires. The information collected can also be used to connect the families to community recourse and referrals. Once the home visitor has collected the data it is entered into a data base and the data is analyzed once a month by the MIECHV administration.

Another aspect of MIECHV funding is the support programs receive for quality improvement. It is expected the program self-evaluates and reflect on

392 *Appendix A*

areas that are needing improvement. Afterwards, the program is to conceptualize specific, measurable, achievable, relevant, and time bound (SMART) goals to improve on the program's specific needs. Once the program has successful improved the area of need, they are given opportunities to share the process and success with other home visiting programs in our state.

Working with Multiple Systems is Complex

Home visiting is a preventive method to support pregnant mothers and other parents by offering weekly home visits that promote positive parent child interactions, focus on global parenting concerns like attachment, discipline, health, nutrition, safety, sleep, routines and transitions, and breastfeeding. The family is also given an opportunity to focus on family well-being. Discussions of family wellbeing may include family strengths, setting goals, families overall health and wellbeing. The home visits give pregnant mothers and parents a safe place to learn about skill building, parenting skills, and learn how to be their child's first and most important teacher. The previously mentioned areas of family wellbeing strengthen the concept that leads parents to be self-sufficient families. Education and awareness of healthy living is strengthened by ongoing discussions, handouts, and hands-on activities. The goal of bringing information to families is not only to educate but to provide the tools necessary to stop a challenge from developing. Empowering families to participate in all aspects of the program (home visits, socialization, policy council, community events, etc.) supports the development of confidence of parenting skills.

The family system interacts with other systems in a bi-directional manner. For example, a family will sometimes find an EHS-HBO program via referrals from another agency. Sometimes since the get-go, or during the course of home visiting, families will find themselves in challenging situations that require extra support. EHS-HBO programs collaborate with agencies within the community to guide connections of services for families. Depending on the family's ability to connect with a resource, EHS-HBO will design a crisis intervention plan that helps the family meet their needs. This can look differently on a case-by-case basis. Some families are sufficient enough to follow up with a resource by simply receiving he information; others need support from their home visitor to make the initial call, set up transportation or brainstorm barriers that are preventing a connection with a resource. Home visitors support families in developing the skills needed to meet this crisis and any future challenges that a family might face.

There are barriers and challenges that families face that unfortunately cannot be solved within a day's work. Goal setting and network connections within the community provide the tools for families to prevent crisis' related to chronic challenges. The addition of awareness and link to resources increases the likelihood that a family will get out of poverty, increase school readiness skills, and improve education and employment opportunities.

This particular Early Head Start program provides support not only to the families in this program but to one another. Teamwork and support from each other are essential to the home visiting system. We provide daily opportunities for support, for encouragement, and for bouncing ideas off of one another. The program supervisor is an important part of the team that helps home visitors function smoothly and is available for support whenever needed. There are many moving parts to keeping the program running. This includes the first contact the families have with the administrative assistance to the enrollment specialist, nurse, and several others who are behind the scenes managing the financial aspects of the program's grants. There is constant change happening in the program to not only meet the changing federal requirements, but to run efficiently and provide the best services for the families we serve.

Wishes for the Future

There are days that we wish that we had the ability to wave a magic wand and have better outcomes for the families we serve; some examples that families need would consist of an endless list, but here are a few notable wishes. First, we wish there was funding available for any family that would like to receive home visiting services, it would also be beneficial if families had access to affordable housing within a reasonable time frame. We wish it would be easier to find high quality, affordable childcare up to kindergarten age that is available to families that wish to enter into the workforce. We wish for families to become more comfortable with establishing a support system with those around them. Also, for families to understand the life-long value of social–emotional development and relationship building with their children as infants and toddlers. Lastly, we wish for our families to have access to adequate mental health services in the community and that the stigma of receiving these services was removed.

As for the profession of home visiting, we home visitors wish we were seen as competent professionals and to be compensated accordingly. We wish that there are more training opportunities designed specifically for the home visiting profession available within communities. Developing strong community partnerships with agencies in the community where we can support one another and to be viewed as valued in the community is what we strive for. The list could continue on and on, but our values and beliefs stem from the wish to create huge changes in the lives of our families and the community as a whole. EHS-HBO works to create a community where families cannot only receive parenting support but are also able to connect with the greater community during play groups and events.

References

Administration for Children and Families (2015). *Head Start: Learning Outcomes Framework: Ages birth to five.* Retrieved from: https://eclkc.ohs.acf.hhs.gov/sites/default/files/pdf/elof-ohs-framework.pdf

Administration for Children and Families (2016). *Head Start Program Performance Standards.* Retrieved from: https://eclkc.ohs.acf.hhs.gov/policy/45-cfr-chap-xiii

Gallen, R.T., Ash, J., Smith, C., Franco, A., & Willford, J.A. (November 2016) How do I know that my supervision is reflective? *Identifying Factors and Validity of the Reflective Supervision Rating Scale.* Zero to Three. pp. 30–37. Retrieved from https://bluetoad.com/publication/?i=406117&p=3#{"page":2,"issue_id":406117}

Michalopoulos, C., Lee, H., Duggan, A., Lundquist, E., Tso, A., Crowne, S.S., Burrell, L., Somer, J., Filene, J.H., & Knox, V. (2015). *The mother and infant home visiting program evaluation: Early findings on the maternal, infant, and early childhood home visiting program.* OPRE Report 2015–11. Washington, DC: Office of Planning, Research and Evaluation, Administration for Children and Families, U.S. Department of Health and Human Services.

Office of the Assistant Secretary for Planning and Evaluation (2019). 2019 Poverty guidelines. Retrieved from https://aspe.hhs.gov/2019-poverty-guidelines

Parents as Teachers National Center (2015). *Parents as teachers foundational curriculum* (2015). Retrieved from https://parentsasteachers.org

Squires, J., Twombly, E., Bricker, D., & Potter, L. (2009). *ASQ-3 user's guide* (3rd ed.). Baltimore: Paul H. Brooks Publishing Co. Inc.

Waugh, S. (2019). Director of the Child and Family Research Center at the University of Nevada, Reno. *Selecting parents as teacher curriculum.* Interview.

Appendix C
FLE as an Enhancement to Parents as Teachers

The Head Start Performance Standards stipulate that all EHS-HBO programs must adopt a "research-based early childhood home-based curriculum" (ACF, 2016). Parents as Teachers (PAT) is implemented in many EHS-HBO programs. The 2016–2017 PAT Affiliate Performance Report (PAT National Center, 2017) indicates:

- Over 2016–2017, PAT had 1,273 affiliates, and 182 programs offered EHS services.
- PAT is found in other home visiting programs such as Nurse Family Partnership, Healthy Families America, and Early Intervention services.
- The majority of children served through PAT are birth to 36 months.
- Many parents that participate in PAT have low education, are low income, or have a child with a disability. A small minority are teen parents, immigrant families, or parents with a mental illness.

About PAT

The overarching message of PAT is that parents are their child's best and first teacher (Wagner & Clayton, 1999). This perspective guides the goals of the program, included content, and how the program is actually implemented. This places the parent at the center of the program. The goals of PAT are as follows:

1. Increase parent knowledge of early childhood development and improve parent practices.
2. Provide early detection of developmental delays and health issues.
3. Prevent child abuse and neglect.
4. Increase children's school readiness and success.

(PAT National Center, 2019)

PAT uses four program components to meet its goals: personal visits with parents and children, helping parents make group connections, connecting parents with resources, and screening child development (PAT National Center, 2019). The curriculum provides parenting and child development knowledge over the first three years of life. The logic of the curriculum is as follows:

Figure C.1 Logic Model for Parents as Teachers Curriculum
Source: Adapted from Wagner, Spiker, & Lynn, 2002

Using PAT, home visits are structured around (1) parent–child interactions (developmentally appropriate activities, child development knowledge, observe and encourage parent–child interactions, and reflection), 2) developmentally appropriate practices in the home, and (3) family wellbeing (cultivating protective factors and family activities) (PAT National Center, 2015). More information about PAT can be found at the Parents as Teachers National Center (www.parentsasteachers.org).

FLE Content Area Knowledge as Enhancement to PAT

Knowledge in the ten FLE content areas can serve as an enhancement to a curriculum such as PAT. While PAT provides the framework, content, and procedures home visitors actually follow in practice, knowledge in each content area gives the home visitor more depth and understanding of parenting and child development issues. Additionally, it widens the home visitor's lens to consider the effects of family and contextual processes. The table below lists the ten FLE content areas, and examples as to how knowledge in each area can serve as an enhancement to PAT, especially as implemented with the EHS-HBO population.

FLE Content Area	Examples of PAT Enhancement
Families and Individuals in Societal Contexts An understanding of families and their relationships to other institutions, such as the educational, governmental, religious, health care, and occupational institutions in society.	• Children are nested in a series of nested ecological systems, starting with the family microsystem. The family microsystem is nested within the community and larger culture. • Child development occurs as a result of the bidirectional interactions that

(Continued)

(Cont.)

FLE Content Area	Examples of PAT Enhancement
	occur within the home microsystem, and indirect interactions with larger systems (e.g., parent's access to community health care resources). • Parenting attitudes, values, and practices are influenced by, and interact with surrounding community and cultural contexts. • The dominant culture's attitudes, values, and practices influence all families within the society to some extent. (Wadsworth, Roy, & Watkins, 2015).
Internal Dynamics of Families An understanding of family strengths and weaknesses and how family members relate to each other.	• Parents are sources of support, protection and guidance for their children's development. • Parents and children function within family systems, which can experience stress that affects parenting practices, the home environment, and child development. • Family history and traditions affect parenting practices what parents view as important for their children's development. (Reinke & Walcheski, 2015)
Human Growth and Development across the Lifespan An understanding of the developmental changes (both typical and atypical) of individuals in families throughout the lifespan. Based on knowledge of physical, emotional, cognitive, social, moral, and personality aspects.	• Infancy and toddlerhood are important stages of development, each with their own developmental characteristics. • Expanded knowledge on typical development from prenatal to 36 months. • Signs of atypical development (delays or disabilities) • Child development occurs as a product of natural maturation (nature) and parenting/environmental experiences (nurture).

(Continued)

(Cont.)

FLE Content Area	Examples of PAT Enhancement
	• Parenting practices should be adjusted to meet the developmental age and individual characteristics of the child. (Leventhal, 2015)
Human Sexuality An understanding of the physiological, psychological, and social aspects of sexual development throughout the lifespan, so as to achieve healthy sexual adjustment.	• Human sexuality is an important part of healthy adult development. • The quality of parents' romantic relationships "spills over" to the parent-child relationship. • Education on contraception and pregnancy prevention for parents who do not want to have more children. (Darling & Howard, 2015)
Interpersonal Relationships An understanding of the development and maintenance of interpersonal relationships.	• Parent–infant attachment develops over the first few years of life. Attachment reflects the quality of the parent-child interactions (e.g., sensitivity, responsivity to infant's needs) • Parent–infant attachment "sets the stage" for the child's future interpersonal relationships and development. • Relationships between parents and children change as the child develops and gains new physical, cognitive, language, adaptive, and social skills. • Child development occurs within the context of relationships. (Glotzer, 2015)
Family Resource Management An understanding of the decisions individuals and families make about developing and allocating resources including time, money, material assets, energy, friends, neighbors, and space, to meet their goals.	• How parents allocate material and emotional resources to their child and the home learning environment is dictated by culture and values. • Parents living in poverty may have limited economic and material resources to meet their child's basic needs. • The availability and accessibility of resources impacts child development

(Continued)

(Cont.)

FLE Content Area	Examples of PAT Enhancement
	and parents' abilities to parent effectively. (Moore & Asay, 2015)
Parent Education and Guidance An understanding of how parents teach, guide and influence children and adolescents as well as the changing nature, dynamics and needs of the parent/child relationship across the lifespan.	• Parenting values, attitudes and beliefs are influenced by culture. • Coaching, scaffolding, modeling, and reflective practices help parents learn new ways of interacting with their children and setting up the home learning environment. • Parenting education must meet the needs of families from different structures, cultures, and backgrounds. (Jacobson, 2015)

Family Law and Public Policy An understanding of legal issues, policies, and laws influencing the wellbeing of families.	• Local, state, and federal laws and policies have implications for
	
	  • Child health and development.
	  • Access to identification and intervention services for indivi-duals with disabilities.
	  • Parents' abilities to parent effec-tively and provide necessary materials/resources in their home to promote child development.
	
	• Advocate for family-centered laws and policies
	(Bogenschneider, 2015)

Professional Ethics and Practice An understanding of the character and quality of human social conduct, and the ability to critically examine ethical questions and issues as they relate to professional practice	• Ethical decision-making about rela-tionships with parents and children. • Ethical practices for promoting healthy parent–child interactions and healthy child development • Implement relational ethics in which practices are guided by (and decisions are made) the development of a caring and respectful relationships with parents and children. (Palm, 2015)

(Continued)

400 *Appendix C*

(Cont.)

FLE Content Area	Examples of PAT Enhancement
Family Life Education Methodology An understanding of the general philosophy and broad principles of family life education in conjunction with the ability to plan, implement, and evaluate such educational programs.	• Conduct needs assessments • Design programs/materials that meet the specific needs of the EHS-HBO population • Develop cultural competence when working with families. • Develop goals and specific objectives for parents and children. (Covey, 2015)

Note. CFLE Content Areas reprinted with permission from the National Council on Family Relations

References

Administration for Children and Families (ACF). (2016). *Head Start Performance Standards 45 CFR Chapter XIII September 2016.* U.S. Department of Health and Human Services.

Bogenschneider, K. (2015). Family law and public policy. In M. J. Walcheski, & J. S. Reinke (Eds.), *Family life education: The practice of family science* (pp. 223–234). Minneapolis, MN: National Council on Family Relations.

Covey, M. (2015). Family life education methodology. In M. J. Walcheski, & J. S. Reinke (Eds.), *Family life education: The practice of family science* (pp. 243–251). Minneapolis, MN: National Council on Family Relations.

Darling, C. A., & Howard, S. (2015). Human sexuality across the lifespan. In M. J. Walcheski, & J. S. Reinke (Eds.), *Family life education: The practice of family science* (pp. 177–188). Minneapolis, MN: National Council on Family Relations.

Glotzer, R. (2015). Interpersonal relationships. In M. J. Walcheski, & J. S. Reinke (Eds.), *Family life education: The practice of family science* (pp. 189–202). Minneapolis, MN: National Council on Family Relations

Jacobson, A. L. (2015). Parenting education and guidance. In M. J. Walcheski, & J. S. Reinke (Eds.), *Family life education: The practice of family science* (pp. 213–222). Minneapolis, MN: National Council on Family Relations.

Leventhal, J. (2015). Human growth and development across the lifespan. In M. J. Walcheski, & J. S. Reinke (Eds.), *Family life education: The practice of family science* (pp. 167–176). Minneapolis, MN: National Council on Family Relations.

Moore, T. J., & Asay, S. M. (2015). Family resource management. In M. J. Walcheski, & J. S. Reinke (Eds.), *Family life education: The practice of family science* (pp. 205–212). Minneapolis, MN: National Council on Family Relations.

Palm, G. F. (2015). Professional ethics and practice. In M. J. Walcheski, & J. S. Reinke (Eds.), *Family life education: The practice of family science* (pp. 235–241). Minneapolis, MN: National Council on Family Relations.

Parents as Teachers (PAT) National Center. (2015). *Foundational curriculum*. St. Louis, MI: Parents as Teachers National Center, Inc.

Parents as Teachers (PAT) National Center. (2017). *2016–2017 affiliate performance report, summary*. Retrieved from https://static1.squarespace.com/static/56be46a6b6aa60db b45e41a5/t/5a37eca0085229e36d170e8e/1513614498107/APR_2pgr_2016-2017.pdf

Parents as Teachers (PAT) National Center. (2019). *Evidence-based model*. Retrieved from https://parentsasteachers.org/evidence-based-model.

Reinke, J. S., & Walcheski, M. J. (2015). Internal dynamics of families. In M. J. Walcheski, & J. S. Reinke (Eds.), *Family life education: The practice of family science* (pp. 157–166). Minneapolis, MN: National Council on Family Relations.

Wadsworth, S. M. M., Roy, K. M., & Watkins, N. (2015). Families and individuals in societal contexts. In M. J. Walcheski & J. S. Reinke (Eds.), *Family life education: The practice of family science* (pp. 147–155). Minneapolis, MN: National Council on Family Relations.

Wagner, M. M., & Clayton, S. L. (1999). The Parents as Teachers program: Results from two demonstrations. *The Future of Children*, 9, 91–115.

Wagner, M., Spiker, D., & Linn, M. I. (2002). The effectiveness of the Parents as Teachers program with low-income parents and children. *Topics in Early Childhood Special Education*, 22(2), 67–81.

Appendix D

How to Become Certified in Family Life Education

National Council on Family Relations

Family Life Education is the practice of equipping and empowering family members to develop knowledge and skills that enhance wellbeing and strengthen interpersonal relationships through an educational, preventive, and strengths-based approach. Family Life Educators can obtain the Certified Family Life Educator (CFLE) credential through the National Council on Family Relations (NCFR). The CFLE credential was established and introduced in 1985 in order to establish standards of practice and increase recognition of Family Life Education. The CFLE credential is the nationally recognized standard in Family Life Education and validates a professional's experience and knowledge as a Family Life Educator (National Council on Family Relations, 2019b).

There are many areas and contexts in which Certified Family Life Educators can work, including home visiting, program development, advocacy, community education, academic teaching, administration, health services, journalism, ministry, research, social work, human services, and so much more. In addition to the areas where Certified Family Life Educators work, survey results from the National Council on Family Relations Certified Family Life Educator 2014 job analysis report of CFLEs show that CFLEs work in a variety of organizational sectors including government entities, for-profits, and nonprofits (National Council on Family Relations, 2014). There are additionally CFLEs who are self-employed and own their own business. Results from the survey further demonstrate that CFLEs mainly focus on prevention and/or education, but some also focus on intervention or other methods. CFLEs can work one-on-one with individuals or present to large groups. There are CFLEs in every state and all over the world who work in a variety of settings. What unites them is the Certified Family Life Educator credential that verifies that they meet a nationally recognized standard for the practice of Family Life Education. Following are directions and guidelines for how to become a CFLE.

There are two steps to becoming a Certified Family Life Educator: demonstrating knowledge in the ten Family Life Education content areas and demonstrating work experience in Family Life Education. The minimum requirement for all Certified Family Life Educator applicants is a bachelor's degree from a regionally accredited college or university. All applicants who earned a degree from outside of the United States must provide evidence of degree equivalency by an official credential evaluation service.

Provisional Certification

The first level of this credential is provisional certification, which is for applicants who can demonstrate knowledge in the ten content areas of Family Life Education. This is the best option for applicants who are ready to become certified, but do not have enough work experience in Family Life Education for full certification.

There are many reasons someone may want to be provisionally certified rather than applying for the full certification. Examples include students who have just graduated, people who are making a career change, or people who have no or only a partial amount of work experience in Family Life Education. Provisional Certification also provides a helpful edge when interviewing for Family Life Education jobs.

There are two ways for applicants to demonstrate they have knowledge in Family Life Education: they can graduate from a CFLE-approved program or they can take the CFLE exam. Both processes will be described in detail in the following paragraphs.

CFLE-Approved Program Application

One of the two ways to demonstrate knowledge in Family Life Education is to graduate from a CFLE- approved program. This is an excellent option for anyone who is currently looking to attend a college or university relating to Family Science or for students who have already graduated from a CFLE-approved program There are over 125 colleges and universities located throughout the United States that offer online and/or on-campus CFLE-approved programs. Program degree levels include Bachelor of Arts, Bachelor of Science, master's, and doctoral programs that offer a variety of majors, including but not limited to Family Science, Family Life Education, human development, and many more. In order to become CFLE-approved, these programs worked closely with NCFR to review their curricula to ensure that their offered courses meet the standards of each of the ten content areas. In addition to completion of coursework in each of the ten content areas, there is also a Family Life Education internship or practicum requirement that an applicant must complete while in school. The end result of this curriculum review is a checklist unique to each school and organized by content areas that shows which course(s) a student must take in order to become approved.

Applicants who wish to apply though the CFLE-approved program application must do so within two years of graduation to ensure that their coursework is current. The application itself consists of submitting some basic demographic information and paying an application fee. Applicants must also sign the CFLE Code of Professional Ethics, which is a set of ethical guidelines that all CFLEs are expected to follow as a guide during their Family Life Education work. In addition, applicants must also submit an official transcript demonstrating successful coursework completion. All coursework must be completed with a C– or better. In addition to an application form, applicants must fill out the CFLE-approved program checklist from their school to ensure all the courses have been completed. Another important caveat is that the oldest course on the checklist needs to have been completed no more than seven years prior to the student's graduation date. It is important to note that most checklists include courses that may not be required for the major. It is advised that students carefully look over the checklist as they complete their coursework to ensure that they are meeting all the requirements to become certified.

A student is allowed two substitute courses on the CFLE-approved program checklist. For a substitute course to be approved, it must cover content similar to content from the course that is missing. The NCFR website offers greater detail of required material that must be covered for each content area. If the substitute course was taken at another college or university, a student must submit a syllabus from the year and semester the course was taken. This can be reviewed and approved at the NCFR office before the student takes the course or before the person applies. If the applicant did not complete the internship or practicum listed on the checklist, but has relevant work experience, they can substitute that work experience for the internship or practicum by submitting a work experience summary form and employer assessment and verification form. This paperwork can be obtained by contacting the NCFR office directly. Please see the NCFR contact information listed in the last paragraph of this appendix.

CFLE Exam Application

Another method to demonstrate knowledge in Family Life Education is to take the CFLE exam. This is an excellent option for anyone who did not graduate from a CFLE-approved program but has at least a bachelor's degree from an accredited institution. This is also a great option for applicants who did graduate from a CFLE-approved program but did not apply within two years of their graduation date or did not complete all the courses on the checklist.

The CFLE exam consists of 150 multiple choice questions covering all ten content areas. The ten content areas are covered almost equally, but an applicant can see a breakdown of the percentage of test questions pertaining to each content area on the NCFR website. The exam is offered during testing windows at computer- based testing sites located throughout the United States and the world. The exam is also offered onsite at the NCFR Annual Conference, which is usually held in November of each year. The applicant is responsible for preparing to take the exam, but NCFR does offer a variety of study materials on its website, including suggested readings, sample study guides, sample test questions, and instructions for how to join an exam study group.

Appendix D 405

The exam application consists of submitting basic demographic information, paying an application fee, and signing the CFLE Code of Professional Ethics. The applicant must also submit an official transcript to show that they graduated with the minimum of a bachelor's degree from a regionally accredited university or college.

Full Certification

Applicants who have both knowledge and work experience in Family Life Education are eligible for full certification. For full certification, applicants must demonstrate they have knowledge in Family Life Education by using one of the two methods listed in the paragraphs above—by applying through the CFLE-approved program process or by taking the CFLE exam—and then also by documenting work experience in Family Life Education. As has been discussed, the practice of Family Life Education includes a variety of activities. Those eligible to count as Family Life Education work experience for the purpose of the CFLE credential include but are not limited to: program coordination/administration; program evaluation; needs assessments; marketing of Family Life Education materials and programs; curriculum or resource development; publications; presentations; group facilitation; or community collaboration.

There is a variety of criteria used when assessing relevant Family Life Education work experience. For one, the work must be related to at least one or more of the ten Family Life Education content areas. The work must also be preventive and educational in nature rather than interventive or therapeutic. Additionally, the work must focus on normal family stressors rather than current trauma. In relation to this, the Family Life Educator must work to develop skills and abilities. The work should be intentional; there should be some sort of planned curriculum, program, or lesson involved. Also, the work experience must consider the family as a whole, even if the Certified Family Life Educator is working only with an individual. Other items to note are that the majority of the work should have been performed within the past five years. Unpaid work experience, including volunteering and internships, can be included in work experience. Work earned before graduation may also be considered but must be in addition to post-graduation work.

The application process for full certification requires the applicant to submit a work experience review fee and a summary of their Family Life Education work experience, including information such as job title, organization name, Family Life Education activity description, employment dates, content areas addressed, and total number of hours. The number of work experience hours needed depends on the level and type of degree. Applicants with a doctoral or master's family degree must earn 1,600 hours; applicants with a bachelor's family degree must earn 3,200 hours; and applicants of any degree level with any other major must

406 Appendix D

Table AD.1 Requirements for full certification

Requirements for full certification	Bachelor's degree	Master's or Ph.D.
Family degree	3,200 hours work experience	1,600 hours work experience
Non-family degree	4,800 hours work experience for bachelor's, master's, or Ph.D.	

Note: National Council on Family Relations, 2019a

earn 4,800 hours (Please see Table AD.1 below, National Council on Family Relations, 2019). Another item needed is examples of work experience in Family Life Education, including but not limited to course outlines/syllabi, brochures, handouts, worksheets, table of contents for curriculum, publications, etc. Applicants are requested to send one to three examples of work experience per job listed.

The last item needed in order to apply for full certification is an employer assessment and verification form completed by an employer, supervisor, or colleague. If the applicant is self-employed, they can have an employee or client fill out the verification. The employer verification confirms that the information submitted about the applicant's job title, number of hours worked, and employment dates is accurate. In addition, the employer is asked to rate an applicant's knowledge in the ten content areas and assess a variety of skills, including ethical decision-making, problem-solving, communication, and more. While the preference is to have all work experience verified by an employer or set of employers, applicants must verify at minimum 50% of total work experience with an employer, or with a set of employers if the applicant has had multiple jobs.

Maintaining the CFLE credential

It is important to note that there are requirements for maintaining this certification. Every year, there is an annual maintenance fee that covers the costs of the CFLE newsletter *Network*, CFLE discussion group, and general maintenance of the CFLE program. In addition, provisional CFLEs must upgrade to full certification once they earn sufficient work experience in Family Life Education. People who are provisionally certified must upgrade within five years of original approval.

CFLEs with full certification must recertify every five years to show that they are staying current in the field. In order to recertify, CFLEs must submit 100 hours of continuing education credit in relevant academic preparation, work experience, and/or professional development.

Benefits of Becoming a CFLE

It is clear that time and effort is needed to become a Certified Family Life Educator. Fortunately, there are many benefits to the credential, including increasing one's credibility as a Family Life Educator. Having this certification means one can market to employers, clients, and other stakeholders that they meet a nationally recognized standard in Family Life Education. Having this credential also helps validate one's education and experience. In addition, all CFLEs have access to a CFLE discussion group and CFLE directory, which allow CFLEs to share resources, ask important questions about the practice of Family Life Education, network, and so much more. There are also a variety of other social media platforms that CFLEs can use to stay connected. In addition to the many networking opportunities, there are also leadership positions for CFLEs, including serving as chair of the CFLE Advisory Board and CFLE Exam Committee. The quarterly newsletter, *Network*, keeps CFLEs updated on research, provides resources CFLEs can use, and demonstrates how others with the certification are making a difference in their communities.

Certified Family Life Educators make an important contribution to society by equipping and empowering families to reach their full potential. For more information on how to become a CFLE, please visit our website at ncfr.org/cfle.

References

National Council on Family Relations (2014). *National Council on Family Relations Certified Family Life Educator 2014 job analysis report*. Unpublished job analysis report.

National Council on Family Relations (2019a). *Requirements for full certification* [Table]. Retrieved from https://www.ncfr.org/cfle-certification/become-certified/work-experience-full-certification

National Council on Family Relations (2019b). *What is family life education?* Retrieved from https://www.ncfr.org/cfle-certification/what-family-life-education

Index

Page numbers in **bold** refer to figures and *italics* refer to tables.

ABC-X model 253, 258–259, 280, 287
academic outcomes 347
academic program review, NCFR 4
Achieve OnDemand 39, 349, 355–356
action plans 34
adaptive culture 84, 86, 280, 286, 288
Addams, J. 1
addiction issues 217
Administration for Children and
  Families 300
adolescence 319–320, 322–323, 340;
  risk-taking 16
adolescent mothers 325, 327
adult competencies, supporting 318–340; attitudes
  336–337; coaching and collaborating to support
  child development 333–334, 335, 336–337; coaching
  and collaborating t to support parent efficacy and
  self-sufficiency 334, 337; FLE content areas 319; FLE
  methodology 329–331, *331*, 336–337; human
  growth and development 322–325, *324*, 332–334;
  knowledge 319–331, *324*, *327*, *329*, *331*; mental
  health 321–322; parenting 320–321; parenting
  education and guidance 325–326, *327*; skills
  331–336; societal contexts 327–328, *329*, 335–336
adult development 302, 305–306
adulthood 305–306
adult learning 329–330, 336–337
Adverse Childhood Experiences 33, 164
advocacy 287, 310
African Americans: children 222; families 274, 275; low-
  income group mothers 34; teen birth rate 320
agency preparation 55–56
Ages and Stages Questionnaire 192–193,
  298, 384
aggression 105
Ainsworth, M. 105
Allen, K. 9, 350
American Academy of Pediatrics 162
American Heart Association 166
andragogy 302

anger management 146
ARCH National Respite Network and Resource
  Center 274
Arcus, M. 5, 232
Asay, S. M. 33, 247
assessment 18, 34, 187, 188, 209; application 196; basics
  188–190; child development 192–193; FLE content
  areas 188; FLE methodology 197–198; internal
  dynamics of families 199–200; methods 190–191;
  needs 197, 199; and observation 189; parent–child
  interactions 191, 199; of parenting 190–192;
  parenting education and guidance 194–195;
  practices 197; process 189; reliability 189; tools 190;
  use 190; validity 189
attachment 84–85, 112–113, *113*, 216; disorganized
  105, 108, 322; importance of 105; insecure 105, 225,
  322; issues 108; role 107–108; secure 104–105,
  108, 225
attachment bond, the 105
attachment relationships 20, 216, 225
attachment theory 84
attitudes 39; diversity and inclusion 288–289; family
  partnerships 259; health and safety 181; infant/
  toddler behavior 231–232; observation 206–207;
  professionalism 312–313; reflective practice 82,
  96-97; relationship building 120–121; supporting
  adult competencies 336–337; supporting
  development and learning 148–149
authoritarian parenting 216
authoritative parenting 216

balance 58
Bandura, A. 321, 326
Baumrind, D. 216
bed sharing 173
behavior change, and parenting 320–321
behaviors 83
being with families 58, 172, 207, 244
beliefs 83
Best Practices in Online FLE 8–9

Index 409

bias 188–189
bidirectional 106, 109, 121
bioecological model 38, 170
birth defects 160
Black land grant colleges 2
Bogenschneider, K. 251, 277–278
Bowlby, John 104
brain, the 108, 160
breastfeeding 161, 168, 175
Bredehoft, D. J. 3
Brigance Infant and Toddler Screen 298
Bronfenbrenner, U. 38, 170
Brophy-Herb, H. 89
Burgess, E. 2
burnout 200–201, 301

Canada 2
caregiving practices 193
caregiving responses 225
care, relationship-based 58
cars 164
Cassidy, D. 7, 298, 349
CDA Home Visitor Competencies 121–122, 149–152, 179, 207–208, 232–234, 260, 289–290, 310–311, 338–339
CDA Subject Areas and Competency Standards 97–99
center-based childcare 17
Center for the Study of Social Policy 252
certification 3–4, 402–407; approved program application 403–404; benefits of 407; coursework 404; employer assessment and verification 406; exam application 404–405; full 405–406, *406*; internship 403; maintaining 406; minimum application requirement 402; provisional 403; substitute courses 404; work experience 405
Certified Family Life Educators 2, 3–4, 29, 34, 40, 50, 347; application process 56; approved program application 403–404; benefits of certification 407; certification pathway 54–55, 56; certification route 402–407; code of ethics 4, 148, 259, 403; content knowledge 38–40; contribution 407; employer assessment and verification 406; exam application 404–405; full certification 405–406, *406*; internship 403; maintaining certification 406; minimum application requirement 402; provisional certification 403; role 9; and technology 9; value of 60; work contexts 402; work experience 405
certified lactation educators 161
change, theories of 34, 34–35, 43
Chicago, Hull House 1
child abuse 163
Child and Adult Care Food Program 166
child autonomy 232
Childbirth and Postpartum Professional Association 161

child-centered approach 49–65; paradigm shift to FLE 54–56
child cognitive development 20
child development 23, 32, 325; assessment 192–193; cognitive 327; context 133–134, 190; domains 129, 131; family role 133–134; individual differences 134; individuality in 131–132; infant/toddler 215–216; outcomes 33; progression 220; protective factors 33; risk factors 33; role of attachment 107–108; socio-ecological influences 175–176; *see also* supporting development and learning
Child Development Associate 19
child development observations 387
child-home visitor interactions 196
childhood obesity 161
child maltreatment 163, 199–200
child neglect 163
child/parent rights, disability 270–271
Child Protection Services 251–252
Child Protective Services 41–42, 164, 165–166
children: approaches to learning 197; internal working mode 105; nutritional requirements 134–135
Children's Health Insurance Program 251
Children, Youth and Families at Risk (CYFAR) program 3
Child Welfare Information Gateway 199–200
Christie, T. 301
chronic problems 32–33
circle of security 105, 110, 225
Clarke, L. S. 276
coaching 19, 33, 333–334, 349–350, 355; to support child development 335, 336–337; to support parent efficacy and self-sufficiency 334, 337
COAL 87
code of ethics 4, 41, 97, 121, 148, 206, 259, 300–301, 304, 305, 309, 337, 403
coercion 119
coercive cycles of interaction 112–113
cognitive development 327
Coker, A.L. 192
collaboration 22, 29, 33, 59, 85, 107, 163, 166, 194, 224, 232, 242–243, 309, 325–326, 382, 392
collaborative relationships 82, 83, 85, 90, 95, 100
collectivism 247, 273
communicable diseases 163
communication 383
communication processes 120, 146, 288; families 96
communication skills 224
community programs 142
community resources 141–142, 149, 170
community support 60, 133, 138
competencies 97–99, 348–349
competency 82

410 Index

comprehensive approach 384
conceptualization 348
conferences 301
confidence-building 58
confidentiality 41, 278, 300–301, 309
confirmation bias 189
conflict-management 120
conflict management 120, 146, 288
Conger, R. D. 140
consent 278
consumer rights 256
contact information 163
content 38–40
content delivery 31
context 37–38
contextual risks 37–38
contextual theories 38
contraception 244, 245
Cooperative Extension Service 2
co-parenting relationship 106–107, 113
coping strategies, unhealthy 119, 231
co-sleeping 173
cost-benefit analysis 297
Covey, M. 196, 197
cribs 162, 271
Cribs for Kids 162
critical reflection 198
critical thinking 198
cultural competence 35–37, 277, 308
cultural differences 144, 281
cultural discontinuity 271, 282, 288
cultural influences 148, 176, 222–223, 247, 284
cultural respect 289
cultural responsiveness 36–37
cultural sensitivity 271–272
cultural values 83, 110–111, 118, 247, 268
culture 35–37, 131, 273; definition 267–268; and family
    experiences 267–268
cycle of stigma 328

Darling, C. A. 7, 35–37, 50, 223, 245, 298
decision-making 189, 244, 256, 283; ethical 304
deficit approach 36
DeFrain, J. 33
Delphi Method 349
Demick, J. 324
demographics 177, 285
depression 321–322, 324–325, 326, 327, 330
Derman-Sparks, L. 89, 267, 268, 271
DeVellis, R. F. 348
developmental delay 269, 271
developmentally appropriate 203, 219; books 150;
    discipline 220, 228; guidance 234, 235; learning
    experiences 151; parents 191
developmental niche 131, 246, 255, 268
developmental outcomes 129
developmental progressions 385

developmental screenings 384
developmental specialists 112
developmental transitions 332
development and learning, supporting: see
    supporting development and learning
development-centered parenting 347
dialogue, ongoing 36–37
disability 269–270, 283–284; child/parent rights
    270–271; stressors 280
discipline 219, 222, 224, 280–281
discrimination 268
disorganized attachment 105, 108, 322
distal systems 196
diversity and inclusion 266–292; aspects 266; attitudes
    288–289; child/parent rights 270–271; culture and
    family experiences 267–268; education 275–276;
    family law and public policy 269–270, 277–279,
    279, 286–287; family resource management
    273–274, 274, 282–283; FLE Content Areas
    267; FLE methodology 277, 277, 285–286;
    internal dynamics of families 280, 281, 287–288;
    knowledge 267–280, 272, 274, 276, 277, 279, 281;
    least restrictive environment 271; national
    resources 273–274; parenting education and
    guidance 271–272, 272; sensitivity to 178;
    skills 281–288; societal contexts 274–276, 276,
    284–285
divorce rate 2
Doherty, W. J. 5–6, 7
domains of family practice model 6–7
domestic violence 29
dominant culture 84, 271, 282
Donnellan, M. B. 140
dual language learners 268, 272
Duncan, S. F. 250

early adulthood 320, 323, 340
Early Childhood Technical Assistance Center 273–274
Early Head Start 17, 49; holistic approach
    xiv–xv; mission 389; parental focus 30
Early Head Start Family and Child Experiences
    Study 243
Early Head Start Family and Child Experiences
    Survey 22
Early Head Start–Home-Based Option xiv, 49–65;
    context 51; data analysis 52–53; Empowerment and
    Intentionality 57–60, 63–64; FLE approach 50; focus
    group 51–52; Knowledge and Experience in
    Developmental Science and Family Science 56–57;
    limitations 64; major themes 53; paradigm shift to
    FLE 54–56; participants 51, 53–54; performance
    standards 50; philosophy 382; procedure 51–52;
    program philosophy 51; reflection 52; Relationships
    to Previous Literature 63–64; rigor of study 52;
    strengths 64
Early Head Start Home Visiting 15–24; background
    16–19; effectiveness 19–23; evidence-based

Index 411

model 16; and FLE 29–35; focus 17–18; principle 17; statistical effects 21; theoretical assumptions 30

Early Head Start Research and Evaluation Project 19–20

Early intervention services 270, 278–279

ecological perspective 110, 195–196

ecological systems framework 34

ecological systems theory 34, 43, 133–134, 137, 139, 147, 251, 287

economic disadvantage 220

education 31–32, 275–276

educational experiences 308, 354

educational requirements, home visitors 388

Edwards, J. O. 89, 267, 268, 271

effectiveness 19–23

electronic tablets 166

eligibility requirements 243, 382

emerging adulthood 323

emotional environment 164

emotional health 171

emotion development 137

emotion regulation 217

emotions 132

empowerment 31, 57–60, 63–64, 380, 392; preschool parents 77–78, **77**

engagement 21, 32, 107, 249–250, 302, 346

ethical decision-making 207, 304

ethical issues 41–42, 181

ethical obligation 235

ethics 41, 88–90, *90*, 94, 111–112, *112*, 148, 248–249, *249*, 256–257, 309, 399; principles 4; principles approach 248; professionalism 304–305, *305*; relational 181, 248; virtue 248

ethnicity 222–223

everyday learning opportunities 23

evidence 189, 297–298

evidence-based 16, 23, 31, 34, 50, 169, 285, 390

evidence-based information 308

evidence-based model 296, 298

evidence-based practice 297–298, 307, 357

evidence-based programming 297–298

evidence-based programs 303, 308

evidence-informed 356

exam application 404–405

experiential learning 137

Exposure to Adverse Childhood Experiences 164

extension programs 2

Facilitating Attuned Interactions 348

families: African American 274, 275; being with 58, 172, 207, 244; child development role 133–134; characteristics 38; cohesion 224; communication processes 96; community support 138; context 38; culture 273; ecological perspective 110; efficacy 5–6; empowerment 380, 392; engagement 107; home visitor relationships 107; individualistic orientation

247; interaction patterns 216–217; internal dynamics 90–91, *92*, 95–96, 113–114, *114*, 119–120, 139–140, *140*, 146–147, 173, *174*, 178–179, 199–201, *201*, 205–206, 223–224, *224*, 229–230, 252–253, *253–254*, 258–259, 280, *281*, 287–288, 397; learning within 131; Mexican American 274–275; needs 5–6; partnering with 240–261; resource management 247, *248*, 255–256, 273–274, *274*, 282–283, 398–399; respect for 289; responsiveness 107; shared histories 274; societal contexts 93–94, 110–111, *111*, 116–117, 202–203, 274–276, *276*, 284–285, 327–328, *329*, 335–336; stressors 96, 139–140; systems perspective 96; values 250; value systems 121

families of color 268, 280

family case management 6, 9, 50, 70–71, **71**

family-centered approach 29, 49

family-centered services, need for xv

family characteristics 38

family cohesion 224

Family Educational Rights and Privacy Act 278

family experiences 243–244, 267–268

Family impact lens 278, *279*, 286

family interaction patterns 216–217

family investment model 140

family involvement, levels of 5–6

family law 8, 41, 251–252, *252*, 258, 277–279, *280*, 286–287, 306–307, *307*, 310

family life coaching 9, 350

Family Life Education 29–43, 70, 357; approach to home visiting 49–65, *53–54*, *60–62*, 346–351, 379; best practices 7, 34, 38; code of ethics 121, 206; content 38–40; content areas 7, 38–39; content knowledge 367–368, *367–368*; context 37–38; culture 35–37; current study 356–357; definition 6; delivery systems xiv; and EHS Home Visiting 29–35; expansion and professionalization 3–10; focus 7, 347; foundations 30–35; historical perspective 1–10; home visiting model 9–10; as metaframework 348; online learning experiences 8–9; operational components 35–42; overview 378; PAT enhancement 395–400; practice 40–42; principles of 4–5, 348, 351; purpose 50; resistance to 366; strengths-based approach 22, 33–34; theoretical assumptions 30; topics 3; training 354–360, *361–362*, 363–364, *363–364*, **365**, 366–368, *367–368*, *369–370*, 371–373; virtues 312–313

Family Life Educators xiv: certification 402–407

Family Life Educators Code of Ethics 304, 305

family of origin 7, 92, 320, 332

family of procreation 320, 332

family participation 243; human sexuality 244–245, *245*

family partnerships: attitudes 259; family law and public policy 251–252, *252*, 258; family resource management 247, *248*, 255–256; FLE content areas 241; FLE methodology 249–250, *250–251*, 257–258;

412 *Index*

human sexuality 254; importance of 241–243; internal dynamics of families 252–253, *253–254*, 258–259; involvement 241–242; knowledge 241–252, *245, 246, 248, 249, 250–251, 252, 253–254*; parenting education and guidance 246, *246*, 255; professional ethics and practice 248–249, *249*, 256–257; skills 254–259; *see also* relationship building

family planning 244
family practice 7
family practice model 9
family relationships 106–107
family resource management 247, *248*, 255–256, 273–274, *274*, 282–283, 398–399
family science 29
family sociology 1–2
family strengths, building on 22
family stress model 140, 321
family system 106–107, 392; issues 217
family systems theory 34, 35, 43, 133–134, 139, 147, 217, 223–224
family therapy 6, 9, 50, 70–71, 111–112
family violence 199–200
family wellbeing 347, 392
father involvement 21
father-toddler play 21
fatigue 189
Federal poverty level 17
federal supports 133
feedback 219, 302, 348, 355
fidelity 18, 34, 39, 50, 145, 204, 298, 303, 307, 308, 348
first aid 166
first language 276
Fleming, W. M. 7
flexibility 18, 23, 49
food assistance programs 133
food insecurity 133, 140
formal reasoning 322–323
foundational visits 169, 389
foundations: education 31–32; prevention 32–33; strengths-based approach 33–34
Fragile Families and Child Wellbeing Study 222
Framework for Best Practices in Family Life Education 7–8, 356
Framework for Lifespan Family Life Education (Bredehoft) 3, 5, 7
free appropriate public education 269, 275
full certification 405–406, *406*
funding xv, 382, 391–392

García Coll, C. G. 84, 86, 268, 280
Gartrell, D. 216
gender identities 244–245
Getting Ready intervention 23
ghosts in the nursery 84
goals 7, 34, 41, 75, 76, 82, 196–197, 240, 321

goal setting 58
Goddard, H. W. 250
Goldberg, J. 170
Goldstein, Sidney E. 2
goodness-of-fit 135
governance 300
grandparents 330
Guttmacher Institute 244

Hartzell, M. 85, 86, 87
Head Start Act 187, 240
Head Start Early Learning Outcomes Framework: Ages Birth to Five 196–197, 298, 357, 384–386
Head Start Program Performance Standards 17–19, 22, 23, 50, 189–190, *190*, 197, 249, 300, 306, 350, 386
Head Start Project 16
Head Start Reauthorization Act, 1994 17
health and safety 159–182; attitudes 181; basics and background 160–161; breastfeeding 161, 168, 175; care of sick infant/child 163; contact information 163; first aid 166; FLE content areas 159–160, 167; FLE methodology 172–173, *173*, 177–178; health education 166; healthy practices 165–166; home 164–166; household safety 164–165; human growth and development 167–168, *168*, 174–176; human sexuality 171, *171–172*, 177; internal dynamics of families 173, *174*, 178–179; knowledge 160–173, *168, 169, 170–171, 171–172, 173, 174*; parenting education and guidance 168–169, *169*, 176; skills 174–180; sleep 162–163, 168; societal contexts 170, *170–171*, 176–177; socio-ecological influences 175–176
health care 251, 278
Health Insurance Portability and Accountability Act 278
Health Resources and Services Administration 391
Healthy Families America 16, 299
healthy parenting 86, 92, 115, 143, 176, 188, 202, 227, 255, 272, 281, 332, 333–334
helping relationship 107, 166, 242
higher education 348–349
Hispanics 320
Holland, S. 194, 195
home-based program design 18
home economics 1–2
Home Instruction for Parents of Preschool Youngsters 299
home language support 268, 280–281, 283, 284, 285, 287
home learning environments 17, 136
home life, value of 2
home microsystem 131
home safety: first aid 166; health education 166; healthy practices 165–166; household safety 164–165
Home Visiting Evidence of Effectiveness database 16, 23, 299
Home Visiting Rating Scales 41, 50, 72–74

Index   413

home visitor–parent relationships 325
Home Visitor Rating Scales—Adapted and Extended to Excellence 298
home visitors 30; coaching 349–350; competencies 97–99; content knowledge 38–40; culturally responsive 36–37; data entry 387; educational backgrounds 49; educational experiences 354; educational requirements 388; education levels 19; education role 31–32; emotional state 387–388; ethical obligation 235; expectations of 31; family relationships 107; fidelity 34; goals 82; healthy practices 165–166; in-service training 349; job titles 350; paperwork 387; perspectives 386–388; preparation 347; pre-service training 348–349; prevention role 32–33; professionalization 371; qualifications 22–23; quality of practice 41–42; responsibility 197–198; role 9, 350; roles 59; salary 301; social identities 277; strengths-based approach 33–34; training 18
Home Visit Rating Scale – Adapted and Extended to Excellence 107
Home Visit Rating Scales 325
home visits and visiting 15–24, 306–307; approaches 15; and context 37–38; and culture 36–37; data entry 387; effective 72; effectiveness 16; experiences 18; Family Life Education approach 49–65, *53–54*, *60–62*, 346–351, 379; first 387; FLE model 9–10; foundational visits 389; funding xv, 382, 391–392; historical perspective 1, 2; holistic approach xiv–xv; importance of 15–16; ineffective 72; layers 386–388; measures 41–42; orientation 58; paperwork 387; paradigm shift 54, 55, 79; PAT structure 396; planning 389; precision 346, 351; pre-service training xv; qualitative study 49–65, *53–54*, *60–62*; research 15; relational dyad and triad 58; structure and content 23; timing 389; universal 346, 351
household chaos 134
household safety 164–165
household safety checklist 164
housing policies 278
Howard, S. 245
Huff, N. L. 9
Hull House, Chicago 1
Human Development and Family Studies xv
human growth and development 86, *87*, 92, 107–109, *109*, 114–115, 133–135, *135*, 142–143, 167–168, *168*, 174–176, 192, *194*, 201–202, 219–221, *221*, 226–227, 305–306, *306*, 322–325, *324*, 332–334; PAT enhancement 397–398
human sexuality 171, *171–172*, 177, 244–245, *245*, 254, 397–398
humility 58–59

immigration policies 275
immunizations 163
impact evaluation 297
implementation evaluation 297

inclusion: see diversity and inclusion
Incredible Years 132
Individual Education Plan/Program 276
individualistic orientation 247, 273
individuality, in child development 131–132
Individualized Family Service Plan 271
individualized services 39
Individuals with Disabilities Education Act 269–270, 271, 275–276, 278
infant death syndrome 161, 162, 169, 173
infants, nutritional requirements 134–135
infant/toddler behavior 214–235, 227–229; attitudes 231–232; basics 215–216; cues 218; cultural influences 222–223; developmental understanding of 220–221; discipline and punishment 219, 222; family interaction patterns 216–217; FLE content areas 215; guidance 218–219, 221–223, *223*; human growth and development 219–221, *221*, 226–227; internal dynamics of families 223–224, *224*, 229–230; interpersonal relationships 225–226, *225*, 230–231; knowledge 215–226, *221*, *223*, *224*, *225*; parenting education and guidance 221–223, *223*; reducing negative 218–219; skills 226–231; supporting positive 218–219
Infant/toddler development and learning 129; pedagogy 349
Infant Toddler-Home Observation for the Measurement of the Environment 191
Innocenti, M. 357
inputs 35, 43
insecure attachment 105, 225, 322
in-service training 349
Institute for the Advancement of Family Support Professionals 39
Institutional Review Board 51, 360
intentionality 57–60, 63–64
interactions, quality 22
Intercultural Development Inventory 36
intergenerational approach 39
internal dynamics of families 287–288; assessment 199–200; discipline and punishment 224; diversity and inclusion 280, *281*; family partnerships 252–253, *253–254*; guidance 224; health and safety 173, *174*, 178–179; infant/toddler behavior 223–224, *224*, 229–230; knowledge 90–91, 92, 113–114, *114*, 139–140, *140*, 173, *174*, 199–201, *201*, 223–224, *224*, 252–253, *253–254*; observation 199–201, *201*, 205–206; PAT enhancement 397; reflective practice 90–91, 92, 95–96; relationship building 113–114, *114*, 119–120; skills 95–96, 119–120, 146–147, 178–179, 205–206, 229–230; supporting development and learning 139–140, *140*, 146–147
internal working mode 105
interpersonal relationships 112–113, *113*, 118–119, 138–149, *139*, 146, 225–226, *225*, 230–231; PAT enhancement 398

414 Index

intervention conditions 360
interviews 191
intimate partner violence 171, 200, 217
intimate terrorism 200
intuition 198
involvement 21–22

job titles 350
Johnson, L. D. 355
Johnson, Lyndon B 16

Keilty, B. 88–89
Kelly, D. 328
Kirkman, E. 189
Knoche, L. L. 23
knowledge: child/parent rights 270–271; culture and
    family experiences 267–268; diversity and inclusion
    267–280, 272, 274, 276, 277, 279, 281; family law
    and public policy 251–252, 252, 277–279, 279,
    306–307, 307; family partnerships 241–252, 245,
    246, 248, 249, 250–251, 252, 253–254; family
    resource management 247, 248, 273–274, 274; FLE
    methodology 90, 91, 137–138, 138, 172–173, 173,
    196–198, 198, 249–250, 250–251, 277, 277,
    303–304, 304, 329–331, 331; health and safety
    160–173, 168, 169, 170–171, 171–172, 173, 174;
    human growth and development 86, 87, 107–109,
    109, 133–135, 135, 167–168, 168, 192, 194,
    219–221, 221, 305–306, 306, 322–325, 324; human
    sexuality 171, 171–172, 244–245, 245; infant/
    toddler behavior 215–226, 221, 223, 224, 225;
    internal dynamics of families 90–91, 92, 113–114,
    114, 139–140, 140, 173, 174, 199–201, 201,
    223–224, 224, 252–253, 253–254, 280, 281;
    interpersonal relationships 112–113, 113, 138–149,
    139, 225–226, 225; learning within the family 131;
    logic models 298–299; mental health 321–322,
    324–325; observation 188–201, 194, 195, 196, 198,
    201; parenting 320–321; parenting education and
    guidance 86–87, 88, 109–110, 110, 136–137, 136,
    168–169, 169, 194–195, 195, 221–223, 223, 246,
    246, 271–272, 272, 325–326, 327; professional
    ethics and practice 88–90, 90, 111–112, 112,
    248–249, 249, 304–305, 305; professionalism
    297–306, 304, 305, 306, 307; reflective practice 82;
    relationship building 104–114, 109, 110, 111, 112,
    113, 114; societal contexts 87–88, 89, 110–111,
    111, 141–142, 141, 170, 170–171, 195–196, 196,
    274–276, 276, 327–328, 329; supporting adult
    competencies 319–331, 324, 327, 329, 331;
    supporting development and learning 130–142, 135,
    136, 138, 139, 140, 141; variations in program
    models 299–300
Kohlberg, L. 306
Korfmacher, J. 21, 241
Kuther, T. L. 320, 323

language: development 134, 268, 272; first 276; people-
    first 289
language and literacy support 268
Lareau, A. 88
Latino families 222–223
laws 8, 41, 251–252, 252, 258, 269–270, 271, 277–279,
    279, 286–287, 306–307, 310
learning 320; adult 302, 329–330, 336–337; application
    329–330; children's approaches to 197; deep
    understanding 329–330; developmentally
    appropriate 151; experiential 137; within the family
    131; home learning environment 136; integration
    136; planning 329; routines 136
learning environments 308
learning opportunities, everyday 23
Learning Outcomes 385
legal rights 278
legal system 8, 41, 251–252, 252, 258, 269–270, 271,
    277–279, 279, 286–287, 306–307, 307, 310
Lemonade for Life 33
Levels of Family Involvement Model 5–6
LGB parents 244–245
lifespan perspectives 93
Lincoln, Abraham 2
listening 38
literature 49–50, 52; training 354
logic models 298–299
long-term outcomes 383
Luyten, P. 85

macro context 142
macrosystem 251, 287
macrosystem-level initiatives 252
McWilliam, R. 55–56, 357
malnutrition 135, 193
maltreatment 199–200, 216, 217, 251–252
mandated reporters 165
marginalization 84, 268
materials 58
maternal depressive symptoms 322
Maternal Infant and Early Childhood Home Visiting 15,
    50, 299, 391–392
maternal sensitivity 110, 115, 221
maternal stress 217–218
meaning-making 37–38
Medicaid 244, 251
Melrose, K. 189
mental health 148, 191–192, 217, 217–218, 321–322,
    324–325, 327–328, 330, 332
mental states, parents 85
mentoring 334
metacognition 323
metaframework 348
Mexican American families 274–275
microsystems 131
middle adulthood 305–306
milestones 131, 135, 192

Index 415

Mindes, G. 189
mindfulness 89–90, 112
Minnesota Council on Family Relations 4, 248
misbehavior 216
mission-creep 31
Mission Statements 75
mistaken behavior 216
Moore, T. J. 247
Morrill Land Grant Act of 1862 and 1890 1–2
motor skills 105–106
multidisciplinary family service approaches 69–71, **70, 71**
multiple systems, working with 392–393
myelination 135
Myers-Walls, J. A. 6–7, 9, 50

narration 33
National Council on Family Relations xv, 2, 50; academic program review 4; certification 3–4; code of ethics 4; national exam 4
National Family Support Competency Framework for Family Support Professionals 41, 99, 123–124, 152–153, 179–180, 208–209, 234, 260–261, 290, 311–312, 339–340
National Head Start Association 190, 350
national resources 273–274
nature, and nurture 193
needs 38
needs assessment 197, 199
neglect 251–252
Network (CFLE newsletter) 406
neuroscience 17
Next Steps Planning Form 80–81
non-parametric analyses 373
norms 131, 192, 223
Nurse Family Partnership 16, 299–300
nurture, and nature 193
nutritional requirements, children 134–135
nutrition assessments 160
nutritionists 160

Obama administration 307
obesity 161
objectives 34, 189, 196–197
objectivity 189
Oborn, K. M. K. 355
observation 33, 38, 187–210; application 196; and assessment 189; attitudes 206–207; basics 188–190; FLE content areas 188; FLE methodology 196–198, *198*, 204–205; human growth and development 192, *194*, 201–202; informal 189; internal dynamics of families 199–201, *201*, 205–206; knowledge 188–201, *194*, *195*, *196*, *198*, 201; measures 298; parent–child interactions 196, 199; parenting education and guidance 194–195, *195*, 202–203; skills 201–206; societal contexts 195–196, *196*, 204
observational measures 298

ongoing dialogue 36–37
online home visiting training 349
online learning experiences, best practices 8–9
online modules 355–356
operational components 30; content 38–40; context 37–38; culture 35–37; practice 40–42
oral health 161
orchids and dandelions 134
orientation 58
Ounce of Prevention Fund 39, 349, 355–356
outcome evaluation 297
outcomes, positive 32, 34
outputs 35, 43

Palm, G. 248
paperwork 387
parental confidence 85
parental efficacy 23
parental reflective functioning 85
parental sensitivity 115, 116, 118
parental support 132–133
parent behaviors 93
parent–child interaction activity sheets 389
parent–child interactions 23, 49–50, 107, 347, 383; assessment 191, 199; bidirectional 121; coaching 325; observation 196, 199; opportunities 387; sensitive 326
parent–child relationships 17, 50, 105–106; bidirectional 106; flexibility 138–139; knowledge 112–113
parent education 2
Parent Gauge 190, 197
Parent Gauge Needs 383
parenthood, transition to 324–325
parenting 312; assessment of 190–192; behavior 347; and behavior change 320–321; influences on 83–84; programs 8; skills 31
parenting education and guidance 87–88, *88*, 92–93, 109–110, *110*, 115–116, 136–137, *136*, 143–145, 168–169, *169*, 176, 194–195, *195*, 202–203, 221–223, *223*, 227–229, 246, *246*, 255, 271–272, *272*, 280–281, 325–326, *327*, 399
Parenting Interactions with Children: Checklist of Observations Linked to Outcomes 41–42, 191, 298
parenting strategies, evaluation 93, 144, 228
parenting styles 93, 143–144, 216–217, 222–223, 228, 333–334
parent interviews 191
parent questionnaires 191
parents: childhood experiences 84–85, 86; coaching 325–326; as collaborators 194; consent 278; developmentally appropriate 191; empowerment 77–78, **77**; experience 390–391; feelings of dissatisfaction 224; focus on 30; LGB 244–245; mental health 148, 191–192, 217, 217–218, 321–322, 324–325, 327–328, 330, 332; mental states 85; preschool 77–78, **77**; reflective

416   Index

practice 86; resources 132–133; role 106–107, 144, 281; as safe haven 105, 115, 118, 120; as safe place 108; as secure base 105, 115, 118, 120, 123; teenager 322–323; undocumented 275; uninvolved 216
Parents as Teachers 23, 34, 165, 169, 192, 298–299, 299, 325, 347–348, 359, 371, 386, 388–391; FLE enhancement 395–400; foundational visits 389; goals 389, 395; message 395; model 389; program components 395–396
parent satisfaction surveys 59
Part C office 279
participation, family 243
participation quantity 21
people-first language 289
performance standards 17–19, 50
Perkins, F. 1
Perry, W. G. 306
Petkus, J. 9–10, 50, 51, 52, 57–60, 59, 64, 372, 373
philosophical basis 75
planning 18
play 137
Poison Help 165
positive feedback 219
postformal reasoning 323
postpartum depression 322
poverty 2, 15, 32, 87, 108, 110–111, 273, 327; challenges of 37; development and learning impacts 139–140; social contexts 37
poverty level 17
practice 40–42
precision home visiting 346, 351
pregnancy 160, 167–168
prejudices 328
prenatal and neonatal health 160–161
preschool parents, empowerment 77–78, **77**
pre-service training xv, 348–349
prevention 32–33, 43; maternal stress 217–218
primary prevention 32, 43
principles approach 248
principles of family life education 4–5
problem solving 120, 146, 224, 288
procedural safeguards 279
process evaluation 297
process quality 22
professional development 89–90, 296, 300–302, 304–305, 349–350, 354; see also training
professional development modules 358, 359, 360, 364, **365**, 366–367, 372–373, 378–382
professional ethics and practice 88–90, 90, 94, 111–112, 112, 117–118, 248–249, 249, 256–257, 304–305, 305, 309, 399
professionalism 63, 296–313; additional skills 301; attitudes 312–313; code of ethics 300–301; family law and public policy 306–307, 307, 310; FLE content areas 297, 302–303, 312–313; FLE

methodology 303–304, 304, 307–309; human growth and development 305–306, 306, 309–310; knowledge 297–306, 304, 305, 306, 307; policies 300; professional ethics and practice 304–305, 305, 309; skills 307–310
professional organizations 301
Professional Quality of Life Scale 302
professional relationships 301
program design 8; steps in 196
program evaluation 31, 31–32
program evidence 297–298
program fidelity 303
program implementation 330; tailoring 329
program involvement 21–22
program models, variations in 299–300
prosocial behaviors 216
protective factors 36, 37; child development 33
provisional certification 403
proximal environments 131
proximal systems 195
psychological health 171
psychological resources 328
psychotherapeutic perspective 23
public policy 8, 41, 251, 252, 258, 277–279, 279, 286–287, 306–307, 307, 310
punishment 21, 219
purpose statements 75
purposive sample 359–360

qualifications 2, 3, 3–4, 19, 22–23
quality practice 296
questions, open-ended 167

Raikes, H. A. 328
randomized experiment 20
reciprocal interactions 177
redirection 218, 219, 228
reflection 52, 112, 195, 198; role of 84–85
reflective evaluation 195
reflective mindset 198
reflective practice 82–100, 112, 305; attitudes 82, 96–97; competency 82; definition 82; FLE concepts and resources 85–95, **87**, 88, 89, 90, 91; FLE content areas 82–83; FLE methodology 90–91, 91, 95; human growth and development 86, 87, 92; internal dynamics of families 90–91, 92, 95–96; knowledge 82, 83–91; parenting education and guidance 86–87, 88, 92–93; parents 86; professional ethics and practice 88–90, 90, 94; role of 84–85; skills 82, 92–96; societal contexts 87–88, 89, 93–94
reflective supervision 60, 63, 64–65, 304–305, 388
reflexivity 36
Reinke, J. S. 139
relational dyad and triad 58
relational ethics 181, 248
Relationship Assessment Tool 192, 200

relationship-based care 58
relationship building 36, 85, 89, 103–124, 232, 242, 298, 387; attitudes 120–121; core areas 242; FLE concepts and resources 104–114, *109*, *110*, *111*, *112*, *113*, *114*; FLE Content Areas 104; human growth and development 107–108, *109*, 114–115; importance of 103; internal dynamics of families 113–114, *114*, 119–120; interpersonal relationships 112–113, *113*, 118–119; knowledge 104–114, *109*, *110*, *111*, *112*, *113*, *114*; parenting education and guidance 109–110, *110*, 115–116; professional 301; professional ethics and practice 111–112, *112*, 117–118; skills 114–120; societal contexts 110–111, *111*, 116–117; staff–family 318; *see also* family partnerships
relationships: importance of 103; quality 107, 242
research 303
research-based 34, 43
research-based curriculum 197
research-based practices 168, 298
resilience 37–38; building 33
resource management, families 247, *248*, 255–256, 273–274, *274*, 282–283, 398–399
resources: access to 383, 386; community 141–142, 149, 170; multiplicity of 255; national 273–274; psychological 328; supporting development and learning 132–133
respect 289
respite care 274
responsibility 197–198
responsive parenting 161
risk 172
risk factors 36, 37; child development 33
Roggman, L. A. 22, 41, 50, 242, 299, 357
routines, learning 136

safe haven 105, 115, 118, 120
salary, home visitors 301
Sayre, Paul 2
scaffolding 326
school readiness 37, 58
Schreiber, L. 371
secondary prevention 32, 43
secondary traumatic stress 301–302
secure attachment 104–105, 108, 225
secure base 105, 115, 118, 120, 123
self-efficacy 321, 325, 326, 328, 334, 337; sources of 326
self-reflection. 355
self-sufficiency 328, 334, 337
sensitivity 40, 98, 108, 120, 122, 285; maternal 115; parental 115, 116, 118
sensitizing concepts 358
service coordinators 279
service delivery 350
service institutions 170

services, individualized 39
sex education 2
sexuality 171, *171–172*, 244–245, *245*, 254
sexual orientation 244–245
Shaken Baby Syndrome 162–163
Siegel, D. J. 85, 86, 87
situational couple violence 200
skill-building 58
skills 82, 92, 336–337; coaching and collaborating to support child development 333–334, 335, 336–337; coaching and collaborating t to support parent efficacy and self-sufficiency 334, 337; diversity and inclusion 281–288; family law and public policy 258, 286–287, 310; family partnerships 254–259; family resource management 255–256, 282–283; FLE methodology 95, 145, 177–178, 204–205, 257–258, 285–286, 307–309; health and safety 174–180; human growth and development 92, 114–115, 142–143, 174–176, 201–202, 226–227, 309–310, 332–334; human sexuality 177, 254; internal dynamics of families 95–96, 119–120, 146–147, 178–179, 205–206, 229–230, 258–259, 287–288; interpersonal relationships 118–119, 146, 230–231; observation 201–206; parenting education and guidance 92–93, 115–116, 143–145, 176, 202–203, 227–229, 255, 280–281; professional ethics and practice 94, 117–118, 256–257, 309; professionalism 307–310; relationship building 114–120; societal contexts 93–94, 116–117, 147–148, 176–177, 204, 284–285, 335–336; supporting adult competencies 331–336; supporting development and learning 142–148
sleep and sleep practices 162–163, 168, 173, 271–272
Smith-Lever Act, 1914 2
social cohesion 141
social identities 89–90, 277
socialization 17–18, 31, 215–216
social learning theory 321
social models 326
social position variables 86
social support 31, 140, 224
social work 2
societal contexts 87–88, *89*, 93–94, 110–111, *111*, 116–117, 141–142, *141*, 147–148, 170, *170–171*, 176–177, 195–196, *196*, 204, 274–276, *276*, 284–285, 327–328, *329*, 335–336, 396–397
societal trends 144
socio-ecological influences 175, 310
spanking 222
specialized populations 329–330
special needs 269–270, 272, 289; *see also* diversity and inclusion
Special Supplemental Nutrition Program for Women, Infants, and Children 133, 251
specificity 64
spillover 106

418 Index

spirituality 110–111
staff turnover xv
stakeholders 287
Stanley Hall, G. 320
state supports 133
Steinberg, L. 223, 323
stigmatization 328
strategies 34
Strengthening Families Initiative 252
strengths-based approach 33–34, 49, 110–111, 172, 232, 245, 288–289
strengths-based perspective 23, 148–149
stress 252–253
stressors 15, 199, 220, 224, 230, 258, 280; families 96
subjective 189
substance abuse 29, 217
Sudden Infant Death Syndrome 161, 162, 169, 173
supervision 372; reflective 60, 63, 64–65, 388
Supplemental Nutrition Assistance Program 133, 166, 251
Supporting Development and Learning 120–121
supporting development and learning 129–154; attitudes 148–149; community-level family support 133, 138; domains 129; FLE content areas 130; FLE methodology 137–138, *138*, 145; human growth and development 133–135, *135*, 142–143; individuality in 131–132; internal dynamics of families 139–140, *140*, 146–147; interpersonal relationships 138–149, *139*, 146; knowledge 130–142, *135*, *136*, *138*, *139*, *140*, *141*; learning within the family 131; parenting education and guidance 136–137, *136*, 143–145; reciprocal influences 142–143; resources for parents 132–133; skills 142–148; societal contexts 141–142, *141*, 147–148; socio-ecological influences 143
support systems 220
systems perspective 287

Tandon, S. D. 355
targeting 23
team approach 59
technology 9
teenage mothers 167–168, 320, 322–323
teenagers 322–323
teen birth rate 320
teen parents 320, 330
teen pregnancies 320
temperament 132, 216, 221
Temporary Assistance for Needy Families 165–166
teratogens 160, 167
tertiary prevention 32, 43
tests of differences 348
theories 34–35, 38, 43, 303
Thomas, J. 232
Thompson, R. A. 328

time management 256
Title X 244
toxic stress 164, 200
toy-centered approach 10, 50, 54, 55, 63
training 39, 54–56; availability 355; coaching 349–350; current study 356–357; FLE 354–360, *361–362*, 363–364, *363–364*, **365**, 366–368, *367–368*, *369–370*, 371–373; home visitors 18; in-service 349; literature 354; online 349; online modules 355–356; pre-service 348–349; recognition 350
training research study 371; context 358–360; design 357; FLE Content Knowledge 367–368, *367–368*; focus group 358–360; future research 372; intervention conditions 360; limitations 372, 373; measure 357–358; method 357–360, *358*, *359*, *361–362*, 363, *364–365*; participants 358–360, 360, *361–362*; procedures 360; professional development modules 358, *359*, 360, 364, **365**, 366–367, 372–373, 378–382; purposive sample 359–360; qualitative analyses 360, 363, *363–364*, *369–370*, 373; quantitative analyses 360; Question #1 364; Question #2 *363–364*, 366–367; Question #3 367-368; Question #4 *369–370*, 368, 371; results and discussion 364, 366–368, 371–372; sample characteristics *361–362*; video perceptions **365**; weblinks *358*
training videos 355, 358, *358*, *359*, 364, **365**, 366–367
transformative learning 90
transformative learning theory 331
transgender people 245
transition to parenthood 324–325
triadic interaction 298
Triandis, H. C. 247
Triple P-Positive Parenting Program 132
Trivette, C. M. 329
trust 218, 242, 302
tuning in 137, 146, 250
two-generation program 17, 132, 240
two-parent households 107

understanding, commitment to 97
undocumented parents 275
unemployment 29
uninvolved parents 216
universal home visiting 346, 351
University of Nevada, Reno, Early Head Start-Home-Based Option 382–394; background 382–386; collaboration 392–393; eligibility requirements 382; funding 382, 391–392; future 393–394; long-term outcomes 383; parent's experience 390–391; use of PAT 388–391; working with multiple systems 392–393
U.S. Department of Health and Human Services 16

vaccination 163
validity 189, 348
values 75, 97, 121, 206, 223, 250, 268, 271–272, 273, 283, 288–289, 309
Vanier Institute of the Family 2–3
Velderman, K. 109–110
video-recording 106, 109–110
violence 119
virtue ethics 248
virtues 181, 312–313
vulnerable families 15–16
Vygotsky, L. 326

Walcheski, M. J. 3, 139
Walsh, B. A. 348–349, 349
Wasik, B. H. 355
Waugh, S. 390
wellbeing 171, 191
well-child visits 163
White House Conference on Child Welfare, 1909 2
Women, Infants, and Children 161

young adults and young adulthood 305–306, 323